FOOD FACTS

A Study of Food and Nutrition

Delia Clarke M Phil

Elizabeth Herbert B Sc

Produced with assistance from the Kellogg
Company of Great Britain Limited

M

Macmillan Education

First published 1986

Published by
MACMILLAN EDUCATION LTD
Houndmills, Basingstoke, Hampshire RG21 2XS
and London
Companies and representatives
throughout the world

Printed in Hong Kong

British Library Cataloguing in Publication Data

Clarke, Delia
  Food facts.
  1. Food
  I. Title   II. Herbert, Elizabeth
  641.3   TX353

ISBN 0-333-33613-5

Contents

Acknowledgements

Illustrations by Illustra Design.

The authors and publishers wish to acknowledge the following photograph sources:

Jim Brownbill p 6, 67 *Colour plates* 1, 2, 4
Camerapix Hutchison *Plate* 1
J Allan Cash Ltd p 6
Carrefour Ltd p 68
John Darby *Colour plates* (with Delia Clarke)
  2, 5, 6, 7, 8, 9, 10, 11, 17, 19, 20, 21, 22, 24-31
Egg Marketing Board *Plate* 11
FAO p 13, 14
Harrods *Plate* 20
Japanese Information Centre *Plate* 2
Kellogg Co of Great Britain Ltd *Plate* 24
Meat and Livestock Commission *Plate* 18

Meat Promotions Executive *Plate* 14, 15, 16, 20
Milk Marketing Board *Plate* 3
St Bartholomews Hospital p 15
Sharwoods *Plate* 32
Sutton Seeds Ltd *Plate* 32
Tesco p 67
Thorn EMI Domestic Appliances Ltd p 72, 78
TI Tower Housewares p 79
Toshiba p 73
Unwins Seeds Ltd *Plate* 32
Weight Watchers (UK) Ltd p 15
WHO p 14

The authors and publishers wish to thank the following who have kindly given permission for the use of copyright material:

The Associated Examining Board, the Joint Matriculation Board, the Northern Ireland General Certificate of Education Examinations Board, the Scottish Examination Board, the Southern Universities' Joint Board, the University of London School Examinations Department, the University of Oxford Delegacy of Local Examinations and the Welsh Joint Education Committee for questions from past examination papers.

The Controller of Her Majesty's Stationery Office for granting permission to reproduce information from the *Manual of Nutrition*.

British Meat, British Sugar Bureau, Department of Home Economics and Nutrition Education of the Flour Advisory Bureau Ltd, National Dairy Council, Spillers Foods, Van den Berghs, White Fish Authority.

A special acknowledgement is due to the Home Economics Department of Roehampton Institute of Higher Education, for use of their food laboratories.

The publishers have made every effort to trace the copyright holders, but where they have failed to do so they will be pleased to make the necessary arrangements at the first opportunity.

Personal thanks to Denise Johnstone Burt, John Darby, Toni Sharmi and the author's family and friends for their encouragement.

Preface

As each succeeding generation of pupils and students comes forward, teachers and lecturers face exciting new challenges. Today these challenges are nowhere more apparent than in the application of the sciences, physics, chemistry and biology, to the better understanding of food, nutrition and health in everyday living.

During the period when *Food Facts* has been under preparation by the authors there have been many developments in food science and technology, food production, marketing and distribution which have had substantial impact on the increased availability of a wide range of foods in the developed world. Variety has indeed been the spice of life for the great majority of the population throughout the entire year. For the developing world, where the individual and national problems of food supply are very different, the approaches and solutions will not only be different in nature but in time as well. At the same time changing lifestyles have been followed with advantages for some and not for others as regards their overall health and well-being. A new awareness of the association of the foods selected, the meals prepared and consumed with the incidence of the so called diseases of affluence have come to the forefront.

The authors are to be congratulated in their attempt in this first edition to meet the requirements of the appropriate course curricula for Home Economists. They have endeavoured to address the culinary issues that the users of this text will experience in planning attractive nutritious meals.

W D B Hamilton
Director of Scientific Affairs
Kellogg Company of Great Britain Ltd

List of colour plates

Food in Our Lives

The Choice of Food 1

'What do you feel like eating today?'

How often have you been asked that question? Before you begin to answer it, think a little about what it means.

The first thing to consider is that you have a choice of food. In the affluent, developed countries such as North America, Europe and Australia there is an abundant variety of food. Most people make a choice of food at least two or three times a day. However, in the developing countries, such as parts of Africa, Asia and South America, there is very little choice and often insufficient food available. All human beings need food to survive. Food is necessary for growth, for healthy living and as a source of energy. The study of the composition of foods and how the body uses food is known as *nutrition*. The availability of a wide choice of foods makes it easier to choose foods that are nutritionally good for you.

The next consideration is that you are being asked to make a decision. Any decision should be based on facts. The aim of this book is to explain the facts about food: the types of foods available, the effects of processing and preparation, the nutritional value of different foods and the many functions of food in the body. From these facts, you will be able to make reasoned decisions about the foods you choose and enjoy preparing nutritious meals that are a pleasure to eat.

Our individual choices of foods and eating patterns are influenced by many factors. To understand why we eat what we eat, we should consider the influences which are illustrated in Fig. 1.1:

Fig. 1.1 Factors influencing our choice of food

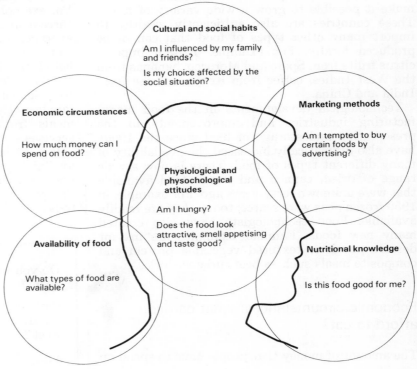

Cultural and social habits

Am I influenced by my family and friends?

Is my choice affected by the social situation?

Economic circumstances

How much money can I spend on food?

Marketing methods

Am I tempted to buy certain foods by advertising?

Physiological and physochological attitudes

Am I hungry?

Does the food look attractive, smell appetising and taste good?

Availability of food

What types of food are available?

Nutritional knowledge

Is this food good for me?

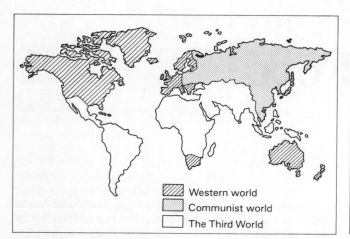

Fig. 1.2 The developed and the developing world

Western world
Communist world
The Third World

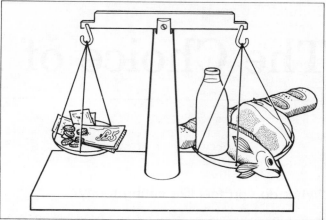

Fig. 1.3 The economic balance

Availability of food

Your choice of food is undoubtedly affected by the types of food available in the country and place where you live.

In the developing countries there is little variety in the types of food available. The climate and the type of land may not be suitable for rearing animals or growing a wide variety of crops. These countries do not have enough money for expensive agricultural developments or to import a wide variety of food from other countries.

In the developed countries, there have been many technological developments in agriculture which make it possible to grow a wide variety of foods. These countries are also sufficiently wealthy to import many other types of food that cannot be produced locally. For example, Britain imports citrus fruits from Spain and Morocco, bananas from the West Indies, coffee from Kenya and tea from India and China.

Technological developments in the food manufacturing industries and improvements in the preservation and storage of food since the 1950s have also dramatically increased the availability of many different types of food. There is now a wide range of dried, canned and frozen food available that were unknown forty years ago. For example, in 1950 frozen peas were scarce; today they are readily available. Food technologists have also created many new foods. Familiar examples are instant dessert powders, textured vegetable protein and composite meals such as beef curry with rice.

Economic circumstances: what can you afford to eat?

The amount of money that people have to spend on

food is crucial to their choice of food. Throughout history food has been a status symbol for rich people. Poor people cannot afford to buy luxury foods such as smoked salmon and caviare. Spending a lot of money on food does not necessarily lead to nutritionally well-planned meals. Many of the cheaper foods are very nutritious, for example locally-grown vegetables, dried beans, eggs and oily fish such as herrings and mackerel. So, if chosen with care, a nutritious diet does not have to be an expensive one.

Throughout the world, people spend differing proportions of their incomes on food: poor people have to spend a higher proportion than rich people. For example, families in Asia spend approximately three-quarters of their income on food, whilst on average, Canadians spend only one-seventh. In some countries, poor people receive some financial help from the government to provide food for their families. For example, in Britain, milk tokens and free school meals are available for low-income families; the elderly can also receive subsidised meals from local welfare centres or voluntary services.

It is an indisputable fact that poverty limits the availability and choice of food. The effect of the uneven distribution of food and wealth throughout the world is one of the major problems in the world today.

Do you know how your family income is spent?

Can you calculate the proportion of your family income that is spent on food each week?

Cultural and social habits: what is your lifestyle?

From infancy, we adopt the eating patterns of our parents: we learn to like the foods our families like. We may not be aware of it but we often absorb our families' attitudes towards food. Food may be used in a number of ways: not only to satisfy hunger, but also to provide comfort, satisfaction, relief from boredom or anxiety, or as a status symbol.

Our family eating-pattern is in turn influenced by both where we live and the culture we come from. Every culture in the world has its own type of eating patterns and style of cooking. These tend to be determined largely by the availability of low-priced, locally-grown foods. For example, rice is a staple food in India, China and Japan, and the potato is an important food in Britain, whereas the yam is widely used in the West Indies and parts of Africa. Wheat is grown in many countries, but is traditionally used in a variety of ways, for example, pasta in Italy and China, bread in Europe, North America and Australasia, unleavened bread such as chapattis and nan in India and the Middle East. Eating patterns also vary regionally within one country due to the local availability of different types of food, and different lifestyles of people who live in that area.

Look at plate 1. Describe the different styles of traditional eating habits for family meals in India, Japan and Great Britain.

Although the availability of certain types of food largely determines the food eaten in any country, religious beliefs of the people can also influence eating habits. The following religions all have special laws:

- *Hinduism* The cow is sacred to Hindus, and they will not eat beef or use any product from slaughtered cows, e.g. beef dripping, gelatine, rennet. Hindus will not use cooking fats containing animal oils or other foods containing animal fats, e.g. some ice cream. Some Hindus will not eat cheese, if rennet has been used in the manufacturing process. Milk, yoghurt, butter and ghee (clarified butter) are acceptable as these are natural products from the cow. Hindus are usually vegetarian and have many days of fasting.
- *Sikhism* Sikhs have similar dietary habits to Hindus, but meat is more generally taken.
- *Islam* The followers of Islam are known as Muslims. The pig is considered unclean and therefore Muslims do not eat pork or any pork products, e.g. bacon, sausages, lard, cooking fats containing animal oils or foods containing animal oil, e.g. ice cream. Other meats must be slaughtered in a particular way, so that no blood remains. It is then known as Halal meat. Alcoholic drinks are prohibited. During the month of 'Ramadan' on the Islamic calendar, Muslims fast from dawn to sunset. At the end of this period there is a three-day feast.
- *Christianity* The influence of Christianity on eating habits varies between different Christian denominations, e.g. Evangelical protestants often abstain from alcohol; some Roman Catholics abstain from eating meat on Fridays.
- *Judaism* Jews are only allowed to eat meat that has been specially slaughtered, soaked and then treated with kosher salt to remove all residual blood. The pig is also considered unclean and orthodox Jews do not eat pork. The consumption of animal fats and oils is not allowed. Meat and dairy products may not be served at the same meal. No cooking is permitted on the Sabbath.

Traditional eating habits are hard to change. However, as people migrate, they take their beliefs with them. They create a demand for their traditional foods. In most large cities all over the world you can now find a wide variety of types of food and many styles of restaurant: for instance, Chinese, Indian, Indonesian, Italian, French. As a result, the effects of many cultural and regional differences are being shared.

Look at plate 2.
Can you name the country of origin of these foods, and find out how you would use them? Try using some of these foods occasionally to add variety to your diet.

Food is also an important part of social life in any country. Certain foods have become almost symbolic of a festive occasion, for example, a wedding cake. Sometimes the meal becomes the most important part of the celebration, and the original purpose may be overlooked, as is perhaps the case with Christmas dinner.

Daily social events often also involve food. Meals are social occasions when people can get together and talk. This might be a casual family breakfast, coffee or lunch with friends, a snack in a bar or a more formal dinner. Snacks are often served at meetings and parties. The purpose of serving food is to make people relax and enjoy the occasion. Food

Fig. 1.4 Eating in different social situations

Fig. 1.5 Convenience foods

frequently gives people something to talk about and 'breaks the ice' at social functions.

Social changes during the past thirty years have also affected our eating habits. Some examples are:

- more mothers are employed outside the home,
- more people live alone,
- people travel greater distances to work,
- people have social activities outside the home.

These changes have affected people's eating habits and the types of food they eat. Some families often have their meals in 'shifts' to accommodate the different lifestyles of family members. The availability of 'take-away' and easily prepared convenience foods allows many people to have more flexible lifestyles. For elderly people convenience foods can provide easy-to-prepare nutritious foods.

Consider the lifestyle of your family. How are the eating patterns affected by the work and social activities of family members?

Changes in lifestyle and eating habits have led to a demand for more 'snack' foods. For some people, 'snacking' has become their regular eating pattern. Snack foods are not necessarily bad for you, but some snack foods have:

- a high proportion of fat and starch. An excess of fat and starch is stored as body fat.
- a high sugar content. Sugar accelerates tooth decay: excess sugar is stored as body fat.

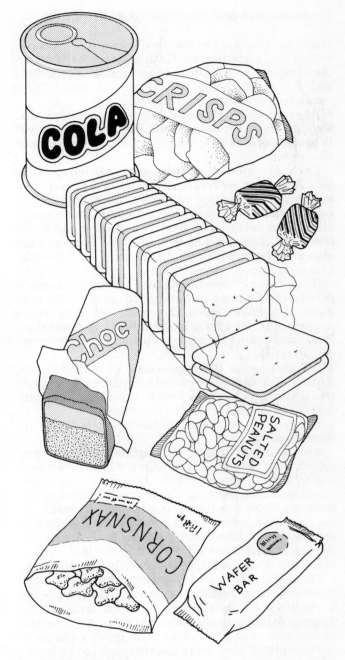

Fig. 1.6 Snack foods

Look at the ingredient list of the snack foods and drinks in your local supermarket.

- Make a list of the snack foods and drinks that you consume in one day.
- Suggest suitable nutritious and appetising alternatives.

Physiological and psychological attributes

How do you appreciate food? For most people, eating is a pleasure. Eating satisfies hunger. However, we also appreciate the appearance, aroma and flavour and the texture of the food. These sensations are often interrelated.

Appearance is probably the first sensation that we judge food by: does it look fresh and attractive? When we look at food we judge both the colour and the texture.

Early experiences of food condition us to relate certain colours with certain foods. If the food is an unfamiliar colour, for example, black potatoes or purple custard, we may reject the food on its colour alone. The colour of a food is a good guide to its freshness. Stale food looks dull. Certain colours are also associated with certain flavours, for example, lemon-flavoured desserts are usually coloured yellow. Many manufactured products contain permitted chemical colourings to make them look more attractive. Since the colour of food is so important in our appreciation of food, we can make a meal more appetising by choosing attractively-coloured foods.

We also judge the appearance of a food by its texture. For example, we can tell just by looking at the texture of a cake whether it will be light and easy to eat or heavy and indigestible.

The *flavour* of a food is identified both by its aroma and its taste.

Aroma is particularly important. We are very sensitive to the smell of certain foods even without seeing them; for example, bread baking, meat roasting, coffee brewing. Good-smelling food stimulates the digestive juices; our bodies are ready for the food even before we have tasted it. The smell of food is also an important guide as to its freshness. We can often detect food that is slightly bad, such as stale eggs or rancid fat, by its smell, before tasting it.

The taste of food is detected by about nine thousand nerve endings, known as taste buds, on the surface of the tongue. Different areas of the tongue are particularly sensitive to four basic tastes: sweet, sour, salt and bitter. The nerve endings in the taste buds then relay the message to the brain, and we can taste the different flavours.

The senses of smell and taste are related. For example, if you have a head cold, food seems to be tasteless, or if you hold your nose it is difficult to detect the flavour of food – try it!

The *texture* of a food in the mouth is also important in determining whether we like certain foods. We appreciate qualities such as smoothness and crispness. These qualities are characteristic of certain foods, and if they are missing the food is unpalatable. For example, do you like lumpy sauce or a soft biscuit?

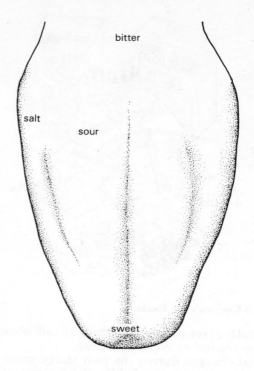

Fig. 1.7 Taste zones of the tongue

Taste a small sample of each of the following foods:

lemon, vinegar, sugar, peas, honey, salted peanuts, salt, watercress, chicory, instant coffee without milk or sugar, red wine.

Make sure each sample passes over the whole surface of the tongue.

Can you identify the predominant taste in each of the foods as it passes over the sensitive areas of the tongue?

All these qualities are important in our appreciation of food. They are the qualities that we remember food by and recall to mind when choosing food. If foods look attractive, smell appetising and taste good, we are likely to want to eat those foods.

Consider the foods you eat today, do they:

- look attractive,
- smell appetising,
- taste good?

Plate 1 Traditional eating habits in family meals in (a) India   (b) Japan (c) Britain

(a)

(b)

(c)

Plate 2 A selection of ethnic foods available in Britain

What motivates you to eat food?

Eating is a comforting habit: it soothes inner tensions and anxieties. For a baby, food is a symbol of love, comfort and security. All our lives, having food available when we need it satisfies our need for security. Being without food, even for a short while, can cause anxiety.

For some people, eating can provide an emotional outlet for loneliness, boredom and depression. At other times, some people eat almost absent-mindedly whilst doing something else, such as watching television or sports. Food is also sometimes used as a reward for example, to congratulate a child for good behaviour. Adults also 'reward' themselves with food or drink.

> In the next few days, consider why you and the people around you are eating, and when they are eating. Is it only because they are hungry, or may there be another reason?

If food is used too often to satisfy these psychological needs, it is easy to eat too much, and may provide only temporary relief: the problems remain!

Marketing methods

Why do you buy the foods you do? Although your choice of food may be controlled by the factors already described, it is also affected by how foods are sold to you. The convenience, hygienic conditions and quality of food in local shops, markets and supermarkets influence a discriminating shopper in the choice of food.

Food manufacturers are well aware that they must produce foods that people want to buy. They conduct market research to find out consumer preferences. Once developed, new products are test-marketed in selected areas for consumer appeal: the quality, the portion sizes, the style of packaging and the price. The product is then marketed nationally.

The price of food affects all shoppers. There is much competition between stores to attract customers. Some stores advertise low-priced goods in local newspapers, others paste large notices on the windows of the shop, to attract people to buy low-priced goods in that shop. Once tempted into the shop, it is easy to buy other products as well.

There is also an 'art' in the way stores display their goods. Have you noticed enormous piles of goods strategically placed on the corner of a gangway to attract attention when approached from any of several directions? Other impulse buys, e.g. sweets, cigarettes, are often placed at eye-level or conveniently near the check-out till. Affluence makes it possible for us to buy these goods, advertising convinces us that we should!

Food advertising is everywhere: on television and radio, newspapers, magazines, window displays and food packages. To be effective, advertisements should persuade you to buy the product. Food is an emotional subject, and manufacturers sometimes use the emotions in advertising their products.

For example, look at the clever photograph in plate 3. The advertisement persuades you to overcome those guilty feelings and enjoy a fresh cream cake!

> Look out for other food advertisements. Does the advertisement suggest a reason why you should eat that food? Does the food look attractive, and if so, why? Is the nutritional value of the food described?

It is also interesting to notice which foods are advertised most frequently, where and how they are advertised. Advertisements for sweets, snacks and drinks occur frequently.

> When do most advertisements on television appear? Are they during the evening, the afternoon or during children's programmes? Are different types shown at different times?

Many food advertisements are designed to appeal to children. Children tend to be more easily persuaded than adults. They may then influence their parents by persistent nagging during shopping trips!

> Consider some advertisements designed to appeal to children. Do they learn anything about good nutrition from them?

Many food manufacturers recognise that people need and want to be told which foods are nutritionally good for them (plate 3(b)). Many food advertisements, for instance those for breakfast cereal products, now feature nutritional information. In addition, many products have descriptions of the nutritional value on the packets. These manufacturers recognise that they have an important role as nutrition educators (see Fig. 1.8).

Nutritional knowledge: what does food do for you?

The extent to which your choice of food is affected by the nutritional value of food depends on how much you know about nutrition: that is, the particular value of foods, the amount of food you need and how the body uses the food you eat. These are all important aspects of nutrition. The next chapter explains the vital importance of choosing nutritionally well-planned meals to keep you healthy. This is a personal challenge: it is your choice of foods that will affect the way you feel. So when you are given a choice, use it wisely: your health will affected by the decisions you make.

KELLOGG'S CORN FLAKES

Ingredients: Maize, sugar, salt, malt flavouring, niacin, iron, vitamin B_6, riboflavin (B_2), thiamin (B_1), vitamin D_3, vitamin B_{12}

Typical nutritional composition per 100 grammes

Energy	348 kcal
	1455 kJ
Protein (N × 6.25)	8.0 g
Vitamins:	
Niacin	16.0 mg
Vitamin B_6	1.8 mg
Riboflavin (B_2)	1.5 mg
Thiamin (B_1)	1.0 mg
Vitamin D_3	2.8 μg
Vitamin B_{12}	1.7 μg
Iron	6.7 mg

A serving of 30 g of *Kellogg's* Corn Flakes provides at least one quarter of the average adult or one third of a child's recommended daily intake of these vitamins; and one sixth of their iron needs.

Fig. 1.8 Nutritional details

The Function of Food 2

Have you ever thought:
- does it matter what kind of food I eat?
- will the kind of food affect the way I feel and the way I look?

You may think that your choice of food does not matter, but before you come to that conclusion, you would be wise to consider the following points:
- why does the body need food?
- what is food?
- how does the body use food?
- how much and what types of food are best for healthy living?

All of these points will be investigated in this chapter.

Make a list of all the foods you eat in one day. For that day, weigh the food you eat. Record the weights accurately. Remember to include all drinks and snacks.

As you read this chapter, you will be able to consider whether your choice of foods is nutritionally well-planned.

1 Why does the body need food?

The simple answer to this question is that the body needs food for growth and repair of cells, to give it energy and warmth and to keep it healthy. This has been shown by many studies of health in different areas of the world:
- where there is little food available, people often suffer from a poor growth rate and many diseases. There is a high rate of infant mortality and life expectancy is short. It has been found that improvements in the amount and types of food eaten alleviate some of these problems.
- where there is an abundant choice of foods available, fewer diseases are prevalent, there is a lower rate of infant mortality, longer life expectancy, and a general improvement in the condition of skin, hair, teeth and physical ability.

In developed countries, many factors have contributed to an improvement in health, such as better sanitation, health care services and higher living standards. Other factors are also important, such as an increasing awareness of the dangers of smoking and alcohol, and the knowledge that sufficient sleep and physical exercise benefit your

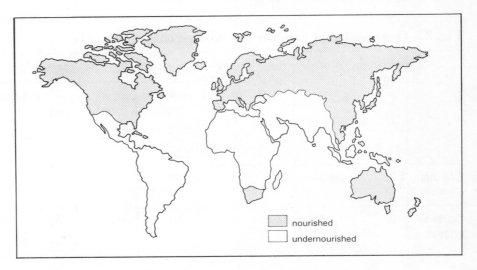

nourished
undernourished

Fig. 2.1 The nourished and undernourished countries

health. In addition, many people believe that the amount and types of food eaten has also been important in making people healthier.

List some examples of indications that show people care about the food they eat, e.g. from newspapers or magazines, from radio and television programmes, and from product advertisements.

How many people do you know who say they are 'on a diet'?

Recent studies of the health of people in various parts of the world have shown that both the *quantity* and the *quality* of food are important factors in keeping people healthy. A knowledge of the quality, i.e. the *nutritional value* of food is essential for a wise choice of foods to keep you healthy.

Nutrition

Nutrition is the study of the chemical composition of foods and how the body uses food. All food is made from chemical substances which are known as nutrients. These are absorbed and used by the body to keep us alive. Water may also be considered as a nutrient, since it is vital for life. The names of the other types of nutrients are:
- proteins, fats, carbohydrates, vitamins and mineral elements.

There are many different nutrients in each of these groups: about fifty are known to be essential to human life. Nutrients vary in chemical composition and each has a specific function in the body. The characteristic of each nutrient is described later (see p. 20). Dietary fibre, although not absorbed, is also essential for healthy living.

Nutrients are needed in varying amounts by the body. It has been found that these amounts vary with the age and sex of the person, and the individual's degree of activity and rate of using the nutrients. The estimated intake of nutrients to achieve healthy living is known as the Recommended Daily Intake (RDI)(see p. 48). Throughout life, water, proteins, fats and carbohydrates are needed in large quantities. They are known as the macro-nutrients and are usually measured in grams (g). Vitamins and mineral elements are needed in much smaller amounts, and are known as the micro-nutrients. They are measured in milligrams (mg), or micro-grams (μg).

$$(1000\,\mu g = 1\,mg; \qquad 1000\,mg = 1\,g).$$

Even though some of these nutrients are needed in such small amounts, they are essential to the *efficient functioning* of the human body.

Most foods are mixtures of nutrients. The composition of foods is shown in food tables (e.g. *The Composition of Foods*, McCance and Widdowson, or *Manual of Nutrition*, HMSO). Some computer programs are also available which incorporate food tables. Most food tables quote the nutrient composition per 100 g of food. Therefore it is important to know the weight of food per portion and understand the use of food tables, if you want to calculate the nutrient content of a meal.

Foods are often popularly identified by the nutrients they contain, that is, whether they contain useful amounts of certain nutrients. For example, cheese is often considered to be a protein food, because compared with other foods it contains a large amount of protein. However, cheese also contains many other nutrients, and the composition varies with the type of cheese: see Fig. 2.2.

Fig. 2.2 Composition of Cheddar and cottage cheese, per 100 g

	water (g)	protein (g)	fat (g)	carbo-hydrate (g)	minerals		vitamins					
					calcium (mg)	iron (mg)	vit. A (μg)	B group vitamins (mg)			vit. C (mg)	vit. D (μg)
								thiamin	ribo-flavin	niacin		
Cheddar cheese	37	26.0	33.5	0	800	0.4	412	0.04	0.50	6.2	0	0.26
Cottage cheese	79	13.6	4.0	1.4	60	0.1	41	0.02	0.19	3.3	0	0.02

Many food manufacturers now recognise that consumers like to know the nutritional value of their products. In Britain, they are required by law to list ingredients in descending order of weight (see Fig. 2.3), but this does not tell you the nutritional value of the food product. Some manufacturers also give nutrition information about their products. These lists often give the nutrient content per 100 g of food, per serving or as an estimate of the proportion of the recommended daily intake of nutrients an average serving will supply.

Fig. 2.3 Nutritional information (a): Allinson's Wholemeal Bread

Nutritional Information

Typical Analysis	Per 100 g	For daily serving of 4 slices (133 g)
Protein	9.5 g	12.2 g
Fat	2.6 g	3.3 g
Carbohydrate	45.6 g	58.4 g
Dietary Fibre	8.5 g	10.9 g

Ingredients

Wholemeal flour, water, yeast, salt, vegetable fat, dextrose, emulsifier, permitted preservative E282.

(b) Food Facts Birds Eye Frozen Peas

Most people know that peas contain vitamin C, but they are also an important source of dietary fibre. One ounce of cooked peas contains on average 3 mg of vitamin C, so that a 3 oz portion can supply about one third of the recommended daily intake.

One ounce of peas contains			
Protein 1.5 g	Fat below 0.5 g	Carbohydrate 2 g
Calories 15		

No one food contains sufficient nutrients for perfect health, so it is important to choose a mixed diet carefully. A *diet* is the total intake of food and drink, and includes all snacks, sweets and alcoholic drinks. A *balanced diet* is one that contains all the nutrients in the required proportion for each person at a particular stage in his life. If the nutrients are not balanced in the diet, the person may become unhealthy and suffer from the effects of malnutrition.

Malnutrition

Malnutrition is defined as an imbalance of nutrients in the diet. The symptoms may include slight depression, tiredness, splitting nails, spotty skin, dry or greasy hair. People suffering from these symptoms may not realise that they may be caused by a poor diet. The effects of a poor diet are not immediate, but are cumulative over several months. Malnutrition may be caused either by:
- a lack of nutrients (undernutrition)
- an excess of nutrients (overnutrition).

Undernutrition

This occurs when the total energy supply and intake of essential nutrients is less than body requirements. In the developing countries, diseases such as marasmus and kwashiorkor occur frequently.

Marasmus most often affects children under one year old. Because they have too little food to eat, their bodies become thin, very weak and eventually they die.

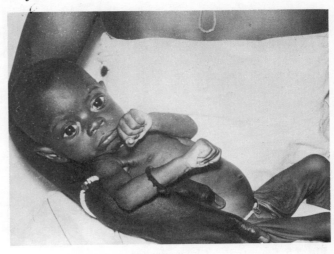

Fig. 2.4 Symptoms of marasmus

Kwashiorkor affects all age groups. The symptoms are retarded growth and retention of body fluids which causes swelling of the abdomen and eventual death. It was once thought that kwashiorkor was a symptom of a deficiency of protein in the diet. Now it is thought that these symptoms may occur when there is insufficient food available, that is, both protein and energy-giving foods. These symptoms occur most frequently during famine conditions.

Many other diseases occur due to the lack of a specific nutrient. These include:
- beri-beri, due to a lack of vitamin B_1 (see p. 33);
- scurvy, due to a lack of vitamin C (see p. 31);
- rickets, due to a lack of vitamin D (see p. 34).

More than half the world's population is suffering from various types of undernutrition. The map on page 11 shows the area where the worst problems of undernutrition occur today.

In the developed countries, undernutrition is extremely rare. However, despite the availability of many different foods some people still eat a diet containing an imbalance of nutrients.

Fig. 2.5 Symptoms of kwashiorkor

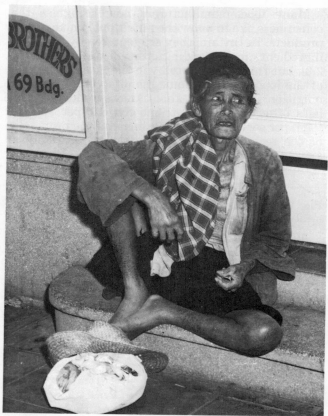

Fig. 2.6 Symptoms of beri-beri

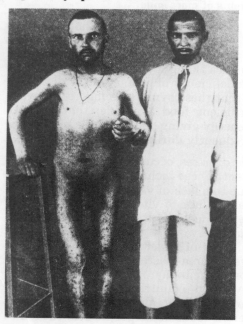

Fig. 2.7 Symptoms of scurvy

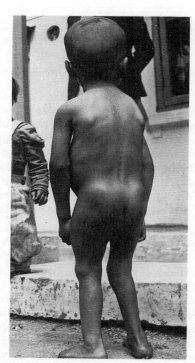

Fig. 2.8 Symptoms of rickets

A few people, especially adolescent girls, suffer from anorexia nervosa (see Fig. 2.9). This illness is caused either by excessive slimming or an eating disorder. It may originate from emotional unhappiness; for example, grief, fear of growing up, instability in relationships with family or friends, unhappiness about body size and weight. The person suffers a drastic weight loss, becomes very ill and cannot eat. In severe cases, death occurs.

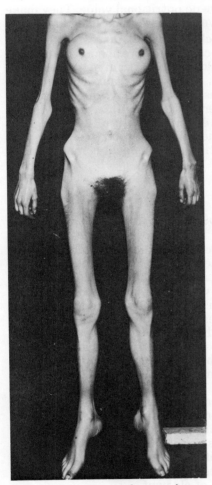

Fig. 2.9 Symptoms of anorexia nervosa

Many people in developed countries suffer from a deficiency of the mineral element iron at some stage in their lives and therefore suffer from anaemia. If the body is deficient in iron, insufficient red blood cells are formed and therefore not enough oxygen gets to the muscles. Anaemic people are usually pale and lack energy (see p. 37).

The diet of many people in developed countries is lacking in dietary fibre. This leads to the problem of constipation. If the symptoms are severe and prolonged they can lead to the development of more serious illnesses (see p. 27).

Overnutrition

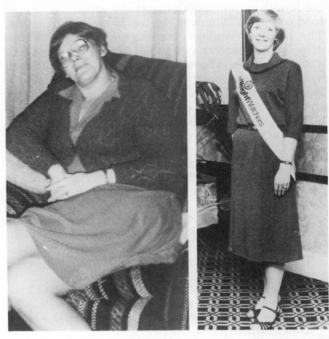

Fig. 2.10 A victim of obesity overcomes

Overnutrition occurs when the total intake of nutrients is greater than body requirements. For example, an excess of food is stored as body fat. Overnutrition is rare in developing countries but is common in the developed world. This condition, known as *obesity*, is unhealthy because:
- the extra body weight puts an excessive strain on heart, lungs and blood circulation,
- obese people are more susceptible to high blood pressure, heart disease, chest infections and diabetes.

An excess of sugar in the diet is known to accelerate tooth decay and gum disease. Decay

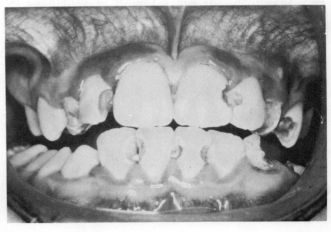

Fig. 2.11 Tooth decay

starts when bacteria which are normally present in the mouth combine with the sweet, sticky residue of food to form a film over the teeth, known as plaque. The bacteria convert the sugars to acids which dissolve the protective enamel coating on the teeth and form holes. These symptoms can be minimised by reducing the sugar content of the diet (e.g. sugar, sweets, cakes), and by regular, thorough cleaning of the teeth and gums.

Summary

There is scientific evidence to suggest that the wrong kinds of diets contribute to the higher rate of cancer and coronary heart disease in developed countries.

The problems associated with nutrition show the importance of a wise choice of nutritionally well-balanced foods in the diet.

The foods we eat must supply the nutrients we need to:
- build and repair body cells and tissue;
- supply energy and warmth;
- regulate all body processes and protect the body from disease.

Fig. 2.12 The general functions of the nutrient groups

Tissue-builders	Energy-givers	Regulators and protectors
proteins	fats	vitamins
some mineral elements	carbohydrates	mineral elements
	proteins if eaten in excess	
water		water
		dietary fibre

The categories in Fig. 2.12 are not exclusive as some nutrients have several functions. Some nutrients are also dependent on the presence of others to be effective. The specific characteristics of each are described in the next section.

2   What is food?

Food is composed of many chemical substances. They are responsible for the structure, colour, flavour and nutritional value of the food. Most of these chemical substances occur naturally in the food. Others are added by food product manufacturers. The chemical substances that give colour and flavour to foods are present in very small quantities and have no nutritional value. They make food look attractive and taste appetising.

The remaining chemical substances in food are called *nutrients* because they are absorbed and used by the body to build new cells, to give it energy and to keep it healthy. The types of nutrients in foods are water, proteins, fats, carbohydrates, vitamins and mineral elements. Dietary fibre, although not absorbed, is also essential for healthy living. To understand how the body uses food (see p. 39), it is necessary to describe the chemical composition of the nutrients.

Chemical composition of nutrients

All food is composed of chemical substances. These substances are made up of millions and millions of units of matter called molecules. Molecules are extremely small. Even a very small spoonful of food will contain millions of molecules. It is the chemical composition of these molecules, and the way they are held together, the *intermolecular bonding*, which determines the texture, the function and the way the body uses the nutrient. For instance, the differences between milk and meat are the result of different chemical composition and the way the molecules in the foods are held together.

Molecules are composed of even smaller units of matter called atoms. Atoms are also held together by bonds, known as *intramolecular bonds*. There are 98 different types of atom already discovered, called elements. However, most nutrients contain only a few different types of element.

Nutrients are broadly classified into two groups, according to which elements they contain:
- *inorganic nutrients* e.g. mineral elements such as calcium, magnesium, iodine, iron and phosphorus and their compounds.
- *organic nutrients* e.g. proteins, fats, carbohydrates and vitamins form the greatest proportion of nutrients in food (excluding water). Dietary fibre is also mainly organic. All organic substances contain carbon atoms, which are bonded to themselves and to hydrogen and oxygen atoms to form molecules. Sometimes inorganic elements, such as sulphur, phosphorus and iron are bonded into some protein and some vitamin molecules.

Proteins are special in that they always contain nitrogen.

To understand how the body uses these organic nutrients, it is necessary to describe the atoms and the nature of the intramolecular bonds which hold the atoms together. This type of bonding is known as *covalent bonding*.

Atoms and covalent bonding

An atom consists of even smaller units of matter: a nucleus and a number of electrons. The nucleus contains almost the total mass of the atom, and is positively charged. The electrons are simply units of negative electrical charge. They have energy and move very quickly around the nucleus in specific volumes of space, known as orbitals. The orbital in which an electron moves is determined by its energy level. Electrons and orbitals bond atoms together, and so build up molecules.

Atoms differ in the size of the nucleus, and the number of accompanying electrons. For example, the hydrogen atom is the smallest atom of all. It has only one electron, which revolves around the nucleus in a spherical orbital.

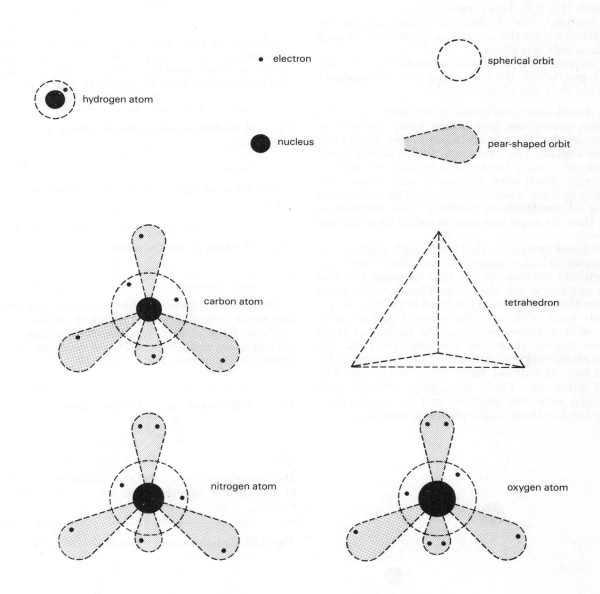

Fig. 2.13 Hydrogen, carbon, nitrogen and oxygen atoms

The carbon atom is larger. It has six electrons. Two of these electrons are located together in one inner spherical orbital. When this orbital contains two electrons it is full. The remaining four electrons are each located in a pear-shaped orbital further away from the nucleus as shown in Fig. 2.13.

Nitrogen and oxygen atoms are larger still. In each case the atom has a large nucleus. Nitrogen has seven electrons, oxygen has eight. Both nitrogen and oxygen have the same arrangement of orbitals as the carbon atom. Two electrons are located in the inner spherical orbital. The remaining electrons are in four pear-shaped orbitals further away from the nucleus. When a pear-shaped orbital contains two electrons, it is full. This means that:

● for nitrogen, one of these orbitals contains two electrons whilst the remaining three orbitals each contain only one electron,

● for oxygen two of these orbitals contain two electrons, whilst the remaining two orbitals each contain only one electron.

The distribution and quantity of electrons within an atom determines how atoms bond together to form molecules. Atoms are more stable when their orbitals contain two electrons. When atoms react, the molecule that is formed will contain full orbitals of electrons. Each atom will lose or gain one or more electrons to form a stable molecule. This losing and gaining of electrons is bonding. The number of bonds that the atom can form is called its *oxidation number*.

Sometimes two atoms that have single electrons in their outer orbitals approach each other and the two orbitals overlap. When this happens the two atoms can share the electrons. This forms a bond between the two atoms. This bond is called a *single covalent bond*. For example, when a carbon atom reacts with a hydrogen atom, the hydrogen atom becomes stable. It shares one electron from the carbon atom, making the number of electrons in its orbital two. It will not form any more bonds. The carbon atom has three remaining orbitals each containing only one electron and could therefore form a further three single covalent bonds.

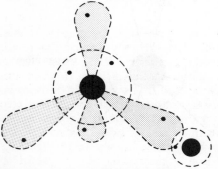

Fig. 2.14 A single covalent bond between carbon and hydrogen

Single covalent bonds are usually written with lines representing the orbitals available for bonding. Consequently, the atoms in organic nutrients are usually written as in Fig. 2.15.

Fig. 2.15 The atoms in organic nutrients (single covalent bonds)

hydrogen	H–
oxygen	–O–
nitrogen	–N–
carbon	–C–

Because of the symmetry of the four orbitals of the carbon atom, it is possible for different carbon atoms to share electrons. This creates a *carbon-to-carbon covalent bond* as shown in Fig. 2.16.

Fig. 2.16 Carbon-to-carbon covalent bond

$$-\overset{|}{\underset{|}{C}}-\overset{|}{\underset{|}{C}}-$$

Long chains of carbon atoms can be formed; see Fig. 2.17.

Fig. 2.17 Chain of carbon atoms

$$-\overset{|}{\underset{|}{C}}-\overset{|}{\underset{|}{C}}-\overset{|}{\underset{|}{C}}-\overset{|}{\underset{|}{C}}-\overset{|}{\underset{|}{C}}-$$

These chains form the basic structure of organic nutrients: proteins, fats and carbohydrates.

These long chains can also be branched, if a carbon atom shares its electrons with two or more other carbon atoms, as in Fig. 2.18.

Fig. 2.18 Branched chain of carbon atoms

$$-\overset{\overset{|}{C}-}{\underset{|}{C}}-\overset{|}{\underset{|}{C}}-\overset{|}{\underset{|}{C}}-\overset{|}{\underset{|}{C}}-\overset{|}{\underset{|}{C}}-\overset{|}{\underset{|}{C}}-$$

It is also possible in certain conditions for carbon atoms to link together and form a ring structure. See Fig. 2.19.

Fig. 2.19 Carbon atoms in ring structure

Fig. 2.20 Carbon atoms in double convalent bond

$$\diagup C = C \diagdown$$

Sometimes *double covalent bonds* are formed between carbon atoms and other carbon atoms when four electrons are shared. In this case, two orbitals of each carbon atom are involved in forming the bond. The double bond is represented in Fig. 2.20.

Carbon can also form double covalent bonds with oxygen and nitrogen atoms. Using these single and double covalent bonds, carbon, hydrogen, oxygen and nitrogen atoms combine in seven common ways to form groups of atoms called chemical groups (Fig. 2.21).

These chemical groups of atoms are represented as in Fig. 2.21.

Fig. 2.21 Chemical groups

Chemical group	Structure of group	Nutrient molecules containing these groups
Hydrocarbon	$-\overset{\mid}{\underset{\mid}{C}}-H$	Carbohydrate
		Proteins
		Fats
Carbonyl	$\overset{O}{\underset{\parallel}{-C-}}$	Carbohydrate
		Proteins
		Fats
Alcohol	$-\overset{\mid}{\underset{\mid}{C}}-O-H$	Carbohydrates
		Fats
Acid	$-C\overset{O}{\underset{O-H}{\diagup\diagdown}}$	Proteins (amino acids)
		Fats (fatty acids)
Ester	$-C\overset{O}{\underset{O-C-}{\diagup\diagdown}}$	Fats
Peptide	$-\overset{\mid}{\underset{}{N}}-\overset{O}{\underset{\parallel}{C}}-$	Proteins
Amine	$-N\overset{H}{\underset{H}{\diagup\diagdown}}$	Proteins

These chemical groups are used to build up the molecular structure of nutrients, and can be seen in the chemical formula. The particular groups used and the way they are arranged in the molecule determines the characteristics of the nutrient.

An example of the way in which a nutrient molecule is built up from various combinations of these chemical groups can be understood by describing the chemical composition and molecular structure of the carbohydrate, glucose.

Glucose

Glucose is a small nutrient molecule made up from hydrocarbon, alcohol and carbonyl chemical groups. When it is refined and dried, as a white powder, it has the chemical formula, as a chain molecule, shown in Fig. 2.22.

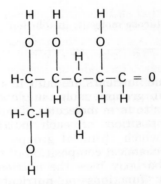

Fig. 2.22 Chemical formula for glucose

This can also be written as

CH₂OH. CHOH. CHOH. CHOH. CHOH. CHO.

The formula is obtained by adding the total number of atoms of each element in the molecule. You will therefore more usually see the formula for glucose written as

$C_2H_{12}O_6$.

Glucose occurs naturally in plants. It is dissolved in solution. The glucose molecule has a ring rather than a chain structure. This occurs because the chain of carbon atoms is very flexible, and it can twist back on itself, allowing the carbonyl group to come close to and react with the alcohol group. The hydrogen atom on the alcohol group moves to the oxygen atom on the carbonyl group and a new C–O single bond is formed, as shown in Fig. 2.23.

In the body, glucose is also in solution in the bloodstream. It is therefore represented with a ring structure.

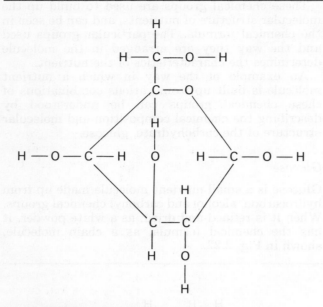

Fig. 2.23 The glucose molecule in solution

Other organic nutrients are built in similar ways from chemical groups using single and double covalent bonds to form molecules of nutrients. The chemical composition of each nutrient varies according to which chemical groups of atoms it contains. The chemical composition of the nutrient affects how the body uses the nutrients in food. These specific functions of nutrients are now described.

The nutrients in food

All food is composed of mixtures of many nutrients. When the function of each nutrient is understood, it is easy to realise the importance of choosing foods that not only look and taste good, but that are also nutritionally good for you. Look at Fig. 2.24.

You can see that some nutrients have several functions. Some nutrients are dependent on other nutrients to function efficiently. The specific characteristics of each nutrient are now described.

Water

Water is essential for human survival. The body can survive weeks without food, but death occurs within a few days without water. About 70% of the body weight is water. It is found in all parts of the body: in all cells, body tissues and blood. Water is not stored in the body, and the water loss must be replenished daily. A lack of water causes dehydration and this produces feelings of fatigue, headaches and digestive upsets.

The main function of water in the body is as a solvent:
- body fluids transport nutrients around the body;
- oxygen and carbon-dioxide are carried in the blood stream;
- the enzymes in the digestive system (see p. 40) are carried in liquids, e.g. saliva in the mouth, gastric juices in the stomach, bile and intestinal juices;
- waste products are removed in solution from body tissues and organs. The kidneys filter waste products which are carried away in urine.

Water in the body also protects the central nervous system, lubricates all joints and has the ability to regulate normal body temperature. It retains heat and prevents a quick rise in body temperature when heat is absorbed. Water also causes cooling when it evaporates from the surface of the skin as perspiration.

Water is lost from the body in four ways: urine; perspiration; in breathing out; and in the faeces.

Water is taken into the body in three ways: drinking liquids; in foods; and some water is released during the metabolic processes in the body (see p. 44).

The volume of water taken into the body should equal the volume lost each day, as shown in Fig. 2.25.

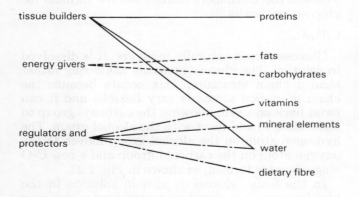

Fig. 2.24 The general function of the nutrient groups

tissue builders — proteins
energy givers — fats
— carbohydrates
— vitamins
— mineral elements
regulators and protectors — water
— dietary fibre

Fig. 2.25 Average adult man - water exchange/day

input:	2.6 litres/day	*output:*	2.6 litres/day
drinks	1.5	urine	1.5
foods	0.8	perspiration	0.6
metabolic		lungs	0.4
changes	0.3	faeces	0.1

In a normal healthy person, living in average conditions, this balance is usually well maintained.

Water is supplied in the diet as drinking water, and as a component of many other drinks and foods such as milk, meat, fruit and vegetables.

Proteins

Proteins are essential to life, as all living cells are built from protein molecules. Proteins are used by the body for:

● growth of new cells;
● repair of cells in body tissues.

The main sources of protein are milk, cheese, meat, fish, eggs, soya beans and nuts. Cereal grains and cereal products also supply valuable amounts of protein as they form a large proportion of the diet.

Look at the top photograph in plate 5.

It shows various foods, each of which supplies 10 g of protein.
List: (a) the animal foods,
  (b) the vegetable foods that contain a good supply of protein.

The chemical structure of proteins

There are many plant, animal and human proteins, which vary in chemical structure. However, all proteins are built from amino acids in long three-dimensional chains of molecules. Amino acids are molecules that contain an amine group, NH_2, and an acid group (COOH)(see p.19). Amino acid molecules therefore contain carbon, hydrogen, oxygen and nitrogen atoms. It is the presence of nitrogen that makes proteins unique and essential to life. The body cannot obtain nitrogen from any other source. Sometimes other inorganic elements, e.g. sulphur, phosphorus and iron, are also linked into the chain.

There are twenty-two different amino acids. Various combinations of these amino acids can be arranged in many different ways. As amino acid groups join, they form larger molecules known as *peptides*. As more amino acids react with peptides, very large chains of amino acids are formed called *polypeptides*. These polypeptides combine in branched and twisted chains to form protein molecules.

The protein molecules can be built up from many different amino acid molecules. For example, insulin, which is found in the pancreas, is a polypeptide built up from 51 amino acid molecules. Urease, which is found in soya beans, is built up from 4500 amino acid molecules.

The quality of protein (biological value)

Because proteins vary in the number, type and arrangement of amino acids present in their molecules, the quality of the protein also varies. The quality of a protein is expressed as its *biological value*. It has been found that eight amino acids are essential for tissue grown in adults. These are isoleucine, leucine, lysine, methionine, phenylalanine, threonine, tryptophan and valine. Children need two additional amino acids which are arginine and histidine. Proteins which supply all the essential amino acids are said to have a high biological value. These proteins are found in milk, cheese, eggs, meat, fish and soya beans. However, some proteins do not contain all the essential amino acids; they are said to have a low biological value. These proteins can compensate for each other's deficiencies if eaten together, and in large quantities, e.g. a vegetarian diet which contains proteins in nuts, mixed vegetables, cereal grains and cereal products.

Each protein has its own chemical name. Some examples are:

collagen: meat, fish (connective tissue)
elastin: meat (muscle fibres)
gelatine: meat, fish
casein: milk, cheese
lactalbumin: milk
lactoglobulin: milk
ovalbumin: egg white
lipovitellin: egg yolk
gliadin: wheat
glutenin: wheat

When heated, all protein molecules change in chemical structure. The proteins are said to be 'denatured': that is, they harden and lose their elasticity. This process is known as coagulation (see p. 41).

Protein in the diet

Fig. 2.26 Recommended Daily Intake (RDI) of protein

children		adults			
0–2 years	30 g	women	18–55	most occupations	55 g
2–5 years	40 g			active occupations	65 g
5–9 years	50 g		over 55		50 g
boys					
9–12 years	60 g	men	18–35	sedentary occupation	70 g
12–15 years	70 g			active occupation	80 g
15–18 years	75 g		35–65	sedentary occupation	65 g
girls				active occupation	80 g
9–18 years	55 g		over 65		60 g

The recommended daily intake of protein, as shown in Fig. 2.26, varies with age, sex and occupational activity. Why do you think this is so?

To ensure an adequate supply of essential amino acids, it is recommended that one-third of a day's protein intake should be of high biological value proteins, and that some protein should be eaten at each meal.

Look at the top photo in plate 5. These foods all supply 10 g protein. Plan a day's menu that supplies your recommended daily intake of protein including both high and low biological value proteins.

In most developing countries - parts of India, China, Africa, South America, - the traditional diet is based on cereal products, such as rice. Because the protein content of cereal products is of low biological value, the diet of people in these areas of the world may be deficient in some essential amino acids, for example lysine.

Recently there have been many attempts to improve the protein content of people's diet in these areas of the world by:
- educating the people to understand the importance of adequate nutrition;
- developing new strains of rice, millet and wheat with higher protein content;
- encouraging the growth of cereal and pulse crops such as soybeans and peas which have higher protein content than the starchy root crops of cassava and yam;
- encouraging the development of poultry and fish farms. These animals have short life-spans and develop quickly and are, therefore, cheap to rear;
- distributing dried milk powders to mothers and children in school and instructing them how to use them;
- producing fortified products, i.e. cereal grains with additives of amino acids, vitamins A and D, and calcium. Some examples of these products are 'Fortifex' made from maize and soybean in Brazil, 'Ariac' made from ground nuts and skimmed milk powder in Nigeria, and 'Lactone' made from ground nuts, skimmed milk powder, wheat and barley in India.

In contrast, people in developed countries receive an abundance of protein in the diet. It is wasteful to include too much protein in the diet: any excess is broken down during the digestive process, nitrogen is excreted, but excess carbon, hydrogen and oxygen is stored as body fat (see p. 15).

Protein in your diet

From the weights of food in your day's menu, use food tables or a computer program to calculate the amount of animal and vegetable protein in your diet.

Does the total represent an adequate intake of protein for you?

The main sources of high biological value protein are from animal sources; that is, meat, fish, milk, cheese and eggs. These products are very expensive and slow to produce in comparison with cereal grain

---

Using food tables or a computer program, work out the protein content of an average serving of these foods, assuming the portion size to be as follows:

white bread 50 g	beef 100 g	pineapples 50 g
wholemeal bread 50 g	chicken 100 g	apples 100 g
cornflakes 25 g	bacon 50 g	bananas 100 g
rice 25 g	sausage 100 g	potatoes 100 g
spaghetti 25 g	herring 100 g	yams 100 g
Cheddar cheese 25 g	cod 100 g	baked beans 100 g
milk 150 ml		haricot beans 100 g
eggs 50 g		peas 100 g
yoghurt 150 g		peanuts 150 g

Show the protein content of an average serving of these foods in descending order in a bar chart. For each food, calculate the percentage of the recommended daily intake of protein for you that these portions would supply.

crops. Therefore, there has been much research into producing protein foods more efficiently:

1 The most notable advancement has been the use of soya bean to manufacture a product called textured vegetable protein (TVP) (see p. 180). The soya bean is of high biological value, and is easy and cheap to grow in many areas of the world.

2 Imitation dried milk can be made by a complicated process from protein in green leaves (this is a manufacturing process similar to that achieved by the dairy cow). Several forms of this type of milk powder are now produced.

3 Several experimental plants are now producing a single-celled protein from yeast which is allowed to grow on the waste products from oil refineries. Protein for animal feed has already been developed in this way. Perhaps one day it may also be available for humans.

These experimental ways of producing protein are perhaps the beginnings of new food processes which may avert a protein crisis in the twenty-first century. As consumers, we should be willing to explore ways of presenting these products in appetising meals.

Fat

The term 'fat' includes both oils and fats. Oils are liquid and fats are solid at room temperature. They have a similar chemical structure and similar functions in the body. Fat is a useful nutrient in the diet because:
- it is a concentrated source of energy;
- it is essential to the structure and function of body cells;
- several vitamins (A, D, E and K) are fat-soluble;
- fat is stored under the skin where it acts as an insulator;
- fat is digested very slowly, therefore it prevents hunger sensations for longer than other nutrients.

Fats are widely distributed in both animal and plant foods, either as solid fat or as an oil. In some foods, the fat is visible, as on fatty meat. In other foods the fat is invisible, e.g. as in eggs, mayonnaise, gravy. In these foods, the fat is finely distributed as an emulsion (see pp.182–184).

Chemical structure of fat

Fats belong to the chemical group, esters. Fat molecules are formed by the reaction of one alcohol molecule, glycerol ($C_3H_8O_3$) and three fatty acid molecules. The fatty acid molecules contain chains of different lengths of carbon and hydrogen atoms

each ending with an acid group. Some fatty acids exist with 16, 18 or 20 carbon atoms in the chain. When fatty acids react with glycerol, a triglyceride is formed. This is more usually called a fat.

Fig. 2.27 Reaction to form a fat

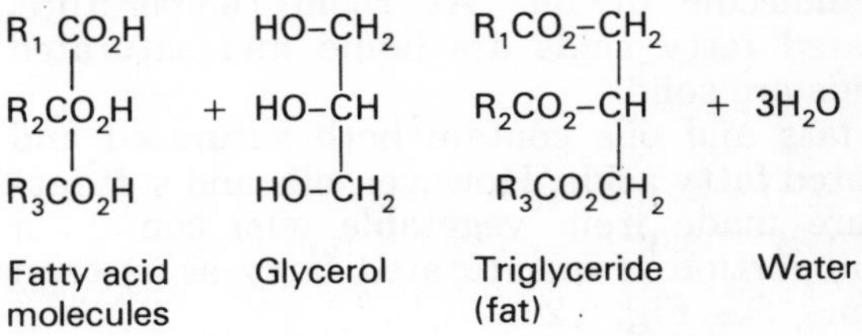

$$
\begin{array}{cccc}
R_1 CO_2H & HO-CH_2 & R_1CO_2-CH_2 & \\
R_2CO_2H & +\ HO-CH & R_2CO_2-CH & +\ 3H_2O \\
R_3CO_2H & HO-CH_2 & R_3CO_2CH_2 & \\
\text{Fatty acid} & \text{Glycerol} & \text{Triglyceride} & \text{Water} \\
\text{molecules} & & \text{(fat)} &
\end{array}
$$

Note: R_1, R_2 + R_3 represent a chain of fatty acids

There are at least forty different fatty acids. Many occur together in one food; for example, milk contains sixteen different fatty acids.

The chemical formulae of three of the fatty acids present in foods are shown in Fig. 2.28. The long chains of carbon and hydrogen atoms are shown as (CH_2).

Fig. 2.28 Chemical formulae of three fatty acids

Myristic	$CH_3 -(CH_2)_{12} CO_2H$
Palmitic	$CH_3 -(CH_2)_{14} CO_2H$
Stearic	$CH_3 -(CH_2)_{16} CO_2H$

Because these molecules contain only carbon-to-carbon single covalent bonds (that is, every possible single bond is formed), the molecule is said to be *saturated*. They are examples of molecules known as *saturated fatty acids*.

Some fatty acids contain carbon-to-carbon double covalent bonds. These molecules are said to be *unsaturated*. If the fatty acid molecule contains only one double bond, it is said to be *monounsaturated*, e.g. oleic acid. If a fatty acid contains two or more double bonds it is said to be *polyunsaturated*. The following are examples of some of the polyunsaturated fatty acids which are commonly found in foods:
- linoleic acid: contains 2 double bonds
- linolenic acid: contains 3 double bonds
- arachidonic acid: contains 4 double bonds

Some polyunsaturated fatty acids, e.g. linolenic and arachidonic, are known to be essential to the efficient functioning of the body. They are known as *essential fatty acids* (EFA). They are found in vegetable oils. They must be obtained from food as the body cannot synthesise them from any other source.

The presence of double bonds in the fatty acid chain determines the final nature of a fat. Whether the fat is:
● hard like the fat on meat;
● soft like tub margarine;
● liquid like vegetable oils;
is determined by the type and number of fatty acids in the molecule of fat. At room temperature, unsaturated fatty acids are liquid and saturated fatty acids are solid.

Most fats and oils contain both saturated and unsaturated fatty acids. However, oils and soft fats (which are made from vegetable oils) contain a higher proportion of unsaturated fatty acids than animal fats. See Fig. 2.29.

Fig. 2.29 Proportion of fatty acids in corn oil, butter and egg yolk.

	saturated fatty acids (%)	unsaturated fatty acids (%)
corn oil	17	83
butter	52	48
egg yolk	49	51

Fat in the diet

The proportion of fat in the diet is greater in affluent countries than in the developing countries. For example, the percentage of total energy value of the diet (see p. 49) which is obtained from fat is approximately 41% in the USA, 43% in the UK, but only 13% or less in India.

The main sources of fat or oil in the diet are shown in Fig. 2.30.

Fig. 2.30 The main sources of fat or oil in the diet

Animal sources	Vegetable sources
butter	vegetable oils e.g. sunflower, corn, olive, peanut, soya, cotton seed, coconut and palm oils
lard	
dripping	margarine and cooking fats (made from vegetable oils)
suet	nuts
	whole cereals, e.g. oatmeal, wheatgerm
milk, cream	
cheese	
eggs	
oily fish	
meat	

It is important to remember that many com-posite dishes also contain fat, e.g. pastry, cakes, sauces, salad dressing.

Using food tables, calculate the amount of fat in each portion of food that you ate on the day you recorded your diet. Which foods supplied most fat? Calculate the total amount of fat you ate on that day.

Because of recent research, nutritionists now suggest that only 30–35% of the energy value of a diet should be supplied by fat (see p. 50). It is thought that in developed countries, people should reduce their intake of fat to achieve a better nutritional balance. There are several simple ways to reduce the fat intake:
● reduce the amount of fried foods in the diet;
● trim excess fat from joints of meat;
● avoid spreading fat thickly on bread, scones, etc;
● use skimmed milk whenever possible, especially in cooked dishes, e.g. sauces, custards, cakes;
● avoid eating large helpings of cream and hard cheeses;
● reduce the intake of cakes and pastries.

It is, however, important to remember that some vegetable oils, which contain polyunsaturated fatty acids, supply the essential fatty acids (EFA) such as linolenic acid. The use of vegetable oils in preference to animal fat where possible in cooking will ensure a supply of these essential nutrients.

It is also believed by some nutritionists that the use of polyunsaturated fats in the diet reduces the level of cholesterol in the blood. Cholesterol ($C_{27}H_{45}OH$), a fat-like substance, is found in all animal tissue. It is synthesised in the liver and transported in the blood. Some foods contain a high proportion of cholesterol, e.g. egg yolk, butter, cream, cheese, dripping, fat in meat, suet and lard. Poultry and fish are low in cholesterol. Fruit and vegetables do not contain any.

It is thought that when too much cholesterol has accumulated in the blood, it is deposited along the walls of the arteries. If this happens, the arteries become narrower. This may increase the chances of a blood clot forming, and a possible heart attack occurring. The association between the level of cholesterol in the blood, and the incidence of heart attack is possibly one cause of heart diseases.

It is obviously nutritionally wise to reduce the total amount of fat in the diet. Excess fat in the diet is only stored as excess body fat, and as such it can be harmful to health.

Plate 3 Styles of advertising

(a) cream cakes

Already she was more deeply involved than she cared to admit...

Naughty. But nice.

(b) hamburgers

To enhance their beef, McDonald's have found the perfect additive. Nothing.

We say no to a lot of ingredients when we're preparing the beef for a McDonald's Hamburger.

Flavour enhancers are out. Colour enhancers are out. Fillers, binders and preservatives are out. So what's left in? 100% pure beef, that's all.

Our philosophy is, start off with the best and you won't need to beef it up later on.

Which is why we choose cuts like lean chuck, brisket and flank.

Not surprisingly, our hamburgers are rich in many nutrients.

A Quarter Pounder,* for instance, will give you two-fifths of your daily need for protein. As well as one-third of your daily need for Niacin, an essential B vitamin, and one-quarter of your daily need for Iron.

Naturally our beef also contains some fat, but we take great care not to add any more.

So while we could choose to cook our hamburgers in fat, what do we use? Nothing, of course.

NUTRITIONAL FIGURES FOR A QUARTER POUNDER						
(Percentage of Recommended Daily Amounts for an Average Adult)†						
Protein 41.6	Calcium 17.2	Iron 26.0	Thiamin 26.0	Riboflavin 4.3	Niacin 33.5	Energy 16.5
Energy: 413 kcals		1728 kJoules			Fat: 20.7 grams	

†Department of Health 1979

McDonald's

At McDonald's we've got time for you.

Plate 4 Stages in the life cycle of healthy people

Plate 5

(a) Foods supplying 10g of protein

300 ml milk
200 ml natural yoghurt
750 ml double cream
80 g egg
40 g Cheddar cheese
75 g cottage cheese

35 g chicken
45 g minced beef
70 g bacon
75 g sausage

20 g textured vegetable protein
40 g peanuts
45 g red kidney beans
90 g walnuts

113 g wholemeal bread
195 g baked beans
175 g peas
1400 g carrots
475 g potatoes
3300 g apples
1250 g oranges

(b) Foods supplying 10g of dietary fibre

6 g Vita Fibre Bran tablets
(16 tablets)
16 g Toasted Bran
22 g bran
37 g ALL-BRAN Cereal
42 g dried apricots
62 g dried prunes

117 g wholemeal bread
370 g white bread

136 g baked beans
128 g peas
400 g potatoes, baked with skin
770 g apples

Plate 6 Foods supplying the RDI for a 15-year-old girl

(a) vitamin A (750 µg)

(b) vitamin B₁ (0.9 mg)

(c) vitamin C (30 mg)

(d) vitamin D (2.5 µg)

(e) calcium (600 mg)

(f) iron (15 mg)

Carbohydrates

Carbohydrates are important nutrients because they:
- supply energy for all activities (see p. 49);
- supply energy to maintain the normal body temperature;
- supply indigestible fibrous materials to aid digestion (see pp. 26-27);
- are important in the structure of cells.

Most carbohydrates are plant products. They are the sugars, starches, cellulose, protein and lignin in plants. A large proportion of the food we eat contains carbohydrates, for example cereal products, vegetables and fruits. Some carbohydrate in the form of glycogen (see p. 43) is stored in the liver.

The chemical structure of carbohydrates

Carbohydrates are large molecules built from carbon, hydrogen and oxygen atoms. All green plants contain a substance called chlorophyll in their leaves. They use this chlorophyll, energy from the sun, carbon dioxide from the air, and water from the soil, to manufacture carbohydrates in their leaves. The process is called photosynthesis.

$$\frac{\text{Carbon}}{\text{dioxide}} + \text{water} + \frac{\text{energy}}{\text{from sun}} \xrightarrow[\text{chlorophyll}]{} \text{carbohydrate} + \text{oxygen}$$

At first very simple carbohydrates are formed. They are known as *monosaccharides*, because they contain a single sugar molecule $C_6H_{12}O_6$ (see p.19).

As the process of photosynthesis continues, the single monosaccharide molecules are linked together to form larger molecules (see p. 16). They are known as *disaccharides* ($C_{12}H_{22}O_{11}$). (A molecule of water (H_2O) is lost as the reaction occurs.)

Eventually these disaccharides are joined in chain-and-branch chain formation to form large complex molecules (see p. 19). These are known as *polysaccharides*. Their general formula is $(C_6H_{10}O_5)n$, where 'n' represents the number of monosaccharide molecules in the chain.

Both polysaccharides and disaccharides are broken down in the body to monosaccharides during the process of digestion. Monosaccharides are then split to release energy for all body activities, carbon dioxide and water (see p. 44).

Types of carbohydrates

(a) *Monosaccharides* ($C_6H_{12}O_6$): Glucose, galactose and fructose. These are known as simple sugars. Although all these three monosaccharides have the same chemical composition, they differ in the arrangement of atoms within the molecule. The body is able to use all these simple sugars to produce energy (see pp. 44-45). Glucose is found most abundantly.

Glucose is found in fruits, honey, onions and sweetcorn. It is also available as a powder, tablets, or a colourless liquid. It is often used in the confectionery, jam-making and brewing industries. When food is broken down by the body, glucose is formed. It occurs in the blood of all animals because blood carries glucose around the body to the cells where it is needed. The level of glucose in the blood is regulated by the hormone insulin, which is secreted by the pancreas.

Fructose occurs in honey and in the juices of fruits and plants. It is the sweetest of all sugars.

Galactose is present in milk combined with glucose.

(b) *Disaccharides* ($C_{12}H_{22}O_{11}$): Sucrose, maltose and lactose.
All disaccharides have the same chemical composition, but different arrangements of atoms within their molecules (see p. 19). Disaccharides are all white crystalline solids which dissolve in water. The most common disaccharide is sucrose.

Sucrose is obtained from cane and beet sugar plants (see p. 195). It is formed by the joining of two monosaccharides, glucose and fructose. It is the most common sugar in everyday use.

Lactose (*milk sugar*) is found in the milk of all mammals. It tastes the least sweet of all sugars. Lactose is formed by the joining of two monosaccharide molecules glucose and galactose.

Maltose is found in germinating cereals and malt products. It is formed when two molecules of the monosaccharide glucose are joined together.

(c) *Polysaccharides* ($C_6H_{10}O_5)n$: Polysaccharides vary in chemical composition because of the different numbers of monosaccharides they contain in long chain-and-branched formations (see p. 19). The most common polysaccharides found in foods are starches and cellulose.

Starches contain many monosaccharide units. There are at least 3000 monosaccharide molecules in a small starch molecule. The properties of starches are different from sugars, i.e. they are not crystalline, nor sweet and will not dissolve in cold water. Starches occur in plants in microscopic granules. The size and shape of the granules depends on the plant from which they come. This structure affects their use in food preparation (see pp. 211-212).

Cellulose is a complex branched chain of approximately 5000 monosaccharide molecules. Cellulose is found in plant cell walls. It forms hair-like fibres which will not dissolve in water. It cannot be digested by humans, but has an important role in the diet as dietary fibre.

Carbohydrate in the diet

In Britain, about two thirds of food eaten is carbohydrate: in poorer countries the proportion is much higher.
The main sources of carbohydrate in the diet are:

Food containing starches
all cereals: wheat, oats, rice, maize
all cereal products: flour bread, cakes, biscuits, pastry, cornflour
pasta: spaghetti, lasagne
vegetables: potatoes, parsnips, turnips

Food containing sugars
cane and beet sugar
treacle, golden syrup, honey
all manufactured foods containing sugar: e.g. baked products, jams, soft drinks
fruits
some vegetables, e.g. parsnips, peas, sweetcorn and tomatoes

> Using food tables, calculate the amount of carbohydrate in each portion of food you ate on the day you recorded your diet. Which foods supplied most carbohydrate?

Carbohydrates usually supply the largest proportion of energy to the body.
Any excess carbohydrate is converted by the body into fat and stored in the tissues (see p. 45).

Therefore carbohydrates should be eaten only in sufficient quantity to satisfy hunger, after the need for other nutrients in the diet is satisfied. Therefore no recommended daily intake of carbohydrate is suggested in food tables (see p. 48).

Dietary fibre

Some parts of food are not digested or absorbed by the body. It is now realised that this part, once known as roughage but now known as dietary fibre, is very important for good health.

> Look at the bottom photograph on plate 5; which of these foods do you eat regularly?

Dietary fibre aids the process of excreting solid waste products from the body. The removal of waste products is vital, as they are potentially toxic to the body.
Dietary fibre absorbs water, and makes the residue of foods in the large intestine bulky and soft. This solid residue, known as the faeces, is pushed along the lower part of the large intestine, the colon, by muscular contractions of the intestinal wall. This action is known as peristalsis. The faeces finally collect in the rectum and pass out of the body regularly. This process usually requires very little effort, provided that the faeces are bulky and soft.
If there is insufficient dietary fibre to absorb water to make the faeces bulky and soft, the muscles of the colon have to contract more than usual to make the faeces pass along. This results in the faeces being small, hard and difficult to expel. This causes abdominal discomfort and a feeling of nausea. This condition is known as constipation.

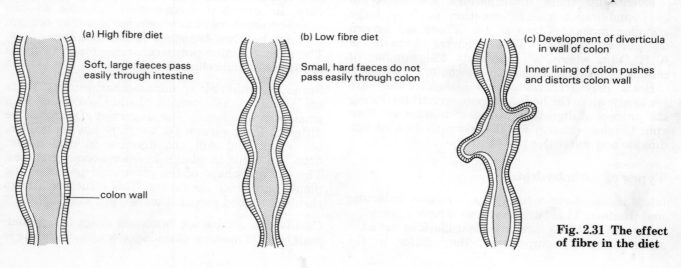

(a) High fibre diet

Soft, large faeces pass easily through intestine

colon wall

(b) Low fibre diet

Small, hard faeces do not pass easily through colon

(c) Development of diverticula in wall of colon

Inner lining of colon pushes and distorts colon wall

Fig. 2.31 The effect of fibre in the diet

If constipation is prolonged the inner lining of the colon may become distorted, sometimes inflamed and painful. This condition is known as diverticular disease. Part of the treatment for this disease is a high-fibre diet.

The main sources of dietary fibre are cereal grains, especially bran, fruits and vegetables.

Dietary fibre is a mixture of several complex chemical substances. Among them are cellulose, hemi-cellulose, pectin and lignin. They are all part of plant cell walls. Animal tissue contains no dietary fibre. The proportions of these different constituents of dietary fibre vary from plant to plant. The ability of dietary fibre to absorb water is dependent on the proportions of these chemical substances in the plant cell walls. Wheat bran contains 44% dietary fibre and has a high water-holding capacity (it can absorb up to six times its own weight). As a result it is one of the most concentrated sources of dietary fibre. Nuts and pulses (i.e. beans and peas) are also good sources of fibre. Apples, pears and potatoes also provide useful amounts if eaten with their skins.

It is estimated that an average British diet contains only 10–20 g of dietary fibre per day but nutritionists suggest that at least 30 g would be healthier.

Fig. 2.32 Dietary fibre content of some common foods

	Portion size	g/dietary
white bread	80 g (2 large slices)	2.0
wholemeal bread	80 g (2 large slices)	7.0
brown bread (not wholemeal)	80 g (2 large slices)	3.6
KELLOGGS ALL-BRAN	40 g (average serving)	11.0
KELLOGGS CORN FLAKES	30 g	0.8
bran	5 g (1 × 15 ml spoon)	3.1
muesli	50 g	4.0
baked potato	200 g (eaten with skin)	5.0
baked beans	225 g (one small can)	16.5
fresh or frozen peas	100 g	9.0
kidney beans (canned)	100 g	6.8
dried apricots	30 g	6.8
sweetcorn	100 g	5.7
wholewheat pasta	50 g (dry weight)	5.7
spring greens	100 g (boiled)	4.3
carrots	100 g	3.4
banana	150 g (average size)	3.4
orange	225 g (average size)	2.5
apple	150 g (average size)	2.2
brown rice	50 g (dry weight)	2.4
white rice	50 g (dry weight)	1.4
peanuts	50 g	4.0
wholemeal flour	25 g	2.7
brown flour	25 g	2.1
white flour	25 g	1.0

Using Fig. 2.32 and plate 5(b), suggest some ways in which you could increase the dietary fibre content of your meals.

Vitamins

Vitamins form a group of organic nutrients, each with a chemical name. For simplicity, most of them are usually identified by a simple letter, e.g. vitamin A, B(group), C or D. They are often classified as:
- water-soluble vitamins, such as B-group and vitamin C,
- fat-soluble vitamins, e.g. vitamins A, D, E and K.

Vitamins are essential nutrients because:
- they promote health, affect the ageing process and help prevent disease;
- they regulate the building and repair of body cells;
- they help regulate the chemical reactions which release energy in body cells.

Normally a well-balanced diet will contain all the vitamins in the recommended quantities, but as some foods are very poor sources of certain vitamins it is essential to choose appropriate foods.

Vitamins are irregularly distributed in very small quantities in a wide range of foods. The main sources and characteristics of each vitamin are detailed on pages 30–35.

Look at plate 6, (a) to (d), and make a table to show the foods which contain the most abundant supply of each vitamin.

Examine your diet plan, and using food tables or a computer program, list the sources of each vitamin in turn.

Look at the section on vitamins pp. 30–34 and see if these foods are likely to have suffered any loss of vitamin content before you consumed them.

Calculate the amount of each vitamin that you consumed.

Refer again to the section on vitamins (pp. 30–34). Was the amount of each vitamin adequate for you?

It is very rare for people in the developed countries to suffer a severe deficiency of vitamins (which causes serious diseases). Some people, however, may suffer mild deficiencies. The symptoms of mild vitamin deficiency include tiredness, broken nails, poor condition of skin, hair and teeth. These symptoms may be due to a shortage of one, or of several vitamins. The amount of each vitamin needed to promote health is greater than the amount needed to prevent disease. It is important therefore to ensure that there is a plentiful supply of foods containing vitamins in the diet.

Vitamins are needed in minute quantities, and are measured in milligrams (mg) or micrograms (μg). It is difficult to measure exactly the amount of vitamins absorbed each day, as the vitamin content of food is affected by:

- *freshness, storage, processing and cooking conditions*;
- *drugs*, e.g. aspirin prevents the total absorption of vitamin C. Over three hundred drugs contain some aspirin. Contraceptive pills affect the blood levels of several vitamins. Antibiotics reduce the body's supply of vitamin B.
- *alcohol*, which hinders the absorption of folic acid: one of the B group vitamins;
- *smoking*, which reduces the vitamin C level in the blood.

Vitamin losses in food preparation

Vitamins are unstable. Losses are caused by enzyme activity in the food (see p. 81), oxidation, heat, light, alkalinity and solubility in water or fat (see the section on vitamins pp. 30-34).

All foods lose some vitamin content as they are stored and go stale or as they are processed, and as they are cooked.

(a) *Freshness and storage of food*

Some vitamins are lost by enzyme activity and oxidation as foods become stale (e.g. it is known that 30% of vitamin C in cabbage is lost after storage for one day). Enzymes are:

- inactive below -18°C (frozen food storage);
- increasingly active at 10°C-70°C (room temperature, and preliminary cooking temperatures);
- destroyed above 85°C (cooking processes).

All food should therefore be used as fresh as possible. If it necessary to store food, keep it in as cool a place as possible; or freeze those foods that do not lose quality on freezing (see p.89).

(b) *Processed food*

There is some vitamin loss in all methods of processing foods. The water-soluble vitamins, B-group and vitamin C, are the most susceptible.

- *dried foods*: There is a great loss of vitamins in dried foods, e.g. approximately 50% loss of vitamin C in fruit and vegetables, approximately 65% loss of thiamin (vitamin B_1) in dried meats. The loss of vitamins is less in accelerated freeze-dry techniques.
- *canned and vacuum-packed foods*: There is considerable loss of vitamins, especially in the canning process. Chemicals are sometimes added to preserve vitamin content, for example sulphites preserve vitamin C.
- *frozen foods*: The nutritional value of frozen foods (particularly fruit and vegetables) is often higher than 'fresh' products because the processing plant is very close to the growing point of the crop. However, some losses occur during preparation and storage of frozen foods:
  5-10% of vitamin C is lost in the 'blanching' process prior to freezing;
  50% of vitamin C is lost in frozen fruit and vegetables which are stored at -18°C for over one year; there is a slight loss of thiamin in frozen meats. (The rate of freezing affects the amount of drip on defrosting. The drip contains B-group vitamins.)

(c) *Cooking conditions*

Vitamins (especially B-group and vitamin C which are water-soluble) are readily destroyed by poor cooking techniques (see pp. 169-171). The vitamin content of the cooked food is dependent on:

- *nutrient content of food used*: For example, there is a greater concentration of vitamins in outer leaves and skin of fruit and vegetables.
- *effect of oxidation*: Some of the vitamin B group and vitamin C are destroyed by oxidation, or by the action of the enzyme oxidase, which is released from plant tissue. The greater the surface area of the food exposed to the air, the greater the nutrient loss.
- *effect of alkalinity*: an alkaline solution (e.g. sodium bicarbonate) rapidly increases the rate of destruction of vitamin C. Thiamin is also destroyed in alkaline conditions, e.g. raising agents will reduce thiamin content of baked products.
- *solubility in water*: vitamin B group and vitamin C dissolve in water. For example:
  cooking fruit - 10% loss of vitamin B group and vitamin C (acidity of fruit helps to stabilise the vitamins).
  cooking green vegetables - 40% loss of B group vitamins; 70% loss of vitamin C (see experiment p. 170 and plate 8(c)).
- *solubility in fat*: vitamins A and D are fat-soluble. These vitamins are lost in fat drippings in cooking.

- *effect of heat*: vitamin B group and vitamin C are very sensitive to the effect of heat. Vitamin C is destroyed at low temperatures, B-group vitamins at higher temperatures.
- *effect of method of cooking*: the method of cooking may also affect the loss of vitamins; prolonged cooking in a large volume of water causes the greatest loss. There is some evidence that pressure cooking and microwave cooking retain more vitamins than conventional methods of cooking.

With reference to Fig. 12.3 on pp. 169–170, plate 8(c) and the experiments on pp. 170–171, give a reasoned description of the method of cooking green vegetables so as to retain maximum vitamin C content.

Vitamin additives

Since the Second World War, when poor health was recognised as a public health problem, British government legislation has required the addition of certain vitamins to basic food commodities. The first foods to be enriched with vitamins were:

flour (white)	vitamin B group	
	thiamin	0.24 mg/100 g
	niacin	1.60 mg/100 g
margarine	vitamin A	900 μg/100 g
	vitamin D	8 μg/100 g
infant milk powders	many vitamins	

These foods are fortified to make their nutritional value equivalent to the natural product. Natural products vary in nutritional composition throughout the year; the fortified products are constant in nutritional value.

As new products are developed, effort is made to make the nutritional value equivalent to the natural product. For example, textured vegetable protein (TVP) is fortified with B-group vitamins (thiamin, niacin and B_{12}) to resemble the nutritional value of meat.

There is also some voluntary enrichment of nutritional value by product manufacturers who want to improve the quality of their product, e.g.

breakfast cereals: most types have a wide range of vitamins added
orange juice: vitamin C
instant mashed potatoes: vitamin C

Do you think that these additions fulfil a real need, or are they an advertising gimmick? Give a short reasoned answer with examples.

Plan a breakfast menu to show the use of some manufactured goods which have been enriched with vitamins.

Vitamin pills

There has been much publicity about the need for vitamins in the diet and there has been a great increase in the number and type of vitamin pills available. This may lead to the temptation to supplement the diet unnecessarily.

List the types of vitamin pills available at your local chemist. Note the nutrient content of each type, and work out the cost of one day's supply.

Fortification of staple foods in developing countries

The addition of vitamins to a staple food product such as rice, has been developed and used commercially in Taiwan, Japan, USA, Egypt, Mexico and Yugoslavia. Vitamin A is added to tea in India, and to sugar in Guatemala; but there are many difficulties to large-scale fortification in developing countries, as food is often processed in small, hand-operated factories, and control is therefore impractical.

Know your vitamins

From the section on vitamins (pp. 30–34), and plates 9–12, answer the following questions:

1 Is vitamin A needed at each meal? If not, why not?
2 Name three foods which are good sources of vitamin A.
3 What is one of the main functions of the B-group vitamins?
4 Which B-group vitamins are essential for

the release of energy, which are important in using protein and fatty acids?

5 Which B-group vitamins are essential for the formation of haemoglobin, (red blood cells) and therefore help to prevent anaemia?

6 Are B-group vitamins stored in the body?

7 Name three foods that are good sources of B-group vitamins.

8 Why is vitamin C needed in the diet each day?

9 Name two foods that would supply the daily recommended intake of vitamin C.

10 Is there any difference in vitamin C content between raw and cooked cabbage? Why do differences occur? (Refer also to 'Cooking green vegetables', p. 170 and plate 8(c).)

11 What is the main function of vitamin D in the diet?

12 Suggest ways of increasing the vitamin D content in a vegetarian diet.

Vitamin A

The chemical name for vitamin A is *retinol* because its function is to protect the retina of the eye. Retinol is only found in animal sources but the body can convert carotenes found in vegetable foods into retinol. These sources are, therefore, also considered as sources of vitamin A (see below).

Characteristics
- pale yellow oil
- fat-soluble

Functions
- increases ability to see in dim light
- needed to keep a thin layer of cells covering the eyes and eyelids, lining of lungs, and respiratory tract

Recommended Daily Intake
Children 1-7 years 300 μg
Adults 750 μg (women during lactation 1 200 μg)
Vitamin A can be stored in the liver, and so is not needed at every meal. A great excess of vitamin A (i.e. 100 times recommended intake) is poisonous: hypervitaminosis A gives fragile bones, intense bone pain, enlargement of liver and spleen, peeling skin, loss of hair.

Main sources
- liver
- herring and fatty fish

- cod and halibut liver oils
- eggs
- milk, cheese, butter (variable supply dependent on season)
- margarine (constant supply, as vitamin A is added by law)

Vitamin losses
- by oxidation
- rancidity in fats
- unaffected by normal cooking process, but losses occur at higher temperatures, e.g. frying and with prolonged heating

Deficiency symptoms
Mild deficiency:
- skin becomes dry and rough
- retina of eye is unable to react quickly to changed light intensity

Beta-carotene

This is the most abundant carotene found in food. It is converted to vitamin A in the small intestine. Only part of the β-carotene molecule can be absorbed, therefore more β-carotene is needed to give equivalent retinol (vitamin A). It is estimated that 6 μg β-carotene is equivalent to 1 μg of retinol.

Characteristics
- bright yellow/orange-coloured oil
- fat-soluble

Main sources
- apricots
- carrots
- tomatoes
- green colour in green vegetables

Deficiency symptoms
Serious deficiency:
xeropthalmia disease:
- dry sore eyes, bacterial conjunctivitis
- can cause death among children
- prevalent in developing countries
- vitamin A is sometimes known as the anti-xerophthalmia vitamin.

Look at plate 6(a) and note the weight of certain foods that is needed to supply 750 μg of vitamin A. How could you increase your intake of vitamin A?

B-group vitamins

The characteristics of the main ones are listed in the chart on p. 32-33. Because many of the B group have similar functions and are found in similar foods, we refer to them either as B-group vitamins or the vitamin B complex. B-group vitamins cannot be stored in the body, and an adequate supply is required daily.

One of the main function of B-group vitamins is to aid in the metabolic processes of carbohydrates, proteins and fats. The daily intake is often related to the amount of food consumed. Average estimates are listed overleaf.

Some B-group vitamins are manufactured by bacteria in the large intestine, but antibiotics may kill these bacteria, so it may be important to take extra B-vitamins in the diet if antibiotics are prescribed.

> Look at plate 6(b) and chart overleaf and say which foods are good sources of the B-group vitamins.

Vitamin C (ascorbic acid)

Characteristics

- white crystalline substance
- soluble in water
- a strong reducing agent
- destroyed in alkaline solution
- destroyed by heat
- destroyed by oxidation

Functions

- to make connective tissue that binds body cells together
- essential in manufacture of blood and cell walls of blood vessels
- related to metabolism of amino acid, tryosine
- related to cholesterol metabolism
- possible resistance to infection. No definite evidence that vitamin C prevents the common cold.

Recommended daily intake

RDI varies in different countries. British recommendations (see below) are lower than in many other countries.
children 1-11 years 20-25 mg
children 11-15 years 25-30 mg
adolescents 15-18 years 30 mg
adults 30 mg/day
pregnancy 60 mg
during lactation 60 mg

Any surplus is excreted in urine. No problems of overdose; it is therefore wise to ensure a plentiful supply of vitamin C. Vitamin C content of body is very low during infections, so it is important to boost vitamin C intake during illness.

Main sources

In some fruits and some vegetables:

- peppers
- blackcurrants
- broccoli and brussel sprouts (raw)
- cabbage
- strawberries
- oranges and other citrus fruits
- melons
- tomatoes
- potatoes (especially 'new' potatoes)
  Note: potatoes are often a good source of vitamin C in the diet, because of the large amount eaten.
- fruit juices are often enriched with vitamin C.
Note: It is not widely distributed in foods, so it is important to include these foods in the diet.

Vitamin losses

- a very unstable vitamin. Great care is needed in food preparation to retain vitamin C. All plant cells contain an enzyme, oxidase. When released from cell structure (e.g. during chopping of fruit and vegetables) oxidase destroys vitamin C. There is a 50% loss with careful handling: at least 75% loss in careless handling.
- reheated foods lose more vitamin C content: a further 25% loss after 15 minutes; 75% loss after 1½ hours.
- long storage of fruit and vegetables in warm atmosphere: 90% loss.
- quick freezing retains vitamin C better than any other method. (Blanching destroys enzyme oxidase.)

Deficiency symptoms

Mild deficiency:

- walls of small blood vessels become porous. Blood escapes and tiny blood spots appear under skin. Skin becomes spotty, small cuts and scratches are slow to heal. Gums swell, teeth become weaker. These symptoms have been noticed among some old people, some poor families and some immigrants in Britain.

Serious deficiency:

- long-term shortage leads to disease (scurvy), very rare in Britain. The symptoms are bleeding teeth, malformed brittle bones, weakened muscles (including heart muscle) and anaemia.

> Look at plate 6(c) and say which foods are good sources of this vitamin.

Characteristics

Functions

Daily Recommended Intake
(B group vitamins not stored in the body; no harm if excess is taken.)

THIAMIN (B₁)

- soluble in water
- stable to dry heat (but not prolonged cooking at high temperatures)
- destroyed by alkalis

- essential for the release of energy from carbohydrates
- needed for growth and normal functioning of nervous system
- maintains muscle tone

children varies with age, 0.3–1.0 mg
average adult woman 0.9 mg
average adult man 1.2 mg

RIBOFLAVIN (B₂)

- soluble in water
- destroyed by light
- fairly stable to heat
- not much affected by oxidising agents
- not affected by acids

- involved in metabolism of proteins, fatty acids and carbohydrates, therefore has an effect on growth rate

children varies with age 0.4–1.7 mg
average adult woman 1.4 mg
Average adult man 1.7 mg

NIACIN (or nicotinic acid)

- fairly soluble in cold water, very soluble in hot water
- fairly stable to heat, acids and alkalis
  The body can convert an amino acid tryptophan, to niacin. 60 mg tryptophan is equivalent to 1 mg niacin.

- involved in the use of (metabolism) of proteins, fatty acids and carbohydrates therefore has an effect on growth rate
- essential for healthy skin and nerves

children varies with age 5–16 mg
average adult woman 15 mg
average adult man 18 mg

PYRIDOXINE (B₆)

- solid
- soluble in water
- fairly stable to heat
- sensitive to oxidation

- affects the use of (metabolism) of proteins, especially the conversion tryptophan to niacin (see above)
- acts as catalyst
- essential for formation of haemoglobin (red blood corpuscles)

artifically-fed babies 0.4 mg
children 1.5 mg
adults 2 mg

FOLIC ACID

- water soluble
- stable in acid conditions

- essential for formation of red blood cells

300 µg
400 µg in pregnancy and for nursing mothers

COBALAMIN (B₁₂)

- red crystalline substance
- soluble in water
- stable to 100 °C
- affected by strong acids and alkalis
- affected by light

- essential for formation of red blood cells
- essential for nervous system

3.0–4.0 mg
Asians and vegetarians (i.e. those who do not eat any meat products) are advised to drink at least 500 ml milk per day

Main sources	Vitamin losses	Deficiency symptoms
At present thiamin is added to white flour, by law natural cereals, e.g. oats. Most breakfast cereals are enriched with thiamin brown rice (four times more thiamin than white rice) offal: liver, kidneys milk, eggs fruit and vegetables	• 70% loss in milling wheat • 50% loss in meat cookery • 25% loss in vegetable cookery • Many manufactured breakfast cereals have suffered thiamin loss. Most breakfast cereals are enriched with thiamin. • Oats contain 14 times more thiamin than puffed wheat.	*Mild deficiency*: fatigue, depression, irritability, forgetfulness. *Serious deficiency*: In developing countries a disease called beri-beri is prevalent. There are two types of beri-beri. The symptoms are: dry beri-beri: muscle wasting; loss of sensation to skin; paralysis wet beri-beri: arms legs and abdomen swollen; enlargement of heart; death.
Liver, kidneys, milk, meat, eggs, green vegetables. Some riboflavin manufactured by bacteria in intestines.	• destroyed by ultra-violet light (NB riboflavin loss in milk in clear bottles, especially in sunlight). Little lost in ordinary cooking.	poor growth rate eye problems sores and cracked lips tongue becomes cracked and magenta-coloured inflamation in folds of skin between nose and mouth
Meat and poultry, especially offal yeasts meat extracts fish wholewheat flour fortified white flour Manufactured by bacteria in intestine. Milk and eggs contain the amino acid tryptophan, which can be converted in the body to niacin.	• 80–90% loss in milling wheat • little loss in normal cooking processes	Deficiency very rare in Britain. Serious deficiency is a disease called pellagra: rough red skin on neck and hands, tongue inflamed, weakness, depression, dizziness and eventual death. Pellagra is common in countries where maize (corn) is the staple cereal, as niacin in maize is not absorbed by the body.
Widespread in foods. Good sources: Liver, kidneys, fish, yeast and yeast products, whole grain cereals, eggs, some vegetables.	• unstable when milk is heated • 20–40% loss B_6 on cooking frozen vegetables	Deficiency rare in humans, but infants may suffer convulsions if there is a shortage: hence B_6 is added to dried milk powder. May cause pre-menstrual tension.
Liver, kidneys, dark green leafy vegetables, whole grain cereals, wholewheat bread, pulses (i.e. peas, beans, lentils) and oranges.	• by oxidation • extraction by cooking water • sensitive to sunlight	*Mild deficiency*: tiredness *Serious deficiency*: anaemia
Liver, kidneys, meat, eggs, milk, cheese. (There is no vitamin B_{12} in vegetable or cereal foods.) Some breakfast cereals have vitamin B_{12} added.	• by oxidation • extraction in cooking water • sensitive to sunlight • reduced by strong acids and alkalis	*Serious deficiency*: insufficient red blood cells leading to pernicious anaemia. Asians and vegetarians are 'at risk'.

Vitamin D (cholecalciferol)

> Look at plate 6(d), and say which foods are good sources of this vitamin.

Often called an anti-rachitic vitamin; it is the anti-rickets vitamin.

Humans can also synthesise some vitamin D from the action of sunlight on dehydro-cholesterol in the skin. (This is known as vitamin D_3.)

Characteristics
- soluble in oils and fats
- can be stored in the body

Functions
- essential, with calcium and phosphorus, for development of strong bones and teeth
- promotes quicker healing of bone fractures
- essential in the intestine so that calcium can be absorbed

Recommended Daily Intake
children and adults 10 µg
- vitamin D can be stored in fatty tissues of body.
- massive doses of vitamin D can lead to an increase in calcium in blood vessels, kidney and heart. Patients are sick, have headaches and lose weight.

Main sources
Few foods contain vitamin D, so it is important to include these foods in the diet.
There are two main sources of vitamin D:

(a) *Animal fats* and fortified foods
- cod and halibut liver oils
- herrings and mackerel
- egg yolk
- liver
- margarine
- some breakfast cereals, fortified with vitamin D
- infant milk powders are fortified with vitamin D
- vitamin supplements for children and pregnant women

(b) *Action of ultra-violet rays* in sunlight on a layer of fat beneath the skin. This fat contains dehydro-cholesterol, which is converted to vitamin D (cholecalciferol) by ultra-violet rays.
This is a very important source of vitamin D in the diet. Housebound people, i.e. invalids, the elderly, and those whose culture dictates that they stay indoors, and are completely covered up, are particularly at risk of vitamin D deficiency.

Vitamin losses
- not affected by ordinary cooking process

Deficiency symptoms
- in a baby, deficiency of vitamin D leads to soft bones, the child develops deformed legs – a disease known as rickets (see Fig. 2.8);
- in adults, prolonged deficiency leads to oesteomalacia (a bone disease);
- Asians are particularly 'at risk' of a vitamin D shortage: their skin does not manufacture as much vitamin D as a white skin; some groups of Asian women stay indoors and wear clothes that cover most of the body; Asians do not eat meat which is a main source of dietary vitamin D.

Vitamin E

Characteristics
- soluble in fats
- stable to heat and acids
- unstable to alkalis and ultra-violet light
- powerful anti-oxidant

Functions
- as an anti-oxidant (especially important in delaying rancidity by oxidation in oils and fats)
- in some animals, vitamin E is essential for reproduction
- research on vitamin E in human diet is still in progress, but there is evidence that it is essential

Recommended Daily Intake
- requirement related to intake of polyunsaturated fatty acids
- a normal diet will contain adequate amounts
- can be stored in the liver, and fatty tissue

Main sources
Fairly widely distributed in food:
- wheat germ, oatmeal
- corn oil, soya bean oil
- margarine, butter (in summer time)
- eggs
- liver, meat
- leafy green vegetables contain a little

Vitamin K

Characteristics
- fat-soluble
- heat-stable
- affected by irradiation

Functions
- needed for clotting of blood

Recommended Daily Intake
Normal diet provides adequate supply.

Main sources
Widely distributed in food:
● eggs, milk
● green leafy vegetables
● pig's liver
● can be synthesised by bacteria in the body

Mineral Elements

These nutrients are *inorganic compounds* which appear as 'ash' when all the carbon, hydrogen, oxygen and nitrogen in foods are burnt. Mineral elements in the body, or in food, may be found as a simple inorganic salt (e.g. sodium chloride-salt) or as part of a complex organic molecule (e.g. some proteins contain sulphur).

Mineral elements enter the body fluids and cells, and are needed in definite amounts in definite places. They are so interrelated that it is difficult to define their specific functions.

Altogether nineteen different mineral elements are essential to the body, but many are needed in very small amounts (and probably act as catalysts). They are known as *trace elements*.

There is a wide variation in the amount of different mineral elements in the body. Figure 2.33 shows the approximate amounts of mineral elements in the body of an adult man.

Fig. 2.33 Mineral elements in the body of an adult man (in grams)

calcium	1050	iron	2.8
phosphorus	700	zinc	2.5
potassium	245	manganese	2.1
sulphur	175	copper	1.25
chlorine	105	iodine	0.35
sodium	105	chromium	0.075
magnesium	35		

There are also minute amounts of the trace elements: molybdenum, cobalt, silicon, tin, fluorine, selenium. Although the list may look formidable, in actual practice, if care is taken to include sufficient calcium, iron and iodine in the diet, there will be an adequate supply of most of the other mineral elements.

Mineral elements are widely distributed in very small amounts in food. Some foods such as white flour and breakfast cereals are enriched by the addition of mineral elements.

Calcium and phosphorus

Look at plate 6(e) and see which foods are good sources of the mineral element calcium.

These mineral elements are often considered together because both are needed together for growth and maintenance of bones and teeth. The chief material that gives hardness to bones and teeth is calcium phosphate. Before birth, the bones of the foetus are cartilage (a firm, but flexible material like the end of your nose, or ear lobe) but as calcium phosphate becomes enmeshed in the cartilage, bones and teeth become stronger. This process is known as calcification. The absorption of calcium is controlled by vitamin D in the body (see p. 34), and the deposition of calcium phosphate is controlled by a hormone produced by the parathyroid gland (at the back of the neck).

There is a special need for both calcium and phosphorus in the diet of pregnant and nursing mothers, growing children, old people, and after bone fractures.

Both mineral elements also have important independent functions in the body.

Calcium

Calcium is necessary:
● for normal clotting of blood;
● to maintain a normal rhythmic heartbeat;
● for normal functioning of nerves and muscles.

Fig. 2.34 Recommended Daily Intake of calcium (mg)

boys and girls
0 – 1 year	600
1 – 9 years	600
9 – 15 years	700
15 – 18 years	600

men	500
women	500
pregnant women and nursing mothers	1200

Effects of deficiency of calcium in the diet:

● in *children*, poor bone formation. The legs may become deformed (a disease called rickets) as when there is a shortage of Vitamin D.
● in *adults*, calcium is removed from bones and teeth to fulfil its other essential functions, with

the result that bones become weak, and eventually deformed (a disease called osteomalacia to which elderly people are particularly susceptible). Both children and adults suffer tooth decay, and white flecks underneath the nails.

Main sources of calcium in the diet (see plate 6(e))

milk
cheese
white bread (calcium carbonate ($CaCO_3$) is currently added to white flour to increase its nutritional value)
'hard' water (i.e. water that contains dissolved calcium salts)
beer
canned fish

Fig. 2.35 Calcium content of commonly-eaten foods

	mg/100 g food	mg/average serving	size of portion
white bread	92	46.0	50 g
wholemeal bread	226	13.0	50 g
Cheddar cheese	810	402.5	50 g
double cream	50	12.5	25 ml
milk	120	180.0	150 ml
eggs	56	28.0	50 g
canned sardines	409	204.5	50 g
winter cabbage	58.2	58.2	100 g

There is approximately 1 kilogram (1000 g) of calcium in the bone structure of an adult man. 700 mg is removed and replaced daily from bone structure. (1 pint (500 ml) milk would supply this amount of calcium).

Calcium salts dissolve in water; therefore it is important to use water used for cooking in gravies and soups. If there is excess calcium in the diet, it is excreted in the urine and in the faeces.

Availability of calcium to the body

Calcium is not always available to the body. Some foods which appear to be 'good' sources of calcium in the diet may not supply much calcium to the body. It is estimated that there is less than a 40% absorption rate of calcium. For example:
● in green leafy vegetables, calcium may be closely linked with cellulose which is indigestible;
● it is thought that phytic acid present in whole cereals and pulses, and oxalic acid present in rhubarb and spinach, precipitate calcium and prevent absorption of calcium;
● excess fat hinders calcium absorption.
It is important, therefore, to include a plentiful supply of foods which supply calcium in the diet.

Examine your day's diet: list the main sources of calcium.
Using food tables, check that the amount of calcium was sufficient for your needs.
If not, suggest ways to increase the calcium content of that day's diet.

Phosphorus

Found in all living tissues, in the molecules of the nucleic acids (RNA and DNA). Phosphorus is present in organic form as part of protein structure, and in the inorganic form as phosphates.

Functions

● building bone and teeth structure
● energy transfer and storage
● almost every metabolic process in the body: muscle energy, carbohydrate, fat, protein and nerve tissue metabolism depends on it
● it is concerned with the transport of fatty acids
● it is a constituent of blood

Recommended Daily Intake

Diets usually have adequate amounts, with no widespread deficiency problems.

Main sources

Milk, cheese, nuts, meat, fish, eggs. Most foods rich in calcium are also rich in phosphorus (but not vice-versa).

Iron

Functions

Needed in the formation of red cells in the blood.
Blood is a watery fluid (called plasma) containing millions of protein cells, minerals and oxygen. There are two types of blood cells:
    red corpuscles: approx. 4-5 million in an adult
    white corpuscles: approx. 5-8000 cells/ml of blood.

The colour of the red cells comes from a pigment called *haemoglobin*, which is a complex protein with *iron* in its chemical structure. Red blood cells have a short life, approximately 6 weeks, then they are broken down and replaced by new cells from the bone marrow.

Oxygen molecules (which have been absorbed

through the very thin walls of the lungs into the bloodstream) attach themselves to the haemoglobin in the red corpuscle and are transported around the body. All living cells need oxygen, so it is essential that there is sufficient iron in the diet to create haemoglobin, which, in turn will carry oxygen in the bloodstream to the cells that need it. Blood carrying oxygen is bright red in colour (arterial). When the oxygen has been used, and the blood is returning to the heart through the veins, it is a dark purple red.

Fig. 2.36 Recommended Daily Intake of iron (mg)

boys and girls

0– 1 year	6
1– 3 years	7
3– 7 years	8
7– 9 years	10
9–12 years	13
12–15 years	14
15–18 years	15

women

18–55 years	12
55 & over	10

pregnant women and nursing mothers 15

men 10

Teenage girls and women who lose blood at menstruation need an increased supply of iron for replacement of more blood cells.

Pregnant women and nursing mothers also need more iron from their food to build their babies' blood as well as their own. Iron tablets are sometimes prescribed at this time.

There is normally 14.5 mg iron/100 ml blood. Each day, iron is lost in sweat, urine, skin cells and bleeding. Men lose 1 mg/day; women 3 mg/day in menstrual periods and pregnancy. Some iron is stored in the liver, so it is not essential that the recommended allowance is taken daily, but the recommended daily intake is in excess of these losses because much iron is not absorbed.

An excess of iron is poisonous. (Hence it is important to keep iron pills out of children's reach.) To prevent an excess of iron from the food we eat, the intestine regulates the amount of iron absorbed at any one time. (This safeguard system is called the mucosal block.)

Main sources of iron in the diet

Look at plate 6(f) and see which foods are good sources of this mineral element. Which of these foods do you eat or drink regularly?

- liver, kidney, heart
- eggs
- bread
- vegetables, potatoes and green leafy vegetables
- drinking water

Because of the difficulty in ensuring a regular supply, iron is currently added to flour in Britain (by law). Several breakfast cereal manufacturers also enrich their products with iron; look at the breakfast cereals available and list the ones that have iron added to them.

Absorption of iron

It is estimated that only 10% of the iron in food is absorbed by the body.

The calcium, phosphorus balance in the diet is important, as an excess of phosphorus reduces the absorption of iron by forming insoluble salts. Cellulose in green vegetables, and phytic acid in cereals prevent the total absorption of iron.

Before absorption, iron must be in its reduced state (ferrous), so it is important that there is a plentiful supply of vitamin C (a reducing agent) in the diet as most of the iron in foods is in the ferric state. Iron added to fortify breakfast cereals is already finely divided and in its reduced state. Once absorbed, iron is carried by the blood to the bone marrow where some is used for formation of red blood cells (a process also needing copper).

The remaining iron is returned to the blood plasma and transported to the liver and spleen, where it can be stored; normally 600–1500 mg is stored in an average adult.

Effect of a shortage of iron in the diet

Red corpuscles are formed which have insufficient haemoglobin molecules. This condition is called *anaemia*. The blood cannot carry sufficient oxygen to the body cells, which then cannot work efficiently.

The muscles are easily fatigued, the heart beats faster and the person is tired and listless.

Fig. 2.37 Iron content of some commonly-eaten foods

	mg in 100 g food	mg/average serving	Size of serving (g)
white bread	1.80	0.90	50
wholemeal bread	2.88	1.44	50
cornflakes (fortified)	6.70	2.00	30
porridge	0.47	0.70	150
liver	21.70	21.70	100
beef	4.60	4.60	100
cod	1.00	1.50	150
eggs	2.53	1.26	50
spring greens	1.33	1.33	100
potatoes	0.48	0.72	150
cocoa	14.30	1.43	10

Look at your diet plan:
Using food tables, which foods supplied iron in your diet?
Did you receive an adequate supply? If not, suggest ways to improve the iron content of that day's diet.

Iodine

Of the 35 mg of iodine in the body, 8 mg are found in the thyroid gland at the back of the neck. The gland uses iodine to make the hormone thyroxine which regulates the metabolic rate of the body.

Recommended Daily Intake: 140 µg

Good sources of iodine: fish and vegetables
In some areas iodine is dissolved in drinking water. Iodine is frequently added to salt, and sold as iodised salt which if regularly used ensures a good supply.

Effect of deficiency of iodine

If there is a prolonged shortage of iodine in the diet, the thyroid gland is stimulated to grow, and appears as a lump in the throat (goitre). In areas of the world where soil and plants are deficient in iodine, goitre is a common disease.

Fluorine

Essential for hardening tooth enamel. Fluorine is frequently dissolved in drinking water, and there is a small amount in tea and fish.
Research and national surveys among groups of children have shown less tooth decay amongst children whose drinking water contains some fluorine, so medical experts now recommend 'fluoridisation' of drinking water.

Fluorine tablets and fluoride toothpaste (which contain fluorine in the form of tin fluoride) also reduce tooth decay in childhood. Excess fluorine can cause a mottling effect on tooth enamel, so do not exceed recommended dose.

Sodium and chlorine

Sodium and chlorine are needed together as sodium chloride (salt). The importance of salt in the diet was recognised in Roman times, when soldiers were paid in salt (salarium). This is origin of our word 'salary'.

The body needs salt to maintain volume and osmotic pressure of tissue fluids in the blood.

Chlorine is also used to make hydrogen chloride in the stomach.

Sodium molecules are also needed to activate some enzymes, transport carbon dioxide in the blood, and conduct nerve impulses.

In normal body functions excess salt is lost in urine and sweat, but in certain kidney, heart and liver diseases excess salt will accumulate and retain excess water.

In Britain the average consumption of salt is 15g salt/day. This is far in excess of needs. Recent evidence has shown that too much salt in the diet may affect blood pressure and can be harmful.

Potassium

● necessary for cell formation
● concerned with protein metabolism
Most foods, except cream, fats, white bread and polished rice contain some potassium.

Sulphur

● contained in some protein molecules
● also present in vitamin B (thiamin)
Good sources are eggs, meat, milk, cheese.

Copper

● a component of many enzymes
● needed as a catalyst in production of haemoglobin in the blood
Good sources: fish and liver.

Magnesium

● involved in enzyme activity
● necessary for synthesis of proteins, fats, carbohydrate and nucleic acids
● concerned with functions of muscles
Good sources: green leafy vegetables (it is a component of chlorophyll)
cocoa, chocolate, nuts and wholegrain and bran-rich cereals.

Manganese

● component of some enzymes
● concerned with energy release
● available in whole cereal grains, pulses, green leafy vegetables
Deficiency never observed in man.

Zinc

● component of some enzymes
● concerned with energy release
Good sources meat, whole and bran enriched cereals, pulses.

Molybdenum

● essential for metabolic breakdown of nucleo-protein derivatives
● may be concerned with iron metabolism
Very small amounts are needed; human deficiency never detected.

3 How does the body use food?

The body is a very complicated organism in which many processes are happening at the same time. These processes are continuous, day and night.

The food we eat is used in every part of the body. It must supply all the nutrients needed:
● to build new cells,
● to provide energy for all activities, including breathing, heart-beating and all physical exercise,
● to regulate all processes and protect the body from disease.

The body therefore needs nutritionally well-balanced food regularly to maintain these basic functions.

There are three important stages in the way in which the body uses the nutrients in food. These stages are:
● digestion of nutrients: most foods have to be broken down physically and chemically to reduce the size of the molecules before the nutrients can be absorbed.
● absorption of nutrients: the nutrients are absorbed into the bloodstream so they can be transported around the body.
● metabolism and storage of nutrients: the absorbed nutrients are carried in the bloodstream to the body cells where they are metabolised; that is, used, or stored for future use.

Digestion of nutrients

All food is physically broken down by the action of the teeth in the mouth, and by muscular movements of the wall of the alimentary canal. The alimentary canal is a continuous tube eight or nine metres in length, which runs from the mouth via the stomach and intestine to the anus. The muscular movement of the canal walls churns, mixes and breaks down the food into a semi-solid mixture. This wave-like motion is called peristalsis, and it moves the food along the alimentary canal (see Fig. 2.38(a)).

Most food is also changed chemically during the process of digestion. The large organic molecules of nutrients in food e.g. carbohydrates, proteins and fats (see pp. 16-19), are broken down by a series of chemical reactions. These reactions are caused by *digestive juices* secreted along the length of the alimentary canal. The digestive juices contain mucus, hormones and enzymes:
● *mucus* lubricates the passage of food through the alimentary canal, and protects the canal wall from the action of enzymes.
● *hormones* are chemical substances secreted by the endocrine glands, e.g. the thyroid, the pancreas,

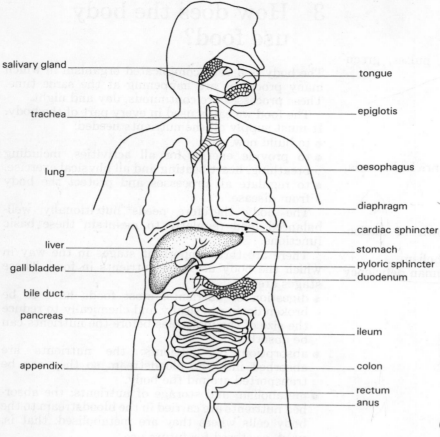

Fig. 2.38 (a) The digestive system

salivary gland

tongue

trachea

epiglotis

lung

oesophagus

diaphragm

cardiac sphincter

liver

stomach

gall bladder

pyloric sphincter

duodenum

bile duct

pancreas

ileum

appendix

colon

rectum

anus

(b) Absorption of nutrients in the ileum

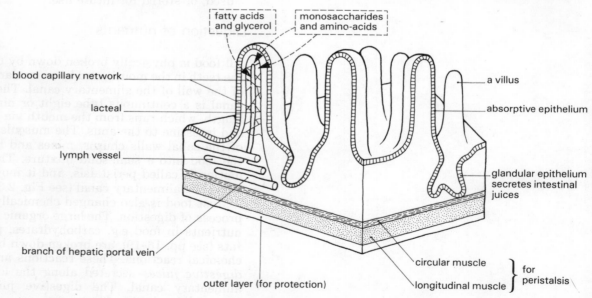

fatty acids and glycerol

monosaccharides and amino-acids

blood capillary network

a villus

lacteal

absorptive epithelium

lymph vessel

glandular epithelium secretes intestinal juices

branch of hepatic portal vein

circular muscle

longitudinal muscle

} for peristalsis

outer layer (for protection)

the pituitary. They pass into the bloodstream, and so are circulated all over the body. Their action affects the rate at which many body functions occur, e.g. rate of digestion and absorption of nutrients, the rate of growth and sexual maturity.

● *enzymes* are proteins. They are secreted in solution by all living cells. They are catalysts, which means they take part in reactions in the body, but they are not changed by the reaction.

The action of each enzyme is specific to one type

Plate 7 Amounts of food and drink supplying 100 kcal

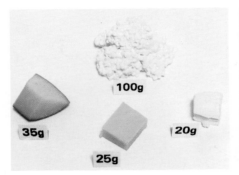

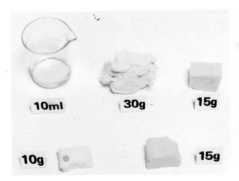

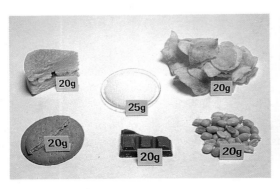

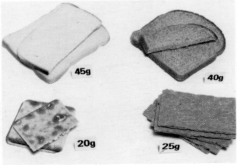

(a)

(b)

Plate 8

(a) Stale and fresh food

(b) Raw, well-cooked and overcooked sausages

(c) Well-cooked and poorly-cooked cabbage

(c)

of substance. Many different enzymes are therefore needed for all the different body functions. Enzymes are affected by temperature, and the degree of acidity or alkalinity (i.e. pH) of the environment.

Many enzymes are secreted at various stages along the alimentary canal. They are known as the *digestive enzymes*. Their function is to break down the large organic molecules of the nutrients into smaller molecules that can be absorbed. Their action is specific to one type of nutrient. For example:

proteinases	act on	proteins	reducing molecular size to	amino acids
amylases	act on	starch	"	monosaccharides
lipases	act on	fats	"	fatty acids and glycerol

Within each group, there are several enzymes. The specific action of each enzyme is shown in the chart on p. 43. These enzymes all work at body temperature. The secretions of the alimentary canal provide the correct pH for the action of different enzymes at different stages in the alimentary canal, e.g. an acid solution in the stomach, an alkaline solution in the intestine.

Stages in the digestion of nutrients

The reactions caused by the digestive juices occur at various stages as food passes along the alimentary canal from the mouth, through the stomach and small intestine.

1 In the mouth

Food is chewed by the teeth: the incisors cut the food, the molars and premolars grind and crush the food. The chemicals in food stimulate special sensory cells on the taste buds on the tongue. These cells send messages to the brain which then interprets the taste of the food. In the mouth saliva, a watery alkaline fluid, is produced continuously. The taste and smell of food also stimulates an increased flow of saliva which helps to moisten the food as it is chewed. Saliva contains an amylase enzyme called ptyalin. Ptyalin breaks down starch (polysaccharide) to maltose (disaccharide).

The chewed moistened food is rounded into a pellet known as a bolus, so that it can be swallowed. The bolus is swallowed directly into the oesophagus which is a tube about 30 cm long connecting the mouth to the stomach. The food is propelled along the oesophagus by peristalsis. This action takes about six seconds. During this time, ptyalin continues to digest starch molecules. As the food

reaches the stomach, a ring of muscle known as the cardiac sphincter dilates to open the entrance to the stomach.

2 In the stomach

The stomach is a thick-walled bag which can hold a considerable amount of food. The muscles in the walls can expand and contract to vary the size. The food is held in the stomach by contraction of the pyloric sphincter muscle, which closes the exit. Food remains in the stomach for two or five hours. The time depends on what is eaten.

In the stomach, the food is mixed with more digestive juices (known as gastric juices). These are produced by deep pits in the stomach wall. These juices contain mucus, hydrochloric acid and enzymes. The mucus lubricates the food and the hydrochloric acid gives a suitable pH (degree of acidity) for the action of the enzymes and destroys most of the bacteria in food.

The enzymes present in the gastric juices are proteinases:
- *pepsin* converts proteins into more soluble, smaller molecules of protein called peptides (see p. 21);
- *rennin* coagulates the protein, casein, in milk to form a clot which can then be digested by the enzyme pepsin.

During the time that food is in the stomach, it is continuously churned by the muscular action of the stomach walls. It becomes a semi-liquid known as chyme. When digestion in the stomach is complete, the pyloric sphincter relaxes and opens to allow small quantities of chyme to pass through into the small intestine.

3 In the small intestine

The small intestine is the longest part of the alimentary canal. It is approximately six metres in length. Food takes about four hours to pass through it. It is here that digestion of nutrients is completed, and absorption takes place (see p. 42). The small intestine consists of two parts: the duodenum and the ileum.

(a) *The duodenum*

The duodenum is the first loop of the small intestine (about 30 cm long). It is a very important area for digestion of nutrients. Digestive juices from the liver (bile), and the pancreas (pancreatic juices) flow into the duodenum. The flow of bile and pancreatic juices is controlled by hormones which are released into the bloodstream from the duodenum. Each of these types of digestive juices is important in the process of digestion:

- Bile is a watery green alkaline fluid made in the liver. It is stored in the gall bladder and passes into the duodenum via the bile duct. Bile contains sodium chloride, sodium bicarbonate and bile salts. The functions of bile are to dilute the chyme, neutralise the acid from the stomach, and emulsify fats. As a result a greater surface area is exposed to the action of the enzymes in the pancreatic juices.
- Pancreatic juice is an alkaline liquid, so that the chyme from the stomach now becomes slightly alkaline. Pancreatic juices contain several enzymes. These are:
  proteinases: trypsinogen is inactive until it meets the enzyme enterokinase from the intestine wall. This converts trypsinogen to the active enzyme trypsin. Trypsin continues digestion of proteins from peptides to amino acids.
  lipases: these convert fats to fatty acids and glycerol.
  amylases: these enzymes complete the conversion of starch to maltose.

(b) *The ileum (Fig. 2.38(b))*

The ileum is a long coiled tube where digestion is completed and soluble substances are absorbed. It is coiled so that it fits into the abdominal cavity. The presence of food in the small intestine causes the secretion of intestinal juice which contains many enzymes. These enzymes complete the digestion of carbohydrates, proteins and any remaining fats. For example, intestinal juice contains:

- amylases which split disaccharides to mono-saccharides,
  maltase splits maltose to glucose
  sucrase splits sucrose to glucose and fructose
  lactase splits lactose to glucose and galactose
- several proteinases which complete the breakdown of peptides to amino acids
- lipases complete the breakdown of any remaining fats to fatty acids and glycerol.

All the nutrients have now been reduced to small soluble molecules. The process of digestion is complete.

Absorption of nutrients

The digested nutrients, together with the other nutrients - vitamins, mineral elements and water -that were already small molecules, are now absorbed through the walls of the ileum. This area of the alimentary canal is specially constructed so that the digested nutrients can be absorbed from it. The ileum has the following features:

- its length means that food takes about four to five hours to pass along it;
- its large surface area over which food can be absorbed is increased by thousands of finger-like projections called villi;
- each villus has a thin lining so that fluids containing soluble nutrients can rapidly pass through;
- each villus is supplied with numerous tiny blood capillaries. The water-soluble nutrients, amino acids, monosaccharides, vitamins B and C and the mineral elements are absorbed through the wall of the villi into the blood capillaries. Some water is also absorbed by osmosis;
- each villus also contains a tiny tube called a lacteal. Fatty acids, glycerol and the fat soluble vitamins (A, D, E and K) are absorbed through the lacteals. Once absorbed, the fatty acids and the glycerol reform fats in the lacteals. The lacteals are connected to the lymphatic system which eventually joins the bloodstream by the jugular vein in the neck. The fat and fat-soluble vitamins are transported round the body in the lymph fluid.

At the end of the passage through the ileum, nearly all the digestible nutrients have been absorbed. The watery fluid remaining is known as chyle. It contains undigested food such as dietary fibre, worn-out cells, large numbers of bacteria, bile fluids and colour pigments. This fluid passes into the next section of the alimentary canal known as the large intestine.

The large intestine is a wider tube than the small intestine. It is about one and a half metres long. Its main function is to absorb water. This takes place along the first section known as the colon. The semi-solid residue which remains is the faeces. The residue passes to the final portion of the tube, the rectum. The faeces may be stored here. They are expelled at intervals through the anus by strong contractions of the muscular walls of the rectum. The food normally stays in the large intestine from 12-24 hours.

If the large intestine becomes infected, e.g. as in food poisoning, the contents pass through quickly before water has been absorbed. This condition is known as diarrhoea. If the contents take too long to pass along the colon because of sluggish muscular action too much water is absorbed. The faeces become hard. This condition is known as constipation. Constipation can be avoided by eating foods that contain dietary fibre (see p.27). The dietary fibre absorbs water so the faeces become sufficiently bulky and soft and are expelled at regular intervals.

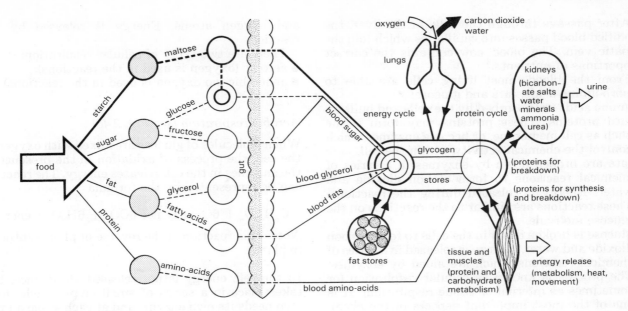

Fig. 2.39 The metabolic chain

Metabolism and storage of nutrients

When the nutrients have been absorbed by the small intestine they are transported around the body to wherever they are required to perform their specific functions. Some nutrients, such as the emulsified fat-soluble nutrients, fats and fat-soluble vitamins A and D, are transported in the lymphatic system to the bloodstream, whilst the water-soluble amino acids, monosaccharides, e.g. glucose, Vitamins B and C and mineral elements, are absorbed directly into the bloodstream and transported around the body.

The tiny blood capillaries in the villi of the small intestine join to form large blood vessels (veins), which all unite to form one large vein known as the hepatic portal vein. This vein carries all the blood containing the absorbed nutrients from the intestine to the liver.

The liver

The liver is a most important organ for the control and storage of nutrients. The hepatic portal vein splits into capillaries in the liver, and the blood and nutrients are then absorbed by the cells in the liver. The liver cells modify the composition and concentration of the nutrients in the blood so that correct concentration of nutrients can be circulated to the rest of the body.

The main functions of the liver

1 The level of glucose in the blood is regulated. The level of glucose in the blood may rise after a meal rich in carbohydrate is eaten. As a result, the pancreatic gland increases the production of the hormone insulin. The liver then removes some of the glucose which causes the level in the blood to fall. If the glucose level in the blood falls too low the liver releases glucose back into the blood to maintain the correct level.

2 Glycogen is formed. Some of the glucose removed from the blood is converted by the liver into the carbohydrate glycogen. In this form, the glucose is stored and is used as an immediate source of energy when required.

3 Fat is formed. There is a limit to the amount of glycogen that can be stored by the liver. Excess glucose is converted into fat by the liver and is carried away by the blood stream to be stored in cells underneath the skin.

4 The level of amino acids is controlled. Protein cannot be stored in the body. If more protein is eaten than is needed for normal tissue-building and repair processes, the liver removes the amino group (that is the part containing nitrogen). This is then excreted by the kidneys in the urine. The remaining part of the amino acid molecule which contains carbon, hydrogen and oxygen atoms is used in a similar way to glucose: that is, to supply energy or to be stored as fat.

5 Reserves of nutrients are stored. In addition to the storage of glycogen and a small amount of fat, the liver also stores some vitamins: A, D and B_{12}, and some mineral elements: iron, potassium and copper.

After passage through the cells in the liver, the modified blood passes into capillaries which join the hepatic vein. The blood now contains the correct proportions of nutrients.

From the blood, most living cells are able to absorb amino acids, fats and glucose:

- amino acids are absorbed by the cells and built up into proteins. These proteins may form tissue such as cell membrane, or become enzymes which control the chemical activity within the cell.
- fats are broken down by enzymes in a series of chemical reactions to form carbon dioxide and water. Energy is released during the reactions. These reactions are similar to the reactions on the glucose molecule.
- glucose is broken down in the cells to form carbon dioxide and water. Energy is released in a series of chemical reactions which are aided by enzymes. The process is known as cellular respiration (or sometimes as internal or tissue respiration). It is one of the most important aspects of the chemistry of living matter.

Cellular respiration

The process of cellular respiration finally splits the glucose molecule which contains carbon, hydrogen and oxygen atoms. Energy is released by the reaction.

There are two types of cellular respiration:
- aerobic (oxygen is used in the reactions);
- anaerobic (no oxygen is used in the reactions).

Aerobic respiration (see Fig. 2.40)

When molecules of glucose are mixed with oxygen in the cell, the process of oxidation in the presence of the enzymes in the cell releases energy. The reaction can be represented by the formula

$$C_6H_{12}O_6 + 6O_2 \xrightarrow{\text{enzymes}} 6CO_2 + 6H_2O + \text{energy}.$$

Note: This reaction is the reverse of photosynthesis in plants.

In the cell, energy is not released all at once, but takes place in a series of small steps. Each small step needs its own enzyme and at each stage a little energy is released.

Anaerobic respiration

This is the release of energy from glucose in chemical reactions that do not require oxygen. In these reactions glucose is broken down to inter-

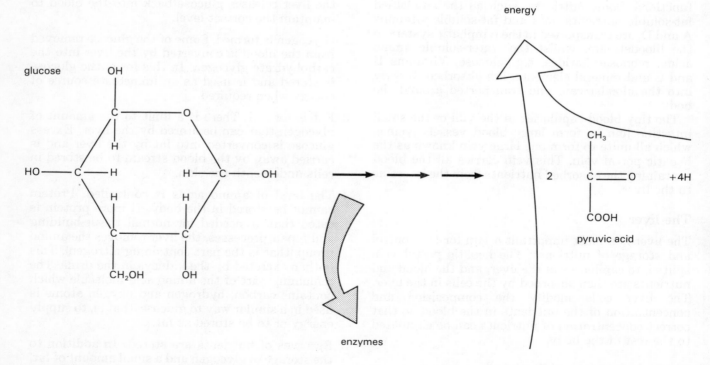

Fig. 2.40(a) Enzymes attack the glucose molecule, and break it into two molecules of pyruvic acid. This breakdown lets energy free.

mediate compounds; less energy is released than in aerobic respiration.

In animal tissue, glucose is broken down to lactic acid.

$$C_6H_{12}O_6 \longrightarrow 2CH_3CHOHCOOH + energy$$

In plants, glucose is broken down to carbon dioxide and alcohol. This process is known as fermentation (see p.248).

Both aerobic and anaerobic respiration occur in the human body. For instance during periods of vigorous activity the oxygen supply may be insufficient to oxidise the nutrients rapidly enough to provide the essential energy so anaerobic respiration occurs. The intermediate products are later oxidised to carbon dioxide and water, hence heavy breathing continues for a while after vigorous activity ceases.

Some energy in the cell is released in the form of heat for example in mammals. This heat keeps them warm. In cold-blooded animals, the heat accumulates and then they use it to move faster. In plants, heat is lost to the surroundings as fast as it is produced. However, energy is also used for the many chemical processes that the cells are involved in, such as:

building proteins
secretion of enzymes

contraction of muscles
electrical impulses of the nerves
breathing
heartbeats.

Consequently, life itself depends on the efficient use of nutrients which are obtained from the food we eat.

Storage of nutrients

If the quantity of food eaten exceeds the body requirements, some nutrients can be stored in the following ways:

(a) *Glucose* About 100 g of glycogen formed from excess glucose in the liver is stored. This is a short-term store of energy: enough for about six hours of life if no other glucose is available. When the level of glucose in the blood drops, the liver releases glycogen and converts it back to glucose to enter the blood stream. About 300 g of glycogen is also stored in the muscles. This is not returned to circulation, but is used by an active muscle in a similar way as glucose. Excess glucose, not stored as glycogen, is converted to fat and stored in fat cells underneath the skin.

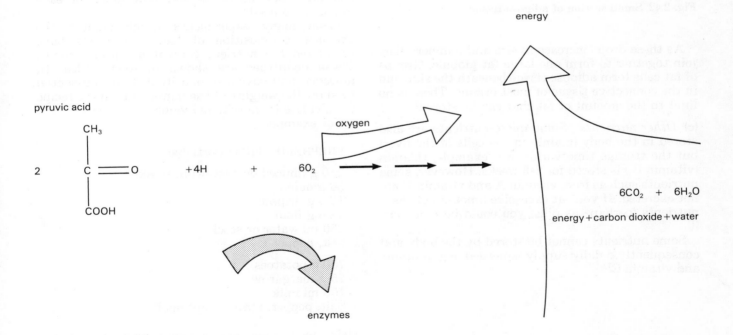

(b) **Each molecule of pyruvic acid containing three carbon atoms is then broken down by more enzymes to form carbon dioxide and water.**

(b) *Fats* Drops of fat accumulate inside certain cells.

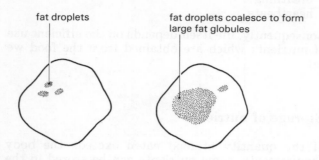

fat droplets

fat droplets coalesce to form large fat globules

Fig. 2.41 Fat droplets coalesce

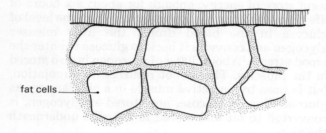

fat cells

Fig. 2.42 Small section of adipose tissue

As these drops increase in size and numbers they join together to form one large fat globule. Groups of fat cells form adipose tissue beneath the skin and in the connective tissue of most organs. There is no limit to the amount of fat that can be stored!

(c) *Other nutrients* Some micro-nutrients are also stored in the body (mainly in the cells of the liver) but the storage time varies. For example, thiamin (vitamin B$_1$) is stored for 2-3 weeks. However, some nutrients such as iron, vitamin A and vitamin D are not excreted. If you eat excessive amounts of these nutrients (perhaps as pills) you could become very ill.

Some nutrients cannot be stored by the body and consequently a daily supply is needed, e.g. proteins and vitamin C.

4 How much, and what types of food does the body need?

How can we judge how much, and what types of food to eat? It has been shown that if too much food is eaten, the excess is converted into body fat: if too little food or the wrong types of food are eaten, people become lethargic, feel irritable and in extreme cases suffer disease, starvation and, eventually, die.

We need just enough food to keep us healthy, build new tissues and transform into energy for all body processes. Appetite can be quite a reliable guide as to the amount of food you need. However, appetite will not necessarily choose nutritionally well-balanced foods. Nor will an unguided choice. For example, apples and plums may look appetising, but these fruits contain little vitamin C, whereas some other fruits, such as blackcurrants, strawberries and oranges, contain abundant supplies of vitamin C. Only an understanding of the importance and function of nutrients and the nutrient content of foods will help you choose foods that will keep you healthy.

Foods are mixtures of many different nutrients in varying amounts. So how do we know which foods contain which nutrients and how much of each nutrient we need?

From many experiments which analyse the chemical composition of foods, scientists have calculated the nutrient content of various foods. These quantities are shown in food tables. If, however, you have a composite dish, it is essential to know the weights of the ingredients in the recipe to calculate its nutritional value.

For example:

SHEPHERD'S PIE (4 portions)

250 g minced beef (stewing steak)
50 g onion
12.5 g dripping
12.5 g flour
250 ml water or stock
salt, pepper

750 g potatoes
25 g margarine
100 ml milk
Salt, pepper, nutmeg (optional)

Using food tables, or a computer program, you can calculate the nutritional value of this dish. Notice that you first have to calculate the nutritional value of a particular weight of each ingredient, then total the nutrients in the recipe. Finally, you can calculate

Fig. 2.43 Nutritional value of Shepherd's Pie (4 portions)

	Energy value		Nutrient content											
	kcal	kJ	water (g)	protein (g)	fat (g)	carbo-hydrate (g)	calcium (mg)	iron (mg)	vit A (μg)	vit D (μg)	B$_1$ thiamin (mg)	B$_2$ riboflavin (mg)	niacin (mg)	vit C (mg)
250 g minced beef	530	2220	172.5	42.5	40.0	0	25	10	0	0	0.17	0.5	20.5	0
50 g onion	12	48	47.0	0.45	0	2	15	0.15	0	0	0.01	0.02	0.2	5
12.5 g dripping	31	133	0.01	0	3.5	0	0	0	0	0	0	0	0	0
12.5 g flour	43	182	1.0	1.25	0.11	0	18.1	0.23	0	0	0.03	0.01	0.35	0
250 ml water	0	0	250.0	0	0	0	0	0	0	0	0	0	0	0
salt, pepper	0	0	0	0	0	0	0	0	0	0	0	0	0	0
750 g potatoes	592	2482	607.5	10.5	0	147.7	30.0	3.75	0	0	0.6	0.02	9.0	3.0
25 g margarine	192	805	4.0	0.05	21.3	0	10	0.07	225.0	2.0	0	0	0.02	0
100 ml milk (100 g)	65	272	87.0	3.3	3.8	4.8	120	0.1	37	0.01	0.04	0.15	0.9	0
Total nutritional value	1466	6143	1069.01	58.05	68.71	165.0	209.1	14.30	262.0	2.01	0.86	0.70	31.2	35.0
Nutritional value of 1 portion i.e. quarter of recipe	366	1535	267.25	14.5	17.1	41.25	52.25	3.57	65.5	0.5	0.21	0.17	7.8	8.75

the nutritional value of one portion. In Fig. 2.43 you will notice a column marked 'energy value'. This is a measure of how much energy the ingredients yield when used in the body. This will be explained later.

To calculate the nutritional value of all food eaten in one day, each portion is analysed in this way. Allowances are made for any losses in nutritional value that may occur during preparation, e.g. vitamin C loss in cooking green vegetables (see Fig. 12.3 on p. 170). The total nutritional value of food eaten in one day can then be calculated.

From your day's menu plan, use food tables, or a computer program to calculate the nutritional value of each item of food. Then total the nutrients to give you the nutritional value of the food you ate in that day.

If it was not possible to record your diet plan for a day, work out the nutritional value of the following menu that was consumed by a 15-year-old boy.

Fig. 2.44 Menu for 15-year-old boy

Breakfast	3 slices toast	(100 g)
	butter	(25 g)
	marmalade	
	coffee with 50 ml milk + 20 g sugar	

Mid-morning	currant bun	(50 g)
	tea with 50 ml milk + 20 g sugar	

Lunch	steak and kidney pie	(150 g)
	crisps	(25 g)
	banana	(150 g)
	Coca Cola	(330 ml)

Supper	cod in batter	(150 g)
	chips	(150 g)
	apple pie	(100 g)
	beer	(300 ml)
	chocolate biscuits	(50 g)
	coffee with 50 ml milk + 20 g sugar	

The next stage in trying to assess whether the food eaten is adequate for you, is to compare the nutritional value of your diet with an estimate of the amount and types of food needed to keep you healthy.

From many studies of the food consumption throughout the world, food scientists have calculated the approximate amount of each nutrient needed by the body. These recommended daily intakes of nutrients (RDI) vary between individuals, their stage in the lifecycle, and their activity level. The chart in Fig. 2.45 gives a guide to the RDI for each age group. Everybody is different.

(a) From Fig. 2.45, list your recommended daily intake of nutrients.
(b) Compare the nutritional value of your day's menu with the RDI for you. Was your diet adequate? If not, was there a deficiency or surplus of nutrients?
(c) Make suggestions as to how your diet could be improved so as to supply the recommended daily intake of nutrients.
(d) Make similar comparisons for the menu for the 15-year-old boy on p. 47.

You will notice in using both food tables and RDI tables that there is another column about *energy values or requirements*. Energy is not a nutrient. The sun gives energy to plants to build molecules of

Fig. 2.45 Recommended daily intake (RDI) of nutrients for each age group

Age ranges years		Energy value kJ (000)	kcal	Protein g	Nutritional values calcium mg	iron mg	vit. A µg	thiamin mg	riboflavin mg	niacin mg	vit. C mg	vit. D µg
Infants												
under 1		3.3	800	20	600	6	450	0.3	0.4	5	15	10
Children												
1		5.0	1200	30	500	7	300	0.5	0.6	7	20	10
2		5.9	1400	35	500	7	300	0.6	0.7	8	20	10
3–4		6.7	1600	40	500	8	300	0.6	0.8	9	20	10
5–6		7.5	1800	45	500	8	300	0.7	0.9	10	20	2.5
7–8		8.8	2100	53	500	10	400	0.8	1.0	11	20	2.5
Males												
9–11		10.5	2500	63	700	13	575	1.0	1.2	14	25	2.5
12–14		11.7	2800	70	700	14	725	1.1	1.4	16	25	2.5
15–17		12.6	3000	75	600	15	750	1.2	1.7	19	30	2.5
18–34	sedentary	11.3	2700	68	500	10	750	1.1	1.7	18	30	2.5
	moderately active	12.6	3000	75	500	10	750	1.2	1.7	18	30	2.5
	very active	15.1	3600	90	500	10	750	1.4	1.7	18	30	2.5
35–64	sedentary	10.9	2600	65	500	10	750	1.0	1.7	18	30	2.5
	moderately active	12.1	2900	73	500	10	750	1.2	1.7	18	30	2.5
	very active	15.1	3600	90	500	10	750	1.4	1.7	18	30	2.5
65–74		9.8	2350	59	500	10	750	0.9	1.7	18	30	2.5
75 and over		8.8	2100	53	500	10	750	0.8	1.7	18	30	2.5
Females												
9–11		9.6	2300	58	700	13	575	0.9	1.2	13	25	2.5
12–14		9.6	2300	58	700	14	725	0.9	1.4	16	25	2.5
15–17		9.6	2300	58	600	15	750	0.9	1.4	16	30	2.5
18–54	most occupations	9.2	2200	55	500	12	750	0.9	1.3	15	30	2.5
	very active	10.5	2500	63	500	12	750	1.0	1.3	15	30	2.5
55–74		8.6	2050	51	500	10	750	0.8	1.3	15	30	2.5
75 and over		8.0	1900	48	500	10	750	0.7	1.3	15	30	2.5
During pregnancy		10.0	2400	60	200	15	750	1.0	1.6	18	60	10
Nursing mothers		11.3	2700	68	200	15	1,200	1.1	1.8	21	60	10

nutrients, e.g. carbohydrates, proteins and fats. Food is therefore a store of energy. When our bodies digest these nutrients, energy is released, and is used by the body for all its activities. It is therefore important in a well-balanced diet that the amount of energy supplied by food is the amount of energy needed by the body for all its functions. This quality is known as the *energy balance* of a diet.

The energy balance

To maintain a constant body weight, the energy input from food must equal the energy output by the body; that is:

energy from food = energy used by the body
= energy to keep body functioning *plus* energy for all activities

For children, and during pregnancy, the energy input should be greater than the energy output. For slimming diets, the energy output must be greater than the energy input from foods.

The amounts of energy obtained from food, and the amounts of energy needed by the body at different stages in the life-cycle, have been measured and recorded by scientists. Energy is measured in either kilocalories or kilojoules.

- *Kilocalories* (kcal). A calorie is a unit of heat. One calorie is the amount of heat needed to raise the temperature of 1 gram of water by 1°C. Because this is a small unit, nutritionists use the kilocalorie (i.e. 1000 calories) as the standard unit of measurement. A little confusion arises as the kilocalorie is often written as a Calorie, with a capital 'C'. This confusion can be avoided by always using the term kilocalorie (kcal).
- *Kilojoules* (kJ). The joule is internationally recognised as the unit of measurement of energy. A joule is the work done in moving a force needed to accelerate a mass of 1 kilogram at the rate of one metre per second. Again, because the joule is quite a small unit of measurement, the kilojoule (i.e. 1000 joules) is used as the standard measurement of energy by nutritionists. Sometimes, the megajoule, MJ, may also be used: 1 MJ = 1000 kJ.

Both these units are used in this book, as it is important that you should be able to read and understand other texts which use either of these measurements. Never try to use the two systems simultaneously. If necessary, you can convert the units as:

1 kilocalorie = 4.186 kilojoules (i.e. approx. 4.2)

Therefore, a simple calculation will convert the units to the alternative system: for example

5 kilocalories = 5 × 4.2 kilojoules
= 21 kilojoules.

These units are used to:
(a) measure the energy requirements of the body,
(b) measure the energy value that can be obtained from food.

(a) How much energy does the body need?

All body processes require energy. For example:
- energy is needed (as heat) to keep us warm;
- muscle cells use energy during movement;
- nerve cells need energy to pass on impulses between brain and other tissues;
- every gland and internal organ needs energy;
- energy is needed to build new cells and replace old ones;
- energy is needed for breathing.

The body uses about three-quarters of its energy needs on functions that make the body work. Only about one quarter of its energy needs are used for muscle movement.

Energy requirements vary with the individual. The speed at which our bodies use food is known as the *metabolic rate*. The energy required just to keep the body warm and all the basic processes functioning is called the *basal metabolic rate* (BMR). BMR is measured when the person is asleep, several hours after the last meal. Basal metabolic rate is affected by size, shape, weight, sex, age, rate of growth, amount of sleep and state of nutrition of each individual. It has been found that:
- BMR is proportionately higher in relation to body weight during periods of growth, for example in children and pregnancy
- men require 10–20% more energy per kilogram of body weight than women.

BMR also varies because no two apparently similar individuals bodies function in exactly the same way. It is also affected by personality; for example, a calm, placid person naturally requires less energy than a nervous person.

Fig. 2.46 Some average values of Basal Metabolic Rate (BMR)

	weight (kg)	Basal metabolic rate kcal(kJ)/kg/day	Basal metabolic rate kcal/kJ/day
infant 1 yr	10	50 (210)	500 (2100)
child 8 yr	25	40 (170)	1000 (4250)
adult woman	55	25 (100)	1300 (5200)
adult man	65	25 (100)	1600 (26 400)

From Fig. 2.46 it can be calculated that an average adult woman needs approximately 0.9 kcal (3.75 kJ) per minute to keep her alive (note: there are 1440 minutes in a day). How much energy would an average adult man require per minute? How much energy would each require during eight hours of sleep?

Any movement or activity uses more energy in addition to that used to keep the body functioning. The more strenuous the activity the more energy is used. The amount of energy used for these activities varies greatly from person to person.

Fig. 2.47 Some examples of approximate energy expenditure (including BMR) for an adult man aged 30, weighing 65 kg

Activity	Average energy expenditure	
	kcal/min	kJ/min
everyday activities		
sitting, reading, watching TV	1.4	6
washing, dressing	3.5	15
walking slowly	3	13
walking upstairs	9	38
work and recreation		
preparing meals, driving; office workers, shop workers, doctors, dentists } *light activities*	2–5.9	10–20
gardening, tennis, dancing; light industrial workers, e.g. plumbers, postmen } *moderate activities*	5–7.4	21–30
coalmining, forestry workers, labourers; squash, swimming, athletics } *strenuous activities*	7.5 and over	over 30

The amount of time spent on various activities gives an indication of the energy required each day. A general guide to the approximate energy requirements at different stages in the life-cycle are shown in Fig. 2.46.

(b) How much energy is there in food?

Some foods have more energy value than others. This is dependent on the chemical composition of the food (see p. 16).

The energy value is often measured by finding out how much heat is given off when the food is burnt. (This is done in a piece of apparatus called a calorimeter.) Although your body does not 'burn' food in this way, the energy the food contains still ends up as heat in the body.

A simple experiment shows how much heat is given off when food is burnt, or used, in the body.

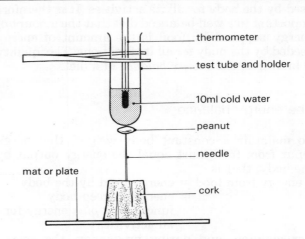

- thermometer
- test tube and holder
- 10ml cold water
- peanut
- needle
- mat or plate
- cork

1 Set up the apparatus as shown. Note the temperature of the water.
2 Light a match, and set fire to the peanut.
3 Describe what happens as the peanut burns.
4 Note the temperature of the water.
5 Can you explain this experiment?

The *energy value* of a food is sometimes known as its *calorific value*. This is because when a known weight of a particular food is burnt in an apparatus called a calorimeter, the energy value is calculated in units of heat given off. It has been found that when oxidised in a calorimeter,

1 g fat yields 9.00 kcal/37 kJ
1 g carbohydrate yields 3.75 kcal/16 kJ
1 g protein yields 4.00 kcal/17 kJ

However, foods are mixtures of nutrients. The energy value can therefore be calculated from the nutrient content. For example, 100 g beef contains

	kcal	kJ
14.8 g protein which yields	59.2 (i.e. 14.8 × 4)	547.6 (14.8 × 17)
28.2 g fat which yields	253.8 (i.e. 28.2 × 9)	1043.4 (28.2 × 37)
∴ 100 g beef yields	313 kcal	1591.0 kJ

Fortunately the energy values of most foods have been calculated, and are listed in food tables or on a computer program. Energy values are also often given in popular publications, such as *Slimming* magazine. As many foods are composite dishes, e.g. shepherds pie, the energy value can be calculated per recipe, per portion or per 100 g (see plate 7).

To assess the energy value of food, it is essential to know the weight of food eaten. This concept has important applications. For example, in a slimming diet, the energy input from food can be reduced just by eating smaller portions. This is perhaps the easiest way to begin reducing the energy value of your diet, without feeling deprived of the foods you like.

However, the most effective way to reduce the energy value of a diet is to reduce the intake of foods that contain high proportions of fat as these foods are the most concentrated sources of energy.

The energy value of food is also often affected by the method of cooking. See Fig. 2.48.

Fig. 2.48 Effect of cooking method on cod and potatoes

	kcal / 100 g	kJ / 100 g
potatoes boiled	79	331
potatoes chipped	236	989
cod poached in milk	69	289
cod fried in batter	199	834

The method of cooking is therefore an important consideration, especially if you are planning a slimming diet.

Look at plate 7. These foods all supply 100 kcal or 420 kJ.

It is also important not to overlook the energy value of drinks. Most drinks contain some sugar or alcohol, which supply energy but few other nutrients. When oxidised, 1 g alcohol yields 7 kcal or 29 kJ. Note that the higher alcohol content, the greater is the energy value, so be particularly careful in your choice of drinks if you are on a slimming diet. See Fig. 2.49.

Fig. 2.49 Volumes of drinks supplying 100 kcal/420 kJ

50 ml spirits, e.g. whisky
150 ml white wine
250 ml Coca Cola
275 ml cider
300 ml beer
1000 ml orange squash.

If you are attempting to plan a nutritionally well-balanced diet, it is important that you understand the nutrient content and energy value of the portion size of each of the foods that you eat. Figure 2.51 shows the analysis of some commonly-eaten foods. Using food tables, look up the nutritional value of other foods you eat regularly.

Using Fig. 2.51, and referring to your RDI of nutrients and energy, work out the percentage of your daily recommended intake each of these foods will supply. Display your results in a series of bar charts, which will look similar to this.

Fig. 2.50 % RDI of nutrients for a 15-year-old girl supplied by 1 glass of milk (250 ml)

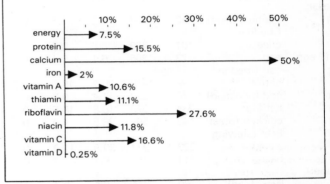

From the figures in this chapter:
- make a list of the most nutritious foods, that is, those that supply several nutrients.
- do all foods contain vitamin C?
- do many foods contain thiamin?
- which is the most important nutrient in milk? Why is this important in the diet?
- how much bread, potatoes, liver and beef would you need to supply your recommended daily intake of iron?

Using the figures in this chapter, work out the nutritional value of the foods you eat in a single day. Is your choice of foods nutritionally well-planned? Suggest any modifications that you consider desirable.

Follow this plan on several days, until you understand the nutrient content of the foods you eat regularly. Now you can plan attractive and appetising meals with the confidence of knowing that the food you have chosen looks and tastes good and is nutritionally good for you.

Fig. 2.51 The nutritional value of average portion sizes of commonly eaten foods

Portion size	Food	Energy value		Nutrient content											
		kcal	kJ	pro-tein g	fat g	carbo-hydrate g	water g	calc-ium mg	iron mg	vit. A μg	thia-min mg	ribo-flavin mg	niacin mg	vit. C mg	vit. D μg
50 g (2 large slices)	wholemeal bread	108	459	4.4	1.3	20.9	20	11.5	1.25	0	0.9	0.80	10.65	0	1.4
50 g (2 large slices)	white bread	116	49	3.9	0.8	24.8	18	50.0	0.8	0	0.09	0.01	1.1	0	0
25 g	butter	185	760	0.1	20.5	0	3.75	3.7	0.05	246	0	0	0.02	0	0.1
25 g	margarine	182	750	0.05	20.2	0	4.0	1.0	0.07	225	0	0	0.02	0	1.9
30 g	cornflakes	122	522	2.8	0.5	28.3	1.0	1.0	2.2	0	0.6	0.5	0.22	0	0
200 ml (1 glass)	milk	130	544	6.6	7.6	9.4	174	240.0	0.2	80	0.08	0.3	1.8	4.0	0.02
150 g	yoghurt (fruit)	142	607	7.2	1.5	26.8	112.5	240	0.3	33	0.07	0.3	1.6	3	0.01
25 g	Cheddar cheese	101	420	6.5	8.3	0	9.2	200.0	0.1	103	0.01	0.1	1.5	0	0.06
50 g (1 egg)	egg	73	306	6.1	5.4	0	37.5	26.0	1.0	700	0.04	0.2	1.8	0	0.8
200 g	cod (fried in batter)	398	1498	25.2	15.0	32.2	128.0	86	1.4	0	0.1	0.1	6.2	0	0
100 g	cod (poached)	76	322	17.4	0.7	0	82	16	0.3	0	0.08	0.07	4.9	0	0
100 g	herring	234	970	16.8	18.5	0	64	33	0.8	45	0	0.1	7.1	0	22.5
100 g	chicken (roast)	142	599	26.5	4.0	0	69.0	9.0	0.5	0	0.08	0.1	15.3	0	0
100 g	beef (stewing steak)	223	932	30.9	11.0	0	57.0	15.0	3.0	0	0.03	0.3	10.2	0	0
25 g (1 rasher)	bacon	111	462	6.1	9.7	0	8	3.0	0.35	0	0.1	0.04	2.3	0	0
25 g	liver (fried)	60	254	6.2	3.4	1.4	14.0	3.5	2.2	4753	0.06	1.07	5.1	3	0.09
50 g (1 thick)	sausage	183	760	5.3	16.0	4.7	22.5	20.5	0.5	0	0.02	0.06	2.8	0	0
100 g	potatoes (boiled)	79	339	1	0	19.7	81	4.0	0.3	0	0.08	0.03	1.1	10.0	0
	(chipped)	253	1065	3	10.9	37.3	47.0	14	0.9	0	0.1	0.04	2.1	10.0	0
50 g	rice	180	768	3	0.5	43.4	6.0	2.0	0.25	0	0.04	0.01	0.7	0	0
100 g	carrots (boiled)	23	98	0.7	0	1.5	93	21	0.5	2000	0.06	0.05	0.7	6	0
100 g	cabbage (boiled)	15	66	1	0	2.3	93	38	0.4	50	0.03	0.03	0.5	23	0
100 g	baked beans	64	270	5	0.5	10.3	74	45.0	1.4	50	0.07	0.05	1.3	0	0
100 g	apple	46	196	0.3	0	11.9	84	4	0.3	5	0.04	0.02	0.1	5.0	0
100 g	banana	76	326	1	0	19.2	71	7	0.4	33	0.04	0.07	0.8	10.0	0
100 g (medium size)	orange	35	150	0.8	0	8.5	86	41	0.3	8	0.10	0.03	0.3	50.0	0
100 g	fruit cake	332	1403	3	11	58.3	21	75	1.8	121	0.08	0.08	1.2	0	1.1
25 g	crisps	133	556	1.5	8	12.2	0.7	5.7	0.07	0	0.01	0.01	0.07	2	0
50 g	peanuts	285	1182	12	24	4.3	2.5	30.5	1.0	0	0.1	0.05	10.6	0	0
330 ml (1 can)	Coca Cola	128	554	0	0	34.6	297	13.2	0	0	0	0	0	0	0
100 ml	orange juice (canned, unsweetened)	33	143	0.4	0	8.5	89	9	0.5	8	0.07	0.02	0.3	35	0

Source: *Manual of Nutrition* (HMSO)

QUESTIONS

1 Explain the reasons why it is important to include food high in fibre content in the daily diet.
Give two examples of foods high in fibre.

2 (a) Name the chemical elements from which fats and oils are formed.
(b) Name six functions of fat in the body.
(c) Why do many middle-aged and overweight men restrict the intake of fat?
(d) Give an account of the digestion and absorption of fat in the body.
(JMB, 1979)

3 (a) Name the chemical elements from which carbohydrates are formed.
(b) Glucose, cellulose and glycogen are three forms of carbohydrates. Where are they found and what is the purpose of each of them?
(c) Why is some restriction in the intake of sugar advisable in the diet of (i) young children (ii) sedentary workers?
(JMB, 1978)

4 Explain what you understand by digestion.
Draw and label a diagram of the alimentary canal.
Describe in detail the digestion processes which take place after food has left the stomach.
(AEB, 1977)

5 What is meant by the word 'nutrition'?
Explain how good eating habits can help prevent the following health hazards: dental decay; rickets; obesity; anaemia.
(London, 1979)

6 (a) Give two reasons why the body requires energy.
(b) The energy used by the body is measured in kilocalories or joules. Give the definition of one of these.
(c) Name the nutrients of which the primary function is to supply the body with energy.
(Scottish, 1979)

7 The foods containing the nutrient carbohydrate are among those most readily available to man.

(a) What are the functions of carbohydrate in the body and what is the effect if eaten in excess of bodily needs?
(b) Carbohydrates consist of simple sugars, double sugars and polysaccharides.
(i) To which group does each of the following belong and what are its food sources? starch; fructose; lactose; glycogen.
(ii) Describe briefly the digestion of starch in the body.
(c) Name the vitamin complex which is associated with carbohydrate metabolism and explain why it is important to include an adequate supply of these vitamins in the diet every day.

(d) What is meant by the terms (i) basal metabolic rate (ii) joule? How many joules per day (approximately) would be required by a boy aged 14 years?
(Northern Ireland, 1978)

8 Name (a) the fat-soluble vitamins, (b) the water-soluble vitamins. State why each vitamin is required in the diet and how you could ensure that it is provided adequately in the family meals.
(Oxford, 1977)

9 In order to build and maintain strong and healthy bones the diet must contain in conjunction with phosphorus the nutrient CALCIUM.
(a) For what other functions in the body is calcium necessary?
(b) State the main food sources of calcium in the average diet.
(c) (i) Name the vitamin which influences the absorption of calcium in the body. What are the sources of this vitamin?
(ii) Why is it important for the following groups of people to have an adequate intake of both calcium and this vitamin?
(1) pregnant women and nursing mothers
(2) babies and young children
(3) the elderly
(d) What is the recommended daily intake of calcium in the diet of the primary school child?
(Northern Ireland, 1979)

10 Food is made up of substances called nutrients. Name these nutrients and give the function of each one in the body.
(Welsh, 1978)

11 (a) State why iron is important in the diet and give the effects which a shortage of iron has on the human body.
(b) Name three foods which are good sources of iron.
(Oxford, 1977)

12 (a) Why is water needed by the body?
(b) How is water introduced into the daily diet?
(Oxford, 1977)

13 (a) Name two micro-nutrients.
(b) Give the function of one of them.
(c) What nutrients are at risk in a vegetarian diet?
(London, 1980)

14 (a) What are nutrients?
(b) Give one example of a major nutrient.
(c) State its recommended daily intake (RDI).
(d) What would happen if this nutrient was:
(i) deficient in the diet for a few days?
(ii) deficient in the diet for several months?
(iii) eaten in excess?
(London, 1980)

15 (a) Give one example of:
a good source of protein
a cheap source of protein
a protein of high biological value
an essential amino acid
the limiting amino acid in cereals.

(b) How can a mixed diet provide adequate supplies of protein cheaply?

(London, 1980)

16 (a) Why is a diet without fat almost impossible to obtain?

(b) What other nutrients are likely to be lacking in a low fat diet?

(c) Where are nutrients listed in (b) obtained:
(i) in a normal diet?
(ii) in a low fat diet?

(d) Why is it considered advisable for most people to eat less fat?

(London, 1981)

17 What are the functions in the body of the following:
(a) Vitamin A
(b) Vitamin B₁ (thiamin)
(c) Vitamin C
(d) Vitamin D?

Name two main food sources of each.

Explain the points to be observed in choosing, storing, preparing and cooking food in order to minimise the loss of vitamin C.

(London, 1980)

Meal-Planning 3

Are you a good meal-planner? Most people in developed countries eat three meals each day, every day of the year. Yet very few people ever consider how fortunate we are to have such an abundance of foods available to give variety to our diet. It is not only the number of meals we eat, but the nutritional quality of the meals that is important. Chapter 2 shows the function of nutrients in the diet. This chapter gives some guidelines on how to use those nutrients in well-planned meals that people will want to eat.

The importance of good meal-planning for health and happiness cannot be over-estimated. It is the responsibility of the skilful meal-planner to make sure that:
- meals are available when needed
- nutritional needs are met
- meals are attractive and enjoyable
- appetites are satisfied
- the budget is not exceeded.

Guidelines for meal-planning

1 *The factors affecting the choice of food*

What people eat is not necessarily what they want to eat. There are many things that may limit the choice of foods eaten:
- family circumstances such as income, lifestyle;
- daily routine of members of the family such as employment, schools;
- individual preferences, traditional habits (see p. 5);
- shopping facilities available locally (see p. 66);
- storage facilities such as larder, refrigerator and deep-freeze facilities;
- cooking facilities and equipment;
- cook's ability and interest in meals.

2 *Meals should never be planned singly*

Except for special occasions, plan meals for at least a whole day, preferably a few days or a week ahead. In this way it is possible to:
- achieve a balance in the diet, by supplying nutrients that are lacking in one meal in subsequent meals;
- plan a balanced diet for individual family members appropriate to their age, sex and occupations;
- provide variety in the diet;
- estimate costs, and adjust menus as necessary;
- plan cooking to save time, effort and fuel;
- make an accurate shopping list.

3 *Plan meals appropriate to the occasion*

Consider the following points before deciding on your menus:
- variety in the type of meal required. It may be lunch, dinner, a snack, a family or a special occasion meal.
- the time of year. Plan more warmth- and energy-giving foods in winter, plan more salads and lighter meals in summer.
- the number of people eating the meal. This will guide you on the type of meal to plan, and the quantities of food to purchase and prepare.
- the personal likes and dislikes of the diners.

4 *The appearance, texture and flavour of food*

Food must look attractive and smell good to stimulate the appetite. The aim in good meal-planning is to provide variety in colour, texture and flavour.

Colour: avoid meals lacking in colour contrast, for example white fish, creamed potatoes and cauliflower followed by rice pudding. Use garnishes, sauces and accompaniments to give extra colour.

Texture: avoid serving all soft, all dry, or all hard textured foods at one meal.

Suggest ways in which you could improve the texture of these meals:

1 Cornish pasty and chips
Cheese and biscuits

2 Macaroni cheese
Chocolate blanc-mange

Flavour: avoid repetition of flavours, and the use of too many bland or highly seasoned foods together. For example fruit as a starter, followed by fruit salad as a dessert, or

tomato soup and a casserole with tomatoes as a major ingredient.

5 *The money available for spending on food*

Here are some tips to help you plan economical meals:

- cost each main meal. This will guide you as to how much you can spend on ingredients, and show where adjustments are necessary.
- use cheaper cuts of meat and types of fish where possible. They are generally as nutritious as the expensive varieties. (Very fatty meat may be less expensive, but may not be nutritious because of the large amount of fat.)
- use foods in season, when they are at their cheapest and best in food value (e.g. runner beans in August and September, tangerines in December and January).
- plan to use left-over foods.
- save money on fuel bills by using full capacity of the oven. Never heat the oven for a single dish. Plan to cook dishes for other meals at the same time. The use of steamer, pressure cooker and microwave cooker will also reduce fuel consumption.

6 *Consider the time available for cooking, cooking facilities and equipment*

Timing is often very important in food preparation.

- It is useless to plan a dish requiring long preparation and cooking when the meal is needed quickly.
- Convenience foods may be quick alternatives that are very useful in some situations.
- Use labour- and time-saving equipment wherever possible, such as electric mixers with blenders, shredding and slicing attachments, pressure cookers, automatic controls, microwave cookers.

Meals in a day

Nutritionists suggest it is advisable to eat small regular meals during the day rather than one huge meal. In this way the body has time to digest the food adequately (see p. 39). People's eating habits vary enormously and are dependent on a variety of factors, such as age and occupation.

There are, however, a number of traditional mealtimes from which patterns of meals have evolved. These are breakfast, lunch, afternoon tea, high tea, evening meal and late-night supper. Meal patterns and times of meals vary with lifestyle and circumstances. The meal pattern must also be

sufficiently flexible to accommodate unexpected events such as arrival of visitors.

Whatever the circumstances, it is important that the total intake of food is nutritionally well balanced. The easiest way to achieve this is to plan meals in relation to other food for the whole day.

Daily requirement of food

The amount of food required daily varies with the specific needs of the individual (see p. 48). A rough guide is:

Water:	At least 1½ litres per day	
Protein foods:		
Milk	adults	250–500 ml
	children	500–800 ml
Meat, fish, cheese, eggs	2 servings per day	
Fruit, salad and vegetables:	2 servings per day	

Foods containing carbohydrate:

root vegetables	1 serving per day
bread, cakes, pastry	only as required to satisfy appetite, after nutritional needs are met.
sugar	only enough to make food palatable.

Foods containing fats and oils:

butter, margarine, cooking fat	not more than 50 g per day
fats naturally in foods e.g. egg yolk, meat; fat in cooked products, e.g. pastry	beware of excess fat in the diet from these sources.

A useful guide to the amount of food to prepare is:

Fig. 3.1 Approximate quantity of food per adult serving

soups	200–300 ml
fruit juice	100 ml
meat without bone	100 g
meat with bone	150–200 g
fish without bone	100–150 g
fish with bone	150–200 g
cheese	50–100 g
potatoes	100–300 g
pasta, rice	25–50 g
green vegetables (after preparation)	100 g
root vegetables (after preparation)	100 g
puddings	100 g
sauces	75–100 ml
gravy	50–75 ml
custard	50–100 ml

Special requirements at different stages in the life cycle

At various stages in their lives, people have special dietary needs.

Pregnant women and nursing mothers

The pregnant woman and the nursing mother must each adapt her diet to provide adequate nutrients for herself and her baby. If the diet is unbalanced, the mother and her developing baby may suffer.

It is particularly important that:
- the building foods are well supplied i.e. the proteins, calcium and vitamin D;
- there is an ample supply of iron. The developing baby stores iron in his blood, liver, spleen and muscles. If the mother does not eat sufficient foods containing iron, the baby's supply will continue to be stored, but the mother may become anaemic (see p. 37). Pills containing iron may be prescribed for the pregnant woman to supplement her diet.
- there is a good supply of fresh fruit, vegetables and salads. These provide vitamin C, and dietary fibre which will prevent constipation.
- carbohydrates and fats are not eaten excessively.

Weight-watching is essential in pregnancy, as excessive weight will tire the mother, and possibly cause undesirable complications. A gain of not more than 10-12 kilograms is desirable. Normal weight should be regained when the baby is weaned.

Babies (0-12 months)

Body growth is very rapid during this period. The diet must therefore contain good supplies of protein, calcium, phosphorus, and vitamins, all in an easily digestible form.

Milk is the most suitable food, either breast milk, or modified cow's milk prepared to resemble breast milk. Milk is very nutritious and forms the basis of the baby's diet for the first few months. Milk is deficient in iron, but the baby has a stored supply of iron, adequate for the first few months. Green vegetables, and iron-rich cereals are introduced gradually to supply iron. There is little vitamin C and vitamin D in milk, therefore vitamin drops are often prescribed. These supplements should be given from when the baby is one month old. In addition a baby needs extra water which can be given in a small bottle between meals. The water must be boiled and cooled.

The introduction to solid foods varies with the individual child. It is wise to encourage the eating of the essential foods and discourage the formation of a taste for sweet foods. New flavours and textures should be introduced gradually. For example:

1-2 months fruit and vegetable juices
3 months a few drops of egg yolk
4 months vegetable soups, finely sieved, or bought, ready-prepared baby foods. Home-made soup can be thickened with sieved or blended vegetables.
4-5 months fine-grained cereals such as well-cooked oatmeal porridge, ground rice, semolina, etc.
6-8 months stewed fruits, milk puddings, thick meat and vegetable soups
8-12 months finely grated cheese, whole egg.

By the end of the first year, most babies are having a mixed diet to supplement the milk, which should still form the basis of the diet.

Infants 1-2 years

The growth rate is not so rapid as it was during the first twelve months, but is still very fast, and energy demands may well be higher. A good diet should be firmly established by now. At first, all food should be sieved, blended or finely minced. As the child acquires more teeth, the sieved puréed foods should be decreased and foods which require chewing should gradually be substituted. Crisp rusks or wholemeal crusts can be given when the child is teething, to teach the baby to bite. Later, pieces of apple or carrot can be introduced, but always with careful supervision to avoid the risk of choking.

Variety, attractive serving, regular meals and a pleasant unworried atmosphere are important aids towards encouraging young children to eat. A routine of three meals a day should now be established to fit in with family meal patterns. Servings of food should be small, as children of this age have small stomachs. Requests for second helpings often delight both the child and the parent!

At least 500-800 ml of milk a day is recommended. Too many sweet foods may blunt the appetite for essential foods. Highly seasoned dishes, and too many fried and fatty foods should also be avoided.

Plan and prepare a day's menu for an infant of 18 months. As both parents are employed, the child is with a child-minder from 9 a.m. to 2 p.m. each day. Give reasons for your choice of foods.

Weigh each portion of food. Calculate the nutritional value. Compare with RDI (see p. 48), and suggest any changes to improve the nutritional value, flavour and appearance.

Toddlers 2–5 years

A mixed diet is continued and quantities are increased to suit the child's appetite. More new foods are introduced, such as salads and stronger-flavoured foods.

Plan and prepare a day's menu for two toddlers aged 2½ and 4 years. Both attend play-school in the morning and want to invite a friend home for tea.

Show how the menu can be adapted to suit each child's preferences, without too much effort.

Calculate the nutritional value of the meals.

Schoolchildren 5–11 years

Growth is very rapid and energy demands are high. The balanced diet should still be followed, with larger helpings of the essential foods being served. Fats may be increased as these are concentrated sources of energy, and are less bulky than carbohydrates in the diet.

It is particularly important that meals eaten at home are nutritionally well balanced, as many children in this age group may be eating away from home at mid-day.

Breakfast is a very important meal and should never be missed, even when time is short.

Plan and prepare a day's menu for two schoolchildren aged 6 and 10. Both take a packed lunch to school. Show the differences in the foods they eat. Compare the nutritional value with RDI (see p. 48).

Adolescents

Growth and energy needs are still very high in this group. Physical activity is often much greater. The changes in the body brought about by puberty make extra demands on the diet. Girls can often become anaemic due to the onset of menstruation, and therefore need plenty of iron-rich foods such as liver, kidneys, meat, green vegetables and wholemeal bread. Some, breakfast cereals are enriched with iron and provide a useful supplement in the diet. Boys and young men need larger amounts of all foods, as they are growing very quickly at this time.

Acne and spots are also common in adolescence. Eating fewer fried foods and more fruit, vegetables, salads, and water, is a great help in clearing the skin.

Increases in weight leading to 'puppy fat' occur quite often at this age, and can cause much distress, especially to girls. Often the fat will disappear gradually as the adolescent gets older, but if slimming *is* undertaken it must be done sensibly (see p. 61).

Plan and prepare a day's menus for a 14-year-old girl and a 16-year-old boy. Both have money to spend for lunch. Comment on their choices. What suggestions would you make? Calculate the nutritional value and compare with RDI (see p. 48).

Adults

Growth usually stops at about twenty years of age, and appetites may become smaller as a result. A balanced diet is still essential for good health. Protein, although not now required for growth, is needed to replace the worn-out cells which are constantly being discarded by the body. Calcium, iron, and vitamin D are also essential.

Dietary needs now vary with the amount of energy expended in daily activities. A balanced diet is essential in all cases, but a person doing heavy manual work will use up more food to provide energy than a sedentary person, so an increased supply of energy-giving foods must be provided (see plate 7).

Describe the lifestyle of a family with two school-age children.

Plan and prepare the day's menu for mother, father and children. Show how the menu and portion sizes are adapted to suit their different needs.

Elderly people

Elderly people should be encouraged to remain as physically active as possible. Even so, they need relatively fewer energy-giving foods as they are probably less active and mobile than when they were younger. It is important therefore to reduce the fat content and possibly the carbohydrate content of their diets.

If too much food is eaten it will be stored as fat and obesity is a dangerous condition. Obesity places a strain on the heart, lungs and digestion. Increased weight causes some joint diseases, varicose veins, ulcers and general fatigue. Because of these conditions, elderly people become even less active, therefore more prone to obesity.

Elderly people need good supplies of:
• protein to provide new cell material as old cells die;
• calcium and vitamin D to avoid brittle bones;
• vitamin A and D to combat infections;
• vitamin B to release energy and build red blood cells;
• iron to build red blood cells and prevent anaemia.

Many elderly people eat unbalanced meals. There are many reasons why this might happen:
• faulty diet habits formed earlier in life;
• ignorance of food values;
• lack of ability and physical stamina to cook proper meals;
• low income. Too little may be spent on protein foods, fruit and vegetables: the bulk is made up with cheaper starchy foods.
• difficulties in shopping for fresh supplies of food;
• ill-fitting dentures or lack of teeth make chewing difficult, so soft starchy foods are preferred to meat, salads, vegetables and fruit;
• digestion may not be efficient, so certain essential foods are avoided, even if they are not the cause of the digestive problem;
• boredom and lack of interest in cooking meals, especially if living alone. The snacks some elderly people choose for convenience may not be nutritionally well-balanced.

There are many ways to help elderly people overcome these difficulties and enjoy the food they eat. The meal-planner must ensure, though, that their food is:
• easy to chew and digest;
• easy to prepare and cook;
• served in small portions;
• a supply of all necessary nutrients in the correct proportions;
• appetising to look at.

Convenience foods may be excellent substitutes for fresh products, especially when shopping and cooking present difficulties for elderly people. Many are available in small quantities. Although convenience foods may seem expensive compared with similar fresh products, they may actually not be so since:
• there is no waste;
• there is little cooking needed, therefore fuel costs are low;

• there is no need to buy the many ingredients that are needed to make some dishes.

There are many nutritious foods that can be stored for long periods and elderly people should be encouraged to keep a well-stocked store cupboard. Many of these products are available in small quantities, such as canned meats, fish, fruit, dried vegetables, beans and lentils, bottled and vacuum-packed fruit juices. A freezer is particularly useful for elderly people.

Ways of encouraging elderly people to eat well-planned meals

Mrs Jones is aged 74 and lives on her own in a residential part of a large town. She has recently been unwell with her hip. She is waiting to have an operation to increase the mobility but until then she is fairly restricted in her movements. She can get about a bit, although she is a little overweight. Her family lives close by and in the area. Where she lives there is a high proportion of elderly people. There is also a local shopping centre and a Day Care Centre nearby. The local library is also just down the road and they often throw out piles of out-of-date magazines.

Imagine you are given the task of planning a week's meals for Mrs Jones. Involve other people and organisations as much as you can, since elderly people enjoy company. Mrs Jones is quite well-situated for local amenities. Can you think of other organisations that might be able to offer help?

Meal-planning for people on vegetarian diets

Vegetarian diets are used by people who, for various reasons (religious, ethnic, moral, or personal taste), do not eat animal flesh. There are two types of vegetarian diets: these are lacto-vegetarian and vegan.

Lacto-vegetarian diets

People following this diet omit all meat, fish and poultry, but include eggs, cheese, milk, butter, and lard. Very few problems exist in planning these diets, since the essential amino acids are supplied in milk, eggs, and cheese, and a wide variety of both sweet and savoury dishes is possible.

Vegans

These are strict vegetarians who avoid eating all meats, poultry and fish and the products from animals: eggs, milk, cheese, butter, lard. Vegans must ensure that they:

- receive an adequate supply of the vegetable proteins that supplement each other, vitamins A, B_{12} and D, and mineral elements (calcium, phosphorus, and iron);
- avoid too much bulk in the diet. The proportion of protein in vegetable foods is less than in animal foods, so larger quantities of vegetables must be eaten. Most vegetables absorb water, and swell during cooking, making the diet still more bulky.
- avoid digestive and intestinal upsets due to excessive consumption of cellulose of vegetables, fruits, and grains;
- avoid lack of variety and lack of flavour.

Sources of nutrients for vegans

Protein pulses (peas, beans, lentils), nuts, cereals, soya beans and soya products, textured vegetable protein products

Fats vegetable fats and oils, nuts and nut products, vegetarian margarines

Carbohydrates all plant foods and grains

Vitamins vitamin A from carotene found in orange, red and dark green vegetables

vitamin B complex from vegetables, dried fruits, cereals and cereal products, yeast, yeast extracts

vitamin C from fruits and vegetables

vitamin D from margarine made entirely from vegetable oils. This is the main dietary source of vitamin D available to the strict vegetarian. Vitamin D is now added to some breakfast cereals as well. Supplementary supplies from vitamin pills may be needed.

Mineral elements

Calcium: from a wide variety of nuts, cereals, pulses, vegetables, fruits and treacle

Phosphorus: most foods rich in calcium are also rich in phosphorus

Iron: yeast and yeast extract, cocoa, chocolate, treacle, wheat germ, soya flour and products, dried fruits, cereals, flour products, some vegetables, and oatmeal

Iodine: water, vegetables, oatmeal, apples, oranges, bread, iodised salt

Vegetarian cookery

Careful planning and cooking is necessary to avoid lack of variety and flavour.

Health stores offer a wide variety of textured vegetable protein foods.

Flavourings can be used freely to avoid insipidness: onions, tomatoes, celery, herbs, yeast and vegetable extracts, garlic, celery or onion salts, spices. The use of sauces adds variety both to flavour and texture of foods.

Suitable dishes include: vegetable hot pot, vegetable pie or flan, soups, risotto, stuffed vegetables (e.g. pepper, marrow, courgettes), mushrooms, pizza, pies made with textured vegetable protein products, nut rissoles and salads.

Meal-planning for overweight people

There are many lists of 'recommended' ideal weights for various types of people, but the most accurate are those which take into account, the height *and* the bone structure (skeleton size, which can alter the weight by up to 4.5 kg between two people of the same height). When the weights for any given height are quoted they are given for small, medium and large bone structures.

Obesity is defined as an excessive accumulation of fat. This leads to a large increase in body weight, 4 kilograms or more over optimum weight. It is a condition which can be very damaging to health and actually shorten life expectancy. It is particularly difficult to lose excess body weight. There are many reasons for obesity: these are some of the most usual:

- *too much food* is eaten for the body's daily needs. Even a small daily excess can build up, and result in an obesity problem over a period. For example, a person who gains 500 g in weight each year between 20 and 40, will be about 10 kg overweight at 40.
- *insufficient exercise* Many people use little energy in their daily work due to mechanisation, both in industry and in the home. Leisure activities are very often passive (for example, watching television).
- *heredity* Obesity often runs in families. It is important to prevent obesity in the very young, to limit the formation of excessive fat cells, that may enlarge later in life and cause obesity. An alternative theory is that fat parents have fat children because the family pattern of eating encourages too high an intake of food, or the wrong kinds of foods are eaten.
- *lowered metabolism* due to glandular disturbances. This is a medical problem, and a doctor should be consulted.

People who are overweight need to be very conscious of their food intake, if they wish to overcome their weight problem. They may need to change their whole pattern of eating.

Slimming diets

Food needs vary between individuals, people have different metabolic rates (see p. 49). One person could be slim and healthy on a diet that would cause obesity in his or her neighbour, so all slimming diets must be planned to suit individual needs. Medical advice should be sought for any major overweight problem.

There are various clubs which aim to help people lose weight by group therapy (see Fig. 2.10).

Two main principles in slimming are:
- the diet should contain adequate supplies of all nutrients.
- slimming should not be allowed to become an obsession, as the body may become unable to accept and process food.

Slimming diets are popular, and magazines often publish different variations from bizarre 'crash diets' to energy value-controlled diets. All have the same aim: to reverse the process of the body storing excess food as fat and to force it to use stored body fat.

The smaller the amount of energy supplied by food, the bigger will be the supplement needed from stored fat, and so the more rapid will be the weight reduction.

Crash diets' may carry this principle to excess. They will undoubtedly lead to sudden weight-loss, but this loss may be quickly regained at the end of the crash diet. They are often not nutritionally balanced, and a too dramatic weight loss can be dangerous.

Energy controlled diets These are based on estimates of how much energy a particular person needs daily. A diet is then planned which will yield slightly less energy than the amount required. The deficit is made up from stored fat, and this will result in a gradual weight loss. A wide variety of foods can be eaten, providing the recommended energy value is not exceeded. Food tables and computer programs list the energy value per 100 g of food, so it is easy to calculate the energy value of a day's meals.

Plan and prepare a day's menu for a mother aged 35 years, which limits the energy value to 1000 kcal or 4200 kJ. Calculate the nutritional value of this menu. Is it nutritionally well balanced?

Meal-planning for invalid and convalescent people

The main aims in planning meals suitable for invalid and convalescent patients are:
- to carry out the doctor's instructions carefully regarding diet, liquids, medicines, rest, etc.
- to provide light, appetising, attractive meals that have good supplies of proteins, vitamins, mineral elements and adequate dietary fibre and water.

The patient usually passes through three phases: illness, recovery, convalescence.

Diets in illness The patient's temperature is usually raised, the patient feels ill, and lacks appetite. A liquid diet only is recommended. This is easily digested, quenches thirst, prevents dehydration from a high temperature, and helps reduce temperature. Water, barley water or clear soups are often recommended by the doctor.

Diets in recovery period When the temperature has fallen and the patient starts to improve, small quantities of solid food can be given. Body-building foods are particularly important, especially easily-digested protein foods, and food supplying calcium, iron, vitamins A, B complex and especially C.

Keep carbohydrates and fats low since energy demands are not great at this stage.

Diets for convalescent period During this period, the temperature is normal, appetite is increasing, and activity is increasing.

A good diet is now needed to build up the patient, and repair tissue damage. Easily-digested protein is needed, and good supplies of calcium, iron, vitamins A, B, and C.

Plan and prepare a day's menu for an adolescent girl who is convalescing after an operation for appendicitis. Give reasons for your choice of menu, and suggest ways you can present the food attractively.

Foods to be avoided in invalid and convalescent diets:

ALL fried foods
fatty lamb, pork, bacon and ham
oily fish
suet pastry and puddings
strong tea or coffee
condiments such as pickles, piccalilli, chutney, vinegar, etc.
highly seasoned, rich foods, such as curry.

QUESTIONS

1 The rising cost of 'living makes careful budgeting necessary for the housewife. Suggest ways in which a housewife could economise on her food bill.
(Scottish, 1978)

2 What special adjustments should be made to family meals when the family includes a toddler?
  Give reasons for your answer.
(Scottish, 1978)

3 (a) What special points would you consider when planning and preparing packed meals for (i) a manual worker (ii) an office worker?
  (b) Plan suitable menus for the packed lunches of each type of worker for two consecutive days to illustrate the points you have made in (a).
  (c) Describe how *one* of these lunches would be packed.
  (d) Complete *one* day's menu for the manual worker.
(JMB, 1979)

4 (a) What do you understand by the terms (i) malnutrition (ii) starvation?
  (b) What are the nutritional requirements of a family in which the mother is at home all day, with children aged 2 and 4 years, and the father is a manual worker.
  (c) Plan suitable meals for one day for this family; include a packed meal for father.
  (d) Explain how your choice in (c) caters for the nutritional requirements of all the family.
(JMB, 1978)

5 Many teenage girls wish to lose weight. Give a full account of the best way to achieve this without endangering health.
  Give details of a diet for one day, suitable for such a girl. Include quantities and an approximate calorific count, and show how all the essentials of a good diet are fulfilled.
(Welsh, 1976)

6 What is meant by obesity?
  Why is it a problem at the present time?
  Explain possible dangers to be avoided if a strict slimming diet is followed.
  Give sensible menus of two consecutive days for an adult office worker who should lose weight.
(London, 1978)

7 Plan the meals for one weekend for a family with teenage children where only a limited budget is available.
(London, 1979)

8 What do you understand by the term 'a balanced diet'?
  What factors would have to be taken into account to ensure a balanced diet by:
  (a) an elderly housebound lady who has a hot meal brought by 'meals on wheels' three days a week?
  (b) a young woman office worker who has a packed lunch every day?
  Plan menus for one day for *one* of these two individuals.
(London, 1979)

9 Three menus are given below. Choose the one most suited for an evening meal for a family consisting of working parents and two teenage boys. Give reasons for your choice.

Menu A	*Menu B*	*Menu C*
Minestrone soup	Fresh grapefruit	Chicken casserole with rice
Beef stew with carrots	Cheese flan	Rhubarb crumble with custard
boiled potatoes	Salad	

(Scottish, 1979)

10 (a) What are the differences between a strict vegetarian and a lacto-vegetarian?
  (b) Explain fully the importance of a well-balanced vegetarian diet.
  (c) Plan a two-course evening meal for:
    (i) a strict vegetarian
    (ii) a lacto-vegetarian.
  (b) What are the disadvantages of vegetarianism?
(Southern, 1978)

11 (a) A recent survey of 4000 school children revealed that 25% of them went to school without breakfast. Suggest reasons for this.
  (b) Discuss the importance of breakfast in the diet of children.
  (c) Give menus suitable for, (i) a winter breakfast (ii) a summer breakfast.
  (d) How could a working mother and her family organise their daily routine to allow sufficient time to prepare and eat breakfast?
(Northern Ireland, 1978)

12 What factors should be considered when planning meals for a family consisting of parents, both working, and two children (a boy aged 16 and a girl aged 14)?
  Plan breakfast, packed lunches and the evening meal for two consecutive days to illustrate the points you have made.
  State the approximate recommended daily kilocalorie requirements for each member of the family.
(London, 1980)

13 The average weekly expenditure on food is a major item in the family budget. How can the mother ensure that, in time of inflation, she can provide nutritious and interesting meals for her family of husband and two teenage children?
(London, 1982)

14 Compare the two halves of each of the following pairs with each other, taking into account nutritional value and aesthetic appeal:

(a) a lunch of bread, cheese, tomatoes, fresh fruit;
   a lunch of sausage and chips, apple pie and custard.
(b) white flour in pastry-making;
   wholemeal flour in pastry-making.
(c) a breakfast of toast and coffee;
   a breakfast of fruit juice, cereal and milk, toast and coffee.
(d) creamed, old potatoes;
   'instant mash'.
(London, 1982)

Shopping for food 4

Are you a good shopper? Most of us believe we are. How many of us would be right? Good shopping is not just the speedy, indiscriminate buying of commodities. It should be a reasoned, considered choice of the good quality, good value products that are suitable for your purpose.

Shopping is such a common activity that we are inclined to take it for granted. We treat it as a chore that must be done, without realising its effect on the living standards, health, security, and even happiness of the family. The wise spending of the family income can mean the difference between a

Fig. 4.1 Guidelines: shopping for food

Planning: be prepared

1 Plan meals in advance.

2 Make an accurate shopping list, including quantities and the quality of goods you need.

3 List commodities in groups according to the types of shop or section of supermarket where they are available.

4 Check supplies of food in stock.

Awareness: be alert

1 Buy from clean, hygienic, well ventilated shops.

2 Avoid impulse buying.

3 Think before you buy

4 Check that the commodity is good value.

5 Compare prices for similar products in several stores.

6 Compare relative prices, small and large packets.

7 Keep a check on what you are spending as you shop.

8 Check weight of product bought.

9 Inspect quality of perishable foods.

10 Check your change.

Thrift: economise where possible

1 Substitute less expensive commodities where possible.

2 Buy the more economical-sized package, whenever possible.

3 Do not be tempted by cut-price offers unless they are a real saving to you.

4 Bulk buying is sometimes cheaper.

5 Use seasonal gluts and preserve commodities where possible.

Knowledge: judge the quality

1 Be sure you recognise good quality products.

2 Have knowledge of manufacturers' and retailers' obligations.

3 Understand labelling of products.
Be able to compare unit prices.
Know relevance of ingredient list.
Understand nutrient content.
Understand date stamping and storage instructions.

4 Know how to make complaints.

Note: 'Net weight' means the weight of goods without packaging. 'Gross weight' means the weight of goods plus packaging.

contented household with all the needs of the family taken care of, and a constant struggle to make ends meet and pay the bills.

As a considerable proportion of income is spent on food, good judgment is needed in order to get the best value for money, and to avoid waste. Being a good shopper is a talent which can be acquired by learning about food and by experience.

To become a good shopper, several qualities are needed: planning, awareness, thrift and knowledge. Look at Fig. 4.1 which gives guidelines on how to become a good shopper.

> Using these indicators as guidelines, look at the food in plate 8, and discuss the quality of all the products shown in these pictures.

Here are some additional guidelines to help you become a well-informed shopper.

1 Labelling of food products

Learn to read and understand labels; they contain a lot of useful information.

The consumer in Britain is protected by laws which aim to maintain safe standards in food manufacturing, distributing and retailing industries. The most important regulations are the Food and Drugs Act (1955) and the Food Act (1984), which aim to ensure that food is pure and wholesome and fit for human consumption. No harmful flavourings, colourings, or additives may be used.

Some additives e.g. antioxidants, have code numbers which must appear, when appropriate, on labels: e.g. sorbic acid is E200.

The Food Labelling Regulations 1980 and 1984 lay down detailed regulations covering the labelling of processed and packaged food. For example, labels on food tins or packages must list all the ingredients in order of their proportion by weight, with the highest proportion first, i.e. if a tin is labelled 'steak, with onions and gravy', the steak must make up the highest proportion, and if a tin of meat is labelled 'solid pack' then it should contain meat only and no liquid. If textured vegetable protein (TVP), i.e. soya protein, appears amongst the list of ingredients, it is a substitute for some of the meat content.

Manufacturers and retailers are prohibited from issuing false or misleading descriptions of food on labels, or in shops, or advertisements; for example, 'cream' cakes must contain fresh dairy cream, not synthetic cream.

Fig. 4.2 Food labels

Other labels on food products

All packaged foods carry a brand name, an ingredient list, the purchase price, sometimes the unit price (i.e. price per kilogram) and a bar code. Some processed foods give nutritional information and some give recipe suggestions.

(a) *Date-stamping – perishable foods*

All perishable, pre-packed products are date-stamped with a 'sell-by' date. This is the last date on which the product should be on sale. Look carefully at sell-by dates on cream, yoghurt, vacuum-packed meats, fresh orange juices.

Make sure the sell-by date has not passed. If possible, choose the products with the longest time yet to elapse before the 'sell-by date'. This gives you the advantage of the longest shelf-life in your home, provided you store the product as recommended.

(b) *Nutrient content*

Many manufacturers label their products with nutrient content. These labels usually give the proportion of protein, fat, carbohydrate, vitamins and mineral elements, and the energy value (see p. 10). Be sure to check whether these quantities are per portion or per package.

(c) *Bar coding*

Many manufacturers are now printing a special code on the package, which looks similar to those in Fig. 4.2 on p. 65.

The parallel bars are codes for the brand, size and recommended retail price of the product. As each product passes through an electronic system at the check-out point, the information on the bar code is recorded on a computer. The computer then records the store's selling price for that item at the check-out point. This is printed out with the name of the item on the till receipt. This information is useful to the customer, so that the receipt can easily be checked later. The computerised system helps stock control in the store by recording stock levels and automatically orders new supplies from warehouses.

2 Safeguards for consumer

The sale of all goods is covered by the Sale of Goods Act (1893) and the Supply of Goods Act (1973). These safeguard consumer's rights as follows:

(a) The goods must be of merchantable quality and must be fit for their purpose.
(b) The goods must correspond with any description given either verbally or written.
(c) The goods must have been bought in a shop normally dealing with such goods.

Complaints

Complaints should be made to the retailer, either in person, by telephone, or by letter, with as little delay as possible. When making a complaint make sure that you have all the relevant information with you, i.e. the unsuitable product, the receipt and, if possible, the date of purchase.

Be polite; ask to speak to the manager. If the manager refuses your complaint, send a letter by recorded delivery to the managing director, or the head office of the firm. If this brings no result, consult the Citizens' Advice Bureau, or the local Consumer's Advisory Centre, or the Trading Standards Officer at the Town Hall or Civic Centre.

As a last resort, there is legal action, and a firm will often be inclined to settle your complaint, rather than have the trouble of being taken to court.

Also most manufacturers offer consumer services; do not be afraid to approach them directly, they are keen that their products are marketed in good conditions.

Types of shop

Where you shop will depend on:
● your family pattern of living
● what shops are available in your area.

The main types of food shop are:
● general stores, street markets, specialist shops
● self-service stores, supermarkets and hyper-markets.

1 General stores

These are almost everywhere except in town and city centres. They are often run by the owner. Most of these shops carry a very varied range of goods, such as groceries, milk, bread, cakes, some vegetables, beverages, cigarettes, sweets, some medicines and household items.

Advantages

● usually near to home, so no transport costs
● often open early and late
● personal service
● may allow credit to regular customers

Disadvantages

● prices usually higher than supermarkets as owner cannot buy goods in large quantities
● the variety of goods and brands may be less than in large stores due to a lack of storage space

Some small shopkeepers link together with wholesale groups to make their businesses more competitive with supermarket trade. The wholesale groups offer inducements such as reduced prices on goods, combined advertising in the local press and on television, regular deliveries, help with modernising shop premises, the advantage of selling the group's 'own-label' goods at prices which compete directly with supermarkets own-label goods, and other services. In return the shopkeeper, whilst still owning and running his own shop, undertakes to buy a large proportion of supplies from the group. There are now twenty-three wholesale groups in Britain of which the six largest are Mace, Spar, VG, Wavy Line, Vivo and Alliance.

2 Street markets and barrows

Because overheads are lower in markets than in shops, goods should be cheaper in markets, and cheaper still on street barrows. Hygienic food handling, quality of goods and prices vary from stall to stall, and care should be taken to judge before buying goods.

Fig. 4.3 A general corner shop

Fig. 4.4 A street market

Fig. 4.5 A greengrocer

Fig. 4.6 A supermarket

3 Specialist shops

These are shops that sell only one type of goods: butchers, greengrocers, fishmongers, bakers, sweets and tobacco, delicatessens, grocers, etc. Quality is usually high and the service is knowledgeable and helpful.

4 Supermarkets and self-service stores

These range from tiny village self-service stores, to the very large supermarkets which supply almost everything needed in the home.

Advantages

- wide choice of goods, both branded and 'own-brand' goods available
- goods always fresh, because turnover is rapid
- prices are often lower, because of bulk buying by the firm
- convenience of 'one-shop' shopping and speed
- self-service gives time to compare goods and prices

Disadvantages

- impersonality
- sometimes difficult to find goods or an assistant

- walking round can be tiring to infirm or elderly people, or difficult for mothers with young children
- cut-price offers are confusing unless you know the normal price
- very easy to be tempted to pick up goods irrespective of whether they are needed
- easy to overspend
- queuing at check-out tills can waste much time

Supermarkets were originally most successful in selling canned, packaged and frozen foods, but now many also sell excellent quality fresh foods. There are many in-store bakeries, large delicatessen sections, butcher departments and 'serve yourself' fruit and vegetables which are proving to be a real inducement to the shopper to buy fruit and vegetables from the supermarket rather than the specialist shop or market. It enables the shopper to hand-pick good quality fruit and vegetables, and weigh the exact quantity required.

5 Hypermarkets

Hypermarkets are larger than supermarkets, and sell an even wider range of goods, including furniture, electrical goods, etc. They are usually situated outside towns, because of the vast acreage of land needed for store plus car parks. They are

Fig. 4.7 A hypermarket

built near main roads as shoppers must come by car or public transport. Goods can be bought in bulk. Hypermarkets offer a wide range of facilities: restaurants and cafeterias, toilets, in-store baking, petrol pumps and delivery of very large heavy items, such as furniture and electrical appliances. Competitive prices attract customers.

6 Computerised shopping

In recent years new computer systems have been developed which allow people to order goods through a computer terminal. The computer needs to be linked to a retail outlet. Experiments are being carried out to see if it is practical to shop for food in this way.

> Can you think of the advantages and possible disadvantages of this type of shopping?

SHOPPING PROJECTS

1 Plan a main meal for each of five days for your family and yourself, stating number of persons and quantities needed. Make out a shopping list for the main ingredients: meat, fish, eggs, cheese, vegetables and fruit.

2 Visit a butcher and price the meats you included in your five-day menus.

Ask the price per kilogram of two cheap types of meat. Suggest a dish or a method of cookery suitable for each of them.

3 Find out the price of plaice at your nearest fish shop (a) whole fish (b) four fillets.

Find out the price of the same number of fillets in breadcrumbs in a frozen food cabinet.

4 Calculate the price per 500 ml of packet soup, and compare this with the price of 500 ml of canned soup.

List the advantages and disadvantages of each type of soup.

5 In the supermarket, calculate how much (if anything) can be saved by buying the largest packet of a given brand of soap powder, as against buying two smaller packets of the same brand (compare weights as well as prices).

Also compare the price of (a) corn flakes (b) toothpaste in a similar way.

6 Visit a large supermarket, and make a comprehensive list of all goods offered under the own-brand label, with their weights and prices. Then make a list of identical goods sold under well-known brand names, also with weights and prices. Where possible, purchase samples of similar products and compare quality differences. Dicuss all your findings.

7 Find out the price of a 100 g jar of Nescafé instant coffee powder in:
(a) a corner shop or general store
(b) a supermarket.

Also compare the price for Nescafé in the supermarket with the price for the store's 'own-brand' instant coffee. Do both sorts of coffee taste the same?

QUESTIONS

1 (a) List the points you would look for when assessing the hygienic standards of a mobile food van.
(b) What rules of hygiene should be observed by the assistant in this type of shop.
(c) Packaging of foodstuffs reduces the number of times a product is handled. Name two packaging materials currently used for packing foodstuffs and state two advantages of each to:
(i) the consumer.
(ii) the shopkeeper.
(d) Why should a packet of vacuum-packed bacon be marked with the date by which it should be opened?
(Scottish, 1978)

2 What are the advantages and disadvantages of shopping at:
(a) supermarkets
(b) individual food shops
(c) open markets?
What preparations does a careful shopper make before going to the shops?
(London, 1981)

The cooking of food 5

The aim in all methods of food preparation is to produce attractive, appetising food and to retain maximum nutrient content. Some foods such as lettuce and strawberries are best eaten raw. It is also important for nutritional reasons that some foods are eaten raw. Most foods, however, must be cooked to make them palatable. The actual changes that take place during the cooking of food are described in each commodity chapter later in this book.

Reasons for cooking food

1 The food is made safe to eat. Cooking destroys harmful micro-organisms: bacteria, yeasts and moulds are destroyed by heat (see p. 82).

2 The keeping quality of food is improved. Bacteria and enzymes that cause deterioration in raw foods are destroyed (see pp. 81-82).

3 Digestion and absorption of cooked food is made easier because of structural changes, e.g. the fibres in meat are tenderised (see p. 155), cellulose in fruits and vegetables is softened (see pp. 171-175) and starch in all cereal products is gelatinised (see p. 211).

4 Some foods become less bulky. The volume of some foods is reduced by cooking, e.g. cabbage, spinach. More of these foods which supply valuable nutrients can be eaten.

5 The flavour of the food may be improved. In cooking, flavours are:
- strengthened, e.g. cooking fresh young vegetables;
- blended, e.g. the combination of ingredients in a casserole;
- altered, e.g. as extractives are developed, and baked products become cooked.

6 Cooking alters the texture of foods, which gives more variety of texture in the diet, e.g. vegetables and fruits soften (see pp. 171-175); eggs, meat and fish become firmer in texture as their proteins coagulate (see pp. 116, 130, 155). Baked products develop a characteristic texture, e.g. cake mixtures, pastries, batters, bread, biscuits according to the recipe used.

7 The colour of cooked food may be improved. Sometimes it is important to maintain and enhance the natural colour of food, e.g. in green vegetables. In some other foods, the colour is improved by cooking, e.g. meat changes from red to an attractive brown colour, baked products change from an insipid yellow to a golden brown colour.

The method of cooking affects the colour changes that take place. For example, boiling, steaming and microwave cooking do not produce such attractive colours in meat and flour mixtures as roasting or baking.

8 Volatile substances are released from food during cooking: e.g. the smell of onions frying, meat roasting, bread baking. These appetising odours stimulate the flow of gastric juices (see p. 41).

9 Cooked foods greatly increase variety in the diet. The ways of eating a particular food are increased, e.g. tomatoes can be eaten raw, grilled, fried or baked, or they can be used as an ingredient in soups, sauces or casseroles.

10 Hot food is more acceptable, especially in cold weather.

The aim in cooking

Whatever the reasons for cooking food, the fundamental aim in cooking is to produce attractive food that people will want to eat. Good quality nutritious food can easily be spoiled by poor cooking.

Look at plate 8(c) and note the differences between well-cooked and overcooked green vegetables.

Overcooking is undesirable because:
- the longer food is cooked, the more nutrients are lost (see Fig. 12.4);

● texture, colour and flavour are spoiled, e.g. fish becomes grey, loses flavour and disintegrates; meat becomes stringy, tough, loses colour and flavour;

● vegetables become soggy, lose their vivid colours and fresh flavours.

To avoid spoiling food by poor cooking methods, it is important to understand what is happening when food is cooked.

How food is cooked

Cooking depends on heat being transmitted to the food, then through the food. The amount of heat and the length of the cooking time vary with the type of food that is being cooked and the method of cooking.

Heat is transmitted to the food by *conduction*, *convection* and *radiation*.

Figure 5.1 shows the methods of heat transfer in a conventional and a microwave cooker.

Fig. 5.1 Methods of heat transfer

Conventional cooker	*conduction*	*convection*	*radiation*
hob	√	√	
oven	√	√	
grill	√	√	√
Microwave cooker	√		√

---

1 Conduction (See Figs 5.10, 5.11 and 5.12 on pp. 74-78 for applications, e.g. boiling, frying, roasting, microwave cooking.) In solids, conducted heat is transferred from one molecule to the next by contact. If the molecules are very close together, the heat is transferred more quickly. Consequently, dense materials are better conductors of heat than less dense materials, e.g. metals are better

conductors than plastic, glass or wood. This is why the handle of a wooden spoon stays cooler than a metal handle when a hot sauce is stirred.

Conduction of heat takes place:

● in the cooking vessel. Heat is transferred through the saucepan or casserole dish by conduction. It is therefore important that saucepans make good contact with the hob (especially solid hot plates and ceramic hobs).

● in the food itself. As heat absorbed on the surface of food passes through the food, heat is transferred by conduction.

2 Convection (See Figs. 5.10 to 5.12 on p. 74-78, for applications, e.g. baking, oven roasting, boiling, frying.) In gases and liquids, heat is transferred by convection. When the molecules are heated they expand, become less dense and rise. Cooler, denser molecules further from the source of heat sink to take their place. Currents of moving molecules are set up in the gas or liquid. These are known as convection currents (Fig. 5.3). Convection is a continuous process.

Convection of heat takes place in:

● the heating of cooking liquids, e.g. water and fat when food is boiled, stewed or fried;

● the flow of hot air in the oven.

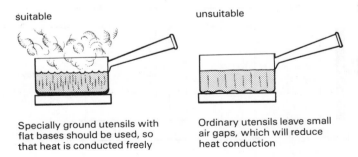

suitable   unsuitable

Specially ground utensils with flat bases should be used, so that heat is conducted freely

Ordinary utensils leave small air gaps, which will reduce heat conduction

Fig. 5.2 Conduction in cooking

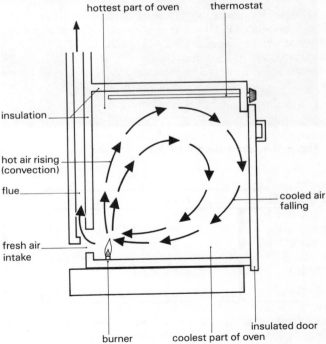

Fig. 5.3 Convection in a conventional oven

(a) *A normal oven*

Convection currents circulate in the oven as shown in Fig. 5.3. Because hot air rises, the top of the oven is the hottest area. The temperature variation between the upper and lowest shelves is often about 20°C.

The advantage of this type of oven is that foods requiring different cooking temperatures can be cooked in the oven at the same time, e.g. an apple pie on the top shelf, a casserole on the bottom shelf.

Fig. 5.4 A conventional cooker

(b) *Fan-assisted oven*

A fan-assisted oven has a circular element combined with a small fan in the back wall of the oven (see diagram). Heated air is forced gently around the oven, instead of relying on convection currents. The advantages of this type of oven are:
● the whole oven heats up quickly;
● the oven is at an even temperature throughout;
● more food can be placed in the oven;
● cooking times are slightly reduced;
● there is slight economy of fuel.

Fan draws air from the oven to the back where it is heated by the element positioned around the fan

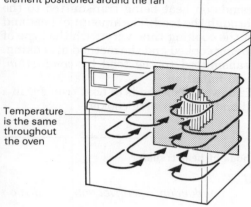

Temperature is the same throughout the oven

Baffles at either side of the back of the oven direct the heated air evenly and quickly into the oven

Fig. 5.5 Convection currents in a fan-assisted oven

3 Radiation (See Fig. 5.10 for applications, e.g. grilling, infra-red grilling, and microwave cooking.) Radiation is the transmission of energy by wave motion. The energy is generated in the form of electromagnetic waves. Electromagnetic waves vary in length and produce different effects according to their length and frequency. Many of them have commercial uses, such as for X-rays and radio as shown in Fig. 5.6.

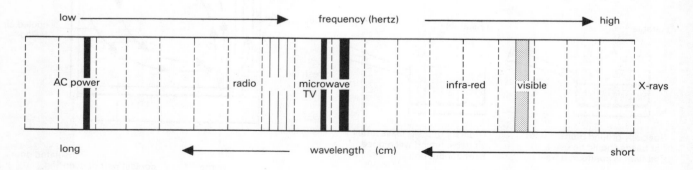

Fig. 5.6 The electromagnetic spectrum

Three types of radiation waves are used in cooking food: the visible red rays, infra-red rays and microwaves. Radiation waves do not warm the space through which they travel but are transmitted through it. When they fall on the food they are absorbed. The absorption of the energy causes the molecules in the food to vibrate and the food is heated.

Not all substances absorb the radiation. Some allow the heat to pass through them without absorbing it (e.g. glass, when the sun heats a greenhouse). Some substances reflect the waves and do not allow them to pass through, e.g. shiny metal surfaces.

(a) *Visible red radiation*

The waves of short wavelength (approx. 1/1000 cm) are used when food is grilled on a normal grill or barbecue. These waves cannot penetrate the food. They are absorbed only on the surface and then the food is cooked by conduction of heat through the food.

(b) *Infra-red radiation*

The waves have slightly longer wavelength than visible red radiation. This type of radiation is used to cook food on an infra-red grill. The food is placed in close contact with the heat source. The waves are able to penetrate the food to a depth of 1 cm. The cooking time is therefore shorter than with conventional grilling.

Fig. 5.7 An infra-red cooker

(c) *Microwave radiation*

Microwaves are the longest waves used for cooking food. They have wavelengths of 1-100 cm. During the Second World War, it was discovered that microwaves would penetrate rain, smoke or fog, which block normal light rays. This potential was developed as radar. It was found that microwaves also had the ability to generate heat. They are now being widely used in microwave cookers. The waves can penetrate food to a depth of 4 cm.

Microware cookers

The microwave cooker looks very simple. It can be plugged into a 13 amp socket outlet. The electricity is passed through a special type of valve called a *magnetron*, which generates electromagnetic waves. These microwaves are carried into the oven which is a sealed metal-lined box. On entering the oven the waves are travelling in straight lines. A rotary metal reflector in the wall of the oven scatters the waves in all directions. When they hit the metal walls of the box they are reflected back into the oven cavity. They are absorbed by the food in the oven. It is important that the waves are not reflected off the dish containing the food. Metal saucepans and aluminium foil containers are unsuitable; paper, polythene, pyrex and china containers allow microwaves to pass through them.

An essential difference between microwave and conventional cooking is that cooking is by time rather than temperature. Very short times are taken for defrosting, heating and cooking most foods.

Fig. 5.8 A microwave oven

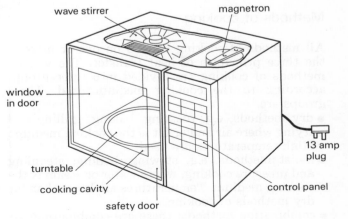

Fig. 5.9 The basic microwave oven

Fig. 5.10 Energy consumption in microwave cooking compared to conventional cooking

Fresh product	Method of cooking	kWh
4 chicken pieces	Microwave	0.4
	Conventional oven	1.14
Topside of beef	Microwave	0.41
	Conventional oven	1.72
Wholemeal bread	Microwave	0.1
	Conventional oven	0.91
Pineapple upside-down cake	Microwave	0.15
	Conventional hotplate/oven	1.02
2 herrings	Microwave	0.04
	Grill	0.21
Brussels sprouts	Microwave	0.1
	Hotplate	0.2
Boiled potatoes	Microwave	0.28
	Hotplate	0.26

Source: Electricity Council Appliance Testing Laboratories

The timer is calibrated in seconds and minutes. The time depends on:
- the type of food (its moisture content, density and thickness);
- the amount of food;
- the power of the oven (usually 500–650 W).

The microwave oven requires less power and uses less electricity output than the conventional oven because all the energy is absorbed by the food. The oven itself and the containers used for the food do not get hot. (Sometimes heat may be conducted from the food to the container, which is why the container may feel warm.)

Methods of cooking

All methods of cooking depend on one or more of the three principles of heat transfer. The various methods of cooking are divided into three groups according to the cooking medium used. These groups are:
- dry methods, e.g. roasting, baking, grilling and frying where air and/or fat is the cooking medium. High temperatures are used.
- moist methods, e.g. stewing, boiling, steaming and pressure cooking, where water or steam is the cooking medium. Temperatures are lower than for dry methods of cooking.
- combination methods; these are combinations of dry and moist methods, e.g. braising.

Fig. 5.11 A pressure cooker

1 Dry methods of cooking

Heat is transferred to the surface of the food by convection or radiation. The interior is cooked by heat conducted through the food. See Fig. 5.15.

Fig. 5.12 Heat transfer in various cooking methods

Method of cooking	Heat transfer to the surface	through the food
baking	convected hot air currents	conduction
frying	convection currents in hot fat	conduction
grilling/ spit roasting	radiation	conduction
microwave cooking	radiation	conduction

2 Moist methods of cooking

Heat is transferred by convection currents in the cooking liquid. At low temperatures, the liquid penetrates the structure of the food and cooks by convection and conduction. See Fig. 5.16.

3 Combination methods of cooking

Heat is transferred to the food first by convection currents in hot fat (a dry method), then by convection currents in the added liquid, and finally by convection and conduction as the liquid penetrates the food (moist methods).

The characteristics of each of these methods of cooking are shown in Figs. 5.13, 5.15, 5.16.

Fig. 5.13 Methods of cooking - combination methods

Method	Definition & type of heat	Some suitable foods	Points of interest
Pot roasting	This is a method of roasting meat in a covered container. The 'pot' behaves like a miniature oven retaining the moisture which escapes from the meat as steam. The meat is browned initially in fat and then continues to cook in the steam. Heat is conducted through the pot, then convention currents in the steam transfer heat to the food. It is finally transmitted through the food by conduction.	meat *beef* – silverside, brisket, topside, thick rib, heart *lamb* – breast, heart, middle neck *pork* – any small joint poultry	Joints of meat with coarser grain can be successfully pot roasted. Very lean joints may be moister if cooked by this method. Vegetables and herbs can be added to enhance flavour. Their juices provide additional moisture. No additional liquid is added to the pot. Cooking times recommended at 180°C: beef – 40 mins per 500 g pork – 40 mins per 500 g lamb – 30 mins per 500 g The meat is normally browned on top of the stove then covered and the cooking continued in the oven although cooking may be completed on top of the stove.
Braising	A very similar method to pot roasting but a little liquid is added to the container after the initial browning. This method is a combination of pot roasting and stewing. Heat is conducted through the pot. Cooking is by convection currents in the pot and conduction rays in the food.	meat *beef* – chuck, brisket, flank topside, silverside, offal *lamb* – middle neck, shoulder chops, offal *pork* – spare ribs, chops, offal vegetables – onions, celery, carrots, leeks, etc.	Originally braising was done in a 'brazier': a container with a special lid which was surrounded by hot coals so both top and bottom heat were supplied. Now braising may be done in an oven at 170°C–180°C or on a very low heat on top of the stove or in a pressure cooker. The meat is browned in fat then placed on a bed of lightly fried vegetables which are covered with either stock or water. Times as for pot-roasting. Excess fat is removed from the liquid which is then all served with the meat.

Fig. 5.14 A slow cooker

Fig. 5.15 Methods of cooking – Dry methods

Method	Definition & type of heat	Some suitable foods	Points of interest
Baking	Foods cooked by heating in an oven. The food is cooked partly by convection currents of dry air and partly by conduction of heat through the food. A metal container is used, e.g. for biscuits where they are in close contact with the tin.	flour mixtures (bread, cakes, biscuits, pastry) potatoes (known as baked or jacket potatoes) baked apples fish made-up dishes e.g. lasagne, shepherd's pie	The surface of baked food becomes crisp and golden brown. If the mixture contains moisture, this gelatinises starch, and softens cellulose. Some moisture is lost by evaporation. Temperatures and cooking times for baking vary, according to the type of food. Temperatures for flour mixtures must be accurate to produce good results.
Roasting	The food is cooked by radiant heat in front of or over a glowing source of heat, e.g. on a rotisserie where the heat of a grill or barbecue is used. The term is also used for cooking meat *uncovered* in the oven although correctly speaking this is baking. Meat that is roasted under cover, e.g. wrapped in foil in a roast-a-bag, or in a covered container, is actually 'pot roasted' (see combination methods chart). This is because some steam is retained in the container instead of evaporating in the oven.	good-quality cuts of meat *beef* – sirloin, fore-ribs, topside, silverside, thick flank *pork* – all cuts *lamb* – loin, best end of neck, leg, shoulder and breast *poultry* For roasting on a spit, joints should be of compact shape with surface fat evenly distributed. Flat joints, e.g. a shoulder of meat can rotate freely and receive heat evenly.	The meat is cooked when a certain internal temperature is reached. This can be checked using a meat thermometer (see p. 155). The cooking time varies with the size of joint, and the method and temperature of cooking. Weight loss in roasting is due to evaporation of moisture and meat juices as dripping. The loss varies with the method of cooking (see roasting meat, p. 155 and plate 19). The weight-loss and shrinkage may be as great as 30% of the original size of the joint.
Grilling Broiling is an American term for grilling.	The surface of the food is cooked by radiant heat. The interior of the food is cooked by conduction as the radiant waves from grills have very short wavelength and cannot penetrate the food. The heat source is a metal grid heated by a gas flame, an electric element, charcoal or wood in barbecues. The temperature of the heat source is very high (280 °C to 980 °C). Heat can be adjusted by a thermostat, or by varying the distance of the food from the heat source. The grill should always be preheated.	small tender pieces of meat not more than 5 cm thick, e.g. steak, chops, cutlets, bacon, sausages, kidneys fish tomatoes, mushrooms bread for toast	Grilling is a very quick and easy method. No cooking liquor is used, but lean meat should be brushed with cooking oil, to protect it from the intense heat. Very little fat is present in grilled foods, as the fat drips away during cooking.

Method	Description	Examples	
Infra-red grill (contact grill)	Infra-red radiant grills emit heat rays of a slightly longer wavelength than those of ordinary grills. The food must be in contact with cooking surface; the heat rays penetrate to a depth of 1 cm from both sides.	steak, chops toasted sandwiches	Infra-red grills are small portable appliances. Food is in direct contact with both sides of the cooking plate, therefore cooking times are short. Foods should not be more than 2 cm thick.
Microwave	Food is cooked by microwave radiation. These radiant waves have a longer wavelength, and penetrate all round the food to a depth of 4 cm. Heat is generated in the food by rapid vibrations of water molecules produced by microwave energy. The interior of thick products is cooked by conduction of this heat through the food.	foods with high moisture content foods normally cooked by moist cooking methods: boiling, steaming, poaching and stewing. defrosting and reheating individual dishes or meals, baked products	Foods absorb microwaves readily, generating heat quickly, so microwave cookers cook quickly. There is no wasted heat energy. Cooking time is influenced by: ● consistency and texture of food ● the thickness of the food ● the power of the microwave cooker ● the amount of food in the microwave cooker Microwave cookers are cheap to operate – low power rating, quick cooking times. Microwave cookers will not crisp or brown foods: some models are available with separate browning devices.
Frying	Food is cooked by total or partial immersion in fat which is heated to temperatures between 150 °C and 220 °C. Convection currents in the fat heat the outer surfaces of the food. The interior is cooked by conduction as heat passes through the food. Dry frying uses only the fat that runs from the food e.g. in cooking bacon. Shallow frying is used for meat and fish which is only partially covered by fat and must be turned during the cooking. Deep frying is when the food is completely immersed in the fat.	small tender pieces of meat – there is always some absorption of fat so lean meats are especially suitable e.g. veal and chicken liver, kidneys, bacon and sausage fish onions, tomatoes, mushrooms eggs potatoes – sautéd in shallow fat, deep fried as chips or croquettes fish cakes fritters	Fats must be heated to a high temperature before food is added. Sudden contact with hot fat causes rapid evaporation of moisture in the food, causing shrinkage and sealing the outside. Juices containing nutrients cannot escape into the fat and the fat is not absorbed too much into the food. Frying gives good colour and flavour and is also used as a first step before other methods of cooking. Most foods for deep frying and some foods for shallow frying are coated to protect their surfaces from the heat and prevent the food breaking up. Batter, egg and breadcrumbs are used. Frying baskets can be used for foods that do not stick, e.g. chips. Choice and care of fat is important. Temperature control is essential. Thermostatically controlled frying pans are available.

Fig. 5.16 Methods of cooking — moist methods

Method	Definition & type of heat	Some suitable foods	Points of interest
Poaching Term used for cooking eggs without their shells, and fish	Food is cooked in simmering liquid (85°C). Usually less volume of liquid than for boiling. Heat transfer is by conduction through the pan, convection current in the liquid and conduction of heat through the food. In an egg poacher, heat is transferred by conduction through the pan, and convection currents in the steam from the top surface.	eggs fillets of plaice and sole cod and salmon steaks	Special pans, egg poachers, are available for poaching eggs. This prevents the egg from breaking due to motion of convection currents in the liquid. An acid – vinegar or lemon juice – is often added to poaching liquid to help keep a firm texture and good colour in fish.
Boiling	Food cooked by totally immersing it in boiling water so that the water is in direct contact with the food. Heat is conducted through the base of the saucepan: convection currents in the liquid transfer heat to the food. Heat is transmitted through the food by conduction. Rapid boiling 100°C – large bubbles break the surface. Simmering – 85°C, very small bubbles gently break the surface.	Vegetables, pasta, rice Tougher cuts of meat *bacon and ham* – collar, hock, streaky or gammon *pork* – belly, hand, head *beef* – silverside, brisket, flank, tongue *mutton* – legs and tongue *boiling fowls* fish – whole or large pieces eggs	Some foods, e.g. pasta, require rapid boiling to prevent the food sticking together and becoming soggy. Other foods, e.g. fish, boiled eggs should be brought to boiling point only to coagulate the surface proteins, then the temperature should be reduced to simmering point. This prevents the food from breaking up by vigorous liquid movements. The liquid is not served with the food, but can be used later in stocks and sauces. Vegetables, herbs and flavourings are added to the cooking liquid of foods cooked for a long time to improve the flavour.
Steaming	Steaming is cooking food in the steam rising from boiling water. Convection currents in the steam transfer heat to the food. Then conduction in the food heats the interior. Steam is used to heat the food directly or indirectly when the food is in a container heated by the steam.	fish fillets or steaks some vegetables, e.g. potatoes sponge and suet puddings Christmas pudding	Steaming makes food very light and digestible. There is less nutrient loss than in other moist methods of cooking. There is little danger of overcooking as this is a slow cooking method. The water must be boiling before food is placed over it so that steam is available. A low heat is necessary to maintain the supply of steam but as some water evaporates a supply of boiling water is needed to top up the steamer especially if the cooking time is long. The lid must fit well and surface of foods must be protected to prevent them becoming soggy as steam condenses, e.g. a pudding basin must have a cover of cooking foil or a cloth.

Pressure Cooking	A pressure cooker cooks using steam under pressure and temperature is increased up to 120°C. Cooking time is reduced. Convection currents in the steam transfer heat to the food, which is then cooked by heat conducted through the food.	Pressure cooker is used for foods which take a very long time by normal boiling or steaming e.g. beetroot, tongue, suet puddings. It is also very useful for stewing, and cooking vegetables quickly, e.g. potatoes.	It is important to follow manufacturers' instructions carefully. Because the food is cooked at a higher temperature than in other moist methods, cooking time is reduced. Care is needed in timing the cooking carefully. It is easy to overcook food. It is important to cool the pressure cooker rapidly under cold running water. This prevents overcooking. Rapid cooling reduces the temperature and consequently the pressure. The lid should never be removed until the pressure has been released, or there may be risk of an explosion.
Stewing	Stewing is cooking food in a small measured amount of liquid which is allowed to simmer and not boil. The liquid is always served with the food. The stew is cooked in a container with a tightly-fitting lid either on top of the stove over a low heat or in a cool oven (temperature 150–170°C). Heat is conducted through the saucepan, then convection currents in the liquid transfer heat to the food. Heat is transmitted through the food by conduction. It is important that the lid fits tightly to avoid evaporation. Oven cooking produces the most successful stew and requires less liquid than stew cooked on top of cooker. Electric slow cookers, multi-cookers, and pressure cookers can also be used for stewing.	Cheaper, tougher cuts of meat can be used (cut into small pieces) *beef* – shin, leg, neck, chuck oxtail, liver, kidney *lamb* – hand-spring, shoulder *chicken* joints *vegetable* stew is ratatouille (mixture of onions, peppers, tomatoes, courgettes and aubergines) Dried fruit	There are innumerable recipes to produce attractive dishes from the cheaper coarser grained cuts of meat. Curries, ragouts, goulash, blanquettes are all stews. The meat is cut up to expose a greater surface area to the cooking liquid which may be water, stock, wine, beer or tomato juice. Vegetables, herbs and spices are added to give flavour and are served with the stew. The liquid may be thickened with flour, cornflour or eggs and cream for rich white stews. For brown stews the meat and vegetables are first browned by frying to give good colour and flavour.
Casseroling	When cooked in an oven, a stew is popularly known as a casserole.		Attractive casseroles (oven to table) mean the stew can be served in the dish in which it is cooked. Fruit is stewed in a liquid of sugar and water or fruit juice.

QUESTIONS

1 (a) Why is it necessary to cook certain foods?
　(b) What factors influence the choice of cooking methods?
　(c) Comment on stewing as a method of cooking using the following headings as a guide:
　　　(i) types of food suitable
　　　(ii) advantages
　　　(iii) disadvantages
(Scottish, 1978)

2 State the reasons for cooking food and give an account of the different methods used in cooking.
　State briefly the effects of cooking on the five main nutrients.
(Welsh, 1976)

3 Everyone is aware of the need to save energy not only because of the high cost of oil, gas and electricity but also because supplies of fuels are limited.
　How can you economise in the use of fuel when cooking meals in a conventional oven? Give examples of meals cooked with extravagent and economic use of the cooker.
　Discuss how modern equipment, e.g. pressure cookers, slow cookers, electric frying pans and microwave ovens, can also help to save energy.

4 (a) Define the methods of heat transference and give examples of their application in the cooking of food.
　(b) Describe briefly with the aid of a clearly labelled diagram, the transmission of heat in a gas oven.
(Southern Universities, 1978)

5 Explain, referring in the scientific principles involved, how heat is transferred to food being cooked on the hob, under the grill and in the oven.
(Northern Ireland, 1979)

6 (a) Grilling and casserole cookery are two popular ways of cooking food. Give a clear definition of each of these methods.
　(b) What are the advantages of each of these two methods?
　(c) (i) Name four different foods which are suitable for grilling.
　　　(ii) Name three cuts of meat suitable for use in a casserole.
　(d) Name three traditional accompaniments to be served with a mixed grill.
(JMB, 1978)

7 What is meant by the term 'casserole cookery'?
　Discuss the advantages and disadvantages of this method of cookery.
　What factors contribute to a successful result when this method is used?
(London, 1978)

8 Discuss the advantages of a microwave cooker in the kitchen. Should it be used alongside or instead of a conventional oven?
　Microwave ovens are considered to be completely safe to use. How have the designers and manufacturers ensured this?

9 (a) What is microwave energy?
　(b) In a microwave oven:
　　　(i) What is the function of the magnetron?
　　　(ii) How are the microwaves distributed evenly throughout the oven space?
　　　(iii) What happens when food absorbs microwaves?
(London, 1982)

Deterioration, safety and preservation of food   6

No food will keep indefinitely in its natural form. Food may lose valuable nutrients before there are visible signs of deterioration. Deterioration may cause food to be wasted. Contaminated food can cause illness, and in severe cases this is known as food poisoning. It is therefore important that we should buy food in prime condition and keep it that way until we eat it. To do this, it is important to understand why food goes bad.

Deterioration of food

All natural foods are slowly and continually changing character and composition. The appearance, smell and flavour of foods are gradually altered. These changes are not always harmful. Cheese ripens to develop flavour and meat is hung to make it more tender. However, there comes a stage when deterioration makes the food unpalatable. Like all other organic matter food deteriorates and decays. Milk goes sour, vegetables wilt and rot, fruits become mouldy and ferment, fats go rancid, meat, fish and eggs go 'putrid'.

Look at plate 9, and describe the changes that you can see in these foods.

These gradual changes that cause deterioration and decay in foods are due to:

(a) enzyme activity in the protoplasm of the food itself

(b) micro-organisms that enter the food from outside.

(a) Enzyme activity

Enzymes are organic catalysts produced by all living cells. In all living things, enzymes are responsible for the normal processes of metabolism. They remain active after death or harvesting and break down animal and plant tissue. For example they cause fruit to become overripe and mushy. In some cases enzyme activity produces more highly flavoured or acceptable foods, such as the enzymes present in freshly killed meat which act on the muscle fibres to make the meat more tender (see p. 141).

Enzymes are very active in temperatures found in a kitchen on a warm sunny day. They can remain very slightly active at very low temperatures such as those found in the freezer. This is why there is a limit to the time food can be stored in a freezer.

As enzymes are mainly composed of protein they are sensitive to heat. Their activity stops when they are heated above 70 °C. This is why cooking and preserving food by heat treatment helps to prevent foods going bad. Heat treatment by blanching is recommended for vegetables before they are frozen (see p. 88).

The activity of enzymes in food makes it easier for the other group of micro-organisms responsible for food spoilage to enter the food.

(b) The activity of micro-organisms

Tiny organisms are present almost everywhere; they occur in all fresh foods, in the soil, in dust, on all surfaces and on the skin of people handling food. Micro-organisms are the most important cause of food spoilage. These micro-organisms are invisible to the naked eye, but can be seen under a microscope. They are capable of multiplying very rapidly in the correct moisture, food and temperature conditions. These conditions must be avoided if the risk of food spoilage is to be reduced. There are three main types of micro-organism: moulds, yeats and bacteria.

Moulds are tiny plants which grown from cells called spores present in the air. They settle and multiply on suitable foods. At this stage they are then visible as a fluffy coloured mass and the food is said to have gone mouldy. Moulds grow most readily in moist conditions, at temperatures between 20 °C and 40 °C. They grow on a variety of foods, particularly meat, cheese, fruit and bread, especially if the food is stored in damp conditions. Moulds may remain active at the low temperatures

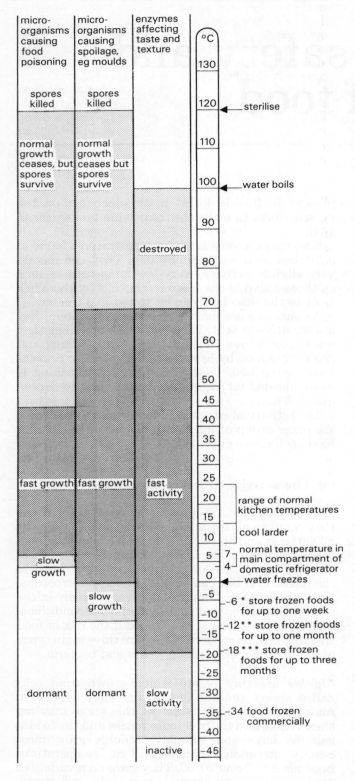

Fig. 6.1 Temperature control of micro-organisms and enzymes

of a refrigerator but they are destroyed by heat above 70 °C. They also like a slightly acid medium and this is why they attack citrus fruit and the surface of jams.

The presence of mould on food does not necessarily mean the food is unfit to eat, but it usually shows that the food is not fresh or has been stored badly. Most people will not eat mouldy food because they find it very unattractive. However, the controlled growth of moulds develops characteristic flavours in blue cheeses (see p. 106).

Yeasts are micro-organisms found in the air and on the skins of fruits. (You can sometimes see they are present as a 'bloom' on the skins of grapes.) They are small single-celled plants, oval in shape and measure 0.0001 cm across. One cell consists of protoplasm and a nucleus. They multiply by a process of budding. Small buds grow on the side of a yeast cell and eventually split forming a new yeast cell (see Fig. 17.1 on p. 248). They grow only on sugary foods.

The activity of yeasts is used in the baking and brewing industries. However, they can cause food spoilage in syrups, fruit, fruit juices and jam, especially as they can survive without air. They grow best at the same temperatures as moulds (20°C–40°C). They are also destroyed by heat and inactivated by cold. Yeasts grow in acid fruits, but not in vinegar (see 'Pickles', p. 88). They survive in sugar concentrations up to 50% but should not grow in correctly made jams which are over 60% sugar. Yeasts do not make food harmful but make it unacceptable by spoiling the taste.

Bacteria are the most widespread of the micro-organisms found in food. They are minute single cells of various shapes. Under ideal conditions, they divide into two every 20 minutes; consequently millions of bacteria may develop in contaminated food in a short time. They are more dangerous than moulds and yeasts because **food may be severely infected but not smell, taste or look bad.** Many types of bacteria present are harmless but some do cause illness (see p. 83 and Fig. 6.2). The bacteria that cause infections in humans are known as pathogens.

As all bacteria thrive in similar conditions, it is important to avoid conditions which favour their growth in order to prevent infection. They are active over a wide range of temperatures. Some like warmth and are active at 75 °C. Others like cold conditions and grow at temperatures as low as −5°C. This may cause problems in storage of foods. Some bacteria can form resting bodies called spores to protect them when the conditions are unfavourable for normal growth, e.g. the wrong degree of acidity or alkalinity, temperature or lack of moisture. Although normal bacteria are destroyed during heat treatment by boiling, some spores survive boiling for hours. They can then resume normal activity when conditions become more favourable and, for example, contaminate some pre-served foods. Bacteria are killed in an acid medium, and therefore they are not a problem in preserving fruits and making jams. The pasteurisation of milk (see p. 96) does not destroy all bacteria in milk but does destroy those bacteria likely to cause disease. Freezer temperatures must be low enough to prevent bacterial activity during storage. Although some bacteria die in the freezer, some remain inactive in the food and start to grow again when the food thaws. The removal of moisture by drying or by the addition of large quantities of sugar and salt make conditions unsuitable for bacteria, and these methods are therefore used in food preservation (see p. 88).

Safety of food

Food poisoning

Food poisoning became a notifiable disease in Britain under the Food and Drugs Act of 1955. Each year the number of cases reported has increased. The general symptoms are an acute attack of abdominal pain, diarrhoea and vomiting which can occur 2-30 hours after eating a meal. The notified cases may be only a small fraction of the actual cases as many mild stomach upsets or 'holiday tummies' may also be due to eating contaminated food. Food poisoning is caused mainly by the action of pathogenic bacteria, or occasionally by chemicals. *Chemical food poisoning* accounts for a small number of cases:

- Some fungi and many berries are poisonous if eaten and each year a few cases of poisoning are reported where people, especially children, have picked and eaten them.
- Traces of metals such as lead, mercury arsenic and cadmium occasionally contaminate food. Pesti-cides and industrial waste also sometimes affect fruits and vegetables.
- Natural toxic substances are found in some foods, e.g. rhubarb leaves, horseradish and green pota-toes but only cause poisoning if eaten in very large quantities.
- Some synthetic additives used in food processing have been found to be toxic. Now all additives undergo thorough investigation before use in food manufacture.

Bacterial food poisoning

Bacterial food poisoning accounts for the vast majority of food poisoning cases.

The main types of bacteria that cause the trouble are shown in the chart on p. 84. They are only harmful if they are present in very large numbers. Millions of bacteria per gram have been counted from samples of food known to have caused food poisoning. Sometimes the bacteria have produced their toxins in the food before it is eaten and the symptoms occur rapidly as soon as the infected food irritates the stomach. Other bacteria do not produce their toxins until they are in the body where they multiply and produce toxins as by-products of their metabolism. These types are most difficult to identify. The symptoms do not appear so quickly and illness of this type may also last longer.

Foods at risk

Protein foods are the ideal media for bacterial growth. Approximately 85% of confirmed out-breaks have been traced to contaminated meat and meat products. Made-up dishes can cause problems if they are not thoroughly cooked or reheated. Also, foods which are eaten without cooking after preparation, e.g. custards, trifles and cream cakes, may be the cause.

Other illnesses spread by food

Some illnesses, e.g. typhoid, cholera and dysentery may be spread by food contaminated by people who are either sufferers or carriers of the disease. The disease-producing bacteria do not grow and multiply in the food but are carried into the new host by the food. They then live in and infect the new host.

Suggest reasons why the number of cases of food poisoning has been increasing in recent years.

Have you noticed cases reported in the newspapers? What were the circumstances of the outbreak and which foods were involved?

Prevention of food poisoning

All infection carried by foods can be greatly reduced by correct and careful handling at all stages of its manufacture, distribution, preparation and storage. Some bacteria will be present in all foods, but the main aims in prevention of food poisoning must be:
- to prevent contamination by harmful bacteria;
- to avoid keeping food in conditions where any bacteria present can thrive and multiply.

Fig. 6.2 The most important bacteria that cause food poisoning

Name	How food is contaminated	Foods affected	Symptoms	Onset	Duration	Special points
Salmonella	Human, animal and insect excreta are direct or indirect source. Meat and poultry may be infected in the slaughter house. Failure to wash hands after use of lavatory may cause infection of food in the kitchen. Door handles, work surfaces and equipment may all be contaminated. Salmonella survive on unwashed hands up to three hours.	Meat, especially cooked meat and poultry, sausages, etc. Duck eggs, shellfish from polluted water, custards, cream, ice cream.	Diarrhoea, vomiting, some fever	12–36 hours	1–7 days	Bacteria themselves cause infection. Most common cause of food poisoning, responsible for two out of three cases. Dangerous in very young and elderly people where it may cause death. Destroyed by adequate cooking. Frozen poultry must be adequately defrosted or it may not reach a high enough temperature to kill salmonella in cooking. See p. 156.
Staphylococci	Present in the nose, throat and skin of many people where they do no harm except to infect cuts and spots. They are introduced into food directly from the hands or by droplet infection (coughs and sneezes) or indirectly from licked spoons or handkerchiefs. Also spread by flies.	Pies, meat, especially cooked sliced meat including ham and bacon. Custards, cream fillings, lightly cooked foods.	Vomiting, diarrhoea, abdominal cramp	1–6 hours	6–24 hours	Toxin is produced in food before it is eaten, so symptoms appear and disappear rapidly and are not serious but unpleasant. Bacteria easily destroyed by heat but the toxin can survive 20 minutes boiling.
Clostridium perfringens (used to be known as Clostridium welchi)	This bacteria lives in the soil and therefore infects fruit and vegetables. It forms spores which can survive in a dry atmosphere and is therefore found in dust, on floors and kitchen surfaces. It also can be found in water and particularly in sewage.	Meat, especially gravies and stews and large joints cooked and allowed to cool slowly.	Diarrhoea, severe stomach pain	8–22 hours	12–24 hours	This bacteria can grow only in the absence of air. The spores are heat-resistant and are not killed by cooking. They germinate and start to multiply as meat and meat dishes cool from 50°C–12°C. The toxin is produced as the host's digestive juices break down the bacterial cells.
Clostridium botulinum	Found in soil and decaying matter and commonly found on vegetables. It does not multiply in air, so fresh vegetables are safe. Other foods may be contaminated from sewage, flies and animals.	Bottled or canned less acid foods: vegetables, meat, fish and meat/fish pastes where processing temperature has not been high enough to destroy spores.	The central nervous system is affected and there is gradual paralysis. Death due to respiratory failure.	13–36 hours	Prolonged illness sometimes fatal (30–65% of cases). An antidote is available but recovery takes a long time.	A very rare disease. The bacteria produces a very heat resistant spore which, if it survives food processing, can multiply without air and produce a very dangerous toxin. Vegetables are not home canned or bottled because of this danger but fruits are safe because they

Food hygiene

There are many regulations controlling the production and distribution of food to make sure it is as safe and fresh as possible when it reaches the shops. From then on it is the responsibility of the consumer in choosing, handling, preparing and storing the food to make sure it is safe to eat.

Choice of food

Here are some tips to guide you:
- Buy from shops which are clean and hygienic.
- Cooked meats, raw meats and poultry should be purchased only from shops which have chilled displays.
- Butchers should keep separate scales, knives, boards, etc. for handling raw and cooked meats. Counters, boards, etc. should be scrupulously clean.
- In self-service shops ensure packaging is intact and 'sell by' dates on perishable foods have not over-run. It is essential that vacuum packs of foods such as cheese and bacon are well sealed and are sold from chilled cabinets.
- At the baker's, cream cakes and pies to be eaten without further cooking should be displayed in a covered case well away from the dust of the preparation area and protected from the customers' coughs and sneezes.
- Do not buy perishable food in excess of requirements.
- Animals should not be allowed in food shops.

Food handling

However carefully we select our food it is essential that it is stored and handled hygienically in the home, if it is to be safe to eat. Here are some tips:

The kitchen and larder should be well-ventilated and kept scrupulously clean. *Surfaces* should be smooth and easy to clean. The use of modern materials such as formica and stainless steel for work tops and vinyl on the floor has removed some of the hazards present in older kitchens where there were cracks and crannies where dangerous bacteria could lurk.

Insects and animals Flies, cockroaches and ants are hazards in the kitchen as they feed on animal faeces then land on food or a kitchen surface and leave behind pathogenic bacteria from their legs. Every effort should be made to keep the kitchen free from flies especially at night where a light left on may attract them in if a window is open. Any food left standing on a kitchen surface should be covered.

Rats and mice are attracted by dirt and decaying food, and special care is needed in food storage areas.

Household pets should not be allowed near kitchen surfaces and human food. Separate bowls should be used for their food and water and hands should always be washed after handling animals.

Equipment should also have smooth easy-to-clean surfaces. Chipped and cracked cups and plates should be discarded. An adequate supply of hot water and detergent should be available for washing up.

Modern automatic dishwashing machines which use very hot water and more powerful detergents are excellent for washing up.

Tea towels and dishcloths should be kept very clean as bacteria can thrive and multiply on damp dirty cloths.

Rubbish bins should be kept clean and covered. The use of plastic sacks inside a rubbish bin is more hygienic. The type that open automatically or with a foot pedal are best as they do not need to be touched by hand.

Disinfectant should be used where necessary in drains and for cleaning rubbish bins, etc.

Personal hygiene in food handling

- Hands should be washed with soap and hot water before and after handling food. Rinsing hands under a tap is not sufficient to kill bacteria.
- Hands should always be washed after using the lavatory.
- Any cuts or spots should be covered with *clean* antiseptic dressings.
- Coughing and sneezing near food should be avoided.
- Nails should be kept short and clean.
- Habits such as smoking or fingering the hair and nose should be avoided.
- Cooks often taste the food they are preparing, but licked fingers and spoons should be washed immediately.

Food preparation

- Food and vegetables that have been in contact with soil should be well washed in cold running water.
- Fruit and vegetables that may have been in contact with chemical sprays should be washed and wiped before being eaten.
- Disposable clean rag or paper should be used to wipe poultry, offal and meat. Cloths used for other purposes should *not* be used.
- Raw and cooked foods should not be handled at the same time, as bacteria could easily be transferred by a knife or board from the raw to the cooked food.
- Frozen meat and poultry should be allowed to

Fig. 6.3 What is wrong in this kitchen?

Fig. 6.4 Storage of food in a refrigerator

thaw thoroughly, preferably in a refrigerator, before cooking.
- Foods that have defrosted should be treated as fresh foods and not be left standing around at room temperature.
- All foods to be cooked should be cooked thoroughly.
- Hot food which is to be cooled and eaten cold should be cooled as rapidly as possible to avoid keeping it for a long time at a temperature where bacteria multiply rapidly. As soon as the food is cool, place it in a refrigerator.

Food storage

There are three main areas for storage of food in a modern home:
- the food freezer for long-term storage of perishable foods (see p. 89);
- the refrigerator for short-term storage of perishable foods;
- the store cupboard for dry and canned foods and home-preserved foods.

Ideally there should be a cool larder or ventilated cupboard at a temperature of about 12°C, but as many homes have central heating, specially cooled larder cupboards or refrigerators should be used.

The running temperature of a refrigerator should be about 4 °C as none of the food-poisoning bacteria is active at this temperature. It would be undesirable to run a refrigerator at freezing point. Most refrigerators have freezer compartments where frozen foods can be stored for a limited period of time depending on the *star-rating* of the refrigerator. These compartments are often not cold enough to freeze fresh foods.

Rating		Temperature	Frozen food storage time
one star	*	– 6 °C	up to 1 week
two star	**	– 12 °C	up to 1 month
three star	***	– 18 °C	up to 3 months

All food placed in a refrigerator should be covered to avoid loss of moisture and transference of flavour to other foods. Refrigerators should be kept scrupulously clean by washing with a solution of warm water and bicarbonate of soda. (Detergents may flavour food if used for cleaning the inside of the cabinet.)

The refrigerator should not be used as a general store cupboard. All food should be stored in the most suitable place, e.g. bread becomes stale more quickly in a refrigerator than in a bread bin.

Details of storage for the different food commodities are dealt with in the appropriate chapters.

Preservation of food

Early preservation methods

Our ancestors did not understand why food went bad but they recognised the need to preserve perishable foods and discovered some simple methods. Fire and salt were readily available; consequently smoked, dried and salted products were characteristic of northern Europe because meat, fish, fruit and vegetables had to be preserved for use in the cold winter months. In hot countries the need was to try and extend the short life of perishable foods: milk was fermented to produce cheese and yoghurt, and grapes were made into wine. Later, bottling, canning and eventually freezing processes were developed.

Present preservation methods

All modern food preservation methods are developments of early methods. Science can now explain the fundamentals of food preservation, however, and from these the food industry has made tremendous strides in commercial preservation. The same principles are used when food is preserved in the home.

The *aim* in preservation is to take food at the point where it is most palatable, fresh and nutritious and keep it in that state so it remains safe and appetising to eat. This is achieved by:
- reducing the number of spoilage organisms present in the food;
- destroying any pathogenic organisms;
- preventing further contamination of food during storage;
- preventing multiplication during storage of any organisms still present.

The reasons for preservation

- Commercially-preserved food is much easier to distribute. Food can be safely imported and exported. An increased variety of foods is therefore made available.
- Foods such as fruit and vegetables have a short growing season and preservation makes them available to use throughout the year and avoids wastage of surplus crops.
- Foods bought when they are most plentiful are cheaper and money can be saved by buying and preserving foods at this time.
- Preservation in some cases produces a different form of the product, e.g. grapes when dried produce raisins, sultanas and currants. Other preserved foods, e.g. jams and pickles, add flavour and variety to the diet.

Fig. 6.5 Preserved foods

- Preserved foods are easy to store and are useful in the store cupboard and freezer as convenience foods, which also give variety to the diet.
- Some countries have surplus food supplies, which can be stored and exported in a preserved form.

Methods of preservation

All methods of commercial and domestic preservation make use of one or more of these methods:
- heat treatment;
- drying;
- addition of chemicals;
- freezing.

In these methods, enzymes and micro-organisms are deprived of one or more of their requirements for activity or growth.

Heat treatment

Heat treatment is the most effective method of preserving food. Above the temperatures at which they are active, enzymes are destroyed and micro-organisms are gradually killed. The temperature must be high enough and the time long enough for the purpose. Some of the spore-forming bacteria found on vegetables and in protein foods require temperatures over 125°C to destroy them and this cannot be achieved by domestic methods, so these products should *not* be preserved at home by bottling or canning. In acid foods, such as fruits, the spore-forming bacteria are destroyed at a lower temperature and these foods can be safely preserved in the home.

Methods of heat treatment

- pasteurisation of milk destroys pathogenic bacteria by heat (see p. 96)
- sterilisation destroys all micro-organisms and enzymes in milk and fruit juices, etc.
- ultra heat treatment uses a very high temperature for a short time for milk and cream (see p. 96)
- bottling and canning combine sterilisation by heat with a sealing process to ensure the exclusion of air. The process cooks the foods, which are then ready to eat when the can or bottle is opened.
- blanching is a rapid heat treatment in boiling water given to vegetables and some fruits before they are frozen to destroy enzymes which may remain active at freezer temperatures and spoil the flavour, colour and nutritional value.

Drying

This is the oldest and simplest method of preservation. Micro-organisms, like all other living things, cannot grow and reproduce without moisture. The removal of water from food means that the concentration of sugar and salt increases. As water is drawn out of the cells of the micro-organisms by osmosis, they die. Enzymes require less moisture to remain active and this is why some commercially dried foods have to be blanched to kill the enzymes before drying.

Originally foods were spread out in the sun to dry naturally and this method is still used today for drying fruits in hot countries and in the home for drying herbs.

Mechanical drying is used commercially for fruit and vegetables. The produce is placed on trays and passed through a tunnel where hot air is circulated and blown over it until the moisture content has been reduced to 25%. Dehydration removes even more moisture and is also used for some vegetables such as potatoes, onions and for milk and eggs. Dehydrated foods contain 2%–10% moisture.

The most recent development in commercial drying is known as AFD (accelerated freeze drying) where the food is first frozen and the moisture is removed from it while it is still frozen (by a process called sublimation). Freeze-dried products have an open texture which rehydrates quickly to give a product of good colour, texture and flavour but they are fragile and easily oxidised and need careful packaging. The process is used for some vegetables, instant coffee and for complete meals.

Addition of chemicals

Salt, sugar and vinegar are the common chemical preservatives and they have been in use for centuries. Strong solutions are formed and water from the cells of micro-organisms in removed by osmosis.

Sugar must be used in large quantities to act as a preservative as in *jam-making* (see p. 177). Bacteria do not thrive if the sugar concentration is 40%–50%, but yeasts and moulds can develop; a concentration of 60% sugar is therefore recommended. Sugar is also used to preserve certain fruits and fruit peels by crystallisation. The water present in the fruit is exchanged for a strong sugar syrup by allowing the fruits to soak in a strong sugar solution.

Salt is used as a preservative for meat, fish and vegetables. Because meat, fish and vegetables can now be preserved by freezing, salting is used less. Bacon and ham are still preserved by salting.

Vinegar contains acetic acid and most micro-organisms do not like an acid medium. The pH in *pickles* is usually 3–3.5 and most bacteria cannot survive below pH 4.5. Other preserves may use a combination of acid, sugar or salt, e.g. chutneys (see p. 177).

Many other chemicals are poisonous to micro-organisms but are also poisonous to humans, so only a few can be used as preservatives. Some chemical substances may be added legally to certain foods and are known as 'permitted preservatives' and are used commercially in certain foods. The one used most frequently is sulphur dioxide which is added to soft drinks, fruit juices, sauces and sausages. It may also be used for the short-term storage of fresh fruits, e.g. bananas on board ship or in jam factories. Other permitted preservatives include benzoic acid and ascorbic acid which alter the pH of the food and make it unsuitable for the growth of micro-organisms.

Chemicals in wood smoke help to preserve food by smoking combined with the effects of heat and drying.

Freezing

Freezing is the method of food preservation most frequently used today and is still expanding to replace other methods of preservation especially for fruit, vegetables, fish and meat. Freezing is popular because:

- almost all foods are suitable for freezing;
- a high proportion of the nutritive value, colour, flavour, appearance and texture of the fresh food is retained.

In addition, a wide variety of appetising convenience foods can be stored in the home including commercial products or meals prepared at home when time is available.

> Discuss the advantages of freezing as an method of preserving food for a working mother, a farmer's wife, an elderly couple and a keen gardener.
>
> Suggest a list of foods which are particularly useful to store in the home freezer.
>
> There are a few foods that cannot be frozen successfully. What are the main ones?
>
> Why is it important to choose top quality fresh food for freezing?

The principles of freezing

Freezing converts the water in food into ice crystals. The water does not freeze at 0°C, because dissolved solids present lower the freezing point, but all the water in foods will be frozen when the temperature is -10°C and the micro-organisms are unable to grow. Some bacteria are killed but some remain and can become active again when the food thaws. Enzyme action is slowed down but not destroyed. Therefore the temperature to *store* frozen food is lowered to -18°C. Enzymes which attack fat are still active; meat with a lot of fat consequently has a shorter storage life than lean meat. Blanching before freezing destroys enzymes that would cause vegetables to deteriorate quite rapidly.

It is important that *fresh foods* should be frozen very rapidly so that a large number of very tiny ice crystals are formed in the cells as they cause less damage when food is thawing. Food frozen slowly forms large ice crystals which damage the cells and cause the food to lose flavour, texture and nutritive value as there is more loss of juices in the form of 'drip' as the food thaws.

Commerical freezing is carried out at below -30°C using blast freezers where food is placed on trays on refrigerated shelves and cold air is blown through them. Sometimes foods are immersed in or sprayed with liquid nitrogen and freezing is extremely rapid so foods retain their original shape and appearance.

Home freezers should have a special fast-freeze switch which lowers the temperature of the freezer to -25°C for freezing fresh food. *It is important that the temperature is lowered before the fresh food is added or the temperature of the freezer will rise above the safe level of -18°C.* For the same reason only a small amount of food should be frozen at a time: usually 10% of the freezer capacity.

Packaging food for the freezer

All food placed in a freezer must be carefully packed in airtight, waterproof wraps or boxes. As much air as possible should be squeezed from polythene bags after filling and they should then be sealed tightly with wire ties. A headspace of 1-2 cm should be left at the top of plastic boxes used for freezing soups, stews, etc. as the food expands during freezing. The air circulation in the freezer causes moisture to be lost from unwrapped or badly wrapped food. The quality of the food is lowered and in some cases

> *Home food preservation*
>
> Examine the popular methods of preserving food at home: jam-making, bottling, pickling, freezing and drying (of herbs).
>
> Make up a chart to explain how the processes used in each method prevent enzyme action and the growth of micro-organisms in the food.

drying known as 'freezer burn' can be seen on protein foods as a discolouration.

All foods placed in the freezer should be labelled clearly with the name and the date. Foods should be used in the order they were frozen and recommended storage times should be observed.

Instructions for preparing, storing and thawing frozen foods are provided by freezer manufacturers and in many books.

QUESTIONS

1 What are the causes of food contamination?
What steps can be taken to minimise it?
What extra precautions against food contamination need to be taken in shops?
(London, 1980)

2 Give six rules a housewife should follow to prevent the contamination of food.
(Welsh, 1978)

3 Discuss the statement that the preservation of food is one of the oldest skills known to man.
When is it worthwhile to preserve food at home?
Select a suitable method for each of the following foods: red cabbage, garden peas, plums, strawberries. Describe the principles used in each of the methods you choose.

4 What is a micro-organism? Describe the micro-organisms that may be found in food. List ways in which their presence may be (a) of use (b) harmful.
What are pathogenic bacteria? How can they be transmitted to food in a kitchen? What are the important rules for personal hygiene when handling food?

5 The preservation of food is important for economy and variety in the diet. Discuss this statement and give examples to illustrate your answer.
(Scottish, 1978)

6 Why has the freezer become increasingly popular for preserving food in the home? Describe ways in which it has replaced other methods.
Name five foods for which freezing is particularly successful.
Name five foods you would not place in a freezer.

7 Why is it important to pack foods efficiently before they are frozen?
What is meant by:
(a) freezer burn
(b) head space
(c) fast freeze switch?

8 Inadequate food hygiene can cause food poisoning.
(a) Name three bacteria which can cause food poisoning, describing briefly the symptoms they cause.
(b) Make a list of foods which are most readily contaminated.
(c) What conditions favour the growth of bacteria?
(d) How could you avoid bacterial contamination of food in your kitchen?
(Northern Ireland, 1979)

9 As a food handler in your own home explain how you would make sure that the hygiene in the kitchen and your own personal hygiene were consistently maintained at a high standard.
(AEB, 1979)

10 What special precautions would you take when handling and preparing the following foods? Give reasons for your answers.
(a) cooked ham and chicken to be sliced and eaten cold
(b) fresh cream trifle
(c) frozen chicken to be served as hot roast chicken
(d) shepherd's pie made with cooked meat

The Foods We Eat

Part 2

Milk, cream and yoghurt   7

Milk

Milk is produced by all female mammals to feed their young. At first milk is the only source of nourishment. It is a highly nutritious food. In some areas of the world, people drink goats', sheeps' and buffalo milk throughout their lives. Cows' milk is the most widely consumed, however.

Production of cows' milk

As milk is a liquid food rich in nutrients it is an ideal medium for the growth of micro-organisms. It must be produced and marketed under very hygienic conditions. If not, it can become a dangerous vehicle for infection.

In the past, cows often carried disease. Tuberculosis and brucellosis were both common diseases and were caused by bacterial infection of the cow. The bacteria were transmitted in the milk to humans. Since 1960, the British farmer must have his cows certified free from tuberculosis, (the TT test) and obtain a licence to sell milk. Both tuberculosis and brucellosis are extremely rare in Britain today.

Milk can also be infected by harmful bacteria after it has left the cow. Diseases which could be spread in this way are typhoid, diphtheria and dysentery. All diseases can be extremely dangerous for humans. It is therefore of vital importance that the hygienic conditions operate both on the farm and at the dairy.

Milk production on the farm

Milk is made from the food the cow eats and the water she drinks. In spring and summer the cows graze out of doors and the fresh grass provides all the nutrients they need. A cow may eat up to 70 kg of grass a day. The winter diet is usually based on grass that has been conserved by the farmer during the summer either as hay or silage, and supplemented by concentrated foods such as cattle cake, sugar beet pulp, kale and potatoes.

After a cow has had a calf she produces milk for about forty weeks. These cows are known as dairy cattle. The calves are taken from their mothers soon after birth and taught to feed from a bucket. The cows are then milked twice daily: early morning and late afternoon. Their milk yields are highest (often 20 litres/day) about three to four weeks after calving. The following year another calf will be born to the cow and the cycle continues. The female calves are reared and in time, they are mated, will calf and produce their own milk. Male calves born to dairy cows are reared as beef cattle for meat production (see Fig. 11.1).

At the dairy farms, the cows are milked by a milking machine. This operates like a suckling calf and is painless for the cow. A cap is placed on each teat and the milk is drawn off by a vacuum pump into pipe lines leading to a refrigerated vat. The milk is rapidly cooled, because it leaves the cow at her body temperature, and in this state it is an ideal medium for the growth of micro-organisms. Some milk is bottled and sold as *untreated milk*. The remainder is collected daily by a large insulated milk tanker that visits several farms, and delivered to a central dairy. About two-thirds of the milk produced is used as liquid milk or cream. The remainder is made into yoghurt, cheese and butter.

Processing milk at the dairy

When the milk arrives at the dairy, it is tested to make sure that it has not been watered down or infected and that nothing has been added. Some of the milk is specially processed, for example, skimmed or homogenised, before heat treatment (see Fig. 7.3).

Heat treatment

All milk is heat-treated before it is bottled or cartoned. This destroys any harmful bacteria and improves the keeping quality. Several processes, which vary in temperature and time of treatment, are used. These are:
(a) pasteurisation: this has very little effect on the flavour and nutritional value of the milk
(b) ultra-heat treatment (Long Life): this alters the flavour of the milk slightly but hardly affects the nutritional value

(c) sterilisation: this gives the milk a different flavour and colour.

The details of each of these methods of heat treatment are given in Fig. 7.3. Milk is graded according to the heat treatment it is given, and these grades are defined by law. They can be recognised by the colour of the carton or the colour of the metal foil tops added during the bottling process.

The bottles are first thoroughly washed and rinsed. They are then tested to make sure that they are sterile. Bottling is done on a high-speed machine which takes bottles from a moving belt and fills them automatically with the correct amount of milk and seals each one with a foil cap. A modern machine can fill and cap 600 bottles per minute. Similar automatic packing machines seal milk in sterilised cartons. After packing, milk goes to supermarkets or to a depot where it is kept in a cold room, until it is taken out for delivery by milk roundsmen.

Britain is one of the few countries in the world still to have regular deliveries of milk to each house. This probably accounts for the fact that Britain consumes far more milk than most other countries.

Fig. 7.1 Approximate average annual consumption of whole milk per head (1983)

Britain	123 litres
Italy	54 litres
Denmark	77 litres

In most countries the price of milk is controlled by and, often, subsidised by government.

Composition and food value of milk

Liquid milk varies in composition according to the breed of cow, her food, and several other factors. The milk from a large number of cows is mixed together at the dairy so that it is more uniform in composition and nutritional value. By law the composition of milk cannot be altered after milking.

Whole milk is the most complete of all foods. It contains nearly all the essential nutrients. Whole milk must contain a minimum fat content of 3%.

Skimmed milk has the cream removed. The composition is changed as most of the fat and fat soluble vitamins are removed. Because there is less fat in skimmed milk, other nutrients are proportionately increased when the nutrient content of a similar volume of milk is compared.

Fig. 7.2 Average composition of whole milk and skimmed milk

	Whole milk %	Skimmed milk %
water	87.5	90.2
protein	3.3	3.5
fat	3.8	0.2
carbohydrate	4.8	5.0
minerals	0.5	0.7
Energy value per 100 g	65 kcal 272 kJ	33 kcal 142 kJ

Using food tables work out the percentage of your daily recommended intake of nutrients which is supplied by a glass of milk, i.e. 250 ml.

The nutrients in milk

(a) Protein

The proteins in milk are of high biological value; that is, they contain the essential amino acids. The principle milk proteins are casein, lactalbumin and lactoglobulin. (See p. 21.)

Casein occurs only in milk. It coagulates when milk goes sour because of the acid present, causing the milk to curdle. Casein is also precipitated by the enzyme rennin during digestion and extracts of this enzyme are used to coagulate milk to make junket and in cheese-making.

Lactalbumin and lactoglobulin are not coagulated by acid or rennin and remain in the liquid whey when milk has curdled or when whey is separated from curds in the cheese-making process. These proteins are coagulated by heat, and can be seen as a skin on the surface of boiled milk.

(b) Fat

The fat in milk is suspended in tiny droplets as an oil-in-water emulsion (see p. 183).

Make a microscope slide of a drop of milk.

Observe the oil (i.e. fat) and water phases in the milk.

When milk has been left to stand for some time the fat globules clump together and rise to the top of the bottle because they are lighter than the watery solution. They form a layer of cream on the surface. If the milk has been homogenised the fat globules are sufficiently small to remain distributed throughout the milk.

(c) *Carbohydrate*

The carbohydrate in milk is lactose. Milk is the only natural source of this disaccharide (see p. 25). Lactose is not as sweet as sucrose and therefore fresh milk tastes only slightly sweet. It is readily converted to lactic acid by the action of bacteria in the milk. This is the main cause of milk turning sour. Lactose is not as soluble as sucrose and may crystallise out in condensed milk and ice cream.

(d) *Mineral elements*

Milk is especially rich in calcium and phosphorus, but the amount of iron present is not adequate for human requirements. Iron is therefore one of the first nutrients that must be given to supplement an infant's diet of milk (see p. 57). Other mineral elements are present in adequate amounts.

(e) *Vitamins*

Milk contains all the main vitamins, but by the time it reaches the consumer very little vitamin C is left. The small amount present is reduced by heat treatment and exposure to sunlight. Vitamins A and D are present in the cream and the pigment carotene present gives milk fat a yellow colour. The fat-soluble vitamins increase in the summer when the cows are feeding on grass. Milk is also an important source of the B vitamin, riboflavin. However, this vitamin deteriorates quickly with exposure to sunlight. It is important therefore not to leave milk standing in a light sunny position. A small amount of vitamin B_1 is also present, but is reduced by heat treatment and exposure to sunlight.

The properties of milk, and their use in food preparation

The chemical composition of milk affects how it reacts in food preparation. The main factors to be considered are that milk contains a very high proportion of water and, in proportion to the other nutrients present, a high proportion of protein. The effects of these characteristics can be seen in the following situations.

Grades of milk

1 bottle each of pasteurised, homogenised and untreated farm-bottled milk.
1 bottle sterilised milk.
1 carton UHT milk.
1 carton skimmed milk.
Small glasses or beakers for each milk.
1 Compare the cost of 1 litre of each milk.
2 Examine the bottles. Is there a separate cream layer? How much cream is there?
3 Pour a little of each milk into the glasses. Compare the colours.
4 Taste and compare the flavours of the different milks.
5 If possible, examine ordinary and homogenised milks under a microscope. Describe the appearance of the fat globules.

1 Heating milk in a saucepan

On heating milk in a saucepan, several changes can be seen.

Warm a sample of milk slowly in a saucepan. Observe the changes and where possible, note the temperature at which a change occurs:

● steam rising from the surface
● the formation of a skin on the surface
● bubbles forming under the skin
● the temperature at which milk boils
● the precipitate on the base of the pan.

On being heated, some of the water in the milk is converted to steam and evaporates from the surface. Small bubbles of air are seen on the top. The fat globules also tend to rise to the surface, giving it a slightly creamy colour. As heating continues, the proteins in milk coagulate. The lactalbumin and lactoglobulin form a skin on the surface of the milk. On further heating, the milk boils, and the pressure from the bubbles of steam forces through the skin. The boiling point of milk, 86 °C, is lower than that of water, because of the solids it contains.

Fig. 7.3 Grades of milk

Grade	Heat treatment	Colour of foil top	Keeping quality	Characteristics and uses
(1) *Untreated* (Farm-bottled, ordinary)	None	GREEN (ordinary)	1 day in a cool place, 2–3 days in a refrigerator	A special licence is required by the farmer to supply this milk.
Channel Islands or South Devon		GREEN with a single gold stripe.		Very visible cream line.
(2) *Pasteurised* ordinary	The milk is heated to 72 °C for at least 15 seconds and then rapidly cooled to below 10 °C. This kills any pathogenic micro-organisms and reduces the numbers of other organisms, so it is safer for human consumption.	SILVER	1 day in a cool place, 2–3 days in refrigerator	The most popular grade. Has a definite cream line. General use for beverages, cereals and in cooking.
South Devon Channel Islands	Treated as ordinary pasteurised milk.	GOLD	2–3 days in refrigerator	Milk from Jersey, Guernsey and South Devon breeds, which has a higher butter fat content and more cream (minimum 4% butterfat). Has a rich creamy flavour, a deeper colour and very distinctive cream line.
Skimmed	Treated as ordinary pasteurised milk.	BLUE (if in bottle) but usually obtained in cartons from supermarkets		Cream has been removed so there is a low fat content. The milk is bluish white in colour. Very suitable for people on slimming diet.
Semi-skimmed	Treat as ordinary pasteurised milk	RED and SILVER stripe	2–3 days in refrigerator	Half the cream has been been removed so the fat content is only about 1 ½ %.
Homogenised	The milk is warmed, then forced through a fine aperture to break up the fat globules so they remain evenly suspended throughout the milk. The milk is then pasteurised.	RED	2–3 days in a refrigerator	No cream layer as fat globules are evenly suspended in the milk. Smoother, creamier taste and is easily digestible. Popular with caterers and by consumers in other EEC countries.
(3) UHT *Ultra Heat Treatment* (Long Life)	Homogenised milk is heated to at least 132 °C for 1 second. All micro-organisms are destroyed.	PINK (if in bottle) but usually purchased in date-stamped cartons	About 4 months without refrigeration, if unopened. After opening treat like ordinary milk. Observe the 'use by' date on the carton.	Colour is similar to ordinary homogenised milk; slightly different flavour. No cream layer. Excellent store cupboard emergency supply. Very popular in countries with no home deliveries. Very useful on holidays, for camping, boats, caravans, etc.
(4) *Sterilised*	Homogenised milk is bottled and sealed and then heat-treated to *above boiling* point (100 °C) for approximately 30 minutes, then cooled. All micro-organisms are destroyed.	Traditionally sold in crown corked bottles	2–3 weeks without refrigeration if container is unopened. After opening treat like ordinary milk.	The high temperature and long sterilisation time give the milk a 'cooked' flavour and more creamy appearance due to the slight caramelisation of the sugar. Makes rich creamy milk puddings.

2 Baked products

In all baked recipes where milk is used as an ingredient (such as batters, scones and cakes), the water in the milk is converted to steam in the heat of the oven. Steam acts as a raising agent. This effect is particularly apparent when making batters (see pp. 218–219).

3 Curdling of milk

Because milk contains both protein and a high proportion of water there are some situations where the protein coagulates and separates away from the liquid part of the milk. This is known as *curdling*; it gives the milk a slightly lumpy appearance. Curdling can be caused by heat, acids, enzymes or the incorrect use of gelatine.

(a) *The effect of heat*

Milk may sometimes 'curdle' if it is added to very hot coffee, because the milk has become very slightly acid.

(b) *The effect of acid*

This effect is most obviously noticed when milk goes sour. The bacteria in milk change the lactose into lactic acid. The increased acidity coagulates the protein casein, and sour milk has a lumpy appearance and a very acid taste. This effect is used in the cheese-making process.

Other acids have a similar effect on milk. Curdling can also happen in food preparation wherever milk is used together with an acid in a recipe. It occurs readily if the milk is warm, e.g. cream soups, lemon puddings. If the milk is thickened with starch before the acid is added, curdling is prevented.

(c) *The effect of enzymes*

The enzyme rennin coagulates the casein in milk, as in the process of digestion (see p. 41). This enzyme can also be extracted from calves' stomachs. It is marketed as a liquid called *Rennet*. This is a dilute concentration of rennin, which will lightly 'set' milk to form a junket.
Rennet is also used in a stronger solution in the cheese-making process (see p. 105).

(d) *The effect of incorrect use of gelatine*

Gelatine may cause milk to curdle if it is added to hot milk. To prevent this, gelatine should always be dissolved in hot water and added to cold milk. The gelatine should always be added to the milk (not milk to gelatine), as this ensures that the gelatine is added gradually and can be thoroughly mixed into the milk.

Convenience forms of milk

Some milk not required for immediate consumption, and the skimmed milk remaining after the manufacture of butter and cream are preserved by *canning* or *drying*. The removal of some or all of the water concentrates the milk in a less bulky form and provides convenience foods for the consumer which are easier to store and have a much longer shelf-life than fresh milk. These products contain all the nutrients of milk, with the exception of thiamin and vitamin B_{12} which are partially destroyed by heat in the manufacturing processes.

Canned milks

There are two types of canned milk; evaporated and condensed. Both products are sterile, and have at least a twelve-month shelf-life.

(a) *Evaporated milk is unsweetened, concentrated* milk produced from whole or skimmed milk. The milk is evaporated in large steam-heated vacuum pans until it contains about 31% solids. It is then canned, sealed and sterilised by heat. The processing alters the flavour and destroys some of the water-soluble vitamins.

(b) *Sweetened condensed milk* may be produced from whole or skimmed milk. It has a considerable amount of sugar added before it is evaporated so that it contains about 71% solids. After canning and sealing, sterilisation is unnecessary as the amount of sugar present is sufficient to preserve the contents of the tin.

Examine canned milks obtained from your local shops. What information is given on the labels?

Reconstitute the milks as recommended and taste them. How does processing affect the taste?

Dried milks

Dried milk (i.e. milk powder) is produced by removing most of the water in milk by evaporation. Most milk powders are made from skimmed milk and are therefore low in fat. Some are made from whole milk but cannot be stored for long as the fat becomes rancid. A third type of dried milk has the animal fat of milk replaced with a vegetable fat which stores well.

Dried milk may be reconstituted and used as liquid milk, or used in its powder form in cooking, for example in custards, or added to baked products. It is used extensively in catering and forms part of many convenience foods. Dried milk powders are useful where milk is to be kept for a long time, such as on sea voyages. They are easy to transport in bulk so they can be exported to countries where milk production is difficult because of the climate.

Milk powders are hygroscopic, i.e. they rapidly absorb moisture from air, becoming lumpy and stale in flavour. To prevent this they must be stored in airtight tins. In these conditions low fat milk powders have a shelf-life of several years.

How many types of dried milk are available in your local shops? Are they whole milk or skimmed milk powders?

What information is given on the labels?

Are the milks easy to reconstitute and what do they taste like?

Fig. 7.4 Composition of milk powders (in grams per 100 g)

	whole milk powder	skimmed milk powder	skimmed milk with vegetable fat added
protein	26.3	36.4	27.5
fat	26.3	1.3	23.5
carbohydrates	39.4	52.8	41.7
calcium	1.02	1.2	0.9
water	2.9	4.1	2.8
energy value	490 kcal	355 kcal	470 kcal
	2051 kJ	1512 kJ	1966 kJ

Convenience milk products for infant feeding

The composition of cows' milk is different from human breast milk. It is now recommended that unmodified cows' milk, evaporated, or dried milk powders are not used for feeding infants under nine months old. Special types of canned and dried milks

are now made commercially, which have been modified to suit the particular needs of young babies:

● the proportion of protein is reduced;
● the lactose or sugar content is increased;
● the type of fat may be changed;
● the proportion of some minerals may be reduced;
● calculated quantities of vitamins and minerals are added

These milks are produced in dried and liquid forms. It is essential that they are used exactly as the manufacturer recommends.

Uses of milk in food preparation

In addition to its use as a beverage, milk is used in many ways in food preparation either as an essential ingredient or to enrich recipes where it is used to replace water, e.g. sauces, cake recipes.

---

1 Make a list of the uses of milk in food preparation:
(a) as an essential ingredient
(b) as an addition or substitute for other liquids in order to enrich a recipe.
2 Explain how dried and canned milks extend the ways in which milk is used in recipes.
3 There are many canned and packet convenience foods on the market containing milk, e.g. canned rice pudding. List those you see in your local supermarket.

Cream

Cream is produced from whole milk by a process of separation. Cream contains all the main constituents of milk but in different proportions. A number of different types of cream are made. They vary in the amount of fat they contain. However, all types of cream contain more fat, less water and proportionally less of the other constituents of milk.

Production of cream

Cream can be separated from milk in a number of different ways. The simplest and traditional way is to allow the milk to stand for about 24 hours and

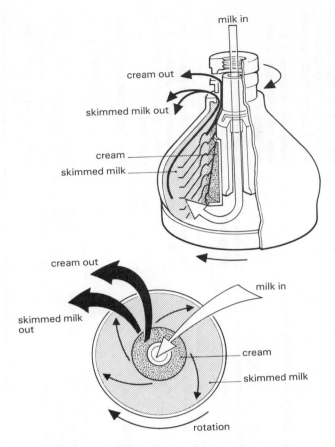

milk in

cream out

skimmed milk out

cream

skimmed milk

cream out

milk in

skimmed milk out

cream

skimmed milk

rotation

Fig. 7.5 How cream is separated

then skim the cream from the surface by hand. This method is not very efficient as much of the fat remains in the skimmed milk. Commercially, the cream is separated from the milk by means of a mechanical separator. The milk is first heated to between 32–49°C, then transferred to the separator, which spins round at a high speed like a centrifuge. The cream, which is lighter, flows towards the centre whilst the heavier skimmed milk is thrown towards the outside of the separator vat. The cream and skimmed milk are collected from two different outlet pipes. The cream is then cooled rapidly to 4.5°C. The fat content of the cream may be varied at this stage by adjusting a control valve.

The following creams are produced. (See plate 10(a).)

Fig. 7.6 Minimum fat content of cream %

half cream	12
single cream	18
sterilised canned cream	23
whipping cream	35
double cream	48

Fig. 7.8 on pp. 100–101 shows the methods of heat treatment for these different types of cream.

In Britain, The Cream Regulations (1970) specify the legal minimum percentage of fat for each variety. The cream must be labelled in accordance with these specifications. Certain additives are permitted in some varieties of cream, for example, whipped cream may contain sugar and stabilisers.

(a) Examine the varieties of cream available in your local supermarket.

(b) Do the different-coloured foil caps make it easy to recognise the different types?

(c) Is the cream well labelled? Carefully compare what the creams contain.

Composition and food value of cream

Cream is an oil-in-water emulsion. The composition of cream varies according to the fat content (see Fig. 7.6).

Fig. 7.7 Nutritional value of cream

Nutrient	%	
	single cream	*double cream*
water	71.9	48.6
fat	21.2	48.2
protein	2.4	1.5
carbohydrate	3.2	2.0
minerals	0.4	0.2
energy value	195 kcal	447 kcal
per 100 g	815 kJ	1868 kJ

The amount of water present varies with the fat content. When the fat globules rise to the surface they are surrounded by a layer containing some of the proteins, lactose and minerals of the milk. The other solid constituents of the milk remain in the skimmed milk. Cream is a good source of the fat-soluble vitamins A and D.

The properties of cream: whipping

The fat in cream is suspended in the water phase in the form of small globules. Each globule is surrounded by a protein/fat membrane. When cream is whipped, tiny air bubbles are forced into it and a

Fig. 7.8 Grades of cream

Type	Legal minimum fat content	Heat treatment	Processing	Keeping quality	Uses
Half cream (sometimes called 'top of the milk')	12	pasteurised (79.5°C for 15 seconds)	Usually homogenised to prevent the cream separating during storage	In refrigerator 2–3 days (summer) 3–4 days (winter)	Thin pouring cream for coffee, fruit and cereals.
Single cream	18	pasteurised	Homogenised to prevent separation and to increase viscosity. Sealed with red foil cap.		Pouring cream, ideal in coffee, on cereals or fruit. Addition to dishes using meat, fish, cheese and eggs and in sauces. Will not whip.
Whipping cream	35	pasteurised	Not homogenised as homogenised cream does not whip satisfactorily. Sealed with green or purple foil cap.		35% fat is the minimum necessary for a cream to whip. This is the best and most economical cream for any purpose requiring whipped cream for decorating soufflés, etc. Whips to twice its volume.
Double cream	48	pasteurised	Slightly homogenised. Blue foil cap.		A rich pouring cream to serve with fruit. Floats on coffee or soup. Can be whipped more easily if 1 × 15 ml spoon of milk is added to 125 ml cream.
Double cream (thick)	48	pasteurised	Heavily homogenised to make it extra thick.		Served with a spoon as it does not pour easily. It will not whip.
Double cream (extended life)	48	pasteurised	Homogenised then vacuum sealed in bottles. Heated to 115°C for 12 mins.	2-3 weeks in refrigerator	It will spoon and lightly whip.
Sterilised half cream	12	sterilised	Homogenised. Put into cans and sealed then heated to 115 °C for 20 mins and cooled rapidly.	Unopened up to two years. Open as for fresh cream	Pouring cream with a slight caramel flavour due to high temperature in processing. Convenient form in the store cupboard.
Sterilised cream	23		As for sterilised half cream		A thicker cream which tastes like the half cream. It can be spooned but will not whip.
'Long life' single cream	18	UHT	Homogenised. Heated to 132°C for 1 second and cooled immediately. Packed in foil-lined packets.	Unopened 6–8 weeks. If open, as fresh cream	Similar flavour to pasteurised cream. Ideal for picnics and holidays. Small individual packs are served with coffee in many restaurants.

Name	Type	Fat %	Processing	Storage	Description/Uses
Long life whipping cream	UHT	35	Homogenised. Heated to 132°C for 1 second and cooled immediately. Packed in foil-lined packets.	Unopened 6–8 weeks. If open, as fresh cream.	Similar flavour to pasteurised cream. Whip straight from refrigerator. Whipping may take longer than fresh cream.
Long life whipped cream	UHT	18	Homogenised. Heat-treated as above. Packed in aerosol container. Nitrous oxide is propellant gas.	3 months in refrigerator	Instant, very frothy whipped cream. Produces large volume. Use immediately before serving, as this cream rapidly loses volume.
Clotted cream (mainly made in Cornwall & Devon)	special	55	Heated in shallow pans over boiling water for about 1hr to temperature of 82°C. After slow cooling the crust of cream is skimmed off. Packed in cartons with gold foil tops.	2–3 days in summer 3–4 days in winter Long-keeping variety in tins. 4–10 weeks.	A very thick cream with a distinctive yellow colour. Served with scones and jam or with puddings and fruit.
Soured cream		18	This is not cream that has deteriorated but is artificially soured by use of specially cultured bacteria to give it a piquant refreshing taste. Packed in cartons with green foil tops.	2–3 days in a cool place. Up to 7 days in refrigerator.	Texture of thick cream. Added to dishes in cooking, e.g. cheesecake, goulash. Excellent served with jacket potatoes and soup and party dips. Used in salad dressing.

foam is formed (see p. 100). Each air bubble is surrounded by a very thin layer of protein which acts as a stabiliser. Some liquid fat is released from the fat globules. They are then able to stick together in clumps round the air bubbles. A stable stiff foam is formed and the cream becomes thick.

In order to whip easily, the cream should:

● be fresh and cold;
● have an average fat content of 35–40%;
● not be homogenised ('Long Life' varieties are homogenised, and therefore take longer to whip).

Under the right conditions whipping cream should whip to twice its original volume. Single cream does not contain a high enough proportion of fat to whip. Double cream can be whipped but better results are obtained if it is diluted slightly with milk to reduce the fat content.

Cream can be overwhipped. When this happens, the fat globules release more liquid fat, and then stick together in large clumps or butter granules. The air bubbles in the foam collapse. Yellow butter granules are left floating in a watery liquid, giving a curdled appearance. This fault cannot be rectified. Cream that is too thick is likely to do this before the foam is formed.

(a) Structure of cream before whipping

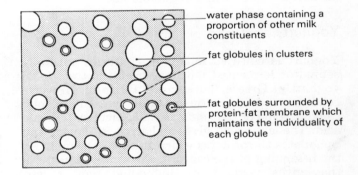

water phase containing a proportion of other milk constituents

fat globules in clusters

fat globules surrounded by protein-fat membrane which maintains the individuality of each globule

(b) Structure of cream after whipping

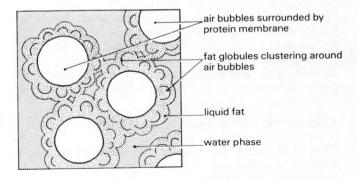

air bubbles surrounded by protein membrane

fat globules clustering around air bubbles

liquid fat

water phase

Fig. 7.9 Whipping cream: changes in the physical structure

Alternatives to cream

Imitation cream resembles cream in appearance and is usually made by emulsifying vegetable fats with dried egg, gelatine and flavourings. It is used frequently by caterers. It can be very easily contaminated and may be the cause of some cases of food poisoning.

Non-dairy whip is a mixture of skimmed milk and vegetable oils. Its consistency and flavour are similar to those of cream. It is useful for people wishing to reduce the amount of animal fat in the diet.

Ice cream is a useful convenience food for desserts and is available in many flavours.

Dairy ice cream is a combination of milk and cream. The word 'dairy' indicates that the fat present is all milk fat whereas ordinary ice cream is usually made from skimmed milk and vegetable fat. Ice cream can also be made in the home and many recipes contain cream or evaporated milk.

Coffee creamers are not milk products at all but are used to replace milk or cream in coffee usually in the form of an easily-dissolved powder or granules which can be added directly to hot coffee. They are made from glucose and vegetable fat.

Yoghurt

Yoghurt is cultured milk. For centuries naturally soured or fermented milk has been the traditional yoghurt of Greece, Turkey and Bulgaria. In warm conditions, the bacteria naturally present in milk convert some of the sugar in milk, lactose, to lactic acid. The lactic acid gives a sharp acid flavour and coagulates the proteins which thickens the milk. At the beginning of the century, the strain of bacteria that gives yoghurt its individual flavour was isolated and named *lactobacillus bulgaricus*.

Nowadays, milder yoghurts are produced by first destroying most of the bacteria naturally present by heat treatment. A culture of the yoghurt bacteria, *lactobacillus bulgaricus*, is then inoculated into the milk under carefully controlled hygienic conditions. This produces a milder-flavoured yoghurt. It is known as natural yoghurt. Yoghurt can be produced both commercially, and in the home.

Commercial manufacture of yoghurt

The milk used for the preparation of yoghurt depends on the type of yoghurt required. If a fluid, acid yoghurt is preferred, (such as in Greece) whole milk or skimmed milk is used. To obtain a milder yoghurt with a semi-solid consistency, whole milk or

skimmed milk is partially evaporated and skimmed milk powder may be added. Yoghurts made from skimmed milk are either low in fat (containing less than 1.5% fat) or fat-free (containing less than 0.5% fat).

The milk mix chosen is treated as follows:
1 It is homogenised as this gives a yoghurt with a creamy smooth texture.
2 The homogenised milk is pasteurised to destroy most of the bacteria naturally present.
3 After cooling the milk is inoculated with the yoghurt culture and then incubated at a temperature of 42-45°C for 2½-3 hours. The desired acidity is reached and the yoghurt sets.
4 After incubation the yoghurt is cooled to 4.5 °C and stored at this temperature. The souring organisms are still active during storage and the acidity increases slowly. This limits the storage life of yoghurt and it eventually becomes too acid to be palatable.

Types of yoghurt

Natural yoghurt has no added flavouring but the flavour and texture vary slightly according to the milk used.
Fruit-flavoured yoghurt has fruit juice syrup added before it is incubated.
Whole or real fruit yoghurt has whole fruit in a sugar syrup stirred in after it has been incubated. Nuts are also added to some yoghurts.

Yoghurt drinks, ice creams and yoghurt-flavoured whips are also available.

In your local supermarket, look at an example of natural yoghurt, fruit flavoured yoghurt and whole or real fruit yoghurt. Compare the sugar and fat content of each one. Why do you think they vary so much?

Making yoghurt at home

There are various appliances for making yoghurt at home. Fresh natural yoghurt can be used a starter to produce yoghurt at home since it contains the correct bacteria. UHT (Long Life) milk or sterilised milk are the best types of milk to use as they are already homogenised and sterile so need not be treated before use. If fresh milk is used, it must first be boiled to destroy any bacteria that could cause 'off' flavours in the milk. Skimmed milk powder, honey, jam, fruit or nuts can be added.

Experiment: *To find conditions suitable for preparation of yoghurt.*

1 litre UHT milk
2 × 15 ml spoon natural yoghurt
Heat the milk in a saucepan to 43°C. (Check temperature is correct with a thermometer.) Stir in fresh natural yoghurt. Pour the mixture into a clean, warmed, wide-necked vacuum flask or small jar. Close the flask securely and leave undisturbed for the yoghurt to set:

(a) remove and refrigerate one portion after 3 hours
(b) remove and refrigerate one portion after 8 hours
(c) leave the remainder in the flask overnight and them remove and refrigerate.

Taste the three samples of yoghurt and measure their acidity using indicator papers. Which one do you prefer?

Composition and food value of yoghurt

Yoghurt contains all the nutrients of the milk from which it is made. If dried milk is added in its preparation the yoghurt will also contain extra protein. Yoghurt is a very easily-digested food. It is therefore especially useful for young children, convalescents and elderly people. Most commercial yoghurt made from skimmed milk has a low energy value.

Fig. 7.10 Nutrient content of low fat yoghurt

Nutrient	natural %	flavoured %	fruit %
water	85.7	79.0	74.9
fat	1.0	0.9	1.0
protein	5.0	5.0	4.8
carbohydrate	6.2	14.0	17.9
minerals	0.8	0.8	0.8
energy value per 100 g	52 kcal 216 kJ	81 kcal 342 kJ	95 kcal 405 kJ

Using food tables, work out the percentage of your daily recommended intake of nutrients which is supplied by one small carton of yoghurt, i.e. approx. 150 g.

Uses of yoghurt in food preparation

Yoghurt can be served at breakfast, either alone, or as an accompaniment to cereals. For desserts, it can be eaten alone or as an accompaniment for fresh or cooked fruit. It is also an alternative to cream served with puddings and pies. Some dessert recipes include yoghurt as an ingredient e.g. cheesecake. Natural yoghurt is an ingredient of many sauces, soups and salad dressings. It is also added to casseroles to sharpen and improve the flavour. Small cartons of yoghurt are useful for picnics and packed lunches.

Other cultured milk products

Buttermilk is a liquid by-product of the manufacture of butter (see p. 184). It contains some protein, lactose and minerals. It is treated with a special culture to give it an interesting fresh flavour. It is sold in cartons as a drink which may be flavoured with fruit juice, coffee or other flavourings. It is used traditionally to make scones, soda breads, etc.

Soured cream is made in a similar way by inoculating single cream with a special culture (see Fig. 10.7).

Care and storage of milk, cream, ice cream and yoghurt

Milk

Milk is a highly perishable food. Great care is taken to ensure that the milk on sale is in good and safe condition. Similar care must be taken in the home. In Britain, where milk is delivered, it should be taken indoors immediately. This avoids the fat becoming rancid, and the loss of the B-group vitamins. If this is not possible it should be placed in a cool place out of direct sunlight and where birds cannot peck the foil caps. Milk should be stored in a refrigerator or cool larder. Any jugs used for milk should be scrupulously clean and covered so that dirt and flies do not contaminate the milk. It is best to keep the milk in the bottle in which it was delivered as this was sterile when filled. In the refrigerator milk should be covered to stop it absorbing strong flavours. Old and new milk should not be mixed. Milk should always be used in the order it was delivered. Figure 7.3 on p. 96 gives the recommended storage times for the different grades of milk.

Cream

Fresh cream should be treated like fresh milk (see p. 103 and Fig. 7.8). Whipped cream should be kept in the refrigerator in a clean covered container and used the same day. Synthetic creams should also be stored in the refrigerator as they too are ideal media for the growth of bacteria.

Double cream and clotted cream freeze quite well but single cream does not. Whipping cream can be stored in the freezer for up to three months. It freezes more successfully when whipped. Rosettes of piped whipped cream can be frozen uncovered and then be stored in a polythene box. They are placed frozen on the food they are to decorate.

Ice cream

Ice cream can only be stored in the freezer compartment of a refrigerator or a home freezer, as follows;

*	freezer compartment	1 day
**	freezer compartment	1 week
***	freezer compartment	1 month
deep freeze		up to 3 months

Ice cream should not be refrozen after it has melted as the texture is affected. It may also be contaminated with harmful bacteria.

Yoghurt

As yoghurt contains live acid-producing bacteria, it is essential that it is stored in a refrigerator. The cartons should be date-stamped and if correctly stored will be palatable for several days after the date marked.

The recommended storage times are:

larder	1 day if cool
refrigerator	5-7 days
freezer	not recommended for natural yoghurt; fruit varieties 1 month

In the freezer, natural yoghurt tends to separate but by whisking after thawing it may be possible to recombine the liquid without loss of flavour or food value. Some of the sweetened fruit varieties freeze quite well. Those bought already frozen may contain added stabilisers and emulsifiers to prevent separation.

QUESTIONS

1 'Milk is a perfect food.' Discuss this statement showing your knowledge of the nutritional value of milk.

Explain how the farmer takes care to produce clean milk and how you would store it in the home.
(AEB, 1977)

2 Write a short paragraph on each of the following with reference to milk.
   (a) pasteurisation
   (b) homogenisation
   (c) sterilisation
   (d) ultra-heat treatment
How could you identify these four different forms of milk in your supermarket? Explain when you would purchase each of the varieties.

3 Give a scientific explanation for each of the following:
   (a) the formation of a skin on milk when it is heated
   (b) the curdling of milk when making a cream soup
   (c) single cream will not whip.

4 Explain the importance of milk in the diet. List ways in which it can be used in food preparation. Discuss the value of dried and canned milks as substitutes for fresh milk.

5 Discuss the value of yoghurt for a person on a slimming diet. How would you make yoghurt at home? Are there any advantages in making your own yoghurt?

6 Explain what happens to a bottle of milk that is left standing on the doorstep in the sunshine all day. What advice would you give to someone who is out at work all day and has milk delivered in the morning?

State the important rules for the storage of milk and cream.

7 Why should you not refreeze ice cream?

Plate 9   Signs of deterioration in food

Plate 10

(a) A selection of dairy foods

(b) A selection of hard cheeses

1. Tendale (low-fat Cheddar)   2. Wensleydale
3. Leicester   4. Huntsman (Double Gloucester
with Stilton)   5. Parmesan   6. Gouda
7. Cheddar   8. Double Gloucester   9. Cheddar
with walnuts   10. Edam   11. Emmenthal
12. Gorgonzola   13. Caerphilly   14. Lancashire
15. Sage Derby   16. Port Salut   17. Cheshire
18. Red Windsor   19. Roquefort   20. Gruyere

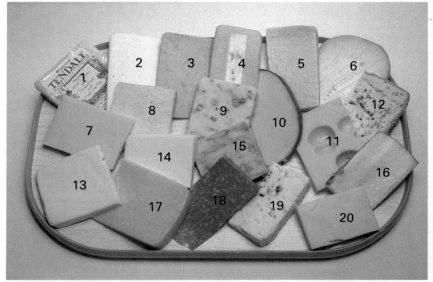

(c) A selection of soft cheeses

1. Camembert   2. Cottage cheese   3. Quark
4. Lymeswold/Cambozola   5. Feta   6. Ricotta
7. Low fat soft cheese   8. Brie   9. Curd cheese
10. Full fat cream cheese

Cheese

Cheese is the oldest way of preserving the nutrients in milk in a compact, concentrated and palatable form. It has probably been made since the earliest domestication of animals (about 9000 BC). Cheeses were traditionally made in farmhouse kitchens. A small amount is still produced in this way and is called farmhouse cheese. However, the majority of cheese is now successfully produced on a large scale in creameries (cheese-making factories).

Cheese is produced in all the important dairy-farming areas of the world. Australia, New Zealand, Canada, France, Switzerland, Holland and Denmark export an enormous variety of cheese. Britain imports cheeses from all these countries and also produces a number of well-known varieties of cheese of which a small proportion is exported.

There are more than 500 varieties of cheese made today. Most are made from cows' milk, but cheese is also made from goats', sheeps' and buffalo milk. Many of the cheeses are named after the places where they were first made or after the towns where they were first sold. Other names refer to the shape of the cheese or the milk from which the cheese is made. No two cheeses are identical if they are made in different places because of variations in local grasses, herbs, water and climate, as well as differences in manufacturing processes. They vary in taste, texture, hardness, colour and smell. Cheese is concentrated milk; 500 ml of milk is used to produce 50 g of cheese. During the cheese-making process, most of the milk protein coagulates, trapping nearly all the fat. The solid clot formed is known as *curd* which will form the cheese. Water and lactose drain away. This liquid is known as the *whey*. Cheeses can be classified in many ways but the simplest way is to divide them into *hard cheeses* which are pressed during their manufacture to squeeze out liquid and *soft cheeses* which are not pressed and therefore contain more liquid.

Hard cheeses

Hard cheeses are cheeses with firm textures as they are pressed heavily during their manufacture to extract most of the whey. There are many types of hard cheese, e.g. Cheddar, Double Gloucester, Gorgonzola, Edam.

Look at plate 10, (b) and (c). Find out the cost of each of these cheeses. How many of them have you tasted?

All these cheeses are made in similar ways. As the manufacture of Cheddar cheese includes all the major stages of cheese-making typical of hard cheeses, its production is described here.

The production of Cheddar cheese

1 *Delivery of milk* Whole cows' milk is brought to the creamery from many different farms.

2 *Pasteurisation* The milk is pasteurised to destroy any harmful bacteria (see p. 96). The pasteurised milk is cooled to 21°C before being pumped into enormous stainless steel vats. The vat is surrounded by a hollow jacket so the cheese can be heated or cooled during manufacture.

3 *The ripening of the milk* The milk must be slightly acid (i.e. sour) to develop the correct texture and flavour of cheese. A starter culture of lactic acid bacteria is added. This process can be more carefully controlled than natural souring and takes only about half an hour.

4 *Renneting* This process coagulates the milk. The temperature is raised to 30°C and rennet is added. Rennet contains the enzyme rennin which causes the milk to clot as it does in the digestion process (see p. 41). The liquid whey separates from the curd and is allowed to drain away.

5 *Cutting the curd* After about 45 minutes the curd is solid enough to cut into small pieces with mechanical cheese knives. The whey is able to drain more easily from the small 1 cm cubes.

6 *Scalding* The curd is heated. Steam is passed through the hollow jacket surrounding the vat for 45 minutes. During this scalding the curds are stirred continously by revolving paddles and heated slowly to about 41°C. This cooking process causes

the curds to shrink, expelling even more whey, so they become firmer and springy in texture.

7 *Pitching (setting)* After scalding, the curd is allowed to 'pitch' or settle in the vat. It shrinks again and begins to matt together. More whey is drained off through a grid at the bottom of the vat.

8 *Cheddaring* After pitching, the curd is cut into 20 cm square blocks which are piled up and repiled at 10 minute intervals. This completes the draining of the whey. During this time the curd loses its rubbery texture and becomes more silky.

9 *Milling and salting* The curd is broken up into small pieces and salt is added (about 2%) and mixed into the curd. This helps to preserve the finished cheese and bring out the flavour.

10 *Moulding* The salted curd is packed into moulds lined with coarse cloth which stays on the cheese during the remaining processes.

11 *Pressing* The cheese is pressed lightly to ensure that all the whey is removed. The moulds are then put in a powerful horizontal press, sprayed with hot water and left for 24 hours under a pressure of 2-5 tonnes. The hot water produces a thin hard rind which improves the keeping quality.

12 *Ripening* The pressed cheese is date-stamped and taken to the ripening room which is kept at a temperature of 10°C in a very humid atmosphere. This prevents the cheese shrinking due to evaporation. The cheeses are turned frequently to ensure an even ripening. During this ripening period, changes take place in the cheese. The cheese becomes firm in texture, and the rind more pronounced. The flavour of the cheese develops. The ripening time is dependent on the flavour and texture required. For example, a mild cheddar is ripened for three to five months, mature cheddar is ripened for up to a year.

Varieties of hard cheeses

Variations in the processing affect the texture and flavour of the cheese produced.

The factors which affect the texture include:
- the degree of acidity developed in the curd;
- the temperature to which the curd is heated;
- the amount of pressure put on the cheese;
- the length of time in the press.

The greater the acidity, temperature and pressing time, the harder the texture produced.

The factors that affect the flavour include:
- the amount of pressure. Lightly-pressed cheeses have stronger flavours, because there is greater bacterial and enzyme activity in cheeses with a high moisture content.
- the ripening time. Stronger flavours develop with increasing ripening time.

Some cheeses have particular characteristics, for example:

(a) *Blue-veined cheeses*, e.g. Stilton, Gorgonzola. This is caused by a harmless mould growing in air spaces in the cheese. The mould is first introduced into the cheese artificially on fine copper wires. Blue-veined cheeses are usually lightly pressed and have an open texture which gives a greater chance for the moulds to develop. This is essential to give the special strong flavour of the cheese.

(b) *Cheeses with a 'holey' texture*, e.g. Emmenthal, Gruyère. The holes are produced by bacteria which produce a gas during the ripening stage.

(c) *Novelty-flavoured cheeses*. There are several types of hard cheese which are mixed with other flavourings during their manufacture.
- Rutland cheese is flavoured with beer, garlic and parsley;
- Cotswold cheese is Double Gloucester cheese mixed with chives;
- Huntsman cheese is layers of Double Gloucester and Stilton cheeses.

These types of cheese add variety in colour, texture and flavour to the types of hard cheese available.

(d) *Processed cheese* Processed cheese is prepared from a mixture of hard cheeses. It is made by finely grinding the natural cheese and then mixing it with certain salts, water and dried milk. This mixture is heated to 85°C and mixed to a smooth pliable mass. The cheese is then packed in individual portions, blocks, slices or cheese spread. Processed cheese is practically sterile and need not be refrigerated until it is opened. It will keep for a long time. Compared with real cheese it is expensive and in the processing the cheese loses its natural flavour and texture.

Buying hard cheeses

1 Cheese should be bought from a refrigerated display or counter. Specialist cheese counters have whole traditionally-shaped cheeses or blocks which can be cut to order. Vacuum packs, which have a longer storage life, are also sold.

2 Some varieties are available in mild, medium or strong flavours and can be selected according to individual preference.

3 It is best to buy small quantities which can be used within a week.

4 Make sure that the cheese is not dry and crumbly, nor wet or moist on the surface.

Examine the hard cheeses in your local supermarket.

How many types are available? Are they all prepacked?

Can you see traditionally-shaped cheeses?

Does any of the Cheddar cheese you see come from countries other than England? Where was Cheddar cheese originally made?

Fig. 8.1 Types of hard cheeses (see plate 10(b))

Country of origin	Name of cheese and county of origin	Characteristics
England	Cheddar	A golden or orange-red colour with a close firm texture. Large variety of uses. Good cooking cheese. It contains less moisture (maximum 39%) than other cheeses. About 10% is still made in farms and known as Farmhouse Cheddar.
England	Cheshire	White or orange red in colour with a loose crumbly texture. Red Cheshire is obtained by adding vegetable colouring. Blue-veined Cheshire is sometimes obtainable. Some Cheshire is farmhouse-made. Keen, tangy flavour which goes well with fruit and is eaten with cake and biscuits. Can be used for cooking.
England	Derby	A white or honey colour with a moist buttery open texture. The extract of sage leaves is sometimes added to give the green variety known as Sage Derby. Soft mild flavour when young but develops a tangy flavour when mature.
England	Double Gloucester	Manufacture is very like Cheddar. Pale orange in colour with a buttery open texture and a delicate creamy flavour.
England	Leicester	A rich orange-red cheese which is soft and crumbly. It has a rich tangy flavour and is used in cooking because it melts quickly.
Wales	Caerphilly	Lightly pressed and soaked in brine for 24 hours before ripening for a short time. White with a smooth close texture. Delicate, slightly salty flavour. Not a good cooking cheese.
England	Lancashire	White with a soft crumbly texture. Stronger in flavour than Cheddar or Cheshire. Toasts well, ideal for Welsh Rarebit and also used in sauces and to crumble in soups.
England	Wensleydale	Normally white in colour but a blue variety is also made. It has a creamy flavour and was first produced in the Middle Ages by monks of Jervaux Abbey in Yorkshire. Not a good cooking cheese.
England	Blue Stilton	To allow the blue veins to form properly, air is necessary and the cheese must be allowed to ripen very slowly. A white mould grows on the outside forming a wrinkled rind. Rich distinctive creamy flavour. Traditionally accompanied by port.

Country of origin	Name of cheese and county of origin	Characteristics
Denmark	Danish Blue (Danablu)	White with blue-green veins. Soft crumbly texture and a sharp piquant flavour. Table cheese and also used in dips.
France	Roquefort	A semi-hard, blue veined cheese made from ewes' milk. It has a strong, rich taste and is one of the most expensive cheeses.
France	Port Salut	A semi-hard cheese first made by Trappist monks in their monastery at Port Salut. The rind is strong but the curd has a soft rubbery texture and a mild flavour.
Holland	Edam	A mild yellow cheese with a firm smooth texture recognised by its coating of bright red wax. It is eaten in Holland for breakfast, usually cut into very thin slices. It is lower in energy value as it is made from partly skimmed milk.
Holland	Gouda	Similar to Edam but is softer in texture because it is made from whole milk. It is made in a large wheel-shape and has a yellow rind. The flavour depends on the length of time the cheese has been allowed to ripen and mature Goudas have a strong taste.
Italy	Gorgonzola	A semi-hard pale green-veined cheese. Strong, distinctive flavour.
Italy	Parmesan	A very hard cheese made from skimmed milk which takes 2–3 years to ripen. It is straw-coloured with a strong taste and is used a great deal in Italian cookery and served grated as an accompaniment for soups and pasta dishes.
Switzerland	Gruyère	A hard cheese also made in France which is made in wheels about one metre in diameter. It is pale yellow with a mild sweet taste and is recognised by the holes in the curd which are due to special bacteria which produce gas bubbles in the curd.
Switzerland	Emmenthal	Similar to Gruyère but with larger holes and a hard golden-brown rind. It is a difficult cheese to make and requires very good quality milk. It is made in even larger wheels than Gruyère (some weigh 100 kg). It has been copied in other countries including the USA. It has a strong flavour, is excellent for cooking and is used for cheese fondue.

Soft cheeses

The varieties of soft cheese are shown in plate 10(c). How many of these have you tasted? Find out the cost of each.

Soft cheeses can be divided into two groups:
- those that are *ripened* to produce stronger flavours, e.g. Brie, Camembert, Lymeswold;
- the *unripened* cheeses which have a milder flavour. The cheeses in this group must be eaten soon after manufacture as they do not keep well, e.g. curd cheese, cottage cheese, cream cheese.

Ripened soft cheeses

Ripened soft cheeses are made from whole milk. The milk is not soured by a starter culture but acidity is allowed to develop slowly and naturally. The curds are very moist as the whey is drained without any pressure being applied. Cheeses of this group are usually small or flat with large surface areas. During the ripening period special types of mould are introduced and allowed to grow on the surface. Enzymes produced by these moulds alter and soften the curd producing the characteristic texture and flavour of the cheese. The traditional shapes allow the whole cheese to ripen quickly before the outside starts to deteriorate.

To be fully appreciated these cheeses must be chosen carefully as they are in perfect condition only for a very short time. They are soon over-ripe, becoming runny and developing a strong unpleasant smell of ammonia. They deteriorate rapidly because of the moisture present. The best-known varieties, Brie and Camembert, are imported from France. They are so popular that they are also produced in other countries, including Germany and the USA.

Camembert is France's most popular cheese. It is available in wooden boxes 10 cm across. It should feel just soft to the touch when pressed in the centre. If it does not appear to fill the box the centre may be runny and the cheese over-ripe. It does not ripen well after cutting. Foil-wrapped wedges are also available.

Brie is a large flat cheese which is usually cut in wedges. The curd should look smooth and creamy but not runny (over-ripe) or white in the centre (under-ripe).

Many other interesting cheeses in this group can be found in delicatessens and specialist cheese shops. How many varieties of soft cheese can you find in one shop?

Look at the varieties available.

Is the Brie cheese in good condition?

Are any of these cheeses 'blue'?

Are any made from goat's milk?

What can you find out about Lymeswold cheese?

Unripened soft cheeses

Unripened soft cheeses are usually eaten in the country where they are produced, as they must be eaten fresh. The three main varieties are curd cheese, cottage cheese and cream cheese.

Curd cheese is made from whole, partially skimmed or skimmed milk. The texture of the cheese depends on the fat content of the milk used. The coagulation of the curd is brought about by natural souring of the milk. Sometimes the process may be aided by the addition of a starter which controls the fermentation. The curd is drained slowly without any pressure and the cheese has a high moisture content (50-70%). It is also rich in protein and easily digested. As it is so moist, yeast and moulds from the air grow on the surface after a few days and the flavour becomes unpleasant. It must therefore be eaten soon after it has been manufactured. It is used to make cheesecakes.

Cottage cheese was originally developed in America, but it is now a popular cheese in many countries. It is made from pasteurised skimmed milk which is inoculated with a special starter to give it a slightly acid flavour and develop the curd. The curd formed is cut up into small cubes and heated slowly to develop the right texture. The curd is then washed with cool water and drained to remove the whey. Cream and salt are then added and the cheese is packed in cartons and stored under refrigeration.

Cottage cheese has a low energy value but is rich in protein, and it is a very good food for people on slimming diets. It is also used in recipes for cheesecakes. The mild flavour of the cheese goes well with fruit and chives. Many varieties are available.

Cream cheese is a soft cheese made from cream instead of milk. The cream used may be single or double cream which is heated and then either allowed to sour naturally or inoculated with a starter. The curd is drained in muslin and salt may be added. It is usually moulded into small cylindrical, square or round shapes. It is sold in small quantities because it does not keep well. The cheese has a buttery texture as it contains a high proportion of milk fat which gives it a creamy appearance. It is used for cheesecakes, dips and sandwich fillings.

These three varieties of unripened soft cheeses are produced in Britain. They are sold in cartons, which should be date-stamped to indicate their freshness.

France and Italy produce some well-known soft cheeses which are sometimes exported. For example:
- Gervais and Boursin (both French)
- Mozzarella (Italian) used to be made from buffalo's milk but is now usually made from cow's milk. It is excellent for cooking lasagne and pizza, for instance.
- Ricotta (also Italian) is rather like cottage cheese, but smoother in texture. It also gives a good flavour to pasta dishes.

Experiment to investigate the conditions for making curd cheese

Ingredients
500 ml pasteurised milk
Large lemon
Salt

Method
1 Warm milk in saucepan to 38°C.
2 Add lemon juice to warm milk. Leave to stand 2 minutes.
3 Note the changes you see taking place.
4 Test the pH of the mixture.
5 Strain the mixture through muslin in a sieve or colander for 30–40 minutes.
6 Add salt to the cheese, and wrap in film. Chill in refrigerator.
7 Repeat the experiment, using a solution of bicarbonate of soda instead of lemon juice.
8 Repeat the experiment using different temperature conditions.

Conclusions
1 What is the effect of acid or alkaline solution in the mixture?
2 What is the effect of different temperature conditions?

Composition and food value of cheese

The composition and food value of cheese varies according to the milk or cream from which it is made and according to the amount of moisture which is present in the cheese. Only about 50 g of cheese is produced from 500 ml milk. Most of the protein, fat, calcium and vitamin A of the milk remains in the curd. A large part of the lactose and some of the B vitamins are lost when the whey is drained off. Minor changes in the vitamin content also occur during the ripening and storage of the cheese.

When whole milk is used in the manufacture of hard cheeses, e.g. British cheeses, their composition is approximately one-third water, one-third protein and one-third fat. Figure 8.2 shows the difference in composition between Cheddar cheese and cottage cheese, which is made from skimmed milk and retains a high proportion of moisture.

Cheese is an excellent source of protein. An average portion (50 g) supplies about one-fifth of the protein required each day by an adult. It also supplies valuable amounts of calcium, phosphorus and vitamin A.

Fig. 8.2 Composition of Cheddar cheese and cottage cheese

Nutrient	Cheddar cheese grams per 100 g	Cottage cheese grams per 100 g
protein	26.0	13.6
fat	33.5	4.0
carbohydrate	trace	1.4
minerals	3.4	1.4
water	37.0	78.8
Energy value per 100 g	406 kcal 1682 kJ	96 kcal 402 kJ

Using food tables, calculate the percentages of your daily recommended intakes of energy and nutrients that are supplied by (a) 50 g Cheddar cheese and (b) 50 g cottage cheese.

Cream cheese contains more fat and less protein than other cheeses. Because it does not contain carbohydrate, cheese is usually eaten with a carbohydrate food, such as bread, which helps to make the cheese more digestible.

Give examples to show how cheese is often combined with foods rich in carbohydrate.

Which other foods should be added to ensure a balanced meal?

Uses of cheese in food preparation

- For snack meals, e.g. sandwiches, ploughman's lunch, cheese on toast, etc.
- for the main protein ingredient of a lunch or supper dish, e.g. cheese pie, macaroni cheese
- as a cheese course, served at the end of a meal
- for desserts, e.g. cheesecake
- for party titbits and dips
- to improve the flavour and nutritional value of many other dishes. For example, cheese is added to:
  (a) white sauce to accompany vegetables, fish, pasta or in a fondue
  (b) baked products, e.g. pastry, scones
  (c) pasta dishes and egg dishes, e.g. omelettes, soufflés

(d) *au gratin* dishes, i.e. those to be served with grilled cheese topping

(e) garnish dishes, e.g. soups, spaghetti.

Cooking cheese

Low temperatures and short cooking time should be used for cheese cookery. Cheese should only be melted to give a good flavour. Overcooking makes cheese indigestible. As the cheese cooks, the fat separates. The protein over-coagulates and becomes stringy, tough and difficult to digest. If cheese is combined with starch in the cooking process, such as with flour or bread, the fat will be absorbed by the starch. The protein may be digested more easily.

Cheese for cooking is usually grated or thinly sliced so that it melts and cooks quickly. Cheese should be added to a sauce after the sauce has been cooked. The heat from the sauce will melt the cheese. Cheese dishes should always be well-flavoured. Mustard, pepper or Worcester sauce may be used.

Types of cheese to use

Cheddar, Lancashire and *Cheshire* are firm, well-flavoured cheeses, suitable for grilling and flavouring sauces.

Parmesan cheese used in Italian recipes and *Swiss* cheeses are excellent where the cheese has to melt to a smooth, creamy consistency (e.g. in a fondue).

Cream cheese combines well with other ingredients and can be used in a number of desserts.

Processed cheese can be used for cooking because the processing helps to prevent the separation of fat during cooking.

Storage of cheese

Hard cheeses

Cheese must be protected from air, light and heat. If conditions are too warm the cheese becomes 'sweaty'. Oil and mould develop on the surface. The cheese should be covered loosely in aluminium foil or polythene wrap. Greaseproof paper is unsuitable as it will allow the cheese to lose moisture and become dry. Blue cheeses need air and should not be tightly wrapped. They are better stored in polythene boxes.

If a cellar or cold cupboard at a temperature of about 10°C is available it is not necessary to store cheese in a refrigerator. In most homes the refrigerator is the most suitable place for cheese. The cheese should, however, be removed from the refrigerator half an hour before serving to bring out the flavour. The very hard cheeses, e.g. Parmesan and unopened processed cheeses, do not need to be stored in a refrigerator.

Small bits of cheese or pieces that are dry should be grated and kept refrigerated in a tightly-covered jar to use for cooking. Surface mould is not dangerous and can be cut off and the remainder of the cheese eaten. Refrigeration only slows the deterioration of cheese, so it cannot be stored indefinitely.

Cheese can be frozen successfully. It should be frozen when in peak condition and wrapped in polythene in pieces which are likely to be eaten within a week once they are removed from the freezer. Some cheeses crumble very easily after thawing. The wrapped cheese should be removed to a refrigerator and allowed to thaw slowly for best results. Grated cheese can also be frozen successfully, stored in a polythene bag or box.

Fig. 8.3 Recommended storage times for hard cheese

	Type of cheese		
	hard	Parmesan	grated
larder	up to 5 days	1–2 months	2–3 days
refrigerator	1–4 days	—	2 weeks
freezer	3–6 months	6–9 months	4 months

Soft cheeses

Cream, curd and cottage cheese deteriorate quickly after ripening due to their high moisture content.

Fig. 8.4 Recommended storage times for soft cheese

	Brie and Camembert	cream and curd cheese	cottage cheese	cheese spreads	cheese cake
larder	2–3 days	24 hours	24 hours	2 weeks	2 days
refrigerator	1 week	1 week	3 days	1 month	5 days
freezer	up to 3 months	4–6 weeks	not recommended	3 months	2 months

Usually these cheeses have a 'sell by' date on their packets and should be eaten within a few days. They should be stored in a refrigerator in their original packages which are usually foil or plastic tubs.

Camembert and Brie may not be completely ripe when purchased and should be allowed to ripen at room temperature and then placed in a refrigerator, but only stored for as short a time as possible.

Cream cheeses and cheese spreads can also be frozen, as can cheesecakes made from these cheeses but it is not recommended that cottage cheese should be frozen even for short periods.

QUESTIONS

1 Explain the value of cheese in the diet.

Suggest a variety of ways in which cheese may be used in cookery.

What special points should be considered when cooking cheese?

Describe the digestion of cheese.

(London, 1979)

2 What do you understand by (a) a hard cheese (b) a soft cheese?

What are the main differences between the two groups?

Name three British hard cheeses.

Name two blue cheeses.

Name two well-known French soft cheeses.

3 Compare the nutritive value of milk, cottage cheese and Cheddar cheese.

Suggest ways in which the two cheeses can be included in the diet.

4 Explain the importance of cheese in the diet and state the main nutrients it lacks.

What points must be remembered when cooking cheese?

Name a savoury cheese dish which could be used as a main course and say what you would serve with it to make it a balanced meal for active young people.

Name two different types of cheese and say briefly how one could be used in a savoury dish and the other in a sweet.

(London, 1981)

Eggs 9

Eggs are one of the most nutritious, convenient and versatile foods. The most popular eggs eaten are hen's eggs, although the eggs of ducks, geese and turkeys are also sometimes eaten.

Egg production

For centuries egg production was a cottage industry. Farmers kept hens and fed them on household scraps; they would also eat anything they found as they scratched around running freely during the day. About 2% of eggs in Britain are still produced in this way and are known as *free-range*.

Egg production is now a very intensive industry. Farms specialise in either breeding, hatching or rearing chickens for poultry or egg production, as shown in Fig. 9.1.

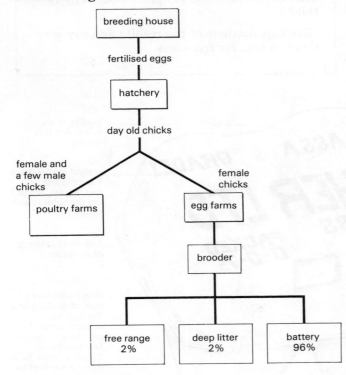

Fig. 9.1 Egg production

At the *egg farms*, day-old chicks are put into a specially controlled room, known as a brooder. The initial temperature of 30°C is gradually reduced until the birds have developed their feathers. The chicks are then reared in one of a number of ways.

A few farms specialise in the production of *free-range eggs* whilst some others rear chickens in *deep litter houses*. These are large sheds where the floor is covered with a thick layer of straw or shavings. Hens of the same age are placed in the building and all start laying eggs at approximately the same time. The hens are all removed at the same time, slaughtered, and used as boiling fowl or processed into chicken products. The building is completely cleaned and disinfected. Then the next batch of hens is brought in, and the process begins again. However, the majority of eggs are now *battery-produced*. There are some very large egg producers who have more than 100 000 hens. The hens are kept in wire cages in sheds where the temperature is carefully controlled. Food and water are provided through chutes in controlled amounts regularly throughout the day. Each hen lays about 250 eggs per year.

It is sometimes said that battery produced eggs lack flavour, but this has not been proved. Taste panels are often unable to distinguish differences in taste between battery, deep litter and free-range eggs.

Whatever the system of production, farmers collect eggs two or three times each day. The eggs are placed in a cool room to await collection by the egg-packing station. The packer collects from farms several time a week.

The grading of eggs

At the packing station the eggs must be **graded for** *quality* and *weight* according to the regulations of the European Economic Community (EEC).

Quality inspection

The eggs are 'candled'. Originally, this meant that the eggs were examined in front of a candle. Now,

113

the eggs are revolved in front of a strong light. The effect is similar to that of an X-ray. Defects in the shell, internal faults such as broken yolks and blood spots, can be seen clearly. There are three quality classes by which eggs are graded in the EEC. These are called class A, B and C eggs, and are shown in plate 11(a).

Weight grading

Under EEC rules class A and B eggs are graded from 1–7 according to the weight. Class C eggs need not be weight-graded.

Fig. 9.2 Weight-grading of eggs (EEC rules)

Grade 1	70 g or over
2	65–70 g
3	60–65 g
4	55–60 g
5	50–55 g
6	45–50 g
7	under 45 g

Packing

After grading, the eggs are packed into trays or boxes. Each box is clearly stamped and will give a considerable amount of information about the eggs it contains, as shown in Fig. 9.3.

Examine egg cartons from your local supermarkets.

Which supermarket had the freshest eggs?

Where were the eggs in the supermarket?

What was the temperature in the supermarket?

Is the week number helpful or would the date of packing be better?

Test for freshness of eggs in the shell

Dissolve 2 × 15 ml spoons of salt in 500 ml cold water in a jar.

Take a new-laid egg, an egg bought from the supermarket and an egg that has been in the kitchen for at least a week and lower each egg into the jar in turn.

Observations

Does the egg float?

Does the egg sink, lie on its side, or stand on end? If so which end is uppermost? Why is this?

Give explanations of the results and say why this is a test for freshness.

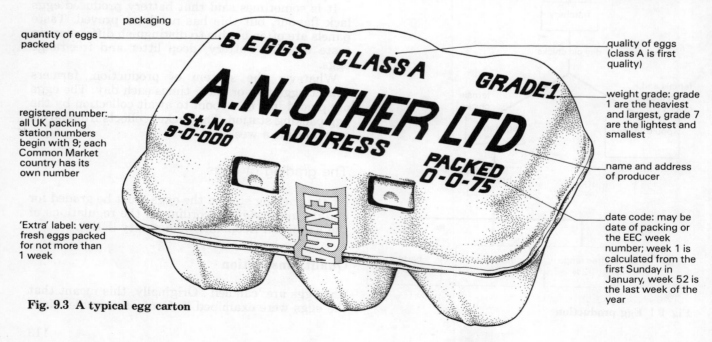

packaging

quantity of eggs packed

registered number: all UK packing station numbers begin with 9; each Common Market country has its own number

'Extra' label: very fresh eggs packed for not more than 1 week

6 EGGS   CLASS A   GRADE 1
A.N. OTHER LTD.
St. No 9-0-000   ADDRESS
PACKED 0-0-75
EXTRA

quality of eggs (class A is first quality)

weight grade: grade 1 are the heaviest and largest, grade 7 are the lightest and smallest

name and address of producer

date code: may be date of packing or the EEC week number; week 1 is calculated from the first Sunday in January, week 52 is the last week of the year

Fig. 9.3 A typical egg carton

Examination of eggs out of the shell (plate 11(a))

Break each of the eggs you used for the last experiment on to a small white plate and describe:

● the size of the air cell;
● the shape and size of the egg yolk and its position in the white;
● the area of the plate the egg covers.

Can you distinguish two types of white and what proportion of each is present?

Into which quality class would you place the eggs?

Structure and composition of eggs

An egg is designed to give protection and food for a developing chick. It is therefore a very nutritious food. There are three main parts: the shell, the white and the yolk.

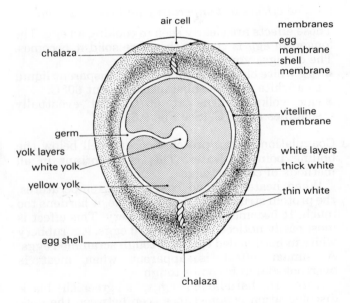

Fig. 9.4 The composition of an egg

The shell forms about 11% of the whole egg weight. It consists of two parts:

● an outer shell composed mainly of calcium carbonate;
● two thin inner membranes composed mainly of phosphates.

The outer shell protects the egg, or the developing chick in a fertilised egg. The shell contains numerous tiny holes, which enable a chick to breath. The shell is therefore porous. The colour of the shell varies from white to deep brown depending on the breed of the hen. Brown eggs tend to be more popular with consumers but there is no difference in the quality of the food value. The strength of the shell is important to producers as thin-shelled eggs break easily. The thickness can be controlled by correct diet and environment.

The two inner membranes lining the shell act as chemical filters to obstruct bacteria which may enter through the porous shell. As an egg cools after laying, the contents contract and the two membranes separate to form a small air pocket between them at the rounded end.

The egg white forms about 58% of the whole egg weight. It has two distinctly visible layers. The egg white immediately surrounding the yolk is thick and viscous. This in turn is surrounded by an outer, thinner, more transparent white.

Egg white is composed largely of protein and water, with only a trace of carbohydrate and riboflavin (Vitamin B_2). Although the main protein present is ovalbumin, other proteins are present, e.g. globulin and albumin. Proteins give the white its foaming property which is a very important characteristic for baking. (See plate 11(b).)

The egg yolk forms the remaining 31% of the egg weight. It is anchored to the membranes inside the egg shell by two rope-like structures known as the chalazae. These hold the yolk centrally in position. The yolk is separated from the white by a membrane known as the vitelline membrane. The colour of the yolk, which is due to the pigment carotene (vitamin A), varies from light yellow to deep orange. The depth of colour can be affected by the diet of the hen, but there is no difference in the food value of pale and deep yellow yolks.

Since the yolk is the main food supply for the unborn chick it is more concentrated, and it contains less water and more protein than the white. About 6 g of fat is distributed in small droplets as an oil-in-water emulsion (see p. 183). Some of this is combined with the mineral element phosphorus, forming substances such as lecithin, which give the yolk the important property of stabilising emulsions. Traces of cholesterol are also present in the yolk fat. Because the fat is finely distributed, it is easy to digest.

Many other minerals are also present in the yolk, for example, iron, magnesium, sodium, potassium, sulphur and chlorine.

The fat-soluble vitamins (A, D, E, K) are found in the yolk. Valuable amounts of the B-group vitamins are also present.

Fig. 9.5 Percentage of nutrients in egg yolk and egg white

	whole egg	egg yolk	egg white
water	65.6	48.5	87.7
protein	12.1	16.6	10.6
fat	10.5	32.6	0.03
minerals and carbohydrates	11.8	2.1	1.5
vitamin groups	ABDEK	ABDEK	B

The value of eggs in the diet

Eggs are an excellent and relatively cheap source of high biological value protein. (See p. 21). They also provide vitamins A, D and riboflavin (B$_2$).

There is a good supply of iron in egg yolk but it is absorbed by the body only if there is also an adequate supply of vitamin C.

Eggs are deficient in vitamin C and carbohydrate, but they are often eaten with foods containing these nutrients, e.g. boiled egg, bread and oranges juice, pancakes with lemon juice.

Although rarely eaten in western countries, the egg shell is edible. It contains many minerals. In some developing countries the shells are crushed and eaten mixed with other foods to form a valuable source of calcium.

> Using food tables or a computer program, calculate the percentage of your daily recommended amounts of energy and nutrients supplied by one egg (i.e. 50 g).

> Discuss the special value of eggs in the diets of:
> ● babies
> ● students
> ● elderly people
> ● slimmers
> ● convalescents.
> (Refer to chapter 2.)

The properties of eggs

There are three main properties of the proteins in eggs which enable them to be used in so many different ways in cookery.

1 Egg proteins coagulate on heating.
2 Egg proteins stretch when beaten and hold air in the structure.
3 Egg yolk proteins are good emulsifying agents.

1 Coagulation

Coagulation is the change from a liquid to a solid. In food preparation, protein coagulation is caused by heat. For example:
● the proteins in meat become firmer in texture (see p. 155);
● the proteins in milk form a skin on the surface (see p. 95).

Like all other proteins, egg proteins coagulate when heated. Coagulation is affected by the temperature used, the cooking time and the presence of other ingredients.

(a) The effects of temperature and cooking time

These effects are clearly seen in cooking an egg. The longer an egg is cooked the more solid it becomes. The changes you will notice are:
● egg white changes from a clear transparent liquid to a white opaque substance at about 60°C.
● egg yolk thickens at 65°C, and eventually solidifies at 70°C. (See Fig. 9.6.)

Coagulation of egg proteins occurs well below the boiling point of water. This is important in all methods of cooking eggs.

When heated beyond coagulation temperatures, the protein structure is denatured, i.e. it hardens too much. It becomes tough and rubbery. This effect is most easily noticed in overcooked eggs, e.g. rubbery white in hard boiled egg, and tough scrambled eggs. A similar effect is apparent when meat is overcooked and becomes tough.

Note: In hard-boiled eggs, a greenish black discolouration is sometimes seen between the yolk and the white. This is a deposit of iron sulphide. This deposit is produced from hydrogen sulphide gas, given off by the egg white on boiling, which combines with the iron in the egg yolk. It is thought that it is caused by prolonged cooking and slow cooking times. This discolouration can be prevented by using fresh eggs, immersing in boiling water, simmering gently for ten minutes and cooling rapidly in cold water.

(b) *The effect of other ingredients*

Eggs are frequently used in varying concentrations and with other ingredients in recipes. These factors affect the coagulation characteristics of eggs.
A firmer set is achieved, and the temperature of coagulation is lowered by:
- an increased concentration of egg proteins (for example, the addition of extra egg to a mixture);
- the addition of salt;
- the addition of acid.

A looser set is achieved, and the temperature of coagulation is raised by:
- the addition of sugar.

The effect of temperature and cooking time and other ingredients on the coagulation of egg proteins can be illustrated in the making of a baked egg custard. The following experiments show the effect of variations from the recommended method.
For other uses of the coagulation properties of egg protein, see p. 123.

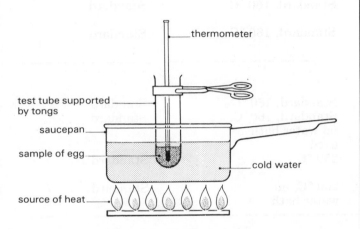

Fig. 9.6 The temperature of coagulation

Experiment: to measure the temperature of the coagulation of egg proteins (Fig. 9.6)
Put equal quantities of the following mixtures into three test tubes:
> lightly beaten egg yolk
> lightly beaten egg white
> lightly beaten whole egg.
Place a thermometer in each test tube. Support the test tube in tongs, and place each tube in turn in a saucepan of cold water. Heat the saucepan, being careful not to let the test tube rest on the base of the pan. Note the temperature at which egg yolk, egg white and whole egg begin to thicken, and finally solidify.

Experiment: to investigate the effects of temperature, cooking-time and other ingredients in a baked egg custard recipe

Procedure: a control sample is made using the standard recipe and method. Other samples with variations from the standard are prepared, and compared with the control sample.

Experiment 1   Control sample

ingredients: 1 egg
1 × 15 ml spoon sugar } standard
250 ml milk

method: 1 Heat the oven to 160 °C.
2 Grease the top rim of a 500 ml dish.
3 Lightly beat the egg and sugar together.
4 Warm the milk until it steams.
5 Stir the warm milk into the egg mixture.
6 Strain the custard into the dish.
7 Stand the dish in a baking tin with 2 cm of warm water, acting as a 'water-bath'.
8 Bake the custard until set i.e. approximately 40 minutes.

To test whether cooked: slip the tip of a knife into the middle of the custard, and press the edges of the slit. If no liquid oozes out the custard is set.

Experiments 2-9: Follow a similar procedure to control sample, with the one variation each time, as shown in Fig. 9.7.

Fig. 9.7 Experiments 2-9: procedure (see text)

Experiment	Variation in Ingredients	Variation in Temperature	Time
1 *Control	Standard	Standard 160 °C	Standard, approx 40 mins
Variation in ingredients			
2 Extra egg	2 eggs	Standard, 160 °C	Standard
3 Egg yolks only	2 eggs yolks	Standard, 160 °C	Standard
4 Extra sugar	2 × 15 ml spoons sugar	Standard, 160 °C	Standard
Variation in temperature			
5 *Cold milk	Use cold milk	Standard, 160 °C	Standard
6 *No water bath	Standard	Standard, 160°C, no water bath used	Standard
7 High oven temperature	Standard	250 °C	Standard
8 *High oven temperature	Standard	250 °C, no water bath	Standard
Variation in baking time			
9	Standard	Standard, 160 °C	Standard + 30 mins

Note: the results of the experiments marked with asterisks are shown in plate 11(c).

To compare samples:
When all samples are baked and cooled, each experimental sample should be compared with the control sample, as follows:
● Note the colour of the top surface.
● Describe the texture of the skin.
● Note if there are signs of shrinkage of the custard caused by evaporation.
● Describe the texture of the custard; is it even, or are small or large air bubbles obvious?
● Cut into the middle of the custard with a knife. Is the custard soft or firmly set?
● Is there any sign of water seeping from the texture of the custard? This effect is known as syneresis.

Observations
1 What is the effect of too high a temperature?
2 What is the effect of overcooking?
3 What is the purpose of a water-bath?
4 What causes air holes in a custard?
5 Explain the differences in the air holes observed in experiments 5 and 8.
6 Explain the differences caused by variation in egg, sugar and milk, i.e. experiments 2, 3 and 4.

2 Foam formation

A foam is formed when a gas is dispersed through a liquid. A very fine 'honeycomb' mesh is formed. Egg white foams easily.

Egg white foams

As egg white is whipped, air is beaten into the mixture. Initially, the egg white is clear, it flows easily and has large bubbles in it. As beating proceeds, the proteins in the egg white stretch, and the large air bubbles are broken into very small air bubbles. These are surrounded by the egg white film and trapped in the mixture, forming a foam. The action of beating creates enough heat slightly to coagulate the egg protein. This gives some stability to the foam. The mixture becomes stiff, opaque, white and glossy. The degree of stiffness of an egg white foam is judged by its appearance.

The quality of an egg white foam is judged by its density and its stability. These are important characteristics in food preparation, as egg white foams are used to lighten and aerate mixtures.

The density of an egg white foam is a measure of the degree of aeration of a foam. The amount of air held in the foam structure determines how effective it will be in lightening a mixture. The more air in the foam, the lighter the mixture will be. The density of a foam can be measured by weighing a volume of the foam in a small container, then weighing an equal volume of water.

$$\text{Density} = \frac{\text{Mass of foam}}{\text{Mass of equal volume of water}}$$

Note: This is a difficult experiment unless you have a very sensitive balance.

The stability of an egg white foam is the extent to which it retains its volume. If the foam is unstable, i.e. it loses air, then the mixture in which it is used will lose volume, and have a heavy texture.

The quality of an egg white foam is dependent on:
- the freshness of the egg white;
- the temperature of the egg white;
- the type of beater and the shape of the bowl used;
- the stage to which the egg white is beaten;
- any additions to the egg white.

Fig. 9.8 Stages in egg white foams (see plate 11(b).)

Stage	Description	Uses
Slightly beaten	Egg white foams. There are large air bubbles.	Clarifying, i.e. clearing soups, such as consommè. The frothy foam coagulates in the warm soup, trapping fine solids. Both are strained off, leaving a clear soup.
Rounded peak	White foam which is very shiny and glossy. The air bubbles are much smaller. Liquid separates out readily.	Sometimes used for soft meringue, i.e. pie topping.
Pointed peak	Very white fine foam glossy and smooth. Very small air cells. More stable foam. Combines easily into mixtures.	Most commonly used in cooking, e.g. meringues, soufflés.
Dry	Dull appearance. Mixture is no longer glossy. Particles are thrown off the whisk. Less stable foam. Does not incorporate well into other mixtures.	Little used in food preparation.

The method of measuring stability of egg white foams and the effect of these variations are shown in the following experiments.

Experiment: to examine the stability of egg white foams

For each experiment, use an electric hand-mixer (unless otherwise stated), beat one egg white to the pointed peak stage (unless otherwise stated) in a medium-sized mixing bowl.

Experiments 1-12 are shown in Fig. 9.10. Make the following observations on each sample, and compare with the control sample, experiment 1.

Observations
1 Note the time taken to reach the pointed peak stage in the foam formation.
2 Transfer the beaten egg white to a funnel standing in 100 ml cylinder.
3 Observe roughly how much foam is in the funnel. After 15 minutes, 30 minutes and one hour (if time allows), record the amount of liquid that has dripped into the cylinder from the foam. Visually, has the volume of foam in the funnel obviously decreased?
4 From your results, answer the following questions.
  (a) Which conditions give the most stable egg white foam?
  (b) Does the condition of the egg white affect the foam produced?
  (c) Does the type of beater used affect the foam produced?
  (d) How would you recommend the addition of sugar in making a meringue?
  (e) Do the results of your experiments support the general findings on p. 122?

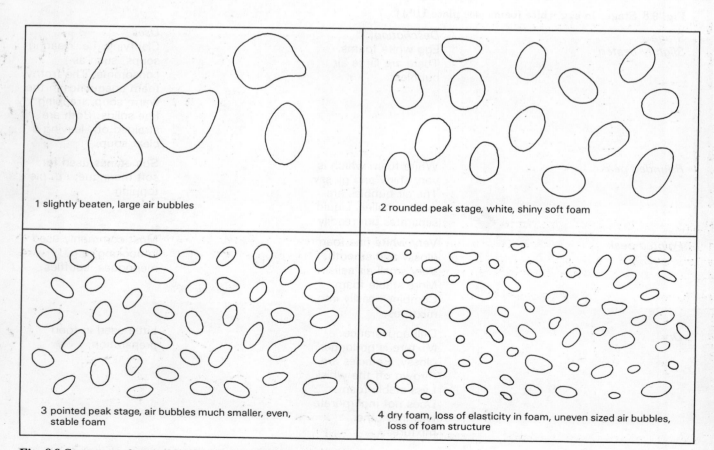

1 slightly beaten, large air bubbles

2 rounded peak stage, white, shiny soft foam

3 pointed peak stage, air bubbles much smaller, even, stable foam

4 dry foam, loss of elasticity in foam, uneven sized air bubbles, loss of foam structure

Fig. 9.9 Structure of egg-white foams (see also plate 11(b))

Plate 11

(a) Eggs, grade A, B and C

Class A (First quality)
Excellent internal quality and has three distinct parts: the yolk (visible under candling as a shadow only), a clear translucent white of gelatinous consistency and an outer layer of thin white.
Yolk central. A small air cell at the broad end of the egg.

Class B (Second quality)
Fair internal quality. The yolk flattening, the two layers of white mingling.
Yolk moving from its central position
Air cell increasing in size.

Class C (Industrial)
Fair internal quality. Rather liquid yolk, breaks easily.
Whites mingled.

(b) Stages in the formation of egg white foam

Stages in whisking egg white (*from left to right*)

1 Slightly beaten Egg white froths: large air bubbles. Used for clearing soups. **2. Rounded peak** White, shiny, soft foam, loses volume quickly. Used for soft meringue pie topping. **3 Pointed peak** Very fine, glossy foam: very stable. Used for meringues, soufflé, etc. **4 Dry** Overbeaten: dull, dry foam; less volume. Little used.

(c) Baked custards, showing the different textures

Effects of temperature variation in egg custard (*from left to right*)

1 Standard recipe Use warmed milk. Bake in warm water bath, 150°C Smooth, homogenous texture. **2 Cold milk** Milk not preheated. Bake as standard recipe. Texture pitted with small air bubbles. **3 No water bath. Standard recipe** Bake, no water bath, 150°C. Uneven texture, Large air bubbles. Moisture seeps out (syneresis). **4 High oven temperature. Standard recipe.** Bake, no water bath, 220°C. Very uneven texture. Large air bubbles. Moisture seeps out. Tough, burnt skin.

Plate 12 White fish and oily fish

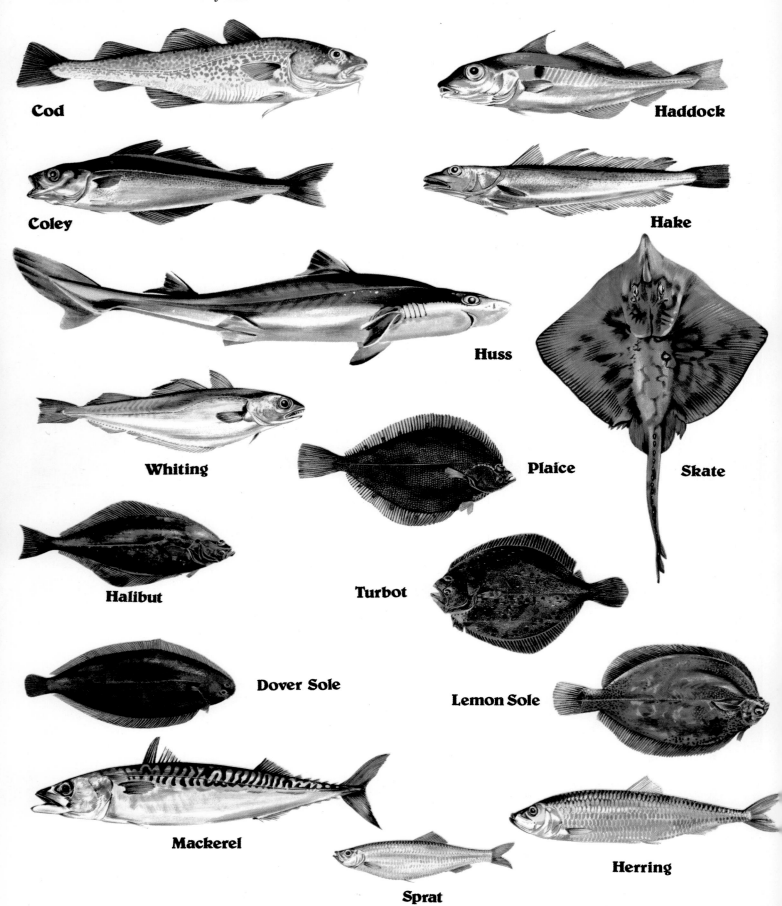

Cod

Haddock

Coley

Hake

Huss

Whiting

Plaice

Skate

Halibut

Turbot

Dover Sole

Lemon Sole

Mackerel

Sprat

Herring

Fig. 9.10 The quality of egg white foams

Experiment	Condition of egg white	Type of mixer	Stage of egg white foam	Additions
1 *Control*	Fresh egg at room temperature.	Electric – hand	Pointed peak	None
Variation in beating time				
2 *Soft peak*	Fresh egg at room temperature.	Electric – hand	Soft peak	None
3 *Dry peak*	Fresh egg at room temperature.	Electric – hand	Dry peak	None
Variation in condition of egg white				
4 *Stale egg*	3–4 weeks old. At room temperature.	Electic – hand	Pointed peak	None
5 *Low temperature egg white*	Fresh egg at refrigerator temperature.	Electric – hand	Pointed peak	None
Variation in type of beater				
6 *Coil hand whisk*	Fresh egg at room temperature.	Coil hand whisk (use wide shallow bowl)	Pointed peak	None
7 *Rotary hand whisk*	Fresh egg at room temperature.	Rotary hand whisk	Pointed peak	None
Variations in additions to mixture				
8 *Egg yolk*	Fresh egg at room temperature.	Electric – hand	Beat for same time as control sample	Add 1 × 5 ml spoon egg yolk before whisking
9 *Acid*	Fresh egg at room temperature.	Electric – hand	Beat for some time as control sample	Add 1 × 5 ml spoon Cream of Tartar (or vinegar)
10 *Sugar before beating*	Fresh egg at room temperature.	Electric – hand	Beat for same time as control sample	Add 2 × 15 ml spoon castor sugar before whisking
11 *Sugar at soft peak stage*	Fresh egg at room temperature.	Electric – hand	Beat for same time as control sample	Add 2 × 15 ml spoon castor sugar at the soft peak stage
12 *Sugar after beating*	Fresh egg at room temperature.	Electric – hand	Beat for same time as control sample	Fold in 2 × 15 ml spoon castor sugar at the pointed peak stage

It has been found that:
- foam formation takes longest by hand-beater;
- foam stability increases with beating time until the pointed peak stage, but then decreases with further beating;
- acidity increases foam stability. The action of acid on egg white is to weaken the elasticity of the protein structure. This allows the foam to stretch more.
- sugar delays foam formation, and produces a heavier texture;
- oils prevent true foam formation.

Do the results of your experiments support these findings?

The effect of heat on an egg white foam
Frequently egg white foams are included in recipes that are baked, e.g. meringues, hot soufflés. On initial heating, the air trapped inside the foam will expand. This increases the volume of foam. On further heating, the proteins in the egg white coagulate, solidifying the fine mesh structure. This gives the very light texture characteristic of mixtures containing an egg white foam.

For use of egg white foams in food preparation, see p. 123.

3 Emulsification: the use of egg yolk as an emulsifier

An emulsion is formed when two immiscible liquids, i.e. liquids that will not normally mix, are mixed together (see pp. 182-183). Water and oil are frequently used together in food preparation. To achieve an emulsion, vigorous agitation is needed (e.g. mixing of an oil-and-vinegar dressing). However, this mixing is only temporary. To maintain a stable emulsion, e.g. in the manufacture of margarine (see p. 189), in the mixing of a rich cake mixture, or in the making of a mayonnaise the addition of an emulsifier is necessary.

Emulsifiers are used in both water-in-oil (w/o), and in oil-in-water (o/w) emulsions (see p. 183). Molecules of the emulsifier surround droplets of the dispersed liquid. This lowers the surface tension between the two liquids, enabling them to combine and form a stable emulsion.

Egg yolk is the most important of the emulsifiers used in domestic cookery because it contains a high proportion of the emulsifier, lecithin. Other emulsifiers used in food preparation in the home are salt, pepper, mustard. Commercially, glycerol monostearate is frequently used.

The ability of egg yolk to emulsify oil and water mixtures is used in rich cake mixtures (see p. 224), and in making mayonnaise.

Experiment: to investigate the stabilising power of some emulsifiers
Prepare four test tubes. Into each one, put 3 ml of cooking oil and 3 ml of vinegar.

Sample 1 This is the control sample.
Sample 2 Add half an egg yolk.
Sample 3 Add 1 × 2.5 ml spoon salt.
Sample 4 Add 1 × 2.5 ml spoon glycerol monostearate, if available.

Cork each test tube. Shake all four tubes vigorously at the same time. Place in a test tube rack. Note the time. Watch carefully and note the time at which each emulsion breaks down into two layers.

Comment on the stability of these emulsions.

Experiment: to investigate the most suitable conditions for making mayonnaise
Experiment 1: control sample
ingredients:

1 egg yolk
250 ml cooking oil } all at room
20 ml vinegar   temperature

method:
1 Put the egg yolk into a small bowl. Beat it with a small wooden spoon or whisk.
2 Add the oil gradually, two or three drops at a time. Beat vigorously.
3 As the mixture thickens, add the vinegar a little at a time to keep the consistency similar to thick cream whilst continuing to beat in the oil.

Experiment 2
Use ingredients at refrigerator temperature. Repeat procedure as control.
Experiment 3
Add all ingredients initially. Beat vigorously.
Experiment 4
Stir ingredients together.

Comment on the results of these experiments, compared with the control sample. What are the most appropriate conditions for making mayonnaise?

The uses of eggs in food preparation

Eggs are very versatile and are extensively used in cookery. They enrich food by adding protein and other nutrients. They improve the colour and flavour of many dishes.

Eggs are used in many ways in cookery because of their various properties:
- they coagulate when heated;
- they have the ability to form a foam;
- they are good emulsifying agents.

1 Coagulation (see p. 116)

The ability of egg proteins to coagulate is used for:

(a) *thickening* When the mixtures are heated they are thickened by coagulation of the egg proteins, e.g. as in egg custards (see p. 117). Eggs have the ability to absorb large quantities of liquid. Some sauces and soups are also thickened in this way. In cake mixtures the coagulation of egg proteins helps to form the supporting framework of the cake (see pp. 219-226).

(b) *binding* Eggs are viscous; they will moisten and bind together a variety of mixtures, e.g. rissoles, croquettes, meat loaves. When the mixtures are cooked, the egg proteins coagulate, holding the food together.

(c) *coating* Beaten egg and breadcrumbs are used as a coating for many foods before frying. The coagulation of the egg on cooking holds the breadcrumbs firmly together, forming a protective coating. This maintains the shape, improves the appearance, retains the flavour and nutrients, and prevents fat from penetrating the food.

2 Foam formation (see p. 119)

The ability of eggs to form a foam is used for lightening. Whole eggs can be whisked to hold air and act as a raising agent for whisked sponge cakes, some soufflés and mousses. Egg whites whisked alone hold even larger quantities of air. This property is used in meringues and also where beaten egg whites are folded into other mixtures, e.g. soufflés.

3 Emulsification (see p. 122)

The ability of egg yolk to emulsify fat or oil and water is used in making oil and butter sauces, e.g. mayonnaise, Hollandaise. Emulsions are also formed when eggs are added to fat and sugar in rich cake mixtures.

Other uses of eggs in cookery

Glazing If eggs are beaten lightly and brushed over the top of pastry or yeast dishes before cooking they give an attractive golden brown glaze to the baked product.

Clarifying Egg whites can be used to clarify stocks, jellies, and home-made wines.

Eggs in the menu

Suggest ways in which eggs are used for breakfast, lunch, dinner, parties, and packed meals.

Describe a balanced meal including eggs in each example.

Which foods are added to provide a balanced meal?

Compare the cost of the protein supplied by two eggs with the same amount obtained from stewing steak, cod, Cheddar cheese and textured vegetable protein.

The importance of eggs in food preparation has led to a wide variety of equipment designed specially for using eggs.

Make a list of all the utensils you can think of for this purpose.

Storage of eggs

Eggs are a highly perishable food and will begin to deteriorate from the time they are laid, especially if the storage conditions are unfavourable. The changes that occur are:

1 Because the shell is porous, there is a continual loss of water from the egg which results in some shrinkage and loss in weight. This can be observed by the size of the air cell which becomes larger in a stale egg (see p. 115). Carbon dioxide also escapes through the shell and the egg white becomes more alkaline. Low temperature storage and a humid atmosphere keep these changes to a minimum.

Micro-organisms may enter the egg through the porous shell and cause extensive changes. The smell of a really bad egg develops when bacterial action produces the gas hydrogen sulphide from the sulphur in the egg protein. Food poisoning bacteria are very rare in hens' eggs but salmonellae sometimes occur in duck eggs. Duck eggs therefore should be well cooked and never preserved.

2 When the storage temperature is too high, water passes from the white to the yolk. The white becomes less viscous and there is a smaller proportion of thick white. The yolk becomes more liquid and the vitelline membrane is weakened. The egg yolk is flatter when the egg is opened. The chalazae weaken and the egg yolk is no longer held at the centre of the egg but rises towards the air cell.

It is important, therefore, that eggs are stored in conditions that will minimise these changes:

(a) Buy eggs that are as fresh as possible. Most shopkeepers keep their eggs in a cool place. The week of packing can be seen on the box (see p. 114).

(b) Do not wash eggs before storing them as this may damage the natural protective cuticle on the shell and micro-organisms may be absorbed by the water and enter the egg through the porous shell.

(c) Keep eggs in a refrigerator or in a cool larder. They may be safely stored up to 4 weeks. Store the eggs pointed end downwards in an egg box or rack. The air cell acts as a cushion between the yolk and the shell as the yolks tend to rise during storage.

(d) Eggs should not be stored near strong-smelling foods, e.g. onions, cheese, as they absorb odours through their porous shells.

(e) Use eggs in the order in which they were bought. If spare yolks or whites are remaining after cooking, they may be stored as follows:
- egg yolks may be covered with water in a screw top jar in the refrigerator for 2-3 days;
- egg whites can be kept for several days in a covered bowl in a refrigerator.

(f) Take eggs from the refrigerator at least half an hour before cooking. They are then less likely to crack when boiled, the whites are easier to whip and they can emulsify the fat more easily in cake-making.

QUESTIONS

1 Why does:
  (a) the white of an egg become opaque and firm when cooked?
  (b) a dark green ring sometimes appear round the yolk when eggs are hard-boiled?
  (c) the yolk of an egg not remain in the centre of the white and possibly break when the egg is broken into a frying pan?

2 (a) State the nutritive value of eggs.
  (b) Why are eggs important when planning meals for the elderly? How can eggs be incorporated into other dishes to give variety in the diet of an old age pensioner living alone?

(JMB, 1979)

3 Explain why eggs
  (a) can be used for meringue topping
  (b) can be used as a coating for deep-fried foods
  (c) can be used to make mayonnaise
  (d) may curdle when egg custard is cooked.

4 With the aid of a diagram describe the structure of an egg. Explain the changes that may take place in an egg during storage. How should eggs be stored to keep them as fresh as possible?

5 Why are eggs particularly valuable in the diet of children? Describe ways they can be used to make them attractive in children's meals.

6 Write brief notes on the following:
  (a) the supply of eggs
  (b) the grading of eggs
  (c) testing eggs for freshness.

Fish

Fish is a valuable protein food. Fish protein is of high biological value and is very similar to meat protein (see p. 142). It is estimated that enough fish is available, all over the world, to supply about 10% of the total protein requirements. The actual amount consumed is much less. Fish makes up only about 1% of the world's protein intake.

Some countries, e.g. Norway and Japan, include large quantities of fish in their diet. However, the British have a tremendous variety of fish available, but eat less than any other country in the North Sea area. About one-third of the fish the British do eat is from fish and chip shops!

Most of the fish caught commercially comes from the sea, however some varieties of fish are found in inland lakes and rivers. These are known as freshwater fish. Trout are the only freshwater fish reared commercially in fish 'farms'.

Classification of fish

All fish, both fresh and sea-water fish are usually classified according to their physical structure and composition.
There are three main groups:
- white fish;
- oily fish;
- shell fish.

White fish (see Fig. 10.6 on pp. 132-3)

Look at Fig. 10.6 and plate 12. Find out the cost of white varieties. How many have you tasted?

Fish in this group are known as white fish because of the colour of their flesh, not their skin. Any fat present in the fish is stored in the liver. Only minute traces are found in the flesh.

There are two main types of white fish:
- the round fish, e.g. cod, haddock and whiting;
- the flat fish, e.g. plaice and sole. They have dark skin on the upper side for camouflage. The skin on the under side is white.

Most of the white fish are sea-water fish and live on the sea bed. They are known as *demersal fish*. They are caught by trawlers which drag their large, open, bag-shaped nets along the sea bed. Small fishing boats fish near to shore and return daily to port with fresh fish. The larger trawlers go further out to sea and are usually away for six to eight weeks. The fish are usually frozen at sea in order to keep them fresh.

There are a few freshwater white fish, e.g. pike, which are caught by amateur fishermen with rods and lines.

Oily fish (see Fig. 10.7, pp. 134-135)

Look at Fig. 10.7 and plate 12. Find out the cost of oily varieties. How many have you tasted?

This group of fish contains fat distributed through the flesh in the muscle fibres. This causes the flesh to be darker in colour than white fish. Unlike meat, fish never contains separate fatty tissue. The average amount of fat present is about 10%, but the actual amount varies from 8-15% according to the time of year.

There are many sea fish in this group, such as herring and mackerel. Most are found swimming near the surface of the sea. They are known as *pelagic fish* and are caught by drifters. The drifter trails a flat net, rather like a curtain. The fish swim into the net and are trapped.

Most of the freshwater fish that live permanently in lakes and streams are also oily fish, such as trout, carp and bream. Salmon and sea trout are oily fish that spend most of their lives at sea but return to the freshwater rivers where they were born to spawn.

Shellfish (see Fig. 10.8, pp. 135-136)

> Look at plate 13(a). Find out the cost of these varieties. How many have you tasted?

All the members of this group live in the sea. There are two main types of shellfish, crustacea and molluscs.

Crustacea have legs with partly jointed outer shells. They include crabs, lobsters, prawns and shrimps. The dense coarse flesh is found mainly in the claws and tail, e.g. in the lobster and crab. This flesh is not as digestible as other types of fish. Most crustacea are sold ready-cooked as they only require simple boiling.

Molluscs have harder outer shells and no legs. They may be bi-valves which have hinged shells like oysters, scallops and mussels. Others have shells in one piece like snails, cockles and winkles. Some molluscs are traditionally eaten raw, e.g. oysters.

Shellfish are highly perishable. They are best when purchased directly from the fisherman. They may be expensive at shops in inland areas because of their very short storage life. The consumption and demand for shellfish, especially shrimps and prawns, has increased since frozen products became widely available. This means that they can be exported and imported, e.g. frozen Norwegian prawns are available all over the world.

Preserved fish

> Look at plate 13(b). Find out the cost of each type. How many of these types have you tasted?

Many types of fish are preserved commercially. Fish is often caught at some distance from where it is to be consumed.

Preservation prolongs the storage life of the fish, both on its way to the retailer and in the home. A high proportion of the fish in our diet is eaten in a preserved form, either frozen, canned or smoked.

(a) *Frozen fish*

Freezing is an ideal process for preserving fish. Most trawlers prepare and freeze their catch at sea, when it is in prime condition. They return to port with blocks of frozen fish fillets weighing 3-6 kg each.

Each year an increasing proportion of fish is processed by frozen food manufacturers. The frozen fish products are available in a number of different forms:
- fillets, steaks and shellfish which can be prepared by any of the methods used for fresh fish;
- ready-coated fish to be cooked as directed on the packet, e.g. fish fingers;
- a large variety of more expensive fish dishes, which only require reheating, e.g. fish in a wine sauce.

Frozen fish is popular because it is absolutely fresh and does not need cleaning.

If the fish is caught and frozen at times when supplies are plentiful, frozen fish may well also be a cheaper alternative to fresh fish at certain times of the year. Regular supplies are available at a constant price.

> - Examine the varieties of frozen fish available in your local supermarket.
> - Compare the price per kg of plaice fillets and cod fillets (uncoated) with the price of the fish at your fishmonger's.
> - Compare the cost of uncoated and coated frozen fish fillets.
> - Examine a fish finger and weigh the amount of fish it contains. Compare the cost per kg of this fish with the cost of 1 kg of cod at your fishmonger's.

(b) *Smoked fish*

Originally smoking was a method of preserving surplus stocks of fish. Smoked fish have a stronger flavour than fresh fish and are now mainly eaten to add variety to the diet. Some, such as smoked salmon and smoked oysters, are very expensive delicacies.

Many countries throughout the world have traditional smoked fish, e.g. Germany and Denmark smoke eels. The most commonly smoked fish in Britain are cod, herring, haddock, trout, salmon and mackerel.

The fish must be salted before it is smoked. It is then hung on rods in an oven or kiln. Hard wood, for example oak, is generally used. Aromatic woods such as juniper and rosemary are sometimes added to give fragrance. The smoke is blown over the fish for varying lengths of time. The fish may be cold-smoked or hot-smoked:
- for cold smoking the temperature of the smoke must not rise above 29°C, and the fish are not cooked, e.g. smoked haddock and kippers.

- for hot smoking the temperature of the smoke is higher. The fish are lightly cooked by the smoke. They can be eaten without further cooking or heating, e.g. smoked mackerel, smoked salmon.

(c) *Canned fish*

The canning process is used for several varieties of oily fish and shellfish. The fish are packed in oil or brine. Some varieties are also available canned in a tomato sauce, e.g. sardines.

Popular varieties of canned fish are salmon, sardines and tuna fish. Mackerel, herring, anchovies, crab, shrimp, prawns and lobster are also canned. The canning process makes available varieties of fish not caught in local waters.

The canned products provide well-flavoured and nutritious meals. They are especially useful for snacks and sandwiches. Small-sized cans are usually available. This means that canned fish is a particularly useful store cupboard item, especially for the elderly.

Fish spreads and fish pastes are also available in cans and jars.

What are the varieties of canned fish available in your local supermarket?

Suggest recipes which make use of canned fish for main meal dishes.

How does the nutritive value of canned fish compare with that of fresh fish?

Fish offal

The only offal of fish that is eaten is the roe. There are two types of roe, hard roe and soft roe. Hard roe, or ova, is the ovary of the female fish, and the eggs can be clearly seen. Caviare is the hard roe of the sturgeon and is a great delicacy. Soft roe, or milt, is from the male fish and has a smoother texture.

Buying and choosing fresh fish

Fresh fish, sometimes known as wet fish, is usually purchased from a fishmonger who will gut, trim, fillet and skin the fish if necessary. Some supermarkets also sell prepackaged, portion-controlled fresh fish which is kept at a temperature of 0–4°C and remains fresh for three days.

Basic cuts of fish

The basic cuts of a fish are very simple and are related to the size of the fish and also the purpose for which it is intended. Fish are sold whole or cut into fillets, steaks and cutlets.

Whole fish

Small fish up to 500 g in weight may be bought whole, e.g. trout, herring, mackerel, whiting, plaice and sole. Larger fish, e.g. salmon, may be poached whole and cut into portions when served.

Fig. 10.1 Cuts of fish

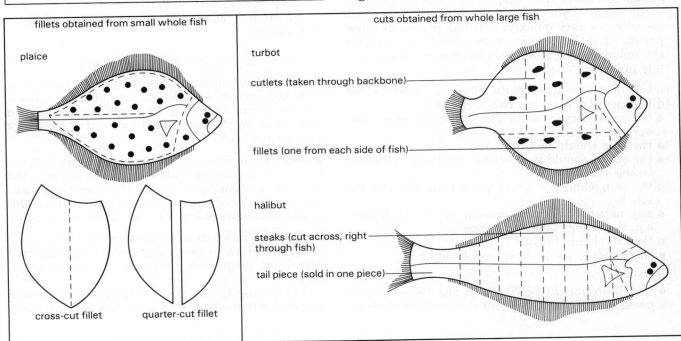

fillets obtained from small whole fish

plaice

cross-cut fillet   quarter-cut fillet

cuts obtained from whole large fish

turbot

cutlets (taken through backbone)

fillets (one from each side of fish)

halibut

steaks (cut across, right through fish)

tail piece (sold in one piece)

Fillets (see Fig. 10.1)

Fillets are cut along the length of a fish. The filleting is usually done by the fishmonger but may be done at home.

From a flat fish, e.g. plaice and halibut, four fillets can be obtained, two long fillets and two shorter fillets. Sometimes a whole side is removed as one fillet and is known as a 'cross-cut fillet'. Cross-cut filleting means that smaller fish can be filleted.

From a round fish only two fillets are obtained. Very large fillets may be cut into pieces and sold by weight.

Steaks (see Fig. 10.1)

Steaks are cut across, right through the fish either from a round or large flat fish.

Cutlets (see Fig. 10.1)

Cutlets are taken through the backbone in the part of the fish from which the gut has been removed.

Tailpiece

The tailpiece is usually too narrow to cut into steaks. It may therefore be sold in one piece from a large fish which has been cut for steaks and cutlets. It is usually cooked whole.

Qualities to look for when choosing fresh fish

Ideally fish should be eaten as soon as possible after it has been caught. This is sometimes difficult in inland areas. Fish should always be chosen from a chilled or iced counter display.

All fresh fish, especially oily and shellfish, deteriorates very quickly. Shellfish may cause food poisoning, if they are not eaten when fresh. Look for the following characteristics to ensure the fish you buy is fresh:

whole fish (Look at plate 8(a) and describe the differences between the two herrings.)
- the eyes should be bright and protruding, not sunken
- the gills should be bright red
- the scales should be plentiful and firmly attached to the skin
- the skin should be moist and a little slimy to the touch
- any natural colouring present should be bright, e.g. the orange spots on plaice
- the tail should be stiff
- there should be no disagreeable odour.

Fillets
- The flesh should be firm and the flakes closely packed together. (Limp and watery flesh is stale.)

- White fish should be pearly white in colour with no discolouration.
- Smoked fish should have a glossy appearance. The flesh should be firm but not sticky.

Shellfish
- The shells should not be cracked or broken.
- Shells of mussels and oysters should be tightly shut. A partly-open mussel which closes smartly when it is tapped is healthy.
- Lobsters, crabs and prawns should have a strong colour. There should be no unpleasant smell.

Structure and composition of fish

The structure and composition of fish are very similar to those of lean meat (see p. 141). The flesh is composed of bundles of short muscle fibres. These are held together by the connective tissue which is all collagen (see p. 142). There is no tough elastin present.

The muscles are divided into flakes between the bones. Some flakes, such as codflakes, are large and easily removed from the bones. Other fish, such as herring, have flesh which is difficult to separate from the bones.

Nutritive value of fish

The nutritive value of fish from the different groups varies. The average composition of white, oily and shellfish is compared in Fig. 10.2.

> What are the main differences in the nutritional composition of white, oily and shellfish?

As fish is usually eaten as an alternative to meat, it is interesting to compare the nutritive value of fish and meat. From Fig. 10.3, write down the main differences in the nutritional value of steamed cod and stewed beef.

Protein is the main nutrient provided by all fish, and it is of high biological value (see p. 21). Because fish contains a higher percentage of water than meat, the percentage of protein present in similar weights of fish and meat is lower in fish than in lean meat.

Fat White fish contains almost no fat. It has a low energy value and is easily digested. It is particularly useful for people on slimming and convalescent diets.

Oily fish has fat distributed through the flesh so it is more nutritious and filling, but not as easily

Fig. 10.2 The nutritive value of a variety of fish (per 100 g)

fish (flesh)	Energy value		Nutrient content											
	kcal	kJ	water	protein	fat	carbo-hydrate	calcium	iron	vit. A	vit. D	thia-min	ribo-flavine	niacin	vit. C
			g	g	g	g	mg	mg	μg	μg	mg	mg	mg	mg
cod (steamed)	83	350	79	18.6	0.9	0	15	0.5	0	0	0.09	0.10	2.1	0
plaice (steamed)	93	392	78	18.9	1.9	0	38	0.6	0	0	0.3	0.10	3.2	0
herring (grilled)	199	828	66	20.4	13 (average summer)	0	33	1.0	49	25	0	0.18	4.0	0
sardines canned in oil (drained)	217	906	58	23.7	13.6	0	550	2.9	0	7.50	0.04	0.36	8.0	0
shrimps (flesh only)	117	493	62.5	23.8	2.4	0	320	1.8	0	0	0.03	0.03	4.5	0
fish fingers (fried)	233	975	61	13.5	12.7	17.2	45	0.7	0	0	0.08	0.07	2.5	0

Fig. 10.3 Composition of steamed cod and stewed beef (per 100 g)

	Energy value		Nutrient content											
	kcal	kJ	water	pro-tein	fat	carbo-hydrate	calc-ium	iron	vit. A	vit. D	thia-min	ribo-flavin	niacin	vit.C
			g	g	g	g	mg	mg	μg	μg	mg	mg	mg	mg
steamed cod	83	350	79	18.6	0.9	0	25	0.5	0	0	0.09	0.09	2.1	0
stewed beef	223	932	57	30.9	11.0	0	15	3.0	0	0	0.03	0.33	3.6	0

digested as white fish. The fat is polyunsaturated, unlike that found in meat.

Shellfish are low in fat but any fat present is high in cholesterol.

Carbohydrate is not present in fish. For this reason fish is often served with food rich in carbohydrate, e.g. fish and chips.

Mineral salts The important mineral salts in fish are calcium and phosphorus, especially if the bones are eaten. Sea fish is also the most reliable source of iodine in the diet. There is very little iron in fish with the exception of sardines, tuna and shellfish. Potassium and sodium are found in all fish.

Vitamins Oily fish are a valuable source of the fat-soluble vitamins A and D. White fish do not supply these vitamins as they are only present in their liver oils which are used to produce vitamin supplements, e.g. cod liver oil. Small amounts of the B vitamins are present, but all fish lack vitamin C.

Extractives Fish contains fewer of the substances

known as extractives than meat (see p. 143). It is the extractives that create the flavour and smell to stimulate the flow of digestive juices. Fish is therefore milder in flavour. It is more suitable than meat for people on light diets.

The effects of cooking

The changes that take place during the cooking of fish are similar to those in cooking meat (see p. 155). The main difference is that there is very little change in the colour of the fish (except shellfish, which change from grey or brown to pink).

Fish is always tender and requires short cooking times. This is because the muscle fibres are short. There is also less connective tissue than in meat. All the connective tissue present is collagen which is converted to soluble gelatine by cooking (see p. 155).

Fish is cooked when its protein has coagulated. This begins at a temperature of about 60°C. As fish is generally cooked in small pieces the heat penetration is rapid. Therefore only moderate oven temperatures are required. The flesh is cooked when it falls into flakes when tested with a fork. Fillets and slices are cooked when a creamy white substance begins to ooze out between the flakes. It is easy to over-cook fish. If this happens, the flesh of white fish becomes dry and falls apart into V-shaped flakes.

Oily fish bake and grill well because their fat prevents them from becoming dry. White fish cooked by these methods require added fat, e.g. brushing with oil.

White fish boil, poach or steam more successfully than oily fish, which tend to break up. Boiled fish may be insipid in taste because some flavour is lost into the cooking liquid which should be reserved for an accompanying sauce.

All fish fry very successfully.

Frozen fish should be thawed before cooking unless it is already coated, e.g. fish fingers can be cooked from frozen.

Storage

Fish rapidly loses its freshness and develops off-flavours because enzymes that cause spoilage are active at low temperatures. Therefore fish should be used as quickly as possible. If storage at home is necessary, fresh fish should be rewrapped loosely in clean paper and a polythene bag and placed in the refrigerator. It should be kept away from other foods that could absorb the fish flavour. Smoked fish should be very well wrapped because of its strong flavour.

Home freezing of fish should be done only when the fish is known to be absolutely fresh.

Fig. 10.4 Recommended storage times: fish

Fish	Larder	Refrigerator	Freezer (- 18°C)
white	use same day	1–2 days	3 months
oily	use same day	1–2 days	up to 2 months
smoked	1 day	4–7 days	up to 3 months
shell	use same day	1–2 days	1 month
cooked	use same day	1–2 days	2 months

Why is frying the most popular method of cooking white fish?

Suggest menus including (a) white fish, (b) oily fish, adding ingredients to ensure the meal is well balanced.

What nutrients have you added to the fish?

What are traditional accompaniments for fish?

Give reasons for their use.

Make a list of the ways in which fish can be used in the menu.

Using food tables, calculate the percentage of your daily recommended amounts of energy and nutrients supplied by (a) 100 g plaice (b) 200 g cod fried in batter (c) 100 g herring. Comment on the nutritive value of these portions.

Fig. 10.5 Types of smoked fish (see plate 13(b))

Name	Points of interest	Uses in cookery
herring 1 kipper	A most popular smoked fish, bought in many varieties. The herrings are split and steeped in brine and then cold-smoked over wood chips. Different flavours of kippers depend on the wood used. Kippers can be bought with the bone in, ready-boned or in 'boil in the bag' packs either fresh or frozen.	Fresh kippers need only stand in boiling water for 10 mins to be cooked. Can also be grilled or fried but has a powerful smell. Can be wrapped in foil before cooking. Cooked kippers make excellent pâté. Raw kipper fillets can be served as a starter.
2 buckling	A whole smoked herring. It is hot-smoked for longer than the kipper, so flesh is lightly cooked. More difficult to find and less popular than kippers.	No cooking required. Usually filleted. Served as a starter or with a salad.
3 bloater	The bloater is a whole herring, dry-salted and lightly smoked. Does not keep as well as other types of smoked herring; should be served within 24 hours of buying.	Grill or fry. Bloater paste is made by mixing the boned bloater with butter.
mackerel	Prepared rather like a buckling and has a very good rich flavour.	No cooking required. Filleted and served with a mustard or horseradish sauce. Makes an excellent pâté.
haddock	Haddock have the head removed, are split, flattened and gutted before being soaked in brine to which a dye is sometimes added; they are then cold-smoked. The best-known are Finnan haddock, originally coming from a village of that name in Scotland. Haddock fillets are smoked in the same way and are more expensive but easier to serve. Arbroath smokies are haddock that have been hot-smoked.	Poached in water and milk and water and served sometimes with a poached egg on top for breakfast or supper. Also used for kedgeree and in omelettes. Made into a mousse for a starter course.
cod	Always filleted. Soaked in brine (often with a dye) and then cold-smoked. Brighter yellow colour with coarser texture and milder flavour than smoked haddock. Cheaper than smoked haddock. Cod's roe is smoked separately and sold by weight in the fish shop or in jars.	Used as an alternative to smoked haddock for kedgeree and fish pies. Beaten to a paste with oil and garlic and served as a starter: 'Taramasalata'.
salmon	A side of salmon is dry-salted or brined then smoked using oak or juniper wood. Has a delicate flavour and soft oily texture. Starts to lose flavour after 12 days and is always very expensive. Now available already sliced in packets which can be kept in the freezer.	Thinly sliced, served with lemon and brown bread as a starter. Used for many cocktail savouries and in quiches, etc.
trout	Whole fish is gutted, dry-salted or brined and cold-smoked. Very perishable but are also available frozen.	Served filleted with lemon or horseradish sauce. Also makes good pâté.

Fig. 10.6 Types of white fish (see plate 12)

Name	Best season	Points of interest	Uses in cookery
Round white fish cod	Oct–April	Most popular and numerous fish caught in northern waters. Weights up to 40 kg are caught. Grey to olive green with dark blotches. Fine flaky white flesh. Usually sold as fillets or steaks.	Can be poached, steamed, baked, braised or fried. Widely used for fish and chips. Also excellent for fish cakes and fish pies.
coley	Sept–April	Medium-sized fish the same shape as cod but nearly black with grey markings. The flesh is coarser and greyer in colour than cod and the flavour is stronger. It provides an inexpensive alternative to cod. (Also known as coalfish or scuttle.)	As for cod. The appearance is improved if a coloured sauce or garnish is used to disguise the grey colour of the flesh.
haddock	May–February	Smaller fish 0.5–10 kg in weight. Recognised by black line down sides of body and a black thumb-mark behind head. Skin is grey-brown on top and white underneath.	Used as an alternative to cod. It is also available smoked.
hake	June–January	Long slender silver fish with a pointed face. Tender white flesh with excellent flavour. More expensive than cod.	Poached, steamed, baked, grilled or fried; serve with a sauce. Can be served cold with aspic or mayonnaise.
whiting	In winter	A small round pearly white fish which may be served whole. Green line down side of body. The flesh is soft and very digestible but deteriorates very quickly.	Very good for invalid and convalescent diets. May be baked or fried whole or may be filleted and poached, fried or served *au gratin*.
huss	All year	Sold with the skin and head removed, cut into fillets. White flesh with not very strong flavour.	Fried or an alternative for fish pies and fishcakes. Used in fish soups.
Flat white fish plaice	May–December	Most common flat fish. Oval in shape. Dark brown colour with orange spots on the upper side and white underneath. Weighs up to 1 kg.	Can be fried, grilled or baked whole. Fillets may be steamed, poached, grilled or fried.

Name	Best season	Points of interest	Uses in cookery
Dover sole	April–January	Most expensive of all flat fish. Oval with very rough brown skin. Weighs up to ¾ kg. Flesh is very firm in texture and is easily removed from the bones.	Fried, grilled, poached, baked or steamed. There is a large number of famous recipes for sole.
lemon sole	May–February	It is rounder than Dover sole with yellowish brown skin on upper side. Flesh is softer with not such a good flavour as Dover sole but it is a less expensive alternative.	As Dover sole.
halibut	July–March	Largest flat fish with long flat narrow body. Can be enormous but best fish is from young halibut. Firm white flesh with excellent flavour but usually very expensive. Sold as steaks or cutlets.	Grilled, fried or baked. Dry flesh, so is best served with a sauce.
turbot	May–July	Average size is 2–5 kg. Firm, rich, creamy white flesh. May be filleted or cut into steaks. Expensive fish.	Grilled, braised or poached.
skate	August–April	Scaleless fish covered with a viscous coating. Rarely seen whole but usually cut into pieces or wings. It has tougher flesh than other fish and is improved if boiled in water and vinegar before final cooking. Flesh is very digestible.	Fried, sautéd or grilled.

Fig. 10.7 Types of oily fish (see plate 12)

Name	Points of interest	Uses in cookery
herring	The average herring weighs about 150 g and is usually served whole. Fresh herrings are shiny silver-blue. They are in season all the year except March and April. *Rollmops* are boned herrings marinated in spiced vinegar. *Kippers, bucklers and bloaters* are smoked herrings (see p. 126).	Grilled, baked or stuffed and baked. Coated in oatmeal and fried. Soused herrings are also popular.
mackerel	Mackerel are slender, 150 g–1 kg in weight with a blue-green striped back and silvery belly. They are caught off the coasts in spring and summer but migrate to deeper waters in winter. The flesh should be very fresh when eaten. It is coarser than herring and very filling.	Can be eaten hot or cold and goes well with a sharp flavouring. They can be grilled, baked, fried, soused or smoked.
pilchard	Can be eaten very fresh but because they deteriorate very quickly they are usually canned in oil or tomato sauce.	Fresh: grilled or fried.
sardine	Named after the island of Sardinia where they are found in large numbers. Very common in Mediterranean.	Fresh: grilled. Especially good cooked on a barbecue as they do on the beaches in Spain.
sprats	Small sea fish rather like a herring but more silvery. Canned as 'brisling'.	Tossed in flour or a thick batter and fried.
whitebait	Young of herring and sprats mixed together and known as whitebait.	Tossed in flour and deep-fried whole, they are served as a first course with brown bread and butter.
anchovy	A small sea fish, usually canned in a spiced oil.	Used as a garnish on pizzas and other dishes because of distinctive flavour.
red mullet	The red colour is due to the fact that the scales have been rubbed and the skin has become red with blood from the fish. Flesh has a very good texture and flavour.	Grilled, baked or fried.
grey mullet	Found in fresh and coastal waters, it has a steel-grey back, striped sides and white belly.	Grilled, baked or poached.
salmon	Salmon spend most of their life at sea, only returning to their native rivers to spawn. The best salmon are caught in the rivers and lochs of Scotland during the season (March–August). Chilled salmon imported from Norway, Japan and Canada is available all the year but does not have such a good flavour. A silvery fish with a pink flesh.	May be poached whole and traditionally served cold with mayonnaise and cucumber. Can also be eaten hot with Hollandaise sauce. Steaks of salmon can be grilled and pieces of salmon can be baked wrapped in foil to keep in the juices. Used for salmon mousse.

Name	Points of interest	Uses in cookery
sea trout or salmon trout	Smaller than the salmon; also spends most of its life at sea and has flesh paler than salmon but pinker than river trout.	As salmon.
trout	Commercial fish farms for trout, where the fish are reared and fed in a protected environment, have meant that trout are more easily available. They may be golden-orange, green or grey. The rainbow trout is one of the most popular varieties.	Poached, deep or shallow fried, grilled or sautéed in butter. Usually served whole.

Fig. 10.8 Types of shellfish (see plate 13(a))

Name	Points of interest	Uses in cookery
crustacea shrimps	The smallest of the crustacea, usually sold cooked, when they are pink. (Uncooked shrimps are grey and should be cooked simply in boiling salt water with no other seasoning.) Because they are small, shrimps are tedious to peel but have an excellent flavour. They are also available ready-peeled or as potted shrimps.	Used for garnishes and in sauces. As shrimp cocktail and in party dips and savouries.
prawns	Larger than shrimps. Caught in the Mediterranean and the Pacific. Often imported and sold frozen. Fresh prawns are sold shelled by weight and by the pint unshelled. The largest prawns are *Dublin Bay prawns (scampi)*.	Used to garnish a number of dishes and in prawn cocktail or salad. Scampi can be deep-fried in batter or made into a variety of casseroles.
crab	Live crabs are grey-brown but they are normally sold cooked when they are brownish-red. Crabs are best in summer and autumn and it is important to obtain them from a safe, clean water area as they may be contaminated by dirty water. The crab is 'dressed' before being served; that is, the white and dark meat are removed from the body and claws. A large crab serves 2–3 people.	Used for soup and served cold with salad or in sandwiches.
lobster	Dark blue when alive, turns bright red when cooked. A lobster will normally serve two people. The flesh is removed from the tail and head; it is all white flesh, unlike the crab.	Served cold; there are also famous hot lobster dishes, such as lobster thermidor.

Name	Points of interest	Uses in cookery
molluscs oysters	Have been eaten by humans since Roman times. Oysters are cultivated in special beds. Normally eaten raw. Ridged green-grey shell should be tightly closed. It is opened before eating by inserting a special knife. They are usually bought by the dozen or half-dozen in their shells.	Served in the opened shell with lemon, pepper, brown bread and butter.
mussels	Smooth oval shell, blue-black. Mussels are cultivated in beds of clear salt water but 'wild' mussels are found in natural rock pools. They should be alive until cooked: that is the shells should be tightly closed or close tightly when the shells are tapped. After cooking all the shells should be wide open. Available in Britain from September to the end of March.	Very quickly cooked in a little water or wine with herbs and flavouring added. Served in the shells or half shells. Eaten with chips in France and Belgium and occasionally eaten raw.
scallops	A rounded shell with a fluted surface which is difficult to open and usually opened by the fishmonger (or may be removed from the shell and sold by weight). They have white muscle and distinctive pink coral.	Cooked with cheese sauce or baked or grilled in the shell.

QUESTIONS

1 (a) State two nutrients, other than fat and protein, in fish.
  (b) The structure of fish is similar to that of meat. Why then does fish require less cooking time?
  (c) Why must fish be coated before it is deep-fried?
  (d) Describe a method of cooking for (i) cod steaks (ii) plaice fillets (iii) a white trout.

(Scottish, 1979)

2 (a) Name the three main groups of fresh fish. Give two examples of each group.
  (b) Explain the main nutritional differences between two of the groups.

  (c) Which foods should be added to fish to produce a balanced meal? Give reasons for your answer.

3 What do you understand by the term 'preserved fish'? Describe three ways in which fish may be preserved. Discuss the value of preserved fish in the diet.

4 What are the important points to look for when buying and choosing fish?
  What are the basic cuts of fish? Illustrate your answer with diagrams.
  What are the main nutritional differences between fish and meat?

Meat, offal, poultry, game; 11 processed meats

Meat is considered an important food commodity because it is an appetising and valuable source of high biological value protein. In western countries, meat is often the focal point of a meal. As the standard of living of a family or a community rises, there is often an increase in the amount of meat products consumed.

Meat is defined as 'any part of cattle, pigs, sheep, goats, horses, asses or mules that is fit for human consumption'. This definition includes both the flesh of the animal known as *carcase meat* and some of the parts cut off when the carcase is prepared. These parts are known as *offals* (from off falls). They include the tongue, tail, head and feet of the animal and also some of the internal organs, e.g. brains, heart, liver, kidneys, sweetbreads and tripe. All types of offal are very nutritious.

The flesh of poultry and game is very similar in structure and nutrient content to meat. It is often served to replace meat in a meal and consequently it is also considered here.

Poultry is the name given to all domestic birds bred and reared for human consumption. The varieties include chicken, turkeys, ducks, geese and pigeons (see Fig. 11.14 on pp. 151-152).

Game is the name given to animals and birds that are hunted. The varieties include grouse, pheasant, partridge, quail, hares and vension. Because availability is limited, game is expensive and consequently eaten only occasionally. It is considered a luxury commodity.

Various types of *processed meats*, e.g. bacon, ham, sausages, pâté are described on pp. 158-162.

Production methods

Since prehistoric times, humans have hunted wild animals. As settlements and communities were formed, animals were slowly domesticated. For many centuries animals were reared in small farms.

Nowadays, modern *intensive farming methods* and large scale processing, distribution and retailing are used to supply the enormous world-wide demand for meat and poultry.

The present day demand is for lean animals with a high proportion of flesh to bone and little fat, so animals are now bred and fed specifically to produce a large number of the right type of animal. Because of controlled feeding systems, animals also reach the desired weight for slaughter at an early age.

The advantages of slaughtering young animals are:

- the animals are small-boned with little fat;
- the flesh is tender (see p. 142);
- it is cost-effective for the farmer. This means that overhead and feed costs are low, but maximum production is obtained.

The production of young animals on the farm is a continuous process, and is controlled according to the season, availability and cost of food, and the particular species.

(i) Cattle

Cattle are reared specifically to produce either meat or milk (see Fig. 11.1).

Beef cattle are cross-bred to produce animals with well-developed backs and hind-quarters as the most valuable meat comes from these parts. In spring and summer the animals graze out of doors as good grass can supply all their growing needs. In the winter they are housed indoors and fed on hay or silage, turnips, sugarbeet and kale. These animals produce the required weight (400-500 kg) in 15-18 months. However, some animals are reared entirely indoors and fed by the intensive cereal feed system with little or no grass or hay. They reach the desired weight for slaughter at 10-12 months.

Veal is the name given to the flesh of young calves. Some veal, known as 'Bobby veal', comes from calves under three weeks of age which have been fed

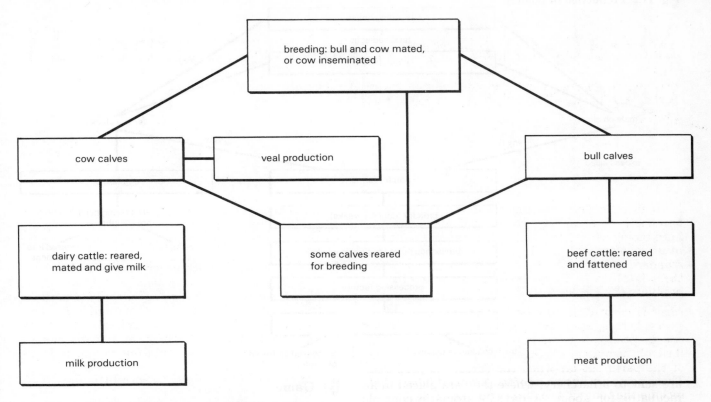

Fig. 11.1 Production of veal, beef and dairy cattle

only on milk. However, most veal comes from animals about four months old and weighing 100 kg. They are reared intensively and fed on a concentrated diet of barley, soya beans, ground nuts and milk.

(ii) Sheep

Sheep are hardy animals, and are kept out of doors throughout the year. Their food is mainly grass, and is supplemented with other bulky foods such as roots, kale, silage and hay with some concentrates in winter.

Lambs are slaughtered at 4–8 months weighing about 25 kg. Only meat from animals slaughtered before they are one year old may be called *lamb*. The meat from sheep older than one year at slaughter is known as *mutton*. All *New Zealand* lambs are slaughtered before they are six months old. Most lamb carcases are exported frozen in refrigerated ships. Hence, New Zealand lamb is available in Britain throughout the year.

(iii) Pigs

Most pigs are now born, reared and fattened indoors in hygienic, airy, damp-proof houses at a constant temperature of 15°C to 20°C. The aim in intensive breeding methods is that each female pig (sow) should produce two litters of approximately eight piglets each year.

The piglets are usually given a carefully controlled diet of cereal, protein, minerals and vitamins. They are slaughtered at four months, weighing about 65 kg.

(iv) Poultry

The most popular poultry eaten are chickens, but production methods are similar for turkey, geese and ducks. In many countries chickens are raised in small flocks and allowed to run free. These are called *free-range chickens*. In western countries chicken-rearing is a highly specialised industry, and most chickens are mass-produced.

Figure 11.2 summarises the production of poultry. From the breeding house the fertilised eggs

Fig. 11.2 Production of poultry

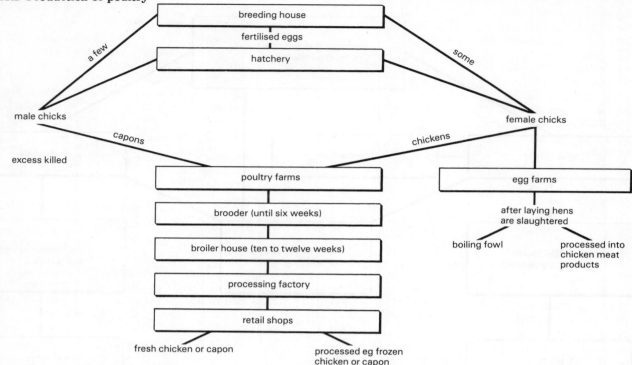

(v) Game

Game is the name given to animals and birds that are hunted, such as grouse and pheasant. Game is protected by legislation in Britain and can be hunted and sold only at certain months of the year, when it is said to be 'in season'. Frozen game is sold throughout the year. Some types of game are reared domestically like poultry, for example rabbit and pheasant.

are sent to a hatchery, where they are placed in an incubator for about 21 days. Automatic controls regulate temperature, humidity, ventilation, and turn the eggs every 4-6 hours. When hatched, the baby chicks are examined for sex. Some male and female chicks are returned to the breeding house to mate and produce more fertilised eggs. Some female chicks are transported to farms to be reared for *egg production*. The remaining female chicks which are to be reared as chickens, and some male chicks to be reared as capons, are transported to farms where they are reared for *poultry production*. Excess male chicks are killed.

At the *poultry farms*, the chicks are put into brooders. These are special rooms where the temperature is maintained at 30°C for the first week, then gradually lowered for the next 5 weeks. When the birds are sufficiently feathered, they are moved into a *broiler house*. Here the chickens are kept in conditions similar to a deep litter house, i.e. a large, well-ventilated room with sawdust over the floor. They are fed a specially formulated diet until an optimum weight is achieved at about 10-12 weeks, for example:

broilers and fryers	1-2 kg
roasting chicken	1½-3 kg
capons	2-4 kg

Then they are transported to a processing factory for preparation for sale as fresh or frozen chicken or capon.

Marketing methods

Beef, lamb and pork

When the animals are ready for sale, they are transported either to an auction market or sold directly to an abattoir. At an *auction market*, the live animals are sold by weight to wholesale butchers. Beef cattle are auctioned individually, the other animals are sold in batches. The buyer must judge the quality of the livestock from appearance only. It is a highly competitive trade as potential buyers bid for stock.

Animals bought at an auction are then slaughtered in an *abattoir*. The abattoirs in Great Britian are strictly controlled by law, so that conditions are hygienic and humane. It is important that the animals are rested prior to slaughter. This increases the tenderness of the meat.

After slaughter the blood is removed quickly. This is because blood, which is warm and liquid, is an ideal medium for the growth of harmful bacteria. The skins and intestines are removed. The only edible part of the intestines is tripe, which is described on the offal chart. Most of the other offal is removed, except the kidneys of pigs and lambs, which are sometimes left in the carcase.

The carcases are then inspected by a meat inspector who ensures that the meat is fit for human consumption and grades it for quality. Lamb and pork carcases are then split into two halves: beef carcases are divided into four quarters. The carcases are then:

chilled to about 5°C. This retards the growth of micro-organisms and also helps to avoid weight-loss by drip and evaporation from the carcase.

hung. Hanging carcases allows time for chemical changes in the muscles that increase the tenderness of the flesh. This is known as the *ageing* or *conditioning* process. After death the muscles of an animal become stiff. This is known as *rigor mortis*. The flesh is very tough at this stage. However, muscle fibres contain about 1% of a starch-like substance called glycogen. Gradually glycogen breaks down and is converted to lactic acid. The meat therefore becomes slightly acid. This acts as a preservative during the conditioning period. As acidity increases, enzymes act on muscle proteins causing them to soften and the flesh becomes tender. The time taken for this conditioning process is dependent on the type of animal:

> *pork* not hung (animals are very young, flesh is tender, *rigor mortis* passes off quickly)
> *lamb* 4 days
> *beef* approximately 10 days

After hanging, the carcases are ready for sale at a meat market to retail butchers. The butcher then joints the carcases as shown in Figs. 11.7, 11.9 and 11.12. Offal is purchased separately from the abattoir.

Poultry

Intensively reared birds, such as chickens, are prepared for sale at a highly automated processing factory. They are slaughtered and plucked. Chickens are not hung as the *rigor mortis* passes off very quickly and the flesh is tender. The heads and internal organs are removed. The off cuts, known as the giblets, include the neck, heart, liver and gizzard, are usually packed separately. The birds are then trussed. Fresh chickens are stored at refrigerator temperature after processing. However, a large proportion of the birds is frozen by the processor and sold by the retailer as frozen poultry.

Game

As game birds are available only in small numbers and have usually been killed by shooting, they are processed by the retailer. They are allowed to hang for several days to develop the stronger flavour associated with game and to tenderise the flesh. The time depends on the customer's preference. They are then plucked, gutted and trussed like poultry.

Composition of meat, offal, poultry and game

(a) Structure

To get the most palatable result, when choosing and cooking meat it is helpful to understand its structure and composition. The structure of poultry and game is very similar to that of meat, and can be examined in the same way. The structure of offal varies and is described on p. 149. Meat and poultry are composed of bone, fat and lean meat.

Bone

This is the skeleton of the animal. Meat is cut and jointed according to the bone structure of the animal. (See Figs. 11.7, 11.9 and 11.12.)

Fat

Fat is deposited:
- under the skin of the animal
- around the internal organs
- as globules of fat embedded in connective tissue in lean meat. This gives lean meat a marbled appearance.

The amount of fat varies with different breeds and their diets. Look at plates 14–16 that show the distribution of fat on joints of meat. The location of the fat varies with the cut of meat. Some cuts have a higher proportion of fat than others, e.g. the breast or belly has more fat than the back or leg of the animal. Fat protects the animal and, in cooking, it helps to retain moisture in the meat.

Lean meat

Lean meat is the muscle tissue of the animal. The structure of lean meat is very important because it determines the way each cut should be cooked (see p. 155). Lean meat is made up of thousands of long slender cells called muscle fibres. Muscle fibres may vary in length from 1–40 mm, and are about 1000 times as long as they are wide. Individual fibres can be seen only under a microscope.

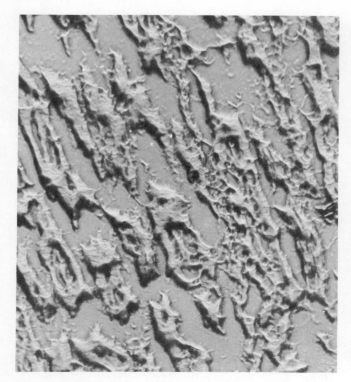 

Fig. 11.3 Fibres of (a) rump and (b) chuck steak

Look at Fig. 11.3. Describe the differences you can see in the structure of these fibres.

The fibres are arranged in bundles which are held together by connective tissue. This is a soluble protein called *collagen*. When dissolved it forms gelatine (see p. 151). Nerves, blood vessels and fat globules are dispersed throughout the bundles of fibres. Many bundles of muscle fibres together make up a muscle. Muscles are attached to other muscles or to a bone by more connective tissue. This is tough and insoluble and is known as *elastin* (often called gristle). It is slightly yellow in appearance.

The muscle tissue gives meat its characteristic appearance. The length of the muscle fibres is one of the factors that affects the tenderness of the meat.

Tenderness is a very important characteristic that determines the quality of meat. Tough meat is difficult to chew and swallow and the flavour may not be appreciated. Tender meat is soft, easy to chew and the flavour is readily detected. There are several factors that affect the tenderness of meat:

- the way the animals are treated before and during slaughter (see pp. 140–141);
- the meat must be hung for the correct length of time to allow the effects of *rigor mortis* to pass off;
- the amount and type of connective tissue present, and the length of the muscle fibres. This is the best guide to judge the quality of meat. As an animal ages, and in muscles that do most work, the muscle fibres become thicker and longer, and the amount of connective tissue increases. The meat becomes tougher. Even within the same animal the tenderness of the meat varies. For example, back and rump cuts, which have not carried the weight of the animal, nor done much physical activity, have short muscle fibres and are therefore tender joints. However, leg, neck and shoulder muscles have carried the weight of the animal and have been very active. These joints have developed longer muscle fibres with a higher proportion of connective tissue and are, therefore, tougher cuts of meat.
- the method of preparation, and the choice of appropriate cooking methods (see p. 155 and Figs. 11.6, 11.8, 11.10 and 11.11).

Look at plate 14 and notice the difference in the structure of the cuts of meat shown, e.g. shin of beef, rump steak.

Suggest reasons for these differences.

(b) Food value

The chemical composition of the flesh of animals is quite similar. Each muscle fibre contains water, proteins, mineral elements and vitamins, and substances known as extractives are dissolved in the water. Fat is distributed in globules between the muscle fibres, and on the outer surfaces.

Water   About two-thirds of the weight of lean meat is water.

Protein   The main protein in muscle cells is *myosin*, with some globulin and albumin. All the proteins are of high biological value (see p. 21).

Mineral elements   The most important mineral element provided by red meat and offal is iron. Iron is present in the muscle pigment, myoglobin (see p. 153). Iron also occurs in haemoglobin, which is a protein present in any blood in the meat. The iron in meat is easily absorbed by the body. Liver and kidneys are especially rich sources of iron. There is less iron in poultry than in the red meats. Small amounts of sulphur and phosphorus are also present in all meats.

Vitamins   Meat is an important source of the B group vitamins, thiamin (B_1), riboflavin (B_2) and vitamin B_{12}. Liver and kidney are particularly good sources of riboflavin (vitamin B_2) and vitamin A.

Extractives   If meat is boiled in water, soluble substances can be extracted. These are known as 'extractives'. Extractives are thought to be responsible for the flavour of the meat and give the appetising smell of meat when it is cooking. These help to stimulate the flow of digestive juices.

Extractives are removed from meat commercially and concentrated to pastes which are known as *meat extracts*. These may be used in soups, gravy and drinks because of their strong meaty taste.

Fat   The amount of fat present varies according to the age and type of animal and the cut of meat. Fat increases the energy value of meat.

Although the chemical composition of the flesh of various animals is similar, the nutritional value of meat, offal and poultry varies according to the proportions of the nutrients in each type, as shown in Fig. 11.4.

It can be seen that liver is particularly nutritious. Other types of offal, especially kidney, also have a high food value. It is also important to remember that the nutritional value of meat from different parts of the same animal is almost identical, e.g. 100 g of a cheaper cut (e.g. chuck steak) is just as good for you as 100 g of an expensive cut (e.g. fillet steak).

In some situations, the method of cooking affects the nutritive value of the meat. For example,
- if meat is fried, there is some increase in the fat content which increases the energy value;
- if meat is cooked in a liquid and the liquor is not served with the meat, soluble nutrients, such as proteins, mineral elements and B group vitamins would be lost.

Which important nutrients are in short supply in meat?

How can these deficiencies be compensated for in meal-planning?

---

	water (g)	protein (g)	fat (g)	carbo-hydrate (g)	iron (mg)	calcium (mg)	vitamin A (retinol equivalent) (µg)	thia-min (mg)	ribo-flavin (µg)	niacin (mg)	vitamin C (mg)	vitamin D (mg)	energy value kcal kJ
beef	64	17.1	22.0	0	1.8	14	0	0.07	0.17	7.3	0	0	266 1107
lamb	53	15.9	30.2	0	1.3	7	0	0.15	0.19	7.4	0	0	335 1388
pork	54	16.0	29.0	0	0.8	8	0	1.00	0.16	7.0	0	0	325 1343
chicken	65	17.6	17.7	0	0.7	10	0	0.04	0.14	9.3	0	0	230 954
liver	69	20.7	8.1	2.0	11.4	14	14 670	0.3	3.10	18.1	16	0.75	162 680

Source: *Manual of Nutrition*, HMSO

Fig. 11.4 Composition per 100 g (raw edible weight average cut)

Using food tables, make a bar chart to show the approximate energy value and protein supplied by 100 g of roast lamb, boiled chicken, stewed steak, grilled fillet steak, fried pork chop, fried liver.

How could you use this information to give advice to a person using a slimming diet?

Cuts and types of meat, offal, poultry and game: cooking methods

The carcases of the larger animals (beef, pork and lamb) have to be cut by the butcher into the sizes and shapes that people want to buy. Each carcase is jointed in a specific way to produce the characteristic cuts of meat seen in a butcher's shop. Look at plates 14-16 to help you recognise the different cuts of meat. It is important to recognise and understand how to use the different cuts. The choice is dependent on the budget, the method of cooking and the type of meal being served, e.g. a main meal or a quick supper.

The following charts show how each animal is jointed, and suggest a suitable cooking method. This will vary according to the part of the animal the cut is taken from. The effects of cooking meat are described on pages 154 to 156.

Beef cattle

Because the beef carcase is so large it is divided into four parts: two hindquarters weighing about 70 kg each and two forequarters weighing about 65 kg each. When the meat is cut into joints, there is a further loss of weight, i.e. bone, fat and drip. The percentages of usable meat, fat and bone are shown in Fig. 11.5. This leaves approximately 190 kg of meat for sale. This is a relatively low proportion of the initial weight of the animal (500 kg), and accounts for the high retail price of beef.

Fig. 11.5 Beef: percentage of meat, fat and bone

	% usable meat	% fat trim	% bone & waste trim
Hindquarter	68	10	16 + 6% kidney and suet
Forequarter	70	10	20

(Veal carcases are cut in a similar way to lamb; see Fig. 11.9, p. 146.)

Fig. 11.6 Cuts of Beef (1) (see plate 14)

An animal which weighs about 500 kg live will provide a carcase and offal which weigh about 270 kg.

Hindquarter (average weight) 70 kg

Cut	Boneless weight	Description	Cooking method
sirloin	7–8 kg	Tender high quality expensive cut. Some fat present. Sold either on the bone including the fillet or without the fillet or boned and rolled.	Roast.
		May be cut into steaks, sirloin or entrecote steak.	Grill or fry.
		Fillet steak, most tender expensive cut (only 1½–2½ kg in each hindquarter).	Grill or fry.
		T-bone steak, popular in America, on bone contains sirloin and fillet.	Grill or fry.
wing rib	4–5 kg	A joint which is part of the sirloin where the three hindquarter ribs are. Does not contain any fillet. Some fat present.	Roast.
rump	6–8 kg	Top quality boneless cut from the hip bone. Usually cut into steaks which are not as tender but considered to have more flavour than fillet steak.	A joint can be roasted. Steaks: grill or fry.

Plate 13 (a) Shellfish

Shrimp

Prawn

Lobster
(uncooked)

Mussel

Oyster

Scallop

Crab

(b) Preserved fish

shin

clod

neck

chuck
and
blade

brisket

ribs on
bone

ribs
(rolled)

flank

fillet

sirloin
on bone
sirloin
off bone

rump

top rump

topside

silverside
(salted)
silverside
(unsalted)

leg

Plate 14 Cuts of beef

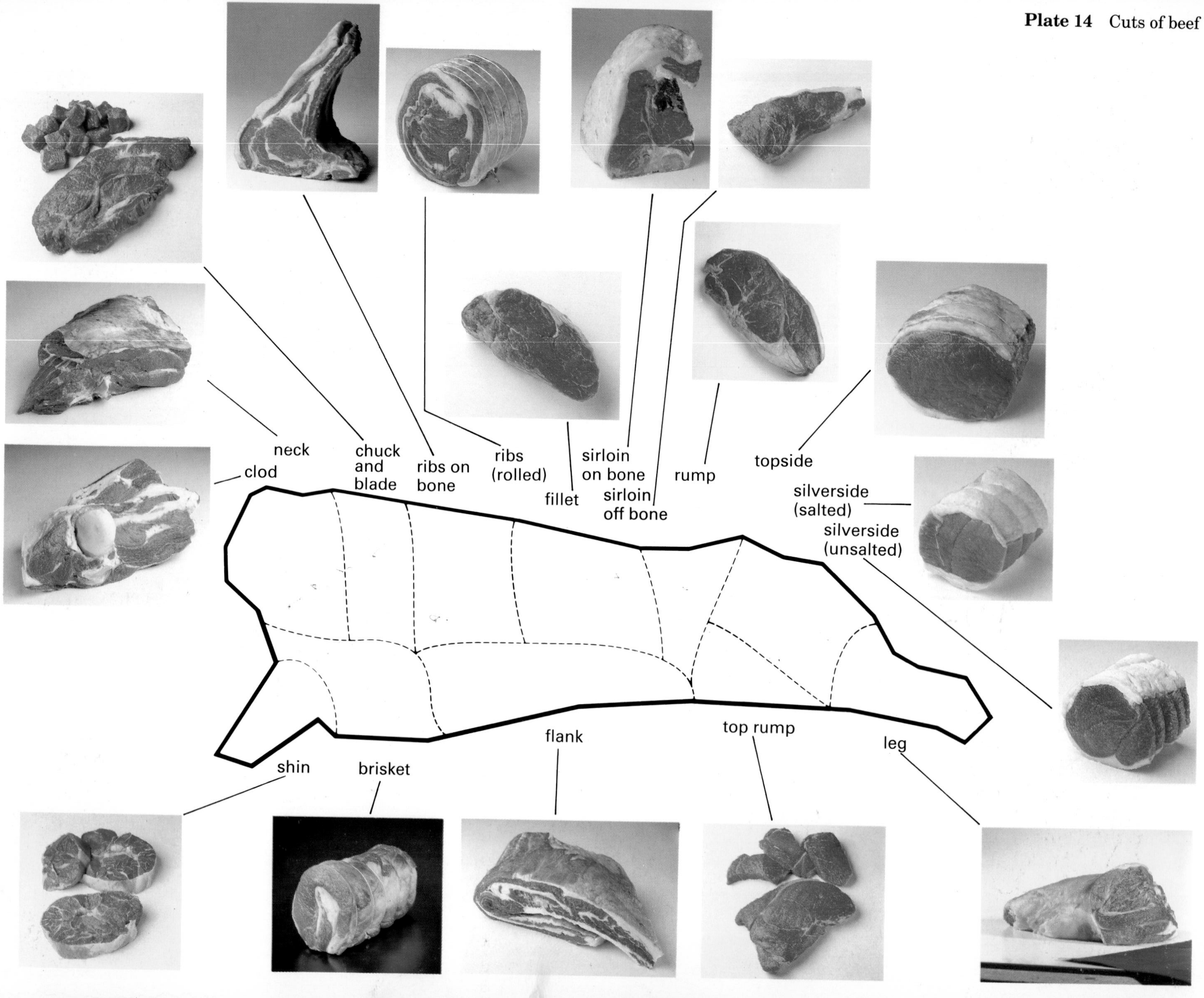

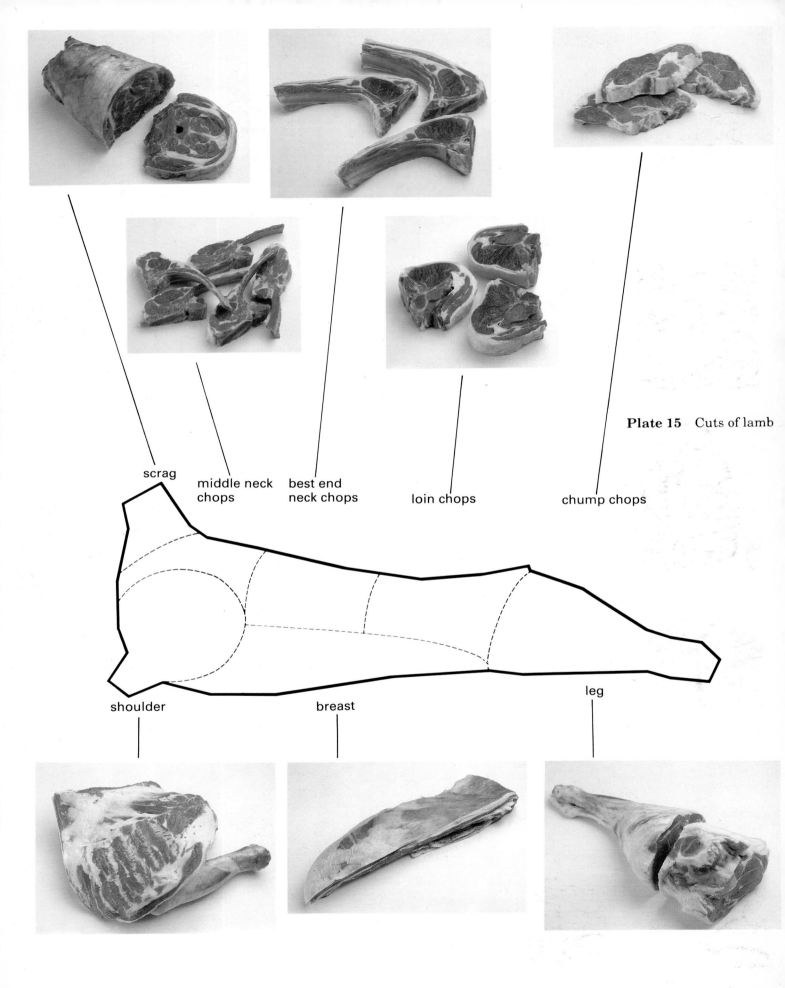

scrag

middle neck
chops

best end
neck chops

loin chops

chump chops

Plate 15 Cuts of lamb

shoulder

breast

leg

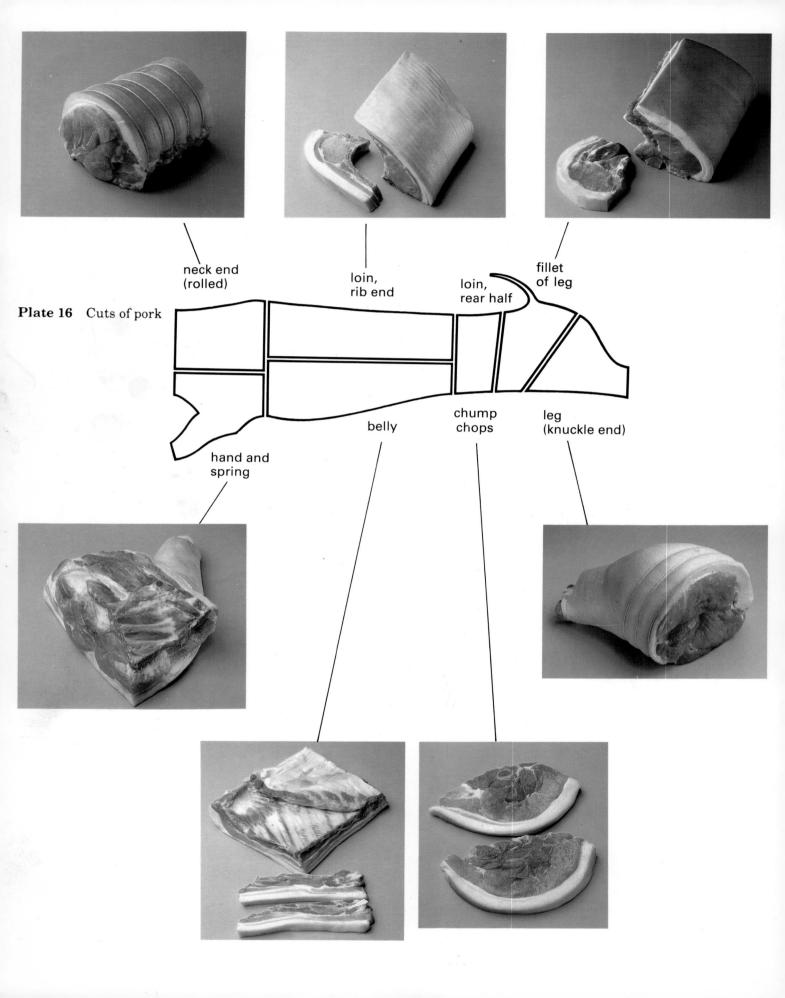

Plate 16 Cuts of pork

neck end (rolled)

loin, rib end

loin, rear half

fillet of leg

hand and spring

belly

chump chops

leg (knuckle end)

Cut	Boneless Weight	Description	Cooking method
topside	9–10 kg	Very lean boneless joint of good quality. Usually sold rolled with a layer of fat tied round it to prevent it becoming dry during cooking. Buttock steaks are sliced from the topside but are not as tender as fillet or rump.	Slow roast or makes excellent pot roast.
silverside	5–6 kg	Medium quality, contains no bone and is very lean. May be sliced very thinly and sold as minute or quick frying steak. Traditional dish of England, boiled beef is prepared from silverside which has been pickled and salted by the butcher. Silver-grey appearance before cooking becomes pink in colour when cooked.	Slow roast or pot roast. Fry. Boil.
thin flank	5–6 kg	Inexpensive cut sometimes inclined to be fat and has a coarse texture. Can be cooked on the bone either fresh or pickled. Boned and trimmed and sold as meat for stews and pies or made into mince.	Pot roast or boil if salted. Stew or braise.
thick flank (also known as top rump)	5–6 kg	Much leaner than thin flank, usually boned and trimmed and sold as joints. May be sliced and called 'frying steak'.	Roast or pot roast. Fry.
leg	3–4 kg	Coarse lean meat with connective tissue which needs long cooking to give tender meat and excellent gravy which forms a jelly on cooling.	Stew or pressure-cook.
kidney and suet	4–5 kg	Suet is removed from kidney and grated for use in stuffing, suet pastry, etc. Kidney is usually sliced, used for casseroles and in meat pies.	Stew or braise.
fat and bone removed in cutting	15–25 kg	Used for dripping or sold for by-products.	

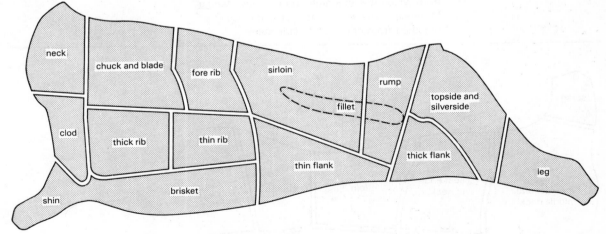

neck

chuck and blade

fore rib

sirloin

rump

topside and silverside

fillet

clod

thick rib

thin rib

thick flank

leg

thin flank

brisket

shin

Fig. 11.7 Beef cuts

Fig. 11.8 Cuts of beef (2) (see plate 14)

Forequarter Average weight 65 kg

Cut	Weight	Description	Cooking method
neck and clod	8–10 kg	Good flavour coarse stewing meat. Usually sold in cubes for stews and pies or as mince.	Stew.
chuck and blade	8 kg	Fairly lean medium quality. A piece can be used as a pot roast but it is usually cut into slices or cubes for braising, stewing, puddings and pies.	Pot roast, stew or braise.
fore rib	5–7 kg (bone in)	Prime quality joint with some fat. Sold on bone or boned and rolled.	Roast.
thick rib and thin rib	14 kg (bone in)	Medium quality meat, usually boned and rolled or cut into steaks for braising. Some fat present.	Pot roast or braise.
brisket	10–14 kg	Inexpensive joint coarse in texture which may have a lot of fat but has an excellent flavour. Sold on or off the bone. Requires long, slow cooking. May be salted or pickled for pressed beef to serve cold.	Pot roast, braise or boil.
shin	2 kg	Good for making stock, soup and brawn. High proportion of connective tissue. Meat and bone cooked together give jellied stock. Meat is also used for stews and pies.	Boil for soups and stock. Stew.
bone and fat (removed in cutting)	15–18 kg		
minced beef		Less expensive than cut up meat because small scraps of meat and some fat can be included. The butcher prepares mince from the tougher cuts, e.g. neck and clod. Mincing makes the meat more tender. Mince requires a shorter cooking time than the cut of meat from which it is prepared and is always tender. More expensive lean mince for hamburgers is prepared from chuck and blade steak.	

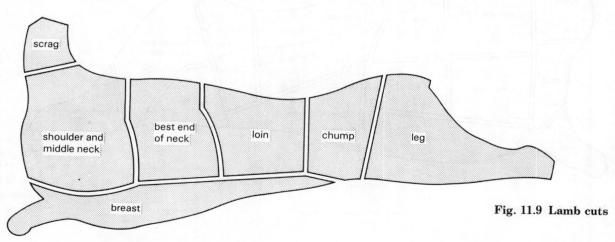

Fig. 11.9 Lamb cuts

Lamb

As lamb is a small animal it is easier to identify cuts and joints. An animal which weighs 25 kg live, will provide a carcase weighing about 17 kg. The wool and skins used for leather are the most important by-products. The gut and intestines are used for sausage casings and tennis racket strings. The butcher has only a small loss as most of the small bones are sold with the meat. He trims about 7% of fat and 1% bone from the carcase as he cuts it into joints. Cuts of lamb are shown in plate 15.

Fig. 11.10 Cuts of meat from a half lamb (see plate 15)

Cut	approx. weight	Description	Cooking method
leg	2 kg	Prime lean roasting joint. If large may be divided into two, the lower end known as the knuckle or shank end and the top as the fillet. Usually cooked on the bone, but may be boned and rolled.	Roast. Knuckle end may be braised or boiled. Fillet end may be fried in slices.
shoulder	1.5 kg	Prime joint usually less expensive than leg. Some people consider it has more succulent flavour due to presence of more fat. Large joints may be sold as two smaller pieces, blade end and knuckle end. May be cooked on the bone or boned and rolled and sometimes stuffed. May also be boned and cut into cubes.	Roast. Pot roast or braise. Cubes may be used for kebabs which are grilled or used for lamb casseroles.
loin (may be sold with kidney and suet)	1.5 kg	May be sold in one piece as a joint or more usually cut into about 6 chops. If both sides of the loin are sold together as one joint this is known as a saddle of lamb. Lean and fat.	Joint or saddle: roast. Chops: fry or grill.
chump	0.5 kg	Usually cut into 2 or 3 chops, which have a large proportion of meat and a small round bone in the centre.	Fry or grill.
best end of neck	1 kg	Can be cooked on the bone or divided into 6–7 lamb cutlets. May be boned and rolled and cut into slices called noisettes. Two best ends of neck are used to make a crown roast or a 'Guard of Honour'. Lean and fat.	In the piece: roast. Cutlets: fry grill or braise. Noisettes; fry or grill.
scrag and middle neck	1–1.5 kg	Middle neck has a coarser texture and is tougher than the best end. It is cut into chops but needs a long moist method of cooking; the basis for Lancashire hot pot and Irish stew. Scrag is often sold and used with middle neck and is also used in soups. Lean meat.	Braise or stew.
breast	0.75 kg	Streaks of fat and lean. Some have a high proportion of fat and if possible a lean breast should be purchased. May be cut into pieces on the bone, or boned and rolled and sometimes stuffed in one piece.	Whole piece makes very economical roast. Slices can be braised or used in lamb stews if lean.

Cuts of Pork

Pigs usually weigh 50-70 kg when they are slaughtered and produce carcases weighing 40-50 kg. As the animal is young all the meat is tender and all the cuts of pork may be roasted or used in a variety of other ways. Most of the cuts are sold on the bone. Some fat may be trimmed off by the butcher. Cuts of pork are shown in plate 16.

Fig. 11.11 Cuts of pork (see plate 16)

Cut	Approx. weight	Description	Cooking method
leg	5 kg	Prime roasting joint. Often divided into fillet and knuckle end. Cooked on the bone or boned and rolled. Slices from fillet end are pork steaks.	Roast. Steaks can be grilled or fried.
chump	1.5–2 kg	3 or 4 large meaty chops cut from the end of the loin from which the leg is removed.	Fry, grill or roast.
loin	4–5 kg	The most valuable part; it can be cooked in a piece as a joint on the bone or boned and rolled. Often cut into chops with or without the kidney present. The tenderloin is the lean meat found under the backbone on the hindloin. May be left in chops or removed whole and sold as separate piece; also sometimes called pork fillet. Chops from the foreloin have longer bones and are more like cutlets.	Roast. Chops are grilled, fried, roasted or braised. Tenderloin: fry or roast.
belly	2–4 kg	Streaks of fat and lean meat: the fattiest pork joint. The thick end has more lean meat and makes an excellent joint. The belly is also sold sliced. This joint may be pickled by some butchers.	Piece: roast or boil. Slices: grilled, fried and in casseroles. Pickled belly: boil. Boneless pieces used for pies and pâtés.
neck end	3–4 kg	Usually divided into *blade-bone* joint and *spare ribs* joint. The blade is normally sold in one piece but the spare ribs may be divided into chops.	Roast or pot roast. Chops may be fried, grilled or braised.
hand and spring	3–4 kg	The fore leg which has coarser meat and more fat than the hind leg. May be divided into two: the upper part, *the hand* is sold as a boned and rolled joint, the lower part, the *shank* or *spring* has the bone left in for boiling, or meat is removed in cubes. Both joints may be sold pickled by the butcher.	Slow roast or boil. Pieces are used for stews, casseroles Pickled joints usually boiled.

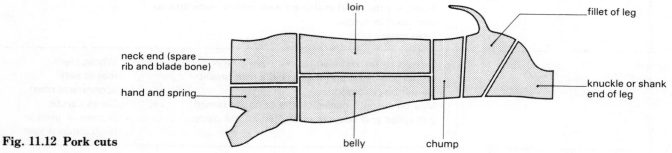

Fig. 11.12 Pork cuts

Types of offal

Look at plate 18 to help you recognise each type of offal.

The types of offal eaten as alternatives to meat are livers, kidneys, sweetbreads, hearts, tails, tongues, tripe, heads and brains. Offal varies in structure according to the type. The hearts, tongues and tails are muscular and contain muscle fibres like carcase meat. They are all parts of the animal which are used continuously during life. The fibres are long and the meats will be tough if not cooked correctly. Tripe contains large amounts of connective tissue, collagen. Therefore it needs long, moist cooking to be tender. Brains, livers, kidneys and sweetbreads are cellular in structure and do not contain any muscle fibres. They are therefore tender.

Offal is very nutritious. All offal supplies protein of high biological value, but little fat. Liver and kidneys are particularly good sources of iron, riboflavin (B_2), B_{12} and vitamin A (see Fig. 11.4).

Always buy offal which is absolutely fresh, and use it as soon as possible as it does not keep well.

For cooking, all fat, membranes and blood vessels should be removed. Offal should be washed in cold water. The method of cooking will depend on the type, texture and tenderness of the offal. The main varieties of offal are described in Figure 11.13.

Which offal do you see in the display at your local supermarket or butcher's shop?

How does the price of offal compare with meat?

Ask if it is possible to obtain varieties of offal not on display.

Fig. 11.13 Types of offal (see plate 18)

Name	Characteristics	Varieties and uses
liver	Cellular in structure with no muscle fibres or connective tissue. Liver must not be overcooked by dry heat or it will be hard. There should not be any green or yellow staining on the liver as it will then taste bitter.	*Calves* very expensive; fried or grilled. *Lambs* stronger in flavour. Most popular and tender for frying in slices. *Pigs* stronger than lambs in flavour and paler in colour. May be soaked in milk or water for 30 mins to remove strong flavour. Sliced and fried; also used for casseroles, pâtés, terrines. *Ox* the best source of iron and vitamin A but coarse with strong flavour. Can be soaked before use and requires long, slow cooking and is braised or used in casseroles. *Chicken* livers have a very delicate flavour and can be sautéd, fried or used for pâtés.
kidney	Similar in texture to liver. They should be plump, a good colour and free from any spots, or smell. If possible buy kidney with suet attached. This helps to keep kidney fresh and the suet can be used for dripping. Always skin kidneys before cooking (with exception of ox kidney which is often sold sliced or cubed). Slit the skin on round side and pull it back to the core. Snip out the core with kitchen scissors.	*Lambs* are best fried or grilled. *Pigs* stronger in flavour and larger, flatter and paler than lamb's kidney. Can be grilled or used in casseroles. Sometimes sold attached to the loin in pork chops or roast and not always available as offal. *Ox* kidney is much stronger, needs longer cooking and is mainly used mixed with beef in puddings and pies. May be casseroled.
heart	Muscular and rather like lean meat in structure but has a denser texture. Hearts bought whole must have the membrane dividing the cavities cut away and any flaps and blood vessels removed.	*Lamb's hearts*: most tender small, 1 portion, often stuffed before roasting or braising. *Calves, pigs' hearts* served in the same way but are usually large enough for 2 portions. *Ox heart* is much larger, usually sold in slices and must be stewed or braised.

Name	Characteristics	Varieties and uses
tripe	Tripe is prepared from the inner lining of the stomach; usually of an ox. It has a high proportion of connective tissue and is usually sold 'dressed' by the butcher which involves 12 hours boiling to convert the tough collagen to gelatine. The only preparation before cooking is to wash in cold water. Tripe is an excellent source of easily digestible protein.	Three kinds of ox tripe are available called honey-comb, blanket and thick seam after their general appearance but all taste the same. Tripe must be tender and as it lacks flavour, it is cut into pieces and boiled for a further 3 hours in a well-flavoured stock. It is traditional to serve it with onions boiled with it.
sweetbreads	The name given to the pancreas of the animal and the thymus gland in the throat. They are cellular in structure, held together by a delicate connective tissue which is removed after blanching. They are easily digested and often recommended for convalescent diets. They must be fresh and have a strong smell which disappears in preparation when they are soaked in cold salted water for several hours. After rinsing they are boiled for 5 mins with a slice of lemon, rinsed again in cold water. Fat, ducts and skin are removed and then the sweetbreads are pressed between two plates until cold when they are ready to use in a recipe.	Pancreas of calf or lamb are the ones usually available in butchers' shops. They may be steamed, stewed, grilled or fried and need an interesting sauce as an accompaniment.
brains	Easily digested but not as nutritious as sweetbreads. They are usually sold in sets and the preparation is like sweetbreads, but they do not require pressing.	Lambs one set (rarely available) gives 1 portion. Calves one set, (the most widely available) gives two portions. Usually poached in a rich stock and served with a sauce.
tongue	Similar in structure to heart and has muscle fibres running in all directions. Tongues can be bought fresh or salted by the butcher. They are frequently served cold. They should be soaked in water for 2 hours if fresh and longer if salted before cooking. They need long, slow moist cooking to make them tender.	Ox weight 1–3 kg usually salted. They are cooked by boiling after which skin, gristle and bone are removed. Served hot with a sauce or pressed in a cake tin and served cold. Calves weigh about ½ kg and are treated as ox tongues. Lambs weigh about 200 g each and one is allowed per person. Several may be pressed together if they are to be eaten cold.
trotters (feet)	Trotters must be cleaned thoroughly and soaked for an hour. Two are required per person.	Pigs simmer with onion and lemon for 2 hours. They are then boned and baked. Also used to make a gelatinous stock (jelly for pork pies). Calves feet are used to make calves-foot jelly by long, slow cooking.
tail	Generally dressed as offal but is really meat. The only tail commonly used is the oxtail which weighs 1–2 kg. There should be an equal proportion of meat and bone and not too much fat. It is usually sold jointed in 5 cm lengths. Soak and blanch before cooking.	Oxtail used for rich stew or soup with vegetables added. If stew is allowed to stand overnight, excess fat can be removed. Pig tails used by some nationalities for the traditional dishes of their countries.

Gelatine

Gelatine is considered in this section as it is prepared commercially by boiling in water the bones, horns and hooves of animals. When the collagen in the connective tissue of meat is cooked slowly it is converted into gelatine. The gelatine obtained is purified and sold either as a powder available in sachets or in sheets known as 'leaf gelatine'.

(i) Use of gelatine

Gelatine has many uses, since when it cools it sets. It is used in jellies, gravies, stocks and many desserts. There are several special points that should be noted when using gelatine if it is to be used successfully.

(a) Gelatine should be stored in an airtight container.

(b) Gelatine must be thoroughly dissolved in a small quantity of hot water. The mixture must not be overheated, or it will become thick and will not mix well with other ingredients. The gelatine should be at the same temperature as the mixture to which it is added.

(c) The dissolved gelatine must be added slowly and stirred well. If added too quickly, the gelatine may set before it is dispersed and cause the mixture to become 'ropey'.

(d) Special care is needed when gelatine is added to milk or cream mixtures. Acid used in the purification of gelatine may cause the mixture to curdle.

(e) Gelatine will not set any mixture containing fresh pineapple, as the fruit contains an enzyme which digests the protein gelatine and the mixture remains liquid.

(ii) Food value of gelatine

Although gelatine is an animal protein it is of low biological value, and used in such small quantities that it is not considered to have any real nutritive value.

Types of poultry

Poultry used to be a luxury commodity eaten only on special occasions, such as Christmas. Modern methods of farming and marketing have resulted in poultry being widely available and much less expensive in comparison with other fresh meat than it used to be. Hence chicken, in particular, is no longer considered such a luxury and is often eaten for everyday meals. Look at plate 17(a) to see the range of poultry available today.

The structure of poultry is similar to carcase meat and is described on p. 141.

Poultry is a good source of high biological protein. It is also low in fat, and is therefore an excellent food for people on a slimming diet. However, the iron content of poultry is less than that of red carcase meat. As the flesh is young it is usually tender, and is easily digested. Chicken is therefore often used in the diets of the young, the elderly and the convalescent. Figure 11.14 shows the types of poultry and suggests suitable cooking methods.

Fig. 11.14 Types of poultry (see plate 17(a))

Name	Average weight	Description	Traditional accompaniment
poussin	½ kg	A very young bird either male or female killed when 5–6 weeks old. Roasted whole or split in half and grilled or fried. Makes 1 or 2 portions.	Veal forcemeat. Sausages. Bacon rolls. Bread sauce. Gravy.
spring chicken	½–1 kg	The name was originally given to open range birds sold during the spring. Now the term is used for small birds which are usually roasted whole. A half bird is usually served per person.	As for poussin.
chicken	1–2½ kg	The most popular bird for roasting, sometimes called by the American word broiler. Over 300 million birds are produced each year. Most are mass-produced (see p. 140) but a few free-range birds are available. They reach the desired weight at 10–12 weeks. 75% are sold oven-ready (frozen or chilled). 5% fresh and the remaining 20% are sold as chicken portions, for frying or casseroles. Allow 250 g per portion.	As for poussin.

Name	Average weight	Description	Traditional accompaniment
capon	3–4 kg	A neutered cockerel which has a longer growing period of 5–8 months and has tender and juicy flesh because of an increased distribution of fat globules in the meat. Considered to be one of the best birds for roasting.	As for poussin.
boiling fowl	1½–3 kg	Usually adult female birds originally used for producing eggs. When they pass their peak egg-laying performance, 12–18 months, they are sold as boiling fowls which need long, slow, moist cooking to make them tender.	Parsley, egg or white sauce. Boiled ham.
turkey	2–15 kg	Frozen turkeys have a large share of the market.	Chestnut stuffing. Sausage meat. Stuffing or veal forcement. Bacon rolls. Cranberry sauce. Gravy.
duckling duck	1–2 kg	Duckling are about 10–16 weeks when slaughtered and usually reared on the batch system like chickens. Can be roasted. Older birds (ducks) may be tough and require braising to make them tender. Contain more fat than chickens. Used also for pâtés and terrines.	Sage and onion stuffing. Apple sauce or orange slices. Gravy or orange sauce.
goose	4–10 kg	Was the traditional Christmas bird before the turkey. Served stuffed and roasted. Meat is darker and contains more fat than most poultry. The bird should be slaughtered at 6–9 months or it may be tough.	As for duckling.
pigeon	¼–½ kg	Birds of either sex are killed at 8–10 weeks of age. Gives 1–2 portions. May be mixed with beef in a pie.	Watercress. Gravy.

Types of game (see plate 17(a))

Birds and animals which are hunted will have led a much more active life and therefore the meat is darker and tougher than poultry meat. To develop the flavours many people associate with game and to make the meat more tender, the game is usually hung after it has been killed.

Buying meat, offal, poultry and game

Meat is a highly perishable, expensive food. The important characteristics of a good quality meat are its freshness, tenderness, texture, flavour and juiciness. Even though it may be difficult to tell the quality of meat just by looking at it, there are several characteristics that will guide you in your choice:

Fig. 11.15 Examples of game caught in Britain

Birds	Season available in Britain
grouse	12 August–10 December
pheasant	10 October–1 February
partridge	1 September–1 February
quail	1 July–30 September
wild duck	12 August–1 March

Animals	
hares	September–March
rabbits	September–April
deer (venison)	August–February

1 Always buy meat from a clean, well-ventilated shop. Check that the assistants are handling the meat hygienically.

2 Meat deteriorates rapidly. Do not buy more than you need, unless you plan to freeze it. An approximate guide of the amount of meat per person is:

without bone: 120-150 g (uncooked weight)
with bone: 150-300 g (uncooked weight)

3 Check that there is not an excessive amount of bone or fat that will be wasted when you prepare the meat.

4 Check that the meat is moist. Meat that has been left exposed to the air for a long time will have a dry surface.

5 Look at the colour of meat (see plates 14-16). Meats naturally vary in colour, but there are some general guidelines to help you choose:

● Beef should be a deep cherry-red, slightly moist in appearance with globules of fat in the lean, visible as marbling. The fat should be firm and creamy-white.
● Veal should be very pale beige/pink, very soft and moist in texture.
● Lamb should have bright pink/brown flesh, with a small quantity of firm white fat.
● Pork should be pale pink/brown. The flesh should be firm and the fat should be white. The rind should not be too thick.
● Offal. Each internal organ varies in colour. Offal from older animals, e.g. ox liver, is always darker in colour than young animals, e.g. lambs' liver. Offal should be brown, and moist in appearance. It should be free from discoloration and unpleasant smell.
● Poultry should have firm, very pale creamy-pink flesh with no visible fat.

The colour in meat is due to the pigment called *myoglobin*. This is the protein which carries oxygen in the muscles. The more myoglobin present in meat, the stronger the colour of the meat. For example, beef is the darkest red, lamb is a medium colour and pork is pale in colour. Poultry has dark meat on the legs and light meat on the breast.

The amount of myoglobin present increases with age. Older animals have darker flesh, e.g. beef is much darker than veal. Myoglobin is naturally a purple-red but in the presence of air it combines with oxygen and becomes a bright cherry-red. Freshly-cut meat has this bright red colour on the surface where it has come into contact with oxygen. If the meat remains exposed to air the bright red fades to brown, which is not so attractive. The quality of the meat is not affected. Refrigerated displays help to keep the desirable red colour in meat longer.

The colour of the *fat* also varies in different meats. The fat of lamb and pork is whiter than that of beef which has creamy-coloured fat because the animals are older when slaughtered.

6 Look at the texture of meat; the length of the muscle fibres and the coarseness of the grain are indicators of the tenderness of the meat (see p. 142). Avoid joints with obvious signs of gristle and excessive amounts of fat. The texture determines the most suitable cooking method (see Figs. 11.6, 11.8, 11.10, 11.11, 11.13 and 11.14). The butcher will advise you if you discuss your requirements with him.

Buying for the freezer

(a) *Carcase meat*

Many people buy carcase meat in bulk to store conveniently in a freezer at home. The meat may be purchased fresh and frozen at home. Some farms and butchers have facilities to freeze and pack the meat. Meat already frozen is also available from frozen-food centres. It is difficult to tell the quality of frozen meat by examining it. Therefore it is especially important to purchase it from a reputable retailer.

If carcases are bought in bulk, it is important to know the amount of freezer space required. The chart below shows the average weight of meat you would expect and the freezer space needed.

Fig. 11.16 Prepared cuts for meat in bulk: weight and freezer space

	Average weight, prepared cuts	Freezer space
Beef		
hindquarter	45 kg	100 litres (3½ cubic feet)
forequarter	45 kg	100 litres (3½ cubic feet)
Lamb		
whole carcase	13.5 kg	42.5 litres (1½ cubic feet)
Pork		
half carcase	22.5 kg	56.5 litres (2 cubic feet)

It is also possible to buy meat packs containing selected cuts or bulk buys of one cut, e.g. six shoulders of lamb, 5 kg minced beef. These are useful for people who do not like all the cuts of meat.

(b) *Poultry*

A large proportion of the poultry available is frozen by the processor. Frozen chickens are much more widely obtainable and less expensive than fresh chickens. They can be bought in supermarkets, or in bulk from a freezer centre and stored in a home freezer.

(c) *Offal*

Do not buy large quantities of offal for freezing. The quality deteriorates rapidly (see p. 149).

As meat and poultry are expensive products, it is particularly important that they are frozen and stored well in the freezer to maintain the original quality. All frozen products should be very well packed. Badly packed meat will develop 'freezer burn', caused by dehydration of the surface. Greyish white marks appear on the surface of lean meat and poultry. They become progressively worse if the meat is stored for a long time. The nutrients in meat are not affected by freezer burn and the meat is quite safe to eat. It may however be dry, brittle and unpalatable. The film used for pre-packing fresh meat is insufficient protection against freezer burn and it should be overwrapped in heavy duty aluminium foil or extra thick polythene bags usually sold as freezer bags. The packs should be clearly labelled, as it is difficult to recognise different cuts after freezing.

When freezing fresh meat or poultry, the temperature of the freezer should be lowered by using the fast-freeze switch 24 hours before the meat is introduced. A large bulk load cannot be frozen all at once as it will take too long to reach the storage temperature. It is better to introduce batches of meat over a period of two days following the freezer manufacturer's loading instructions. The meat must be used in rotation and not left in the freezer too long (see p. 158).

---

1 What are the advantages of buying meat in bulk for the freezer? Are there any disadvantages?

2 Explain why a large quantity of fresh meat should not all be placed in a freezer at one time. How would you deal with it? Give reasons for your answers.

3 What is the best time of year to buy meat for the freezer?

4 What other frozen meat dishes do you see in your freezer centre or supermarket? What are the advantages and disadvantages of these foods?

Cooking meat, offal and poultry

Meat is a relatively expensive commodity. It is often the focal point of a meal and should be well cooked. Correctly-cooked meat should be succulent and tender. Poor cooking can spoil good quality meat and make it dry, tough and stringy. To obtain good results it is important to follow the recommended cooking method for each cut (see Figs. 11.6, 11.8, 11.10, 11.11, 11.13 and 11.14).

Changes occur in the structure of meat fibres during cooking. Can you explain these differences?

All meat is spoiled if it is cooked at too high a temperature. Intense heat causes the meat fibres to become hard, tough and stringy. It is often difficult to tell when meat is cooked. Here are some guidelines to help you cook meat so that it is succulent and tender.

1 The tougher cuts require long, slow cooking by a moist method. When cooked, the pieces of meat should be soft and slightly springy.

2 For more tender cuts that are to be grilled, fried or roasted, personal preference is an important factor. Pork and lamb are usually served well-cooked but many people prefer slightly under-cooked (rare) beef as they consider the meat has more flavour and retains more of its juices.

- For *small cuts* that are to be grilled, fried or cooked in a microwave cooker, the cooked meat should be springy to touch, and the juices run clear when the meat is cooked. For rare beef, the juices will be tinged with blood.

Fig. 11.17 Roasting time/weight of joint

Beef	
Rare	20 mins per 500 g + 20 mins
Medium	25 mins per 500 g + 20 mins
Well-done	30 mins per 500 g + 20 mins
Lamb	
Medium	25 mins per 500 g + 25 mins
Well-done	30 mins per 500 g + 30 mins
Pork	
Well-done	30 mins per 500 g + 30 mins

Notes

1 If a fan-controlled oven is used, roasting times may be shorter and the cooker instruction book should be referred to.

2 For automatic cooking when the meat is put in a cold oven, an extra 15 mins should be allowed.

● For *larger joints* that are roasted, the approximate cooking time can be estimated from the weight of the joint, as for example, in Fig. 11.17.

The oven is preheated to 160°C/Regulo 3 and the time calculated as shown in the chart.

However, the most reliable way to know when a joint is cooked is to insert a meat thermometer into the centre of the thickest muscle. It must not touch a bone. Heat is transferred from the surface of the roast to the interior and the meat is cooked when the internal temperature reaches a certain point according to the type of meat.

Fig. 11.18 Cooking meat: recommended internal temperature

beef	● rare	60°C
	● medium	70°C
	● well done	80°C
lamb		82°C
pork		85°C
chicken		90°C

As described in Fig. 11.13, the varieties of offal are cooked in different ways according to their structure and texture.

The main aims in cooking all meat, poultry and offal are to make them:
● look and taste more appetising;
● tender and more digestible;
● safer to eat by destroying harmful bacteria.

(a) Cooking makes meat look and taste more appetising

Several changes occur when meat is cooked that make it look attractive and smell and taste appetising.
● There is a change in colour from red to brown. This is mainly due to changes in the pigment myoglobin (see p. 153). The brown colour develops above 65°C.
● An appetising smell is produced. Volatile and aromatic substances are released by the cooking process.
● The texture becomes firmer. Proteins in the muscle fibres coagulate above 50°C. Overcooking by a dry heat method tends to make meat too hard and dry.
● Meat juices are squeezed out as the collagen contracts at 60°C. The juices that are lost contain soluble proteins, mineral salts, vitamins and extractives. This loss of juices causes the meat to shrink and lose weight. This may be as much as 30% of the initial volume and weight. The losses vary with the method of cooking. Can you explain the differences shown in plate 19?
● In moist methods of cookery the meat juices pass into the cooking liquid and are usually eaten with the meat as gravy.
● If a dry method of cooking is used some of the juices evaporate and leave a brown savoury coating on the outside of the meat giving a characteristic flavour to roasted, grilled and fried meats.
● The fat melts in dry methods and helps to keep the lean meat moist by reducing moisture loss. Some of the fat runs out and causes further weight loss. It may be collected as dripping. There is less tendency for fat to melt at the lower temperatures used in moist methods but excessive amounts of melted fat should be skimmed from the surface of stews and gravies.

(b) Cooking can make meat more tender and digestible

The meat becomes more tender and palatable. At temperatures of 80-100°C the collagen is softened and converted, in the presence of water, to gelatine which is soluble. This increases the tenderness of the meat as the muscle fibres separate more easily. Overcooking by moist heat causes the fibres to separate completely and the meat is stringy. Look at plate 19 to see the difference in the texture of raw and cooked beef.

It was shown on p. 142 that tenderness is a very important characteristic of meat. However, cuts of meat that have long muscle fibres and contain large amounts of connective tissue will not be tender unless they are cooked by the correct method for that particular cut of meat.

A knowledge of the cuts of meat (see Figs. 11.6, 11.8, 11.10, 11.11, 11.13 and 11.14) is essential so that the correct cooking method is chosen. This depends mainly on the amount of connective tissue present. Cuts with only a small amount of connective tissue can be cooked by dry heat methods, e.g. roasting, grilling and frying, as the meat itself contains enough water to soften the collagen. If large amounts of connective tissue are present, long, slow, moist cooking is necessary. The methods used are those in which the moisture is supplied either by steam (in pot roasting and braising) or boiling liquid (in stewing and boiling) or by a combination of steam and liquid.

However, there are several ways of helping to

tenderise meat before it is cooked. These ways are either:

- to cut the long muscle fibres into small fragments making the meat easier to chew and digest;
- to break down some of the connective tissue, collagen, into gelatine which is soluble in water. Hence the muscle fibres are separated more quickly in the cooking process.

The ways in which these aims are achieved are:

(i) *Fragmenting the muscle fibres*

- Mechanical pounding, i.e. beating with a heavy knife, meat hammer or rolling pin to break up the elastin and the longer fibres.
- Cutting the meat into small pieces before cooking, as in a stew; or scoring the surface with a knife.
- Mincing. Some parts of an animal, e.g. the neck in beef, will never be tender because of the amount of elastin they contain. Hence they will be minced or ground by the butcher to help make them more tender after cooking. Mincing other less tender cuts may mean they can be cooked by methods normally considered suitable for the more tender cuts. For example hamburgers can be fried or grilled like steak.

(ii) *Breaking down the connective tissue, collagen to gelatin*

- Acids may be used in a marinade before the meat is cooked or they may be added to the cooking liquid. For example, vinegar, lemon juice and tomato juice are sometimes used. The action of the acid increases the rate at which collagen is converted to gelatine.
- Commercial meat tenderisers, usually containing enzymes, may be used to break down the proteins of the connective tissue. They are sprinkled on the surface of the meat before it is cooked. Fig. 11.3 shows the change in structure of meat fibres treated with a commercial tenderiser.

Are meat tenderisers available in your supermarket?

Read the label and note the ingredients.

(c) Cooking destroys bacteria and makes meat safer to eat

Meat is a highly perishable food. It is subject to deterioration by the action of micro-organisms in the meat, and by attack from micro-organisms in the air. The temperatures achieved in cooking must be sufficiently high to destroy all micro-organisms.

Special care is needed in preparing poultry to prevent food poisoning caused by salmonella organisms (see p. 84). Although this micro-organism is potentially dangerous, it is easily destroyed by heat. Thoroughly cooked chicken is perfectly safe to eat.

It is extremely important when preparing frozen poultry to:

- ensure that frozen poultry is thoroughly defrosted before use. If poultry is not thoroughly defrosted, the interior may not reach a sufficiently high temperature during cooking to kill all salmonella organisms. The recommended thawing times are:

Recommended thawing time	Room temperature	Refrigerator
chicken 1-2 kg	8 hours	24 hours
turkey 4-5 kg	27 hours	3 days
turkey 10-12 kg	2 days	4 days

- remove giblets as soon as possible;
- avoid raw poultry coming into contact with other foods, especially those which are not to be cooked further;
- thoroughly clean all knives and boards used in preparing the poultry;
- not stuff the internal cavity of large birds. This may prevent the interior reaching a high enough temperature;
- ensure that all poultry is thoroughly cooked. (To kill salmonella organisms, all parts must reach 65°C for 15 minutes.) The cooking time depends on the temperature of the oven. If a meat thermometer is used (see p. 155) the temperature should reach 90°C in the thigh muscle. Alternatively, if a skewer is inserted in the thickest part of the leg, the juices should be clear, not pink.
- take care not to recontaminate a cooked bird with salmonella from surfaces, knives or cloths, as the micro-organisms multiply rapidly between 10-45°C;
- ensure that birds not eaten immediately are either kept very hot or chilled quickly.

Experiments to show the effects of cooking meat

Experiment to investigate the structure of meat

Look at Fig. 11.3. This is the structure of rump steak and chuck steak as seen under a microscope. You may be able to make similar slides, but it is essential to use a very fine fibre and tease it on the slide.

1 Note the difference in the lengths and thicknesses of fibres of raw rump and chuck steak.
2 What is the effect on the structure of the fibres when these samples are
   (a) hammered
   (b) treated with acid
   (c) treated with a meat tenderiser?
3 Note the effect of cooking on the untreated sample.

Experiment to show the effects of various methods of cooking rump steak

3 × 100g rump steak, all of equal thickness.

1 Weigh each sample. Comment on the appearance.
2 Measure the surface area on graph paper.
3 Cook the samples until medium rare, i.e. approx. 5 mins each side for grilling, 2-3 mins each side for frying, 1-2 mins in a microwave oven.
4 If possible, collect the juices that drip from each sample in a 10 ml cylinder. Let the drip cool. Fat will solidify on top. Comment on the amount of drip from each sample.
5 Measure the surface area of the cooked meat sample; compare with the original area.
6 Look at the three cooked samples and describe the changes that have taken place during cooking.
7 Taste each sample. Can you detect any difference in tenderness or flavour?
8 From this experiment comment on the effects of cooking rump steak.

Note: This experiment can be repeated using samples of steak that have been hammered and samples that have been treated with a meat tenderiser.

Experiment to show the effects of various methods of cooking chuck steak

1 Cut 200 g of chuck steak into four equal pieces. Label the samples (a)-(d). Describe the appearance and draw the shape of each sample on graph paper.
2 Treat the samples as follows, noticing all the changes that occur:
   (i) put sample (a) into a small saucepan with 100 ml cold water.
   (ii) put sample (b) into a small saucepan with 100 ml cold water and add 1 × 2.5 ml spoon lemon juice.
   (iii) put sample (c) into a small saucepan with 100 ml boiling water.
   (iv) put sample (d) into a small saucepan with 1 × 5 ml spoon cooking fat or oil. Fry meat on all sides very quickly, then add 100 ml boiling water.
3 Bring samples (a) and (b) to simmering point, being careful not to let them boil.
4 Put lids on all four saucepans. Simmer very gently for one and a half hours, being careful not to let them boil.
5 Turn each sample out into separate glass basins. Label each sample.
6 Describe the appearance of each sample.
7 Draw the shape of each sample on graph paper. Has the size changed?
8 Taste each sample. Comment on the flavour of meat and gravy. Which is most tender? Which is the best-flavoured meat? Which is the best-flavoured gravy?
9 Comment on the changes that take place when cooking chuck steak.

Experiment to investigate the effects of cooking chicken

A chicken contains a high proportion of skin and bone.

1 Weigh and cook a small chicken. Weigh the cooked chicken. Remove all the meat from the carcase and weigh the meat. Calculate the percentage of meat obtained and work out the cost per kilogram. Compare this with the cost of stewing steak. Suggest uses for the skin and bone from the chicken.
2 Compare the cost of chicken portions with the cost of portions which you cut from a chicken yourself.

Storage of meat, offal and poultry

All meat should be stored in a cool place as it is an ideal medium for bacterial growth. If a refrigerator is not available, a cool larder is the best place. All meat should be covered to avoid contamination by dust and flies, and to prevent the surface from drying out.

Storing fresh meat
- *in the coolest part of a refrigerator* (excluding ice box). Fresh meat should be covered with foil or cling film to prevent it from drying out.
- *in a cool larder.* Fresh meat should be covered to prevent flies from landing on it, and to prevent drying out.

Storing cooked meat
Even cooked meat can be contaminated by dust and flies. Therefore, always cover closely with foil or cling film.

Store away from fresh meat to avoid cross contamination. Use cooked meats as soon as possible. Figure 11.19 table shows the recommended storage for cooked meats.

Processed meats

Cured meats, e.g. bacon, ham

Salting and drying were the earliest ways of preserving meat, so that it lasted during the long winter months. The introduction of salt into the meat to preserve it and give it a characteristic colour and flavour is known as *curing*. In traditional methods of curing a small proportion of either sodium or potassium nitrate is included to give cured meat its characteristic pink colour.

Bacon

Bacon has been a popular food for many hundreds of years: ever since humans discovered they could preserve pork by salting it. The traditional bacon and egg breakfast was established in Britain as early as the sixteenth century. Today more bacon is eaten in Britain than in any other country in the world. Only 40% is produced locally; the remainder is imported. Denmark supplies approximately 45% and the rest comes from Holland, Ireland and Poland.

> Many people now buy bacon in joints as well as rashers and use it for main meals. Make a list of ways in which bacon can be served for breakfast, lunch, dinner and in snacks.

Fig. 11.19 Recommended storage times for meat

Meat	Cool larder	Refrigerator	Freezer (at −18°C)
Uncooked			
beef joints	1–2 days	3–5 days	12 months
lamb joints	1–2 days	3–5 days	9 months
pork joints	1–2 days (depends on temp.)	2–4 days	6 months
steak, chops / stewing steak	1 day	3–4 days	4–6 months
mince	use same day	1–2 days	3 months
offal	1 day	1–2 days	3 months
chicken and turkey	1 day or if frozen as soon as it has thawed	2–3 days	6–9 months
giblets	use same day	1 day	2 months
Cooked			
joints	2 days	3 days	1–2 months
sliced meat	1–2 days	2–3 days	1–2 months
shop cooked meat	use same day	1–2 days	not recommended
casseroles	1 day	2 days	6 months unless they contain bacon when 3 months
poultry	1–2 days	2–3 days	1 month

Modern bacon production

The pigs that are to be used for bacon production must have a good proportion of lean to fat and a long back. When they are six or seven months old and weigh about 60–70 kg they are sent to be slaughtered.

1 The head, trotters, tail and internal organs are removed. The carcase is singed to remove the hairs, and split into two sides.
2 The sides are weighed, graded and only those with the correct amount of fat and length of back are used for bacon. The rest of the sides are used for fresh pork, pies and sausages.
3 The sides are cooled to 4°C and automatically injected with brine, which is a salt solution. They are then immersed in a tank of brine for 2–4 days. The brine diffuses through the meat, producing the typical colour and flavour of cured meat.
4 After brining, the bacon is drained and allowed to mature in a cool room for about a week, to develop its flavour.
5 The bacon is now ready for sale as 'green' or 'unsmoked' with a pale rind. All Danish bacon is exported at this stage.

Sometimes certain tender back portions of the pig are cured by a special process which produces bacon

in 2–3 days. This bacon has a mild flavour and is usually labelled 'sweetcure' or 'tender cure'.

Smoked bacon

About half of the bacon is smoked in kilns for up to eight hours using smouldering wood chips or sawdust. The bacon acquires the characteristic flavour and brown rind of smoked bacon. Most retailers sell both green and smoked bacon.

Buying bacon

Bacon must be fresh when purchased. The fat should be firm and white and the lean, pink and moist.

Bacon may be bought either as ready-cut slices (rashers), or as joints. Sometimes the retailer cuts the bacon to the customer's requirements but it is more usually ready-cut, either:
- fresh sliced: ready sliced in piles and weighed to order;
- film-wrapped: marked with cut, weight, price (used for rashers and joints);
- vacuum-packed: in strong polythene packs from which all air has been removed and if unopened the bacon has a longer storage life. These packs are stamped with a 'use by' date and may be more expensive due to the cost of packaging.

Look at the bacon in your local shops or supermarket. Can you tell if it is British or imported? Where does it come from?

Are there ways of recognising the country of origin?

Look at plate 20(a). Can you identify the different cuts shown in this photograph?

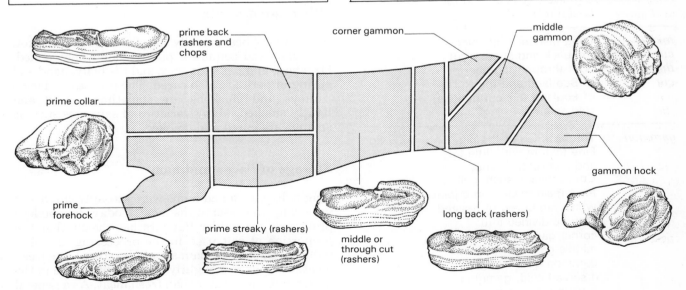

Fig. 11.20 Cuts of bacon

prime back rashers and chops

corner gammon

middle gammon

prime collar

prime forehock

prime streaky (rashers)

middle or through cut (rashers)

long back (rashers)

gammon hock

Fig. 11.21 The main cuts of bacon (see plate 20(a)).

Name	Description and use	Approx. weight boneless
forehock	More fat and coarser texture than gammon. Usually bought as a boneless joint for boiling. Can be used for lentil stew.	3 kg
collar	Similar in texture to forehock. Can be cooked as a joint, boiled or roasted and also sold as rashers.	4 kg (usually cut into several smaller joints)
back	The prime and most expensive rashers with a large area of lean and a layer of fat beneath the rind. May be divided into long back and short back. Grilled or fried. Sometimes cut thickly as bacon chops.	12.5 kg
streaky	The lean and fat are distributed in long strips hence the name 'streaky'. Less expensive. Thinly sliced; grilled and fried. The only sort sold in USA. As the fat content is higher they are used to accompany lean meats e.g. liver, chicken and for bacon rolls.	12.5 kg
middle cut or through cut	Long rashers containing the back and streaky cut right through together. In Scotland and the North of England this cut may be sold as a roll.	
gammon	The back leg of the pig. Fine texture with little fat and a delicate flavour. Cut in thick rashers grilled for a main meal or into joints which are boiled or roasted. May be divided into: corner gammon (1½ kg) middle gammon (3½ kg) gammon hock (2 kg). If served cold, gammon is usually called *ham*.	7½ kg

Look at the bacon counter in your local supermarket. Is the bacon green or smoked?

Is some of the bacon sweet cure?

How many different cuts are available?

How are they packaged?

How much do the average joints weigh?

How do different cuts vary in price?

Speciality hams are produced from whole legs, separated from the carcase before being cured. There are many traditional hams, for instance:

England: York ham
Italy: Parma ham
Belgium: Jambon d'Ardennes
America: Virginia ham.

Each ham is produced differently by variation in the method and the ingredients used for curing. Dry salt is used for some cures. Some hams are not smoked, but others are well-smoked, matured and usually eaten raw.

The term 'cooked ham' is commonly used for both gammon and ham sold ready-cooked and sliced. Cooked ham, like gammon, is from the back leg of the pig and is thus treated in the same way.
Picnic or shoulder hams are the front leg of a pig and are cured like a ham. They are usually sold ready-cooked and boneless and are less expensive than ham or gammon.

Other cured meats

Some cuts of beef, usually the silverside and brisket, are cured and acquire a pink colour when cooked. Ox, sheep and pig's tongues, and the belly, hand and spring of pork are also cured. The breasts of ducks, turkeys and chickens are sometimes cured and lightly smoked. Many varieties of sausages such as salamis are cured and smoked.

Storage of bacon and ham

Originally bacon and hams were strongly cured and very salty to preserve the meat. Today, the modern preference for milder flavours has meant that the proportion of salt used in the processing has been reduced. Bacon and ham should be stored like fresh meat. They have a slightly longer storage life in the larder and refrigerator than fresh meat. As a general rule bacon joints and rashers should be cooked and

Plate 17
(a) Poultry and game

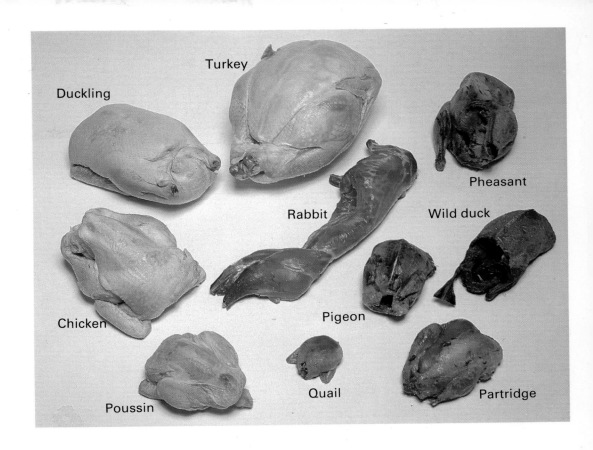

(b) The shrinkage of poultry during cooking

1 Fresh chicken; oven temperature 180°C (preheated). Cooking time 1 hr 40 min; weight loss 19.5%, evaporation loss 18.6%

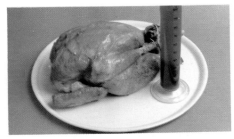

2 Fresh chicken; oven temperature 180°C (cold start). Cooking time 1 hr 50 min; weight loss 19.5%, evaporation loss 12%

3 Fresh chicken; spit roasted, cooking time 2 hr; weight loss 23.6%; evaporation loss 18.6%

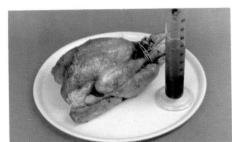

4 Frozen chicken; oven temperature 180°C; cooking time 2 hr 40 min; weight loss 35.4%; evaporation loss 22.8%

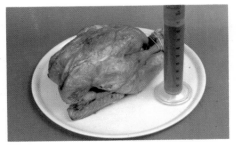

5 Frozen chicken; defrosted in a refrigerator; oven temperature 180°C; cooking time 1 hr 45 min; weight loss 31.6%; evaporation loss 22.3%

6 Fresh chicken; cooked in a microwave oven; cooking time 25 min; weight loss 5%; evaporation loss nil

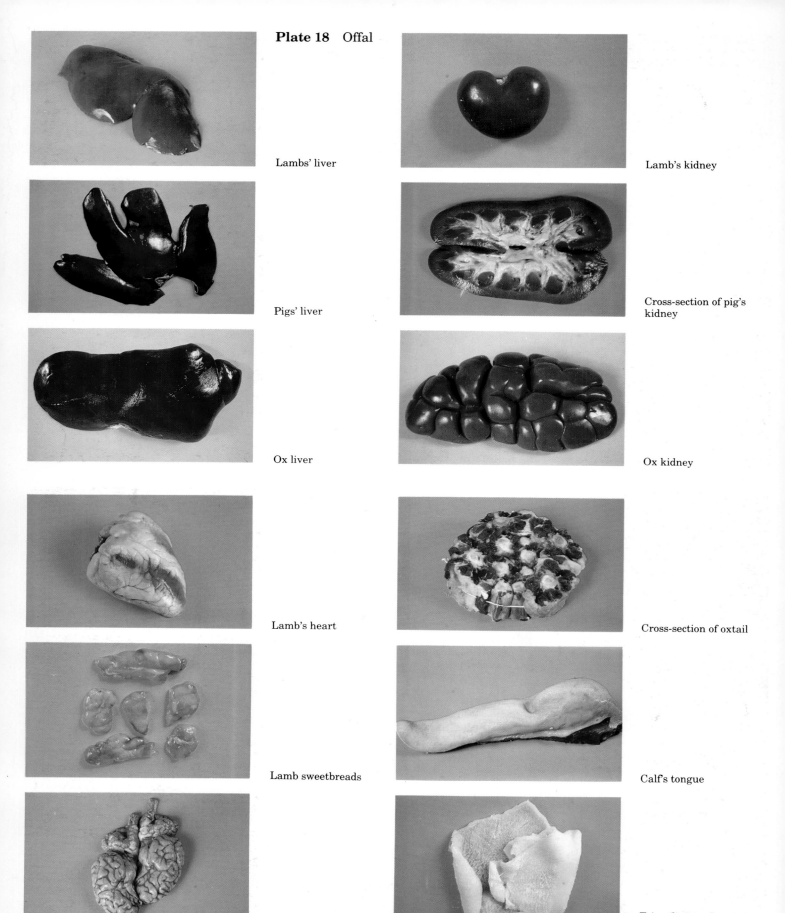

Plate 18   Offal

Lambs' liver

Lamb's kidney

Pigs' liver

Cross-section of pig's kidney

Ox liver

Ox kidney

Lamb's heart

Cross-section of oxtail

Lamb sweetbreads

Calf's tongue

Lamb's brains

Tripe (lining of ox stomach)

Plate 19 Shrinkage of beef
during different cooking methods

1 Fresh, cooked by the searing method;
  oven temperature 215°C for 15 min
  reduced to 170° cooking time 1 hr 3 min;
  weight loss 20.5%; evaporation loss 16.5%

2 Fresh, cooked in a slow oven;
  oven temperature 150°C; cooking time 1 hr
  40 min; weight loss 19.5%; evaporation
  loss 9.6%

3 Fresh, cooked in an automatic oven;
  oven temperature 180°C; cooking time 1 hr
  40 min; weight loss 26.3%; evaporation
  loss 19.4%

4 Fresh, cooked in microwave oven;
  cooking time 24 min; weight loss 8.0%;
  evaporation loss 1.0%

5 Frozen oven temperature 180°C; cooking
  time 2 hr 40 min; weight loss 31.0%;
  evaporation loss 21.4%

6 Frozen, defrosted in refrigerator overnight;
  2.5ml drip; oven temperature 180°C;
  cooking time 1 hr 20 min; weight loss
  19.2%; evaporation loss 9.4%

Plate 20
(a) Cuts of bacon

(b) Sausages

Fig. 11.22 Storage times for bacon and ham

	larder	refrigerator	freezer at −18°C
green and smoked bacon rashers	2–3 days	1 week	1 month
bacon joints	5 days	10 days	1 month (8 weeks smoked)
vacuum-packed bacon	3–4 days	'use by' date if unopened: as fresh after opening	6 months
'boil in the bag' bacon	1 day	2 days	Not recommended
cooked bacon	1–2 days	2–3 days	Not recommended
raw ham	1 day	3–5 days if fresh; up to 4 months for smoked	1–2 months
cooked ham joint	2 days	7–10 days	1 month
cooked ham sliced	1 day	5 days	1 month

eaten within a week of purchase unless bought in date-stamped vacuum packs.

Bacon and ham must have protection from the air and should be tightly wrapped in foil or cling film; greaseproof paper is not suitable as it is porous and allows moisture to evaporate, which dries the surface of the meat. Plastic boxes are unsuitable unless the bacon or ham is first wrapped to exclude the air. Bacon can be frozen but the presence of salt accelerates the development of rancidity, and therefore the storage-life in the freezer is shorter than for fresh meat.

Sausages, pâtés and other processed meats

A great variety of these foods is available. They are important because:
- they are quick to prepare and ideal for snack meals, packed meals and main meals where saving time and effort is important;
- they provide an alternative to meat and poultry and introduce variety into the diet;
- many of them are less expensive than meat or poultry and provide economical meals.

Sausages

Sausages are one of the oldest forms of processed food. Homer's *Odyssey* in the ninth century BC says that 'Man, beside a great fire, has filled a stomach with fat and blood and is very eager to get it roasted'.

Sausages are a very popular food. They are made from a wide variety of minced raw meats and special spices bound with cereal. This mixture is stuffed into either natural skins which are made of animal intestines, or manufactured skins which are made of collagen obtained from the hide of animals. In Britain, the amount of meat sausages contain is controlled by law:
- pork sausages must contain at least 65% meat, of which 80% must be pork
- 50% of the meat in beef sausages must be beef.

Three main kinds of sausage are produced: thick, thin or chipolata and skinless. Sausage meat is also available and used for stuffings and in a variety of recipes. As fresh sausages and sausage meat are highly perishable foods they must be produced, transported under hygienic conditions and sold and eaten as soon as possible. Some sausages and sausage meat contain permitted preservatives.

Examine the types of sausage available in your local shops. Do they contain preservative?

Make a list of the ways sausages are used in the menu for snack and main meals.

A large variety of other types of sausage is also available. Some originate from England, but many are from other European countries, especially Germany. They may be made from cured dried meat, raw smoked meats or cooked meats. They do not usually require cooking before being served unless they are normally eaten hot, e.g. frankfurters and black pudding.

Look at plate 20(b). How many of these types of sausage have you tasted?

Fig. 11.23 Types of sausages

Name	Description	Countries of origin
salami	Probably the oldest type of sausage. They are made from meat that has been cured before processing: usually lean and fat pork, seasoned with salt and spices. Some contain a lot of garlic. Those from hot Mediterranean countries are more heavily spiced than those from northern Europe. They are smoked, dried and hung up in a cool dry place. They keep almost indefinitely. Always eaten raw.	Italy: best known and most expensive. Well-seasoned with garlic. Meat is coarsely chopped. Belgium: available with or without garlic. Milder taste. Denmark: less expensive, rather salty. No garlic, artificially coloured. Also France, Germany, Poland and Hungary.
mortadella	A semi-dry sausage not so heavily smoked as salami and must be kept in a refrigerator. Very smooth; made from cured beef and pork and also contains diced pork fat.	Italy
frankfurter	The world's best-known boiling sausage used for the American 'hot dog'. Made from a mixture of cured pork and veal which is well-smoked and cooked in water. They need reheating for 10 minutes in simmering (not boiling) water.	Germany: named after town of Frankfurt.
black pudding	Made from fresh pig's blood and fat, with oatmeal, onion and seasonings mixed and formed into rings in their skin and cooked in water to which a black dye is added. They are usually served sliced and fried.	England: especially North of England. Similar sausages made in Germany.
polony	Made from finely chopped pork and fat with rice flour, rusks and seasoning formed into rings and cooked for 45 minutes. They are dipped into red polony dye.	England
liver sausage	Found in every European country. Made from finely chopped pig's liver and pig's head meat with corn-flour, onions and seasonings added, then placed in skins and cooked in water. Must be stored in a refrigerator.	England: least highly seasoned. Not smoked. 30% meat content must be liver. Belgium and other EEC countries: often called 'continental' liver sausages. Smoked or unsmoked and more highly seasoned than English variety.

Pâtés

Pâté is the French word for pie. The term should really be used only for a meat or fish dish enclosed in pastry. It is however now commonly used for a large number of meat mixtures made from finely-ground liver, meats and game and cooked in a dish which is often lined with strips of bacon. Nearly every town in France produces its own pâté and probably the most famous is pâté de foie gras, from Strasbourg, made of goose liver. Britain imports pâtés from France and Belgium and some are also manufactured in this country.

Examine the pâtés in your local delicatessen. Where do they come from?

Are they in the dishes they were cooked in?

Suggest when they may be eaten and what you would serve with them.

Other meat products

A number of other meat products are made from trimmings and offal. They include brawn, haggis and faggots.

Canned meats

A large variety of canned meats is available as convenience foods. They include:
- canned meats that are served cold, e.g. hams, luncheon meats, tongue, poultry;
- cured meat (corned beef). The meat is cured and trimmed, coarsely cut and cooked before canning. South America supplies a large proportion of the world's corned meat.
- a large number of prepared meat and poultry dishes are also sold in cans. Special cans are made for meat pies and puddings.
- pastes and pâtés.

What are the advantages and disadvantages of canned meats? Do they taste as good and look as appetising as fresh meat?

How do they compare nutritionally with fresh meat?

Storage

The storage times for the products in this section vary enormously. The fresh sausages and pâtés are highly perishable foods. Others, such as salamis, are so heavily cured and smoked that they will keep almost indefinitely even without a refrigerator.

Fig. 11.24 Storage times for sausages, pâté and bought meat pies

	larder	refrigerator	freezer
pâté	1 day	2 days	1 month
fresh sausages without preservative	1 day	2 days	up to 3 months
fresh sausages with preservative	1 day	2–3 days	up to 3 months
meat pies (bought)	1 day	2 days	not recommended

NB   The storage-life of canned meats is at least 12 months in the store cupboard. The exception is large cans of ham which may require refrigerator storage and have a 'use by' date on the can as the temperatures reached in the canning process may not be adequate completely to sterilise the ham.

QUESTIONS

1 Write a paragraph about each of the following, giving examples of their uses in cookery:
- (a) gelatine
- (b) offal
- (c) accompaniments to roast meat and poultry.

2 What do you understand by the term 'cheaper cuts of meat'? Give three examples of cheaper cuts of beef, lamb and pork.

What advice would you give about cooking these cuts of meat?

What would be the effect on the meat of the cooking method you have suggested?

3 Draw a clearly labelled diagram to illustrate the structure of meat.

Write a paragraph about each of the following:
- muscle fibres
- collagen
- elastin
- myoglobin.

4 State two nutrients other than fat and protein contained in meat.

Do poultry and offal provide the same amounts of these nutrients?

Discuss the value of meat and meat products in the normal diet.

5 (a) Name the principal cuts of either lamb or pork using a diagram to illustrate your answer.
  (b) Suggest suitable ways of cooking the cuts you have chosen.
(Welsh, 1978)

6 The weekly consumption of poultry increased 10 times between 1955 and 1980.

Give reasons for this and explain how you would include poultry in the diet.

Why is it important thoroughly to defrost and cook frozen chickens?

What other poultry do you see in the shops?

What is the difference between poultry and game?

7 Consumers rate tenderness as a very important quality of meat.

What may have been done to meat before you buy it to make sure it is going to be tender when cooked correctly?

Describe ways in which the tenderness of meat can be improved during preparation and cooking in the kitchen.

8 What are the qualities to look for when choosing beef?

What are the advantages and disadvantages of buying meat in a supermarket rather than from a butcher's shop?

Name one expensive and one cheaper cut of beef and

say how you would prepare, cook and serve each one. (London, 1980)

9 Why is the storage life of pork in the freezer shorter than that of beef or lamb?

Discuss the reasons why the storage life of mince and offal is so short.

10 What do you understand by the term 'curing' in relation to meat?

Explain how this process is used in bacon production.

Name three cuts of bacon. Suggest ways you would cook and serve each one.

What is the difference between bacon and ham?

11 How do you account for the popularity of the British sausage?

Describe ways in which sausages are used in menus.

Name four other types of sausage which are eaten in Britain.

Give the country of origin and the characteristics of each one.

12 Describe in detail the information you would expect to find on a tin of beef stew.

How might this information affect your choice of brand?

Discuss the value of having canned meats in the store cupboard.

Fruit, vegetables, nuts, pulses and textured vegetable protein (TVP)

12

Fruit and vegetables are very important commodities in our daily diet for several reasons:
- they make a meal more attractive because of their interesting colours and textures
- fresh fruit and vegetables (including potatoes) supply approximately 90% of the vitamin C in the diet
- they provide fibre and bulk to the diet.

Many different fruits and vegetables are grown throughout the world. There are also many varieties of particular fruits and vegetables. For example:
- *apples* Granny Smith, Cox's Orange Pippin, Worcester, Bramley
- *plums* Damson, Greengage, Victoria, Golden Drop
- *potatoes* King Edward, Jersey Royal, Red Desirée
- *cabbages* January King, Savoy, White Cabbage.

This wide range offers an interesting selection of refreshing fruit and vegetables which add variety to the diet throughout the year. Each country in the world grows fruit and vegetables suitable to its climate. Many countries also import those that are

not available locally or at a particular time of year or to supplement demand.

Fresh fruit and vegetables are highly perishable and should be eaten as soon as possible after harvesting. A large variety of processed fruit and vegetables (i.e. frozen, canned, dried) is also available and their characteristics are described later in this chapter.

What are vegetables, fruit, nuts and pulses?

All fruits and vegetables are plants or parts of plants that are used as food. Many different parts of plants are eaten. For example, spinach is the leaf, carrot is the root, cauliflower is the flower, and cucumber is the fruit of different plants. Nuts are the seeds contained in the fruit of certain plants (see p. 178).

Pulses are the dried seeds from one group of vegetables (see p. 179).

It is sometimes difficult to define what is a fruit and what is a vegetable. Botanically, a fruit is classified as the part of a plant that contains the seed. Traditionally, in food preparation, the fruits of some plants, e.g. marrow, avocado, peppers and tomatoes, are treated and served as vegetables. This conflict arises because vegetables were traditionally used as an accompaniment to a main course. Fruits were traditionally used for dessert. Nowadays, cooks may mix fruit and vegetables in salads or serve fruits as a sweet accompaniment to a main course, e.g. ham and pineapple. This traditional classification is thus rather artificial.

Nutritionally, fruit and vegetables are considered as one group and they provide a similar function in the diet. You will find many areas of similarity between them. This chapter examines fresh vegetables, fresh fruit, processed fruit and vegetables, nuts, pulses and finally TVP (see p. 180).

From the photographs of fruit and vegetables shown in plate 22, pick out those which are grown in Britain. Make a chart to show how they are grown and which areas of the country are the main growing areas.

Name the remaining fruits and vegetables and the countries where they are grown. Note the price of these fruits and vegetables in your local greengrocery shop. Taste as many as you can afford to buy. Suggest ways of using them in the diet.

Fig. 12.1 Classification of fresh vegetables

General term	Part of plant	Examples
green vegetables	leaves	Cabbage, lettuce, endive, spinach, watercress, Brussels sprouts, curly kale
	flowers	Broccoli, cauliflower, globe artichoke
	stems	Celery, asparagus
	fruits	Courgette, marrow, avocado, cucumber. Peppers and tomatoes are unusual in that these fruit turn from green to red as they ripen.
root vegetables	roots	Beetroot, celeriac, carrot, parsnip, radish, swede, turnip
	bulbs	Onion, garlic, leek
	tubers	Potato, Jerusalem artichoke, yam, cassava
legumes and plants that produce pods containing the seed.	pods	Runner beans, French beans, mange-tout, peas, okra
	seeds	Peas, broad beans
fungi	caps and stalks	Mushrooms

Fresh vegetables

Vegetables are usually broadly classified into three groups:
- green vetables;
- root vegetables;
- legumes.

Within these groups they are identified by the part of the plant they come from.

Choice of fresh vegetables

Vegetables deteriorate quickly. To enjoy the full food value, most flavour, crispest texture and most attractive colours they should be used as soon as possible after purchase. Here are some guidelines to help you choose vegetables:

1 Do not be tempted to buy more than you need.

2 Vegetables in season locally are usually at their lowest price and highest food value.

> Make a chart to show which vegetables are available where you live each month of the year.

3 Buy only where you can see the quality of the vegetables. This is sometimes difficult if you buy pre-packed vegetables, or if the retailer selects vegetables for you from behind a display.

4 Choose good quality vegetables:
- *green vegetables* The plants should have crisp fresh leaves with a bright colour. The outer, darker leaves have the higher food value. Beware of vegetables with these removed as it may mean the plant is old.
- *Root vegetables* These should have unblemished skins, free from spongy discoloured patches. Avoid very large root vegetables as they can be coarse-textured. Washed vegetables deteriorate more rapidly than unwashed.

In Britain potatoes are the main root vegetable grown, and 93% of the potatoes eaten are also grown in Britain. They are one of the staple foods of the country. Each person in Britain consumes 100 kg of potatoes every year. About 20% of the crop is made into 'convenience' forms of potato such as instant mashed potato, potato crisps and frozen chips.

There are about forty different varieties of potatoes grown. The early varieties are known as *new potatoes*. They have thin skins which should rub or scrape off. New potatoes are harvested from May to October. Maincrop potatoes are available from August to May and are sometimes known as *old potatoes*. They have firmer skins which are removed by peeling. They can be stored for several weeks in a dark, dry, cool place so they are often bought in bulk, when they are cheaper. The texture and colour of different varieties means that some are more suitable for making chips, e.g. Majestic, and some for mashing, e.g. King Edward and Pentland Hawk. Some people prefer red-skinned varieties which have creamier coloured flesh than the white-skinned types.

● *Legumes*   The pods should be firm, crisp and not too big. The pods should not be too full, or the vegetable may be coarse-textured. There is an enormous variety of peas, beans and lentils. Their seeds are frequently dried are known as pulses (see p. 179).

Look at the potatoes in your local greengrocer's. How many varieties can you find? How do you recognise them?

Which of the varieties you have identified would you recommend for boiling, cooking in their jackets, roasting with meat making chips?

When Brussels sprouts are in season, compare the cost per kg with frozen Brussels sprouts.

Cook both varieties. Compare the colour, texture and taste. How long did it take to prepare each sort?

How many varieties of cabbage are available in your local greengrocer's?

Why is cabbage not a very successful frozen-vegetable?

Composition and food value of fresh vegetables

Although vegetables contain *80-95% water*, they are a significant source of *dietary fibre*, because plant cell walls are cellulose. Cellulose gives the characteristic structure and texture to vegetables and because it is indigestible it helps other foods pass through the digestive system.

Vegetables are also an important source of *mineral elements and vitamins*, expecially vitamin C. The vitamin C content of several vegetables in shown in Fig. 12.2

The colour and flavour are also recognisable features of vegetables. They have no nutritional value but they create a range of distinctive vegetables, which adds interest to the diet, so that people may want to eat more. The *attractive colours* are due to several pigments. For example, the green colour of leafy vegetables is caused by chlorophyll, the red colour in radish, red cabbage and beetroot is due to anthocyanin and the orange-yellow colour of carrots is due to carotenoids and flavones. *The distinctive flavour* is characteristic of each vegetable, and can be recognised by taste and smell. As the plants grow and ripen complicated mixtures of chemical substances are produced. These are present in minute amounts, but produce very specific flavours. For example, the strong smell associated with boiling certain vegetables and the irritating effect on the eyes of peeling onions, are caused by the release of some volatile substances.

The composition and food value of different vegetables vary according to the part of the plant from which they come.

(a) Green vegetables

The *leaves* of green vegetable plants manufacture carbohydrate by the process of photosynthesis. The starches and sugars produced are not stored in the leaves but carried away to other parts of the plant for use or to be stored. Therefore the leaves have a low energy value (see p. 50) and can be included in large quantities in slimming diets. The cellulose walls of leaves are very thin and they maintain their characteristic crisp structure only because of the water they contain. After picking they soon shrivel and wilt, because of the loss of their water supply.

Green leafy vegetables are very valuable in the diet because of the vitamins, mineral elements and fibre they provide. They are nutritionally most valuable when eaten fresh and raw. *Vitamin C* is easily destroyed in wilted vegetables and by the cooking process (see p. 170). The leaves (especially the dark green outer leaves) are also rich in *carotene (vitamin A)*. They are also important sources of the B vitamin, *folic acid*, and the minerals *calcium and iron*. Spinach and watercress are particularly rich sources of *iron*. It is important to remember that the absorption of iron is assisted by vitamin C. Hence it is essential to prepare vegetables so as to retain the maximum amount of vitamin C (see pp. 170-171).

The *flowers* of green vegetable plants, e.g. brocolli

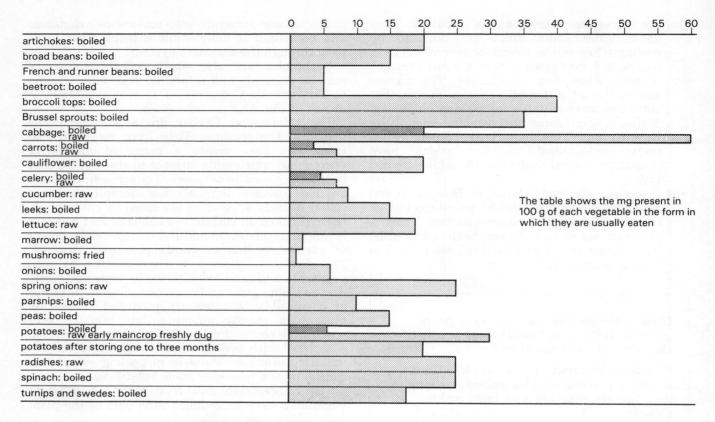

The table shows the mg present in 100 g of each vegetable in the form in which they are usually eaten

Fig. 12.2 Vitamin C content of fresh vegetables (mg/100 g)

or cauliflower, do not store carbohydrate, and so have a low energy value (see p. 50). They are a particularly valuable source of vitamin C.

Stems of green vegetable plants are not storage organs but only the pathways for carrying nutrients from roots to leaves and from leaves to storage organs. They are fibrous and provide fibre and some minerals and vitamins.

The *fruits* of green vegetable plants, e.g. cucumber, avocado, pepper, courgette provide vitamin C and some carbohydrate in the form of starch or sugar as the fleshy portion is a store of food. Many, e.g. the cucumber, have a high water content and therefore have a low energy value. The exception is the avocado pear which contains a high percentage of oil.

(b) Root vegetables

Root vegetables come from plants with large storage organs. They contain the carbohydrates manufactured in the leaves as either starch or sugar. Many of them are, therefore, valuable energy foods.

They are less valuable than green vegetables as a source of Vitamin C.

Tubers, e.g. the potato, provide energy in the form of starch. However, as potatoes contain 80% water, they are a much less concentrated form of energy than bread. The energy value is greatly increased if potatoes are cooked in fat:
- 100 g boiled potatoes provide 80 kcal or 331 kJ
- 100 g chips provide 236 kcal or 989 kJ

Because of the large quantities in which potatoes are eaten in Britain they also provide one-third of the vitamin C in the average diet. The vitamin C content is highest in new potatoes and falls gradually as the storage time increases. Small amounts of protein found mainly just under the skin, iron and the B vitamins are also present.

Yams are similar to potatoes and form the staple part of a Caribbean diet.

The *roots*, e.g. carrots, parsnips, turnips contain more water and therefore supply less energy than potatoes. Carrots are an important source of carotene (vitamin A) and turnips and swedes provide some vitamin C but no carotene.

The *bulbs*, e.g. onions, store the carbohydrate in

the form of sugar, but their main value is their strong flavour which helps to make savoury dishes more interesting and appetising.

(c) Legumes

Legumes are plants that produce pods containing seeds. Those legumes that are eaten whole, e.g. runner beans, are particularly nutritious because the pod is similar in food value to green leaf vegetables, i.e. it supplies fibre, vitamins A and C, calcium and iron; but the seed also contains some protein, carbohydrate, additional vitamin C and some of the B-group vitamins.

Other seeds, e.g. peas, contain high proportions of water, vitamin C, some protein and carbohydrate.

(d) Fungi

Fungi, e.g. mushrooms, are eaten almost entirely for their flavour. They supply a little protein and minerals but only negligible amounts of vitamins.

The use of fresh vegetables in the diet

(a) Raw vegetables

Because vegetables are such an important source of vitamin C which is easily destroyed by heat, it is especially important that some raw fresh vegetables are included in diet. The water-soluble vitamins (C and B-group) and mineral elements are all retained in raw vegetables. It is important to wash all vegetables, to remove any traces of pesticides they may have been sprayed with during the growing period.

It is possible to use raw vegetables to produce attractive *salads* at all times of the year using a variety of the fresh vegetables, fruit and nuts available, e.g. when lettuce becomes scarce and expensive in winter, cabbage can be substituted.

> Make a selection of vegetables suitable for a mixed salad for four people, (a) in summer, (b) in winter.
>
> Prepare and weigh vegetables for one of these salads and calculate how much vitamin C will be supplied by an average portion.

In many countries salads are used as an accompaniment to a main meal. They can be served as a side dish with a main course especially with grilled meats and poultry dishes. Salads are also eaten as a main dish often with the addition of animal protein in the form of eggs, cheese, cold meat or fish.

Salad dressings are added to give flavour and make the salad more palatable. The dressing should always be added to a salad immediately before it is served or the salad vegetables will become limp, soggy and unpalatable. Where salads are being eaten as part of a slimming diet it is possible to substitute ingredients of low energy value in the dressing, e.g. yoghurt or buttermilk.

(b) Cooked vegetables

Some vegetables are always cooked because:
- they are unpalatable when eaten raw and may be difficult to digest
- their texture is too firm or tough. Cooking softens the cellular tissue.

Some vegetables which can be eaten raw are also cooked:
- to reduce the bulk, so that more can be eaten, e.g. cabbage, spinach;
- to alter the texture and make digestion easier, e.g. carrot;
- so that they can be served as a hot accompaniment, e.g. tomatoes, peppers.

The aim in preparing and cooking vegetables should be to preserve their nutritional value and produce an attractive, palatable dish. Cooked vegetables should be tender but firm and the natural colour retained. Some changes in nutritional value, texture, colour and flavour are inevitable.
- nutrient loss
- texture change
- colour change
- flavour change

> Look at plate 8(c), to see the differences between well cooked and over-cooked cabbage.

1 Nutrient losses in cooking vegetables

Vitamin C and thiamin (Vitamin B_1), are both water-soluble and heat-sensitive. Green vegetables lose 50-70%, and potatoes 20-40% of their vitamin C during cooking. If vitamin C can be retained, then other water-soluble nutrients are also retained. The only way to minimise these losses is by understanding and following a very careful cooking proceedure, as shown in fig. 12.3.

Fig. 12.3 Cooking green vegetables

Action	Reason
1 Vegetables should be prepared immediately before use.	Vitamin C is readily oxidised either by exposure of cut surfaces to air, or by the action of the enzyme oxidase present in the plant tissues (see p. 31).
2 Vegetables should be washed thoroughly, but never soaked in water.	Vitamin C is water-soluble, and will be dissolved in the water, if vegetables are soaked.
3 Vegetables should be plunged into boiling water.	The enzyme oxidase is destroyed by a high temperature.
4 Vegetables should be cooked in the minimum of water needed to prevent burning. Any vegetable liquid remaining after cooking should be used in a gravy or sauce.	During cooking, vitamin C, thiamin and soluble mineral salts pass from the plant tissues into the cooking liquid.
5 *Do not* add sodium bicarbonate to the cooking water.	Destruction of vitamins is increased in an alkaline solution.
6 Cook for a minimum time, using a tight-fitting lid on the saucepan. The vegetables should be tender but still crisp.	Prolonged heating increases vitamin loss.
7 Serve immediately.	Vitamin losses are greater when vegetables are kept warm.

If the procedure outlined in Fig. 12.3 is not followed carefully, there will be considerable loss of vitamin C.

The following experiment shows the vitamin C loss in several ways of cooking cabbage, and hence the importance of following the recommended cooking procedure for green vegetables.

Experiment: to investigate the loss of vitamin C in preparing and cooking cabbage

Equipment
Burette
Some 10 ml pipettes with rubber bulbs
Conical flask
Filter funnel and filter paper
Measuring cylinders (100 ml and 50 ml)
Pestle and mortar or liquidiser
DCPIP tablets
Ascorbic acid tablets
20% Metaphosphoric acid
Distilled water
Cabbage samples
Salt
5% acetic acid

Experimental method
Dichlorophenol-indophenol (DCPIP) is a dye which is blue when dissolved in water, red in acid conditions and ascorbic acid reduces the dye to a colourless compound. This dye is used in a titration for estimating the concentration of ascorbic acid in a food. This can change in alkaline or neutral conditions so acetic acid is added to the test sample.
1 Make up the dye solution by putting two DCPIP tablets into a 100 ml measuring cylinder and adding distilled water so that the dye solution is made up to 100 ml. Use the filter funnel to pour the dye solution into a burette held in a clamp.
2 Prepare the food samples by grinding in a pestle and mortar or liquidiser with a few ml of 5% acetic acid. Filter into a 100 ml measuring cylinder, washing out the pestle and mortar or liquidiser with more acetic acid until the mixture is made up to 50 ml. Add distilled water to a total volume of 100 ml.
3 Take 10 ml of acidified food extract, using a pipette with a rubber bulb. Put the solution into a conical flask placed on a white tile below the burette. Note the level of dye solution in the burette (measure the lowest point of the meniscus of the liquid).
4 Add the dye solution carefully. Contents of the conical flask should be disturbed as little as possible during the titration.
5 As the dye solution runs into the conical flask it first turns pink because there is acetic acid in the flask and then the ascorbic acid reduces the dye to a colourless compound. When all the ascorbic acid has reacted with the dye the end point of the titration has been reached and a slight pink colour remains (for at least 15 seconds).

6 Note the second level of the dye solution and work out the volume of dye solution used.

Sample 1: Raw cabbage

Shred 50 g of mixed cabbage leaves (i.e. those from heart, centre and outermost parts). Add 50 ml of 20% metaphosphoric acid and 150 ml water.

Liquidise and pour into a 250 ml measuring cylinder. Add water to make up to 250 ml. Strain liquid through a muslin to remove any remaining solids.

Pipette 10 ml of juice into a conical flask. Titrate against indophenol dye solution, as shown. Repeat until constant readings are obtained.

Sample 2: Cabbage cooked by method recommended for green vegetables

Boil 200 ml water in small saucepan, shred 50 g of mixed cabbage leaves. Plunge into boiling water. Add 1×2.5 ml spoon salt, replace saucepan lid. Cook for 5 minutes. Strain off any remaining liquid. Continue as for sample 1.

Sample 3: Cabbage soaked in water before cooking

Shred 50 g of mixed cabbage leaves. Leave to soak in water for two hours before cooking. Strain off water. Continue as for sample 2.

Sample 4: Cabbage cooked for a long time

Boil 200 ml water in a small saucepan. Shred 50 g of mixed cabbage leaves. Plunge into boiling water, add 1×2.5 ml spoon salt, replace saucepan lid. Cook for 30 minutes. Continue as for sample 1.

Sample 5: Cabbage cooked in a large volume of water

Boil 1 litre water. Shred 50 g of mixed cabbage leaves. Plunge into boiling water, add 1×2.5 ml spoon salt, replace saucepan lid. Cook 5 minutes. Continue as sample 1.

Sample 6: Cabbage put into cold water

Shred 50 g mixed cabbage leaves. Put into small saucepan containing 200 ml cold water and 1×2.5 ml spoon salt. Bring to the boil. Replace the saucepan lid. Boil 5 minutes. Continue as sample 1.

Sample 7: Cabbage kept warm after cooking

Boil 200 ml of water in small saucepan. Shred 50 g mixed cabbage leaves. Plunge into boiling water. Add 1×2.5 ml spoon of salt. Replace saucepan lid. Cook 5 minutes. Strain off any excess liquid. Keep cabbage warm for 30 minutes. Continue as for sample 1.

Observations

1 Calculate the amount of vitamin C in your sample of cabbage. If x is the amount of vitamin C present, and if z ml of dye solution is required, then you have an amount equivalent to $\frac{z}{x}$ mg of vitamin C.

The total volume of 250 ml liquid contains 50g cabbage;

    10 ml liquid contains 2 g cabbage;

    2 g cabbage contains $\frac{z}{x}$ mg vitamin C;

    100 g cabbage contains $\frac{z}{x} \times 50$ mg vitamin C.

2 Record the results of all the experiments on a chart.

3 Explain the variation in results obtained. Which is the best way to cook cabbage to retain a maximum amount of vitamin C?

The following graph shows the type of variation you are likely to obtain from the results of your experiment. Calculate the percentage loss of vitamin C for each cooking method. From these results, describe the method you would choose to cook green vegetables.

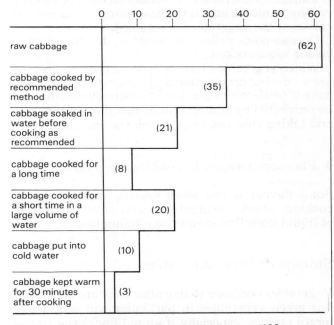

Fig. 12.4 Vitamin C content of cabbage mg/100 g

2 Texture-changes in cooking vegetables

Changes occurring in the texture of vegetables during cooking are due to the softening of the cellulose and the gelatinisation of the starch. Overcooking makes vegetables soft and mushy. Vegetables should be cooked only until they are tender but firm. This means that some of the crispness of the raw vegetable is retained. Potatoes should be cooked until they are soft but not mushy. They tend to break up if overcooked in rapidly boiling water and should only be simmered after reaching boiling point. (A few drops of vinegar or lemon juice provides an acidic liquid which helps to prevent potatoes breaking up.) The cooking-time of vegetables is determined by the amount of cellulose the vegetable contains, e.g. carrots require a longer cooking-time than a green vegetable.

3 Colour-changes in cooking vegetables.

When green vegetables are heated, plant cells release acids which change the bright green colour of chlorophyll to an olive green colour which is less attractive. Some colour change is inevitable but can be kept to a minimum by correct cooking.

The pigments in red vegetables are very soluble in water. If the cooking-water is alkaline, as tap water often is, the colour will change from red to purple or blue. (The pigments behave in the same way as litmus paper does in a chemistry experiment.) The change is reversible and if a small amount of vinegar or lemon juice is added to the cooking liquid the red colour of the vegetables is retained.

Orange and yellow vegetables do not change colour when cooked.

White vegetables have a tendency to go grey or brown during preparation and cooking, e.g. potatoes have a tendency to blacken. The discolouration can be prevented by adding acid (lemon juice or vinegar) and taking care not to overcook the vegetables.

4 Flavour-changes in cooking vegetables

Some flavour is lost when volatile acids escape in cooking. Short cooking-times and small quantities of liquid keep flavour-loss to a minimum.

Storage of fresh vegetables

Vegetables continue to live after they are harvested but green vegetables in particular wilt and deteriorate rapidly, especially if stored under the wrong conditions.

Care should be taken in handling all vegetables as even firm vegetables such as potatoes bruise easily. If the cells are damaged by careless handling, enzymes are released and vitamin C is destroyed. There is always some loss of vitamin C during storage, but a low temperature for storage of green vegetables and a moisture-proof wrapping keep this to a minimum.

Some refrigerators have 'crisper' boxes for salad

storage. Vegetables and salads may be kept in these boxes either unwrapped or in moisture-proof bags, but for as short a time as possible. Lettuce and other green vegetables may also be stored for a short time in a saucepan with a well-fitting lid in a cool place.

Some vegetables become less palatable during storage because the sugar they contain is changed to starch. This happens with peas. These vegetables should also be eaten as fresh as possible.

Firm root vegetables may be stored for longer periods in a cool, dry, well-ventilated place. Potatoes require a dark place and should be stored unwashed in a thick paper not a polythene bag. Warmth makes potatoes sprout, damp causes rot and light makes them turn green. The ideal storage temperature for them is 10-15°C.

Home-freezing of vegetables

Most young fresh vegetables freeze very well. Peas and carrots may be frozen without blanching if they are to be stored for one or two months. All other vegetables should be blanched before they are frozen, to retard the action of enzymes, which would spoil the colour and flavour of the vegetables.

Vegetables should be frozen in quantities suitable for one meal unless the vegetables are suitable for 'free flow' packs (e.g. peas, broad beans and mushrooms). These vegetables can be frozen in a single layer on a tray and packed after freezing into polythene bags or boxes.

Salad vegetables do not freeze well as they

Fig. 12.5 Recommended storage-times: vegetables

	Cool larder	Refrigerator	Freezer (after blanching)
new potatoes	4–5 days	not recommended	6–9 months
old potatoes	2–6 months	1–2 weeks	6–9 months
carrots	1 week	1–2 weeks	6–9 months
green vegetables	1–2 days	5–7 days	6–9 months
peas	unshelled: 1 day	4–5 days in shells. shelled: 1 day	6–9 months
lettuce	1 day		not recommended
tomatoes	up to 1 week (depends on ripeness)	1 week	6 months
cucumber	3–4 days	1 week	not recommended
mushrooms	1 day	2–3 days	3–4 months

become very limp. Tomatoes, mushrooms, peppers and onions are soft when thawed and only suitable for cooking. Potatoes can be frozen as chips or croquettes or in other made-up dishes.

All frozen vegetables should be cooked from frozen and will require a shorter cooking-time than fresh vegetables if they have been blanched.

Fresh fruit

Fruit is usually eaten as a dessert, a snack or in salads (see p. 169). Fruit usually contains the seed of the plant. Fruits are usually broadly classified into four groups:

Type of fruit	Examples
citrus fruits	oranges, lemons, grapefruits, satsumas
stone fruits	plums, apricots, cherries, greengages, damsons
berry fruits	strawberries, raspberries, blackberries, gooseberries, red and blackcurrants, grapes
fleshy fruits	apples, pears, melons, pineapple, bananas

NB Rhubarb does not contain the seed, but is the stalk of a green leaf plant.

Look at plate 22(b). Can you identify each of these fruits? Which fruits are grown in Britain and which are imported? Taste as many as you can afford.

Choice of fresh fruit

Fruit should be eaten when it is just ripe. Under-ripe fruit is often green in colour, the flesh is hard and has a bitter flavour. The starch content is high and the fruit is acid with a sour taste and is difficult to digest.

Ripe fruit is sweeter because the carbohydrate changes into sugar and the acid content of most fruit decreases. The water content increases and the fruit becomes softer, juicier and more pleasant to eat.

Here are some guidelines to help you choose good quality fruit. Notice how many of the criteria are similar to those for choosing vegetables.

1 Do not be tempted to buy more than you need.

2 Fruits 'in season' are usually at their lowest price

and highest food value. Some fruits, especially apples, are kept in cold storage for several months, which gives a constant supply throughout the year, but prices vary widely. Other fruits are imported when they are not available locally, e.g. strawberries, as climatic conditions vary throughout the world at different times in the year. Other types of fruit are always imported, as climatic conditions are unsuitable in Britain for the growth of citrus fruits, peaches, bananas and pineapples. Imported fruits are always more expensive than locally-grown varieties.

Make a chart to show the fruits available where you live each month of the year.

Give examples of the well-known varieties of each fruit.

---

3 Buy only where you can see the quality of the fruit. This is sometimes difficult if you buy pre-packaged fruit. The plastic cover for pre-packed fruit should have small perforations in it. This allows carbon dioxide to escape as the fruit matures, which would otherwise cause the fruit to soften.

If the retailer selects fruit for you – possibly from the back of a display counter – check the quality before leaving the shop.

Also check the quality of fruit sold in punnets, such as strawberries and raspberries. Buy these fruits only from stalls where there is a rapid turn-over. The fruit in the bottom of the punnet deteriorates quickly with the weight of the other fruit on top. It is often preferable to buy these fruits loose.

Beware of handling fruit on a self-service counter until you are sure you want to buy it. Fruit bruises easily with overhandling. A reputable retailer will exchange decaying fruit if it is pointed out at the time of purchase.

4 Choose good-quality fruit.

Fresh good-quality fruit should be under-ripe or just ripe, but never over-ripe. Ripe fruit will feel very slightly soft to touch; under-ripe fruit will be firm to touch, but will soften as it ripens. The fruit should be dry with no bruises or soft patches.

Fruit should be plump and feel quite heavy. They should not be huge, as over-sized fruits often have a coarse texture. Small fruits have a larger proportion of waste than plump fruits.

Beware of thick-skinned citrus fruits: the skin is waste! You can judge the thickness of the skin by its texture:
● thin-skinned fruit has a smooth surface;
● thicker-skinned fruit usually has a pitted surface.

Produce a chart to show the main fruits grown in the place where you live. Show the areas of the country where they are grown commercially.

Give examples of the well-known varieties of each fruit and their use in the diet.

When are the fruits in season?

Consider one type of fruit. Compare quality and price of fruit available:

(a) in a small greengrocery shop
(b) in a supermarket
(c) on a market stall.

Composition and food value of fresh fruit

Fresh fruit is composed mainly of *water* and *carbohydrate*. The amounts of protein and fat in fruit are negligible. The exceptions are olives and avocado pears, both of which have a high fat content.

Fig. 12.6 Water and carbohydrate in fresh fruit (%)

	water	carbohydrate	fibre
banana	71	19.2	1.11
apple	84	12.0	1.93
orange	86	8.5	2.0
lemon	91	1.4	0.9
melon	94	5.2	1.0
strawberries	89	6.2	2.2
blackcurrants	77.4	6.6	8.7

The carbohydrate in ripe fruit is mainly sugar, i.e. sucrose, glucose and fructose. These sugars are readily absorbed by the body. Because of the large amount of water present, fruits have low energy value (see p. 50) so they are valuable in slimming diets. Some carbohydrate is also present as cellulose and pectin. These carbohydrates are not digested but provide some *dietary* fibre. The pectins are important because they give fruit the ability to gel and form jam or jelly (see p. 177).

Fruit is most important as a major source of *Vitamin C* in the diet, especially as many fruits are eaten raw. The amount of vitamin C in different fruits varies widely as shown in Fig. 12.7.

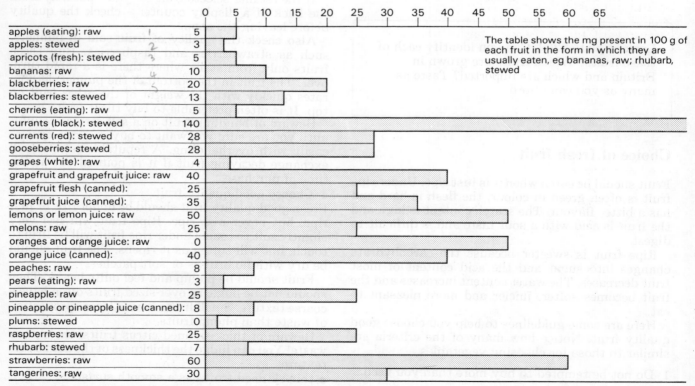

The table shows the mg present in 100 g of each fruit in the form in which they are usually eaten, eg bananas, raw; rhubarb, stewed

apples (eating): raw	5
apples: stewed	3
apricots (fresh): stewed	5
bananas: raw	10
blackberries: raw	20
blackberries: stewed	13
cherries (eating): raw	5
currants (black): stewed	140
currents (red): stewed	28
gooseberries: stewed	28
grapes (white): raw	4
grapefruit and grapefruit juice: raw	40
grapefruit flesh (canned):	25
grapefruit juice (canned):	35
lemons or lemon juice: raw	50
melons: raw	25
oranges and orange juice: raw	0
orange juice (canned):	40
peaches: raw	8
pears (eating): raw	3
pineapple: raw	25
pineapple or pineapple juice (canned):	8
plums: stewed	0
raspberries: raw	25
rhubarb: stewed	7
strawberries: raw	60
tangerines: raw	30

Fig. 12.7 Vitamin C content of fruit in mg per 100 g

Only minute traces of other vitamins and minerals are present in fruit. Carotene (vitamin A) is present in yellow and orange fruits, e.g. apricots, oranges. Eating apples encourages people to chew and use their teeth effectively.

The characteristic colours and flavours of fruit have no nutritional value, but they add interest and variety to the type of fruit available. The colouring and flavouring compounds are similar to those found in vegetables. The colours in fruits are due to the pigments they contain. For example, red, blue, purple and pink colours are due to anthocyanin pigments, orange and yellow colours are due to carotenoid, and creamy white fruits contain flavones. The flavour of fruits is due to mixtures of organic acids, essential oils and volatile substances which give each fruit its own distinctive smell and taste. The organic acids most commonly found are:

- malic acid in apples, pears, peaches, apricots;
- citric acid in citrus fruits and raspberries;
- tartaric acid in grapes;
- oxalic acid in pineapples.

These acids are responsible for the laxative action of fruit because they stimulate peristalsis in the intestine (see p. 26).

The use of fresh fruit in the diet

All fruits should be washed before they are eaten to remove all traces of pesticides they may have been sprayed with during the growing period.

(a) Raw fruit

Much of the fruit we eat is raw. The varied colours, flavours and textures of raw fruit add interest and variety to the diet. Raw fruits are an important source of vitamin C and dietary fibre, and should be included frequently in the diet either as a dessert, salad or a snack.

Most raw fruits, except those with a high acid content, turn dark on exposure to air when they are cut. The discolouration of the cut surfaces is caused by tannin compounds and enzymes present in the fruit coming into contact with air. This effect is most noticeable with white fruits, e.g. apples, bananas. This browning can be reduced or prevented by removing the oxygen, e.g. by adding a sugar syrup to a raw fruit salad; by changing the acidity, e.g. by adding lemon juice; or by blanching as a preliminary stage in freezing, when heat destroys the enzymes.

An enzyme is present in fresh pineapple which digests protein. If fresh pineapple is to be used in a gelatine-set dessert, it is important to blanch the pineapple in boiling water to inactivate the enzyme.

If this is not done, the enzyme partially digests (breaks down) gelatine, which is a protein and this prevents the dessert from setting. This enzyme has been destroyed in canned pineapple by the high temperature used in the canning process.

(b) Cooked fruit

Some varieties of fruit are unpalatable if eaten raw. These varieties are always cooked, e.g. gooseberries, rhubarb. Many other fruits are cooked when used in pies, puddings and in making jams and jellies.

When fruit is cooked it may become more digestible. The changes that occur in cooking fruit are similar to the changes in cooking vegetables (see plate 8(c)). These are changes in nutrient content, texture, colour and flavour.

1 *Nutrient loss in cooked fruit*

Vitamin C (the most important nutrient in fruit) is water-soluble and unstable when heated. Some loss is inevitable. The acids present help to preserve the vitamin C and consequently there is a smaller loss than in vegetable cooking (see p. 170). The liquid (juice) is usually served with the fruit and will contain some of the nutrients which have leeched out of the fruit. The high temperatures and cooking-time required for making jams and jellies mean that most of the vitamin C is destroyed.

2 *Texture-changes in cooking fruit*

The texture of fruit depends on the type and quantity of cellulose present. This also determines the amount of water required for cooking. Berries have very little cellulose and cook quickly in a small amount of water, but apples and pears require more water and a longer cooking time. Moist heat softens cellulose, but sugar strengthens the structure, so where it is desirable to retain the shape and texture of the fruit, e.g. in cooking plums, they should be cooked in a sugar solution. Very hard fruits, e.g. unripe pears should be cooked slightly to soften them before the sugar is added. Fruit that is to be served as a purée should also be cooked before the sugar is added.

3 *Colour-changes in cooking fruit*

Tapwater in hard water areas is alkaline and this may cause red or purple fruits to go blue during cooking. This can be prevented by adding lemon juice to the water. Red fruits such as strawberries tend to lose their colour when heated rapidly. Slow heating helps to retain the bright red colour. White fruits with a tendency to brown due to oxidation also keep their colour better if lemon juice is added to the liquid.

4 *Flavour-changes in cooking fruit*

Some flavour is lost when volatile acids escape in cooking. Short cooking-times and small quantities of liquid keep flavour loss to a minimum. A few fruits, particularly strawberries, develop a sharp, unpleasant flavour if cooked for too long with sugar.

Make a list of the ways in which raw and cooked fruit may be included in the menu.

Suggest ways of using fruit in the diet throughout the year.

Storage of fresh fruits

The enzymes responsible for the ripening process in fruit continue to function after the fruit has reached its peak quality. Some fresh fruits, especially soft berries, spoil very rapidly, become over-ripe, mushy, discoloured and susceptible to mould. These fruits should be purchased in small quantities. Very fresh citrus fruits can be stored for longer periods because of their protective skins. Only apples can be stored for several months in cold storage, or in a cool dark place.

Low temperatures and good air circulation are necessary for fruit storage. A refrigerator is suitable for most fruits. Bananas should not be stored in a refrigerator as the low temperature causes their skins and flesh to blacken. Apples stored for any length of time should be individually wrapped so that any decay will not spread.

If fruit is stored in plastic bags, these should always be punched with small perforations. This allows carbon dioxide to escape, which would otherwise soften the fruit very quickly.

Home-freezing of fresh fruit

Good-quality fruit can be frozen successfully if it is very fresh. Some fruits freeze more successfully than others, e.g. raspberries freeze better than strawberries. Bananas cannot be frozen as they turn black and pears lose their texture because of their high water-content.

Stones should be removed from fruit before freezing as they can give a taste to the fruit if left in. Citrus fruits should never be frozen with their skins on, as the flesh develops a strong bitter taste. Apples are best frozen as a purée to reduce bulk. Some fruits may be frozen and used later to make jam e.g. raspberries. Fruit pies and other fruit dishes can also be frozen.

There are four basic ways of freezing fruit. Blanching is not necessary.

1 *Dry pack* Nothing is added. The washed fruit is packed either free-flow (see p. 172) or in small quantities in plastic bags.
2 *Sugar pack* The fruit is gently mixed with sugar before packing.
3 *Sugar syrup* This method is good for fruits with tough skins or that easily change colour. Fresh lemon juice or ascorbic acid may be added to prevent browning. The syrup is used cold to prevent softening the fruit.
4 *Pulp* This method is for apples and for ripe, soft fruit, e.g. strawberries, to use for home-made mousses, ice-creams, etc.

Fig. 12.8 Recommended storage-times for fruit

	cool larder	refrigerator	freezer
apples	3–5 days up to 6 months in dark cellar	2 weeks	as pulp 6–9 moths
bananas	5 days	not recommended	not recommended
soft berries	1 day	2 days	up to 1 year
citrus fruit	1 week	2 weeks	3–6 months in segments. Whole fruit: unsuitable.
stone fruits	1–3 days	up to 1 week	up to 1 year

Plate 21
Selection of fats and oils, and the
seed plants used in their production

SUNFLOWER

SAFFLOWER AND CORN

RAPESEED

SOYA BEAN

PALM OIL AND COCONUT OIL

Plate 22

(a) Vegetables

(b) Fruits

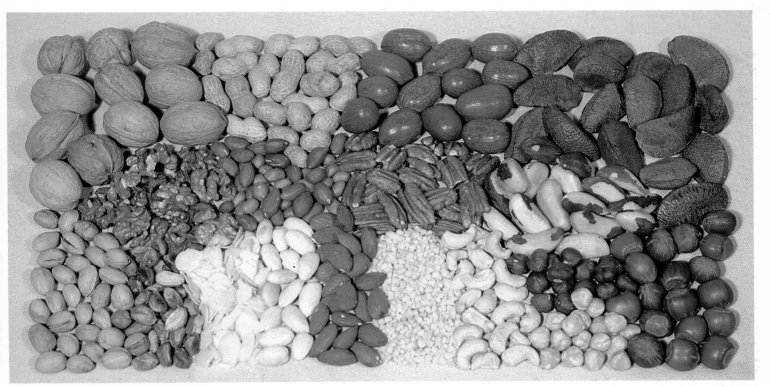

Plate 23 (a) *above* Nuts

(b) *below* Pulses

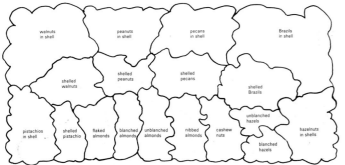

walnuts in shell	peanuts in shell	pecans in shell	Brazils in shell
shelled walnuts	shelled peanuts	shelled pecans	shelled Brazils
pistachios in shell	shelled pistachio	flaked almonds	blanched almonds	unblanched almonds	nibbed almonds	cashew nuts	unblanched hazels / blanched hazels	hazelnuts in shells

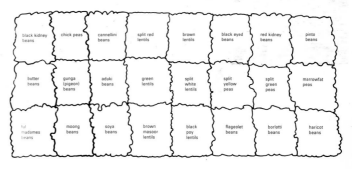

black kidney beans	chick peas	cannellini beans	split red lentils	brown lentils	black eyed beans	red kidney beans	pinto beans
butter beans	gunga (pigeon) beans	aduki beans	green lentils	split white lentils	split yellow peas	split green peas	marrowfat peas
ful madames beans	moong beans	soya beans	brown masoor lentils	black poy lentils	flageolet beans	borlotti beans	haricot beans

(a) Wheat

(b) Maize

(c) Barley

(d) Oats

(e) Rye

(f) Rice

Plate 24 Cereal plants and breakfast cereals

(g) Breakfast cereals   1 Sultana Bran   2 Fruit 'n' Fibre   3 Sugar Puffs   4 Shredded Wheat   5 Weetabix   6 Wheat flakes   7 Hot Oat Cereal   8 Ready Brek   9 Jordan's Oat Cereal   10 Crunchy Nut Corn Flakes   11 Corn Flakes   12 Frosties   13 Coco Pops 14 Rice Krispies   15 Ricicles   16 Bran Buds   17 Bran Flakes 18 ALL-BRAN   19 Bran   20 Start   21 Harvest Crunch 22 Country Store   23 Special K

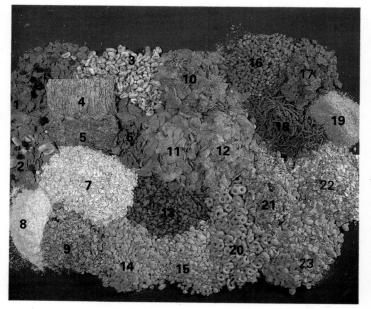

Processed fruit and vegetables

As fresh fruit and vegetables are only available at certain times of the year, and because they are highly perishable foods, 'convenience' forms are very popular and useful. Many fruits and vegetables which have been processed are available dried, canned, frozen or preserved as chutneys, jams, jellies and marmalade.

1 Drying (see p. 88)

Modern methods produce clean, attractive dried fruit. For example, currants, sultanas and raisins are all types of dried grape; prunes are dried plums. Dried frieds such as dates, figs, apricots and apples are also available.

The most popular dried vegetables used are potatoes, onions and pulses.

2 Canning (see p. 88)

A large variety of canned fruit and vegetables is available. Peas and tomatoes were some of the first foods to be preserved by canning, in 1830, and are probably still the most popular canned vegetables today. Baked beans canned in tomato sauce are also a very popular product. Some fruits are more generally available in Britain as a canned product, e.g. peaches, lychees, pineapple.

3 Freezing (see p. 89)

Freezing has proved to be a particularly successful method of preservation for fruit and vegetables because the colour, flavour and vitamin C content of the fresh produce are retained much better than in other methods of preservation.

A large variety of frozen vegetables and fruits are now available. Fruit is also frozen in fruit pies, desserts.

4 Crystallisation (see p. 88)

Some fruits are preserved by placing them in tanks containing strong sugar syrup. The water in the fruits is replaced by the sugar syrup. The fruits are then left to dry: the sugar remains and acts as a preservative.

The crystallised products most commonly used are glacé cherries and candied orange and lemon peel but other fruits are also crystallised and sold as luxury foods to be eaten as sweets or to decorate foods, e.g. pineapple, apricots and lemons. The skin of the angelica plant, the rhizomes of the ginger plant and some flower petals, e.g. violets, are also crystallised.

5 Jam, jelly and marmalade

Fruits contain varying proportions of polysaccharides (see p. 25). Some combine together in ripe fruits to form another carbohydrate: pectin, a gum-like substance, which can be released from the cell walls by crushing the fruit and cooking it for a short time. When the pectin is mixed with the right proportions of acid and sugar, in jam-making, the mixture will set and form a gel.

It is important that the fruit used for jam-making should be just ripe: In under-ripe fruit, the pectin is in an insoluble form, pectose: this can be changed to pectin by cooking with acid. However, in over-ripe fruit the pectin has changed to pectic acid which has lost its setting power, so over-ripe fruit is useless for jam-making. Apart from helping to change pectose to pectin and the pectin to form a better gel, the acid which may occur naturally or be added improves the flavour and colour and prevents crystals of sugar forming during storage.

There should be approximately 60% sugar in the finished jam. A larger proportion causes the sugar to separate as crystals and a lower percentage means that the jam will not keep but have a tendency to ferment and go mouldy (see p. 82).

The keeping-quality of a jam depends mainly on the proportion of sugar, on the right amount of boiling and the exclusion of air and moisture when covering and storing the jam.

6 Pickles and chutneys

Pickling is a chemical method of preservation (see p. 88) in which vegetables and fruits are stored completely covered with spiced vinegar. Chutney is the name given to a hot sweet pickle originating from India, consisting of mangoes and chillies. It is now widely varied and includes fruit, vegetable, spices, vinegar and sugar. It is usually the consistency of jam, but does not gel.

Effects of processing on the nutrients in fruit and vegetables

The processes which cause some loss of nutrients are blanching, heat processing and drying.

Freezing has little effect on nutritional value and as the process takes place very soon after harvesting, nutrients in frozen fruit and vegetables are well retained. Some minerals and water-soluble vitamins are lost when vegetables are blanched before freezing.

Heat processing in canning reduces the amounts of heat-sensitive vitamins, especially vitamin C and the B-vitamins thiamin and folic acid. The loss depends on the time and temperature used for processing and the acidity of the food in the cans. After processing the vitamins remaining are stable as long as the can is sealed. Some soluble vitamins remain in the liquid: hence the liquid in canned foods should be used whenever possible.

Drying in controlled conditions has little effect on most nutrients but about half of the vitamin C is lost. Dried fruits which may contain as much as 70% sugar are therefore considered as useful energy foods and a good source of some mineral elements, e.g. dried apricots are a rich source of carotene (vitamin A); sultanas and currants are rich sources of iron.

Vitamin C lost in drying potatoes and fruit juices may be replaced by adding ascorbic acid to return the vitamin C content to the level found in the fresh produce. This can be determined by reading the pack label. Ascorbic acid is also added to some concentrated fruit drinks, e.g. blackcurrant syrup to replace that lost in processing.

It is important to remember that good quality, well-prepared raw or cooked fruit and vegetables are the best source of vitamin C, but that wilted produce which is badly-prepared with probably contain less of the vitamin than the processed varieties.

Other convenience fruit and vegetable products

Fruit juices and some vegetable juices are available in a variety of forms:

frozen   concentrated natural juice
canned   unsweetened and sweetened varieties
bottled   concentrated and normal strength
cartons   normal strength

as well as a tremendous variety of fruit-flavoured squash and carbonated drinks which also contain fruit. There are also some dried fruit drinks.

Canned fruit pie and flan fillings are also a very popular convenience food. They contain the fruit in a thickened sweetened juice.

Nuts

Nuts are defined as any seed or fruit containing an edible kernel with a hard or brittle shell. They are usually hard and oily.

Our nomadic ancestors gathered fruit and nuts for food, before they hunted animals. Nuts were their main source of protein. The oils present were used for cooking. Powdered nuts were used to thicken and flavour dishes as coconut is used today in curries. The Romans served all kinds of nuts as a dessert. Nuts were especially valuable as they keep almost indefinitely in their shells.

Today, nuts are particularly important in vegetarian cookery as a relatively concentrated form of protein. However, they are deficient in the amino acid lysine, and therefore only of low biological value. As they are also rich in fat they are a concentrated source of energy. They are a good source of the B-vitamins but contain no vitamin A or C. They provide useful amounts of dietary fibre

Shelled nuts are available in many different forms: whole, slivered, chopped, blanched and ground as well as those which are roasted and salted for snacks. Peanuts are particularly popular as snacks, and useful in packed lunches. Note however, their high energy value, so beware of nibbling excessive amounts, especially if you are on a slimming diet!

Nuts add variety in texture, flavour and colour, and can be used in both savoury and sweet recipes. They keep almost indefinitely, so they are a useful store-cupboard product.

What are the main varieties of nuts available in your local supermarket?
Where do they come from?

Suggest ways nuts can be used:

(a) in their different forms in general food preparation
(b) in a vegetarian diet.

Fig. 12.9 Peanuts: composition per 100 g

energy value		nutrient value												
kcal	kJ	water	protein	fat	carbo-hydrate	dietary fibre	Ca	iron	vit. A	vit. D	thia-min	ribo-flavin	niacin	vit. C
		g	g	g	g	g	mg	mg	μg	μg	mg	mg	mg	mg
570	2364	4.5	24.3	49	8.6	8.1	61	2.0	0	0	0.23	0.1	21	0

Pulses

There is an enormous variety of pulses available. Look at plate 23(b) and identify as many as you can.

Pulses are the ripened and dried seeds of some legumes. Other leguminous plants, such as laburnum, produce seeds that are inedible because they contain poisonous substances.

Pulses are all very similar in structure. They consist of two seed leaves or *cotyledons*, which are full of stored food for the plant, a tiny root and shoot and a loose skin. The skins come off easily when pulses are soaked. As they are a good source of dietary fibre, the skins may be ground and added to some types of white flour to replace fibre lost in milling (see p. 204). This type of flour is then used to make fibre-enriched 'white' bread.

Nutritionally, pulses are more comparable with cereal grains than fresh vegetables. Pulses provide more energy and protein than fresh vegetables but lack the vitamin C (see Fig. 12.1). They should not be considered as substitutes for fresh vegetables. They are, however, a valuable food commodity.

Fig. 12.10 Comparison of fresh and dried peas (per 100 g)

	energy		protein	fibre	vitamin C
	kcal	kJ	g	g	μg
fresh	52	223	5.0	5.2	15
dried	103	438	6.9	4.8	0

All pulses are relatively good sources of vegetable protein, dietary fibre and calcium. They also provide iron and some B vitamins. The protein is of low biological value with the exception of that in soya beans which are increasingly used in the manufacture of textured vegetable protein (see p. 180).

● *Lentils* There are many different varieties of lentils. They are indigenous to the Mediterranean countries, India and the Middle East. Some are best known as various types of dhal. The two main types which are generally available are the orange-coloured Egyptian lentil and a French and German type which has a greeny-yellow tint. Lentils are particularly rich in protein. They are used in soups, salads and are a staple vegetarian food.

● *Peas* Peas are native to northern Europe. There are two main types of dried peas available: whole green peas, and split peas which have had the outer skin removed. Some peas are now also processed by accelerated freeze-drying (see p. 88).

● *Chick peas* are the chief pulse crop of India, where they are known as Bengal gram. They are usually split and separated from the husk before cooking.

● *Beans* There are many varieties of beans grown in different parts of the world. They are particularly nutritious as they contain appreciable amounts of protein, calcium, iron and some B-group vitamins. They are particularly useful for use in soups, casseroles, salads as they add interest in colour, texture and flavour.

The main types of dried beans available are red, black and white kidney beans, butter beans and haricot beans (these are the seeds from French beans). Haricot beans are used to make baked beans; even after processing they are relatively nutritious (see Fig. 12.11).

Many other types are also available in large supermarkets and health food stores, e.g. black-eyed beans, flagelots and mung beans (known also as black or green gram). Mung beans, which are grown in China and the United States are also used to produce *bean sprouts*. These are obtained by germinating the seeds in the dark until the sprouts reach the desired length. Bean sprouts contain a good supply of vitamin C.

Most dried pulses require soaking before cooking. Pulses absorb flavour well. They must also be cooked for a long time at a sufficiently high temperature to soften them and make them safe to eat. It has recently been discovered that this is particularly important when cooking dried red kidney beans. At low temperatures these beans contain a toxin which causes food poisoning. It is only at prolonged high temperatures that a chemical reaction changes the toxin to a non-toxic state. Canned red kidney beans are perfectly safe to eat as the canning process has changed the nature of the toxin.

Fig. 12.11 Food value of baked beans canned in tomato sauce (composition per 100 g).

energy value		water	protein	fat	carbo-hydrate	dietary fibre	Ca	Fe	vit. A	vit. D	thia-min	niacin	ribo-flavin	vit. C
kcal	kJ	g	g	g	g	g	mg	mg	μg	μg	mg	mg	mg	mg
64	270	73.6	5.1	0.5	10.3	7.3	45	1.4	0	0	0.07	0.05	1.3	trace

Soya beans

These have been grown and eaten in China and other parts of the Far East for over 4000 years. The Chinese still regard meat as a luxury and depend on the soya bean as their main source of protein. Today soya beans have become an important source of vegetable protein in Western countries, and about 70% of the world's crop is grown in the USA. The beans were originally grown as an oil seed crop (see p. 187), but now the residue left after extracting the oil is equally important. It is an excellent source of high biological protein and is being processed to produce food products which resemble meat but are much less expensive. These products, textured vegetable protein (TVP) are intended as a replacement for or an extension to the meat in our diet.

Production of textured vegetable protein

After the oil has been extracted from the beans they are ground to produce a de-fatted soya flour containing about 50% protein. This flour is mixed with water to form a dough to which colouring and flavouring can be added. The dough is put into a machine which is heated by a jacket of steam.

It is forced through the machine under pressure and 'extruded' or forced out through a nozzle. As it comes into contact with the air it expands into a spongy textured mass. A wide variety of sizes, colours and textures can be obtained by varying the process. Pieces resembling beef mince or diced stewing steak in appearance and texture are usually sold dehydrated and have a shelf-life of about one year.

Nutritional value

TVP is very similar to meat in its nutritional content. Dehydrated TVP must contain at least 50% protein before the word 'protein' can be used to dercribe it on food labels. It contains all the essential amino acids but has a lower proportion of methionine and tryptophan. These amino acids may be added in the manufacturing process. TVP is also fortified with the vitamins and minerals which are obtained in significant quantities from meat: thiamin, riboflavin, vitamin B_{12} and iron. TVP contains a low percentage of fat and therefore can be useful in slimming diets. Some manufacturers add fat during the production to improve the flavour.

Using TVP

The dehydrated TVP has to be rehydrated with two-to-three times its own weight of water. It requires only a few minutes' cooking, if it is used alone. It will readily absorb flavours and therefore it is usually soaked or simmered in hot stock to rehydrate according to the manufacturer's directions.

If it is being used as an extender to mince or a stew, it is cooked with the meat and absorbs the flavours of the gravy. There is no shrinkage in cooking and the pieces of TVP do not lose their texture with longer cooking times.

TVP is often used in the catering trade as an extender to hamburgers, sausages, curries, and in some dried, canned and frozen convenience foods. It is also available in small packets for the domestic market. In this form it is a useful store cupboard product. When skillfully used with interesting flavourings, TVP produces some tasty vegetarian dishes, or it can be used to extend, and therefore reduce the cost of dishes using minced meat or in casseroles.

Fig. 12.12 Beef and TVP: nutrients per 100 g

	Nutrient content protein g	fat g	carbohydrate g	moisture g	Energy Value kcal	kJ
beef (stewing steak, raw)	20.2	10.6	0	69	176	736
TVP (hydrated with 2 parts water to 1 part TVP)	16.3	0.3	10.4	70	108	452

QUESTIONS

1 'The use and versatility of vegetables tend to be undervalued in the diet.' Discuss this statement in relation to choice, use, preparation and service of vegetables.
(London, 1982)

2 Under the headings: Classification, Nutritive value, Effects of cooking; state what you know of the following:
(a) Brussels sprouts
(b) carrots
(c) lentils
Why are fresh vegetables important items of the diet? Describe a method of storing lettuce in order to maintain its fresh condition.
(Scottish, 1978)

3 List the fruit and vegetables that are richest in vitamin C.
What effects do preparation and cooking have on the vitamin C content?
How would you ensure that the fruit and vegetables that you purchase prepare, cook and serve contain the maximum amount of vitamin C possible?

4 Write notes on the following;
(a) cooking green leafy vegetables
(b) stewing fruit
(c) the use of processed fruit and vegetables.

5 How can an understanding of the nature, composition and behaviour of vegetables enable the cook to produce interesting meals which are of a high nutritional standard?
(London, 1981)

6 Name *two* substances which are present naturally in fruit and vegetables and which are responsible for their colour.
How does the colour of some fruits and vegetables change when they are cooked? Why does this happen?

7 (a) What are the main nutrients found in green vegetables and why are vegetables important in the diet?
(b) What points should be considered when buying green vegetables?
(c) List and discuss faults which often occur in vegetable preparation and cooking.
(Southern Universities, 1978)

8 List the varieties of products containing textured vegetable protein available in your supermarkets.
Are they to be used as substitutes or extenders for meat?
Does your local health food shop also sell textured vegetable protein and in what form is it available?

9 Why is textured vegetable protein such a valuable food?
Discuss:
(a) how it may be used in cookery;
(b) its advantages and disadvantages.

Fats and oils

13

A large variety of fats and oils is used in food preparation.

Look at plate 21. Which of these products are available locally? Look at the ingredient list and compare the cost of these products.

This chapter describes the composition, manufacture, suitability and use of fats and oils in food preparation. (For the chemical structure of fats and oils, and the importance of fat in the diet, see chapter 2.)

It is important to realise that fats and oils have a similar basic chemical structure (see p. 23). If they are solid, or semi-solid at room temperature (20°C), like butter and lard, they are known as 'fat'. The term 'oil' is used to describe the fats that are liquid at room temperature, like corn oil and olive oil. Some solid fats, such as margarine and white cooking fats, are manufactured from oils.

There is one important chemical characteristic that may affect your choice of fat. Fats and oils are large molecules built up from long chains of glycerol and a wide variety of fatty acids. The fatty acids vary in chemical composition: some are *saturated*, others are *unsaturated* (see p. 23). Many nutritionists recommend that it is wise to reduce the total amount of fat in the diet, and in particular those fats that contain saturated fatty acids.

Most fats and oils contain both saturated and unsaturated fatty acids, but as a general guide, animal fats contain higher proportions of saturated fatty acids than vegetable oils. (If a label on a packet of fat lists 'edible oils' as an ingredient it will contain a mixture of vegetable, animal and/or fish oils.)

There is also one important physical characteristic of fats and oils that affects their use in food preparation. Fats and oils do not mix with water, i.e. the liquids are immiscible. When two immiscible liquids are forced to combine and form a stable mixture, tiny droplets of one liquid are dispersed in the second liquid. This is called an *emulsion*. There are many situations when fats and oils are mixed with water or a water-based liquid. Examples are the manufacture of margarine and salad dressings, and in cake making.

Fig. 13.1 Degree of saturation of fat

High proportion of saturated fatty acids		*High proportion of polyunsaturated fatty acids*
Animal fats suet lard dripping butter ghee (clarified butter) some fish oils – proportion varies with type of fish	*Mixed animal, fish and vegetable oils* margarines and cooking fats containing 'edible' oils, e.g. Echo, Stork, Blue Band, Krona, Kraft, Cookeen, Trex, Spry. Low fat blends containing buttermilk and vegetable oils e.g. Gold. Low fat spread, e.g. Outline. Clover (spreadable butter) (a blended fat containing cream and vegetable oils)	*Vegetable oils* Sunflower oil Corn oil Other vegetable oils Margarines made from high proportion of sunflower oil, e.g. Flora. Margarine and cooking fats made from vegetable oils, e.g. Kraft Luxury blend Some fish oils, especially mackerel

There are two types of emulsion: the type depends on the proportion of oil and water in the mixture. When the proportion of oil greatly exceeds the water, the mixture is known as a *water-in-oil emulsion (w/o)*, e.g. butter, margarine. Tiny droplets of water are dispersed throughout the oil. This is the most common type of emulsion in food preparation. When the proportion of water greatly exceeds the proportion of oil, the mixture is known as an *oil-in-water emulsion (o/w)*, e.g. milk. Tiny droplets of oil are dispersed throughout the water-based liquid.

The difference in the structures of these two types of emulsion can be seen in Fig. 13.2, and in the following experiment.

Experiment: to examine the structure of emulsions

1 Make microscope slides of
   (a) a drop of milk
   (b) a thin smear of margarine

2 Observe each sample under a microscope. Draw what you can see.

3 Comment on the difference in structure of the two emulsions.

(a) Oil in water emulsion eg milk

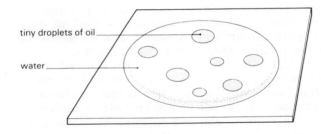

(b) Water in oil emulsion eg butter or margarine

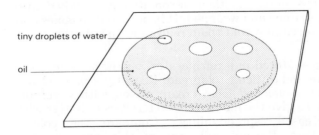

Fig. 13.2 Emulsions

The formation of an emulsion is dependent on:
● the temperature of the liquids;
● the way in which the liquids are combined;
● the amount of agitation of the mixture;
● the type of *emulsifier* naturally present or added.

Emulsifiers are substances that help immiscible liquids to combine and form a stable emulsion. They are used in both o/w and w/o emulsions. Molecules of the emulsifier surround the droplets of the liquid that are dispersed by agitation of the mixture as shown in Fig. 13.3. This lowers the surface tension between the two liquids and encourages them to combine, forming a stable emulsion. The action of emulsifiers used in food preparation is described on p. 122. The formation of emulsions is an important characteristic in the manufacture of fats, and in the use of fats and oils in food preparation.

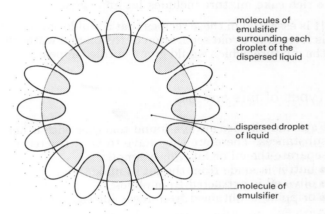

Fig. 13.3 The action of emulsifiers

Fig. 13.4 Pure and emulsified fats

	Natural fats	*Manufactured fats*
Pure fats	lard vegetable seed oils, e.g. corn oil, olive oil	white cooking fats, e.g. Trex, Cookeen
Emulsified fats w/o emulsions (i.e. high percentage fat, low percentage water)	butter (water, fat and emulsifiers naturally present)	margarine e.g. Echo, Stork (water and emulsifiers added during manufacture)
o/w emulsions (i.e. low percentage fat, high percentage water)	milk (water, fat and emulsifiers naturally present)	low-fat spreads, e.g. Outline, Gold (water and emulsifiers added during manufacture)

The fats and oils that we buy can be classified into two groups: that is according to whether they are pure fats or emulsified fats, as shown in Fig. 13.4.

Pure fats may occur naturally, e.g. lard, olive oil; or they may be manufactured entirely from mixtures of pure fats and oils, e.g. white cooking fats (see p. 191).

Emulsified fats contain a percentage of water. The water and emulsifier may be present in the fat naturally, e.g. butter, dripping. Some manufactured emulsified fats, e.g. margarine and low-fat spreads are produced by adding water and an emulsifier.

Both pure fats and emulsified fats are frequently used in recipes which include water or a water-based liquid, for example:
- salad dressings (French and mayonnaise) include oil and vinegar;
- rich cake mixture includes fat and eggs.

It is essential in these recipes that a stable emulsion is formed to avoid separation of the oil and water in the mixture, which would give a curdled appearance.

Types of fats and oils

Fats and oils are always found together with other substances. Therefore they have to be extracted to separate the oil or fat. For example:
- butter is made from the fat in milk;
- olive oil is extracted from olives;
- dripping is obtained from meat juices.

In the past, only a limited range of fats was available. These were mainly from animal sources. During the twentieth century, technological developments have made it possible to extract oil from a wide variety of fish, vegetables and animals.

The main sources of particular fats and oils are shown in Figs. 13.6 and 13.7.

Animal fats

Most animal fats are by-products of slaughtering animals. For example, suet is obtained from beef cattle, and lard is obtained from pigs. Fat is found mainly in layers under the skin of the animal, or surrounding and protecting the vital internal organs, such as the kidneys. The fat is obtained by heating the fatty tissues of the animal carcase. This causes the fat to melt. It is then collected and resolidifies as fat. Most animal fats contain a high proportion of saturated fatty acids (see p. 23).

Fat is also present in milk produced by animals. It is extracted from cow's milk and processed to make cream (see p. 98) and butter.

Butter

Butter is probably the most popular animal fat, because of its delicate flavour. In Britain, some butter is home produced, but most is imported from EEC countries (especially Denmark), and from New Zealand.

Butter is made by churning cream (an oil-in-water emulsion containing 35-40% fat). When shaken or churned, the fat globules clump together to form butter. The excess liquid separates and is drained off as buttermilk. The butter is a water-in-oil emulsion containing about 16% buttermilk dispersed in about 82% fat. The structure of emulsions is described on p. 183. By law, the butter made in Britain must have a minimum milk fat content of 80% and a maximum water content of 16%. Most butter has about 3% salt added, although some is left unsalted.

Manufacture of butter

A small amount of butter is still made on farms and is called farmhouse butter, but the majority is made in modern, automated creameries.

There are two main types of butter: *sweet cream butter* is made from fresh cream; *lactic or ripened butter* is made from cream inoculated with lactic bacteria which produce acid and give the butter a stronger flavour.

The manufacturing process varies slightly according to the type of butter required.

1 At the creamery, the milk is cooled and separated into cream and skimmed milk.
  For *sweet cream butter*, the cream is pasteurised and then cooled to 4-5°C. It is held at this temperature in large storage tanks for about 12 hours to allow the fat globules to harden.
  For *lactic butter* the cream is warmed to a temperature of 15-18°C, a culture of bacteria is added, and the mixture is left to ripen for three or four hours. It is then cooled and left to harden.
2 The mixture is churned in large stainless steel drums. After about half an hour, the butter separates out: the buttermilk is drained off.
3 Salt is added. The drums are rotated for a further fifteen minutes to give a smooth texture.
4 The butter is then automatically weighed into portions and wrapped. It is packed into boxes and stored in a cold room ready for distribution.

When stored in a refrigerator, butter becomes very firm and difficult to spread. Recently a product has been developed from cream mixed with vegetable oils to give the flavour characteristics of butter with increased 'spreadability'. Compare the colour, texture, flavour and cost of this product with butter. Which do you prefer?

Examine packets of butter on your local supermarket shelves.

How are they wrapped?

Which countries do they come from?

Can you tell if the butter is sweet cream or lactic from the label?

Is the butter salted or unsalted?

Is there any other information on the label?

Fish oils (see Fig. 13.6)

Fish oils are obtained by extraction of oil from the whole fish. The most suitable fish are those with a high percentage of oil in the flesh, e.g. herring (see p. 23). These oils contain some unsaturated fatty acids (see p. 23). They are most usually used in the manufacture of margarine and cooking fats. Valuable oils rich in vitamins are also obtained from the livers of white fish, e.g. cod and halibut, but these are not used by the food industry.

Vegetable oils

There are several hundred plants growing in various parts of the world which have seeds containing oil. A few of these are grown commercially to produce vegetable oil for the food industry, for example soya, sunflower, rape, palm, coconut and corn.

Look at Fig. 13.8 on p. 188 and the chart on p. 187. How many of these plants have you seen growing?

Extraction and refining of oils

The oil is either squeezed or pressed by large industrial machines from the hard tough seeds.

All the oils are refined after extraction to:
● neutralise any free fatty acids present which would cause rapid rancidity (see p. 143);
● improve the taste and smell;
● lighten the colour.

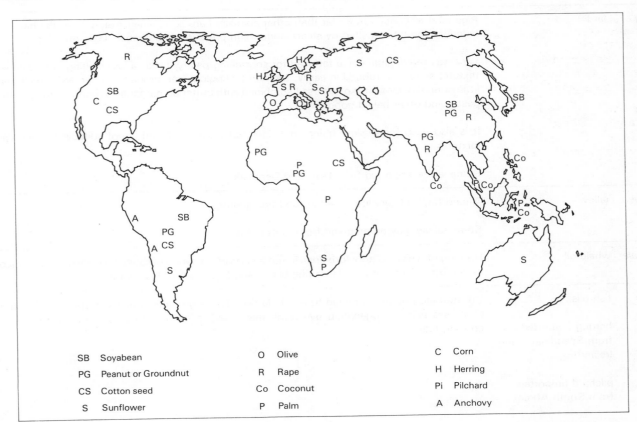

SB	Soyabean	O	Olive	C	Corn
PG	Peanut or Groundnut	R	Rape	H	Herring
CS	Cotton seed	Co	Coconut	Pi	Pilchard
S	Sunflower	P	Palm	A	Anchovy

Fig. 13.5 The sources of oil in the world

Fig. 13.6 Animal and fish fats and oils

	Type of fat	Characteristics and main uses
Beef	suet	A hard fat with a high melting point. It is obtained from around the kidneys of the animal (where it is enclosed in connective tissue). It must be flaked or grated as it is too hard to blend by normal methods, e.g. rubbing in. It can be obtained in a block from a butcher, or grated, in packets, when it is mixed with flour to prevent the pieces sticking together. Mixtures containing suet are usually boiled or steamed to make the fat more digestible.
	dripping	The fat collected when meat is cooked. Prepared by butchers from fat meat trimmings. It is usually brown and flavoured by the meat. Used for shallow frying and making pastry for savoury used. Now less readily available because of modern preference for lean meat.
	tallow	Hard fat obtained from suet. High quality. It is used in margarine manufacture and also for production of soap.
	oleostearin oil	Produced from the intestinal fat which has a lower melting point than kidney fat and can be processed at a lower temperature. Can be used in manufacture of margarine.
	butter	For production see p. 184. Butter is used as a spread, and in some cake mixtures for flavour, e.g. shortbread.
Pig	lard	Pigs tend to contain more fat than other animals. Lard is obtained mainly from the back and kidneys. The fat is melted by steam under high pressure. It is almost 100% pure fat. Lard was the original white fat used for shortening pastry. It has a low melting point and soft texture, so can be rubbed in easily. Modern technology can produce harder lards which have little or no flavour so it is often used combined with butter or margarine to improve the colour in pastry and other baked goods. It is also used for shallow frying, but does not cream well and is not suitable for rich cake mixtures. Some lard is imported from USA and Denmark.
Sheep	tallow	A hard fat, and very little used in food preparation. Some tallow may be prepared from mutton fat.
Whale	whale oil	Hunting of whales is now forbidden in most parts of the world because they are now so reduced in numbers. This is due to large numbers being killed earlier this century.
Fish	fish oils herring (imported from Scandinavia and Ireland) pilchard (imported from South Africa) anchovy (imported from Peru and Chile)	Unsaturated oils are extracted from whole fish. These go rancid quickly, but modern refining processes and hydrogenation overcome this. Used in manufacture of margarine and white cooking fats.

Fig. 13.7 Vegetable oils

Source	Countries where grown	Characteristics and main uses
soya bean (see plate 21)	China, Japan, USA, Brazil	A member of the pea family. The plant produces hairy pods with 2–5 beans in each pod. The beans are smooth, oval and black, green or yellow in colour. Their oil content is low (13–20%), but they are in important source of vegetable protein. They contain 41-50% protein. They are now grown in such large quantities especially in USA that they are a very important source of vegetable oil. They are eaten as a staple food in the Far East. Also used to make soy sauce.
peanut or groundnut	Nigeria, West Africa, China, South America, India	Cultivated in most tropical and sub-tropical countries. Its pods turn down into the earth to a depth of 5 cm where they swell and ripen. They contain about 45% oil and are a very important source of vegetable oil. They are exported as nuts, oil, or as a nutritious spread, peanut butter. This is made from ground peanuts, sugar, salt and emulsifiers. It is especially popular for sandwiches. The oil is often used for salad dressings, for frying and as an ingredient of some margarines. Peanuts are staple foods in countries where they are grown, stewed with meat or roasted.
cotton seed	USA, Sudan, Russia, South America	The oil is a by-product from the plants grown to produce cotton fibres. The seeds are separated from the fibres. The small seeds contain 15–25% oil. USA is the main exporter of cotton seed oil in blends with other oils in the food industry.
sunflower (see plate 21)	Russia, Rumania, Hungary, Argentina, France, Australia, South Africa.	Sunflower is a native of Central America, but its cultivation is now widespread. The plants are 1½–2½ m in height. The oil content of the seeds is about 40%. It contains the highest percentage of essential fatty acids of all vegetable oils used in Britain. It is used for margarines and white fats high in polyunsaturated fats, e.g. Flora.
olive	Italy, Spain, Greece, Mediterranean climate	The ripe fruits of the olive tree produce the best known, finest and most expensive vegetable oils. Each tree bears 10–20 kg fruit each year and the oil is obtained by pressing the olives in oil mills near the olive groves. The oil is mainly used as a table oil for salads and preserving. It is unsuitable for deep frying. Some olives are grown to be eaten as table olives but they have a lower oil content.
rape (see plate 21)	India, China, Canada, Poland, France	Seeds are obtained from several plants of the brassica (cabbage) variety. The crop is grown mainly in China and India but is becoming important because it can also be produced in western Europe and Canada. The seeds contain 35–40% oil.
coconut (see plate 21)	Philippines, Malaysia, Sri Lanka, Indonesia.	Coconut palms grow on the coasts of all tropical countries. The nuts weigh over 1 kg. They have fibrous outer husks and inner kernels which are dried to produce copra. It is exported then to countries who extract and refine the oil. About 63% copra is oil.
palm and palm kernel (see plate 21)	Nigeria, Malayasia, Indonesia, Zaire.	Oil palm is a native of tropical West Africa. It is now cultivated in other areas near the equator. The fruit grows in bunches weighing 15–20 kg and is deep orange, red or brown in colour. Two kinds of oil are obtained from the thick fibrous pulp on the outside. Palm kernel oil is obtained from the inside and is more like coconut oil.
corn	USA	Comes from the seed of the maize plant. The oil has a very bland flavour and is used for all culinary purposes, e.g. salad dressings, in recipes and for deep frying. It remains liquid in the refrigerator and has a low melting point. Contains polyunsaturated fatty acids.

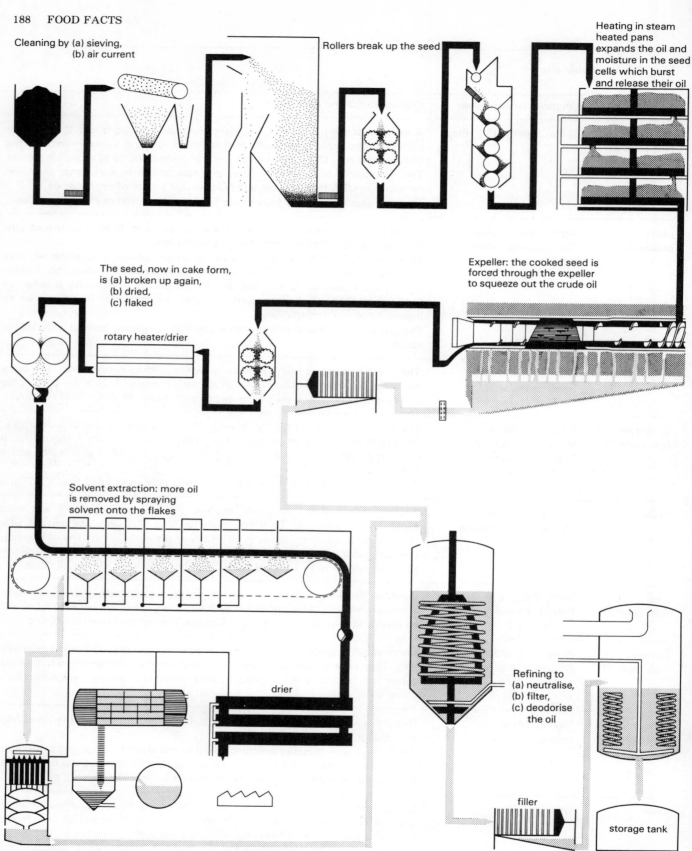

Cleaning by (a) sieving,
          (b) air current

Rollers break up the seed

Heating in steam
heated pans
expands the oil and
moisture in the seed
cells which burst
and release their oil

The seed, now in cake form,
is (a) broken up again,
   (b) dried,
   (c) flaked

rotary heater/drier

Expeller: the cooked seed is
forced through the expeller
to squeeze out the crude oil

Solvent extraction: more oil
is removed by spraying
solvent onto the flakes

drier

Refining to
(a) neutralise,
(b) filter,
(c) deodorise
   the oil

filler

storage tank

Fig. 13.8 The extraction and refining of vegetable oils

Use of oils

The refined oils are used in both the food industry and in the manufacture of other products, e.g. soap, paint, plastics. They are used either as liquid oils, or they can be hardened to give a solid fat.

(a) Liquid oils

There is a wide variety of oils available on the domestic market. Some are pure oils, e.g. olive oil, corn oil. Others are blends of mixed vegetable oils. They vary in price, flavour and hazing temperature (see p. 193). The choice of oil must be appropriate to the specific use (see p. 192).

Examine the liquid oils in your local supermarket and see if the label tells you the source of the oil.

Are some products made from blends of different oils?

List the ways oils are used in their liquid form in food preparation.

Can they be used in this form for cakes and pastry?

Examine and experiment with recipes using oil and discuss the results.

(b) Hardened oils

The process by which oils are hardened is known as *hydrogenation*. This process is possible because most oils contain a high proportion of unsaturated fatty acids (see p. 23). When hydrogen gas is pumped through a blend of polyunsaturated oils, the hydrogen reacts with the unsaturated fatty acids, breaking the double covalent bond and creating some new single covalent bonds in the molecule. Consequently, the oil becomes less unsaturated. The size of the molecules in the oil is increased and the oil hardens. Although most fats and oils contain both saturated and unsaturated fatty acids, oils and soft fats made from vegetable oils contain a higher proportion of unsaturated fatty acids than animal fats.

The oils are mixed with hydrogen and heated in the presence of a nickel catalyst. This weakens the double bonds in the unsaturated fatty acid and hydrogen is taken up. This increases the size of the molecules and hardens the oil.

This process is used in the manufacture of margarine and white cooking fats to harden the blended oils. The consistency of the fat may be modified from a very soft to a very hard fat according to the degree of hydrogenation during the manufacturing process. There is a wide variety of margarines and white cooking fats which vary in texture and in the degree of saturation of the fat.

Margarine

Margarine was invented over a hundred years ago by a French chemist, Mège Mourié. His aim was to find a substitute for butter, which was very expensive at that time. Because margarine is used in place of butter in the diet, legislation has now been passed to ensure that nutritionally the two products are very similar:
- margarine must not be more than 16% water;
- it must be fortified with the vitamins A and D;
- only permitted colouring matter may be used;
- no preservatives may be added.

Originally, margarine was manufactured entirely from animal fats, but now many oils and fats are blended in its production. Look at plate 21 to see the variety of ingredients that may be used in the manufacture of margarine. Because of the wide choice of ingredients, and improvements in the manufacturing process, many margarines are now available that vary in consistency, colour and flavour. These characteristics determine the most appropriate use. For example:
- *for spreading*, the margarine must be easy to use over a wide range of temperatures;
- *for baking*, the margarine must be able to entangle and hold air and be plastic enough to coat flour in pastry mixtures (see p. 233).

These particular characteristics are dependent on the manufacturing process.

The essential differences in the manufacture of margarine and butter are:
- in butter manufacture (see p. 184), cream naturally contains fat, water and emulsifiers;
- in margarine manufacture, the fat and water based liquid have to be brought together and emulsifiers added to form an emulsion. The 'fat' in margarine is usually a mixture of vegetable oils and may contain fish oils. The 'water' is fat-free milk or whey.

There are several stages in the manufacture of margarine as shown in Fig. 13.9. The final nature of a margarine is dependent on:
- (a) the choice of oils
- (b) the amount of hydrogenation
- (c) the amount of churning at the emulsification and crystallisation stage.

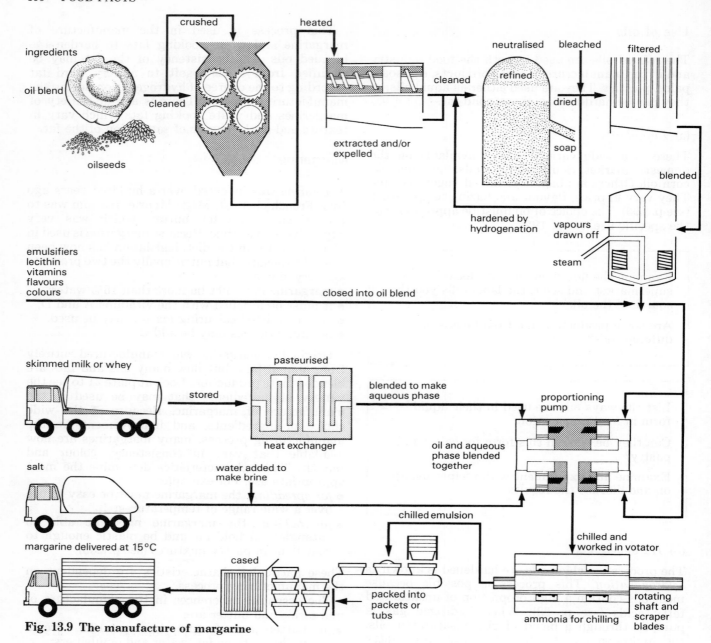

Fig. 13.9 The manufacture of margarine

The stages in manufacture are:

1 *Refining of oils*
  Oil is extracted from the vegetable seeds, filtered, bleached and deodorised.

2 *Hydrogenation of oils* The oils are hydrogenated by bubbling a stream of hydrogen gas through the oils. The oils are kept warm so that they remain liquid. This process is continued until the required amount of hydrogen is bound into the mixture. This is dependent on the blend of oils used, and the required final consistency of the margarine.

3 *Blending of oils*
  Oils from several sources, e.g. many vegetable sources, fish oils and animal fats, are blended together. The blend of oils used is dependent on the type of margarine required.

  Controlled amounts of vitamins A and D are added. Permitted colouring, flavouring and emulsifiers are also added.

4 *Pasteurisation and inoculation of fat-free milk or whey*
  Fat-free milk or whey is delivered to a separate area of the factory. Conditions here are like a dairy. The liquid is pasteurised (see p. 96), and then inoculated with a culture of bacteria to

produce acid from the lactose in milk. This gives the correct flavour.

5 *Salt is added* to the pasteurised liquid.
6 *The formation of the emulsion*
The warmed, hydrogenated oils and the pasteurised fat-free milk or whey are mixed in the correct proportions and pumped into a votator. This is an enormous vat fitted with a central spindle with blades attached.

The mixture is churned rapidly by rotating the blades. The water droplets become very finely distributed throughout the oil, forming a water-in-oil emulsion.

7 *The formation of the fat crystals*
The mixture is cooled rapidly against the sides of the votator. Some of the fat forms tiny, needle-shaped crystals. The minute size of these crystals is very important to give margarine a smooth, soft texture.

The amount of fat crystals and liquid oil in the finished margarine varies in different brands, for example a packet margarine may contain 75% oil and 25% crystals and a tub margarine as much as 85% liquid in oil and only 15% fat crystals. This explains why there is variation in the consistency of different brands of margarine.

8 *Packing margarine*
From the votator the margarine passes to the packing machine where it is weighed, shaped and wrapped, or measured into plastic tubs. It is then transferred to boxes and stored ready for delivery.

Special margarines

Several special margarines are manufactured to meet consumer demand for products with particular characteristics.

(a) *high in polyunsaturates*
There is a demand for dietary fats that contain only vegetable oils, such as corn and sunflower oils, which are high in polyunsaturated fatty acids (see p. 23). All margarines of this type, e.g. Flora, must be clearly labelled 'high in polyunsaturates'. The reason for this demand is that there is a possibility that a diet rich in saturated fats, e.g. animal fats, may be one of the factors contributing to a high level of cholesterol in the blood (see p. 24).

(b) *milk-free*
Some margarines are produced that do not contain any milk, e.g. Tomor. These products are useful for:
● Jewish people
● people who cannot digest lactose or milk proteins
● vegans, i.e. strict vegetarians.

In these margarines only water and salt will be added to the blended oils. (No milk or whey will be used.)

(c) *low-fat spreads*
These are not margarines, as they contain too much water (more than 16%) to be legally called margarines. They must be labelled 'low-fat spreads'. They are emulsions of tiny droplets of blended vegetable oils in water (i.e. o/w emulsion). They contain only half the fat of margarine and butter. They are fortified with vitamins A and D in the same way as margarine.

These products are especially useful for people on slimming diets as they have lower energy values than margarine or butter. They are unsuitable for use in baked products.

Energy value per 25 g

	kcal	kJ
butter	185	760
margarine	185	760
low-fat spread	92	390

Examine the fats counter in your local supermarket.

How many brands of margarine are available? What information do the labels give you?

Are there special margarine and low-fat spreads available? How many brands of these are there?

Are some margarines more expensive than others? Do you consider an average family should buy more than one brand of margarine?

White fats

White fats are manufactured from varying blends of vegetable oils, fish oils and lard, but they do not contain any water. They are useful substitutes for lard as they contain a higher proportion of poly-unsaturated fatty acids (see p. 23). There are several different brands on the market, e.g. Spry, Cookeen, Trex.

Their main uses are for shortening pastry, and frying. Some of these products are aerated (whipped to include air) during their manufacture. This makes them easy to rub in and cream. They have little flavour and are therefore suitable only for cakes using chocolate, ginger or other strong flavours.

Uses of fats and oils in food preparation

Whenever fats and oils are used, they improve the appearance, flavour, palatability, colour, nutritional and energy value of the food.

Fats and oils have two main functions in food preparation. They are used as:

(a) an *ingredient* in many dishes, e.g. cakes
(b) a *cooking medium* when they transfer heat to the food, e.g. when frying.

As an ingredient, fats are used for:

- *spreading* Carbohydrate-rich foods, such as bread and scones are more palatable when served with fat.
- *flavouring* Butter or margarine is added to vegetables, fish and meat to improve and develop the natural flavour. (Herbs and spices may be added to the fat for this purpose, e.g. maître d'hôtel butter). Fat is also used to enrich sauces (see p. 215), and can be used in a number of cake icings.
- *forming an emulsion* Various oils and butter are used in salad dressings and sauces, e.g. mayonnaise, Hollandaise sauces.
- *to improve the keeping quality* Because fat is often emulsified with moisture in baked products, it helps to retain the moisture and prevents them from drying out or going stale too quickly.
- *shortening* This is the term used when flour particles are coated with fat, e.g. in shortbread, shortcrust pastry, biscuits, cakes and scones. (see p. 233).
- *aeration* In rich cakes, fat has the ability to trap and hold air. This helps to give the cake a good volume and texture (see p. 224).

As a cooking *medium* fats are used for:

- *lubrication* In shallow-frying, fat or oil prevents the food sticking to the cooking surface. In baking, fat is used to grease the baking tin.
- *basting* Foods to be grilled and roast meat, poultry and vegetables are basted with fat to prevent the surfaces drying and burning. This also improves the colour and flavour.
- *deep-frying* Oils and fats which can be heated to a high temperature are used to cook a large variety of foods, e.g. chips, fritters, fish etc. (see p. 193).
- *sealing* Fat can be used as a moisture-repelling seal, e.g. melted butter is used to cover pâté.

Choice of fat

There is a large number of fats and oils available on the market. It is important to choose the most suitable product for the specific purpose and to understand the reasons for your choice. Here are some guidelines to help you choose.

(a) *flavouring* e.g. shortbread, butter or a block margarine should be used as the taste of the fat gives the flavour to the product.
(b) *aeration* For rich cakes the fat must also be able to *entangle air* (see p. 224). Butter, margarine and white fat all have this property but if a white fat is used, extra flavouring may be necessary.
(c) *shortening* Lard and white fats which are practically 100% fat *shorten* mixtures best. However, as they have an insipid flavour, they are often combined with margarine to add flavour in biscuits and pastry.
(d) *frying* The fat must not decompose at high temperatures and must not foam. A pure fat or oil should be chosen, e.g. lard, dripping, corn oil.

Sometimes the same fat can be used for different purposes at different temperatures. For example, a block of margarine which is used at room temperature for creamed, all-in-one and rubbed in mixtures, may be suitable for flaky or puff pastry which require a firmer fat if it is used at refrigerator temperature.

Some tub margarines which have very soft textures for spreading should be used straight from the refrigerator if they are used for cooking (see pp. 224, 234).

Recipes can be modified to use different fats. If fats high in polyunsaturated fats must be used for health reasons, they can be substituted in all recipes, but for baking, they should be used at refrigerator temperature. If oils are used for baking, the method of mixing is changed.

Prepare a chart showing suitable fats and the reasons for choosing them for the following:

spreading on bread, making cakes, scones, shortcrust pastry, flaky pastry, shortbread, white sauce, deep-fat frying and greasing tins.

Heating fat and oil

When solid fats are heated they melt. The *melting point* varies for different fats. Oils and fats can be heated to high temperatures before any changes take place. If heating is continued smoke eventually begins to rise from the surface of the fat as the *smoke point* is reached. This indicates a chemical breakdown of the fat. An unpleasant smelling substance called acrolein, which irritates the eyes, is produced from some of the glycerol. Free fatty acids are left in the fat and give it a rancid flavour. The smoke point of different fats and oils varies. The temperature required for deep-frying is 175–200°C and it is important to choose a fat or oil with a smoke point above this temperature. The fats that contain water, salt and emulsifiers start to decompose at a lower temperature than pure fats.

Fig. 13.10 Choice of fats for deep-frying

---

unsuitable	suitable
low fat spreads	pure dripping
butter	lard
margarine	oils and fats specially
olive oil	produced for frying
coconut oil (because it foams)	(these may be blends of
	oils with stabilising
	substances added to
	prevent fat breakdown)

A good quality oil or fat should last for about nine or ten fryings. However the correct use and care of the fat is essential. Fat deteriorates rapidly if:
- it is excessively heated,
- too much food is fried at one time,
- the fat is stored in the pan or exposed to air and light,
- any sediment is left in the fat during storage.

Eventually a fat will:
- foam easily,
- smoke at a lower temperature,
- darken in colour,
- be absorbed excessively by the food which will taste greasy,
- smell unpleasant.

If these symptoms occur the fat should be discarded.

If fat is heated above the smoke point the temperature rises until the *flash point* is reached when the fat bursts into flames. This is usually about 100°C above the smoke point (e.g. for corn oil the smoke point is 221°C and the flash point is 324°C).

Rancidity of fats and oils

When fats and oils spoil they are said to be *rancid*. They develop a disagreeable smell and taste which is very easily detected by the senses. The flavours depend on the composition of the fat, for example the very distinctive taste of rancid butter is due to the presence of butyric acid produced from the butyrin in the butter. Rancidity is caused by:
- *enzymes* which break the fat down into fatty acids and glycerol. These enzymes are destroyed by

heat but can remain active in a freezer where they shorten the freezer storage life of foods containing fat e.g. bacon.
- *bacteria* which do not grow in pure fat but may be present if the food also contains moisture or protein.
- *oxidation* which occurs in unsaturated fats and oils. Oxygen from the air is taken up at the double bonds in the carbon chain (see p. 19). The reaction takes place more quickly at high temperatures and in strong light. Substances known as anti-oxidants may be added to fats by manufacturers to help prevent oxidation occurring.

Storage of fats and oils

Correct storage of fats and oils will delay the onset of rancidity in these products in the home.

Fats and oils should be kept in sealed containers or be well-wrapped in greaseproof paper and foil wrappings to reduce exposure to light and air.

Oils and suet do not need refrigerator storage if a cool dry cupboard or larder is available. Fats may be stored in a refrigerator or freezer. Fats and oils also absorb flavours easily from strongly-smelling foods stored nearby.

Fig. 13.11 Storage-times

	cool dry larder	refrigerator	freezer
oils	2–3 months	-	-
suet (shredded)	1 month	-	-
lard	1 month	6 months	6–12 months
margarine	7 days	3 months	6 months
white fats	1 month	6 months	1 year
butter	5–7 days	4–6 weeks	3 months (salted) 6 months (unsalted)

QUESTIONS

1 State the difference between fats and oils.
  How can an oil be converted into a fat?
  Name three fats and three oils which may be used in food preparation.
  For each, state the source and give examples of dishes where you would choose to use each one, giving reasons.

2 Describe briefly how margarine is manufactured.
  Name three different types of margarine.
  How and why is margarine enriched?
  Compare margarine and butter.

3 What are the important characteristics of fats used for the following purposes? Give reasons for your answers.
(a) spreading
(b) shortening
(c) deep-frying
(d) creaming

4 Explain what is meant by the following terms with reference to fats:
  (a) polyunsaturated
  (b) hydrogenation
  (c) smoke-point
  (d) flash-point
  (e) rancidity.

5 Describe the changes that take place when heat is applied to
(a) butter
(b) corn oil.

6 How do fats and oils make a valuable contribution to the diet? What important points must be borne in mind when choosing, storing and using fats and oils?
(London, 1982)

Sugar

14

In chapter 2 we saw that there are many different sugars, including:

monosaccharides, e.g glucose, fructose
disaccharides, e.g. sucrose.

However, when we consider sugar as a food commodity we think of the crystalline substance used to sweeten foods: granulated, castor, icing, soft brown, demerara and muscovado sugars are all almost pure sucrose.

Sucrose is a natural product. It is created in plants by the process of photosynthesis (see p. 25). It has been extracted from plants for thousands of years, but until the beginning of this century, sugar was a luxury that only the wealthy could afford as it was heavily taxed. During the twentieth century, machinery has been developed which allows large-scale extraction of sugar.

All plants contain some sucrose but only two plants have enough to make extraction of the sugar commercially worth while: sugar cane and sugar beet.

Production of sugar

Sugar is obtained from sugar cane and sugar beet plants. Raw brown sugar is extracted from both plants. This is then refined to become the food commodity known as sugar.

Sugar cane

Sugar cane is a huge grass, rather like bamboo, which grows only in tropical climates. A high rainfall and hot sunshine are essential for its growth. It grows in the West Indies, Central America, Australia and South Africa.

The sugar, which is made in the leaves of the plant, is stored in the stems. The canes are harvested in the autumn. They are crushed in a mill to extract the juices containing the sugar. The juice is boiled to produce a sticky mass of syrup and dark brown crystals. This mixture is spun off at high speed to separate out the syrup. The syrup, known as molasses, is used for making rum. The raw brown crystals are either packaged or exported to be refined to white sugars.

Sugar beet

Sugar beet is a plant rather like a turnip, which grows well in temperate climates, including Britain. The crop is harvested between September and November. The roots are washed and sliced. The slices are soaked in large rotating cylinders of hot water. This draws the sugar out of the plant into the solution by osmosis. The sugar solution is boiled and evaporated. This mixture is spun to separate the molasses and the raw brown sugar crystals, which are then sent to refineries.

The refining process

The refining process has a number of stages, which are summed up in Fig. 14.3. The varieties of sugar available are summed up in Fig. 14.2 and Fig. 14.4.

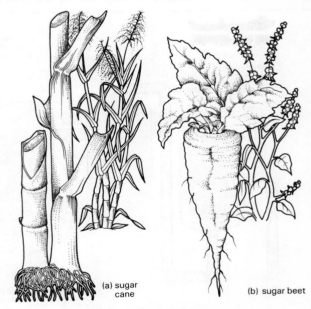

(a) sugar cane   (b) sugar beet

Fig. 14.1 Sugar cane and sugar beet

Fig. 14.2 White sugars

White sugars are all highly refined.

Name	Description	Uses
granulated	The most popular, widely used and cheapest refined sugar. Medium-sized crystals.	Sweetening drinks and fruit. Rubbed in cake mixtures. Sauces. Sweet-making.
castor	More expensive with the smallest crystals of all the sugars. It dissolves more easily than granulated sugar.	Cake-making: the small crystals give a very fine texture (creaming all-in-one and whisked methods). Pastry, biscuits, meringues, soufflès.
icing	Made by grinding sugar crystals to a fine powder. The powder dissolves very easily to form a smooth opaque white paste. A small amount of calcium phosphate is added to prevent lumping in the packet.	Cake icings, some biscuit recipes. Sweet-making. Sprinkled on cakes.
preserving	Specially designed for jam, jelly and marmalade-making. It has large crystals which do not settle in a dense layer at the bottom of the pan. The jam needs less stirring to prevent burning. Dissolves slowly and causes less scum formation.	Domestic preservation. Can also be used to decorate tea breads.
quick-dissolving sugar lumps	Produced from moist granulated sugar which is moulded and then cut into shape. The cubes are loosely formed to allow rapid penetration by liquids.	Convenient form of sugar for sweetening hot drinks. Useful for picnics and parties.
coffee crystals	Vary in size. Largest of all sugar crystals. Designed originally for coffee connoisseurs who liked the first taste of their coffee to be the pure coffee. The large crystals slowly dissolve to make the coffee sweeter.	Sweetening coffee. Multi-coloured crystals are decorative for children's parties on cakes, biscuits etc.

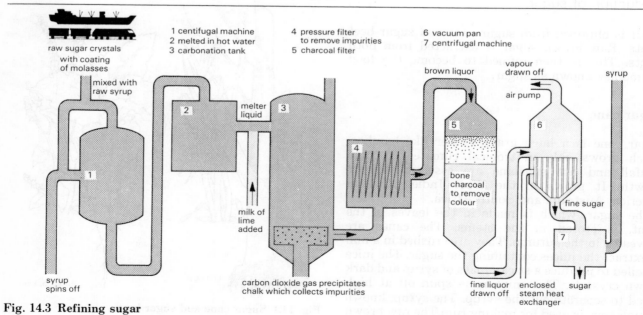

raw sugar crystals
with coating
of molasses

1 centifugal machine
2 melted in hot water
3 carbonation tank

4 pressure filter
to remove impurities
5 charcoal filter

6 vacuum pan
7 centrifugal machine

mixed with
raw syrup

melter
liquid

milk of
lime
added

carbon dioxide gas precipitates
chalk which collects impurities

syrup
spins off

brown liquor

bone
charcoal
to remove
colour

vapour
drawn off

air pump

fine sugar

fine liquor
drawn off

enclosed
steam heat
exchanger

sugar

syrup

Fig. 14.3 Refining sugar

Brown sugars

There are two types of brown sugar: natural and refined. It is easy to confuse the two types, as refined brown sugars are made to resemble the natural product.

Natural brown sugars are made from unrefined raw cane sugar. They are always produced in the country of origin which will be stated on the packet.

Refined brown sugar Many brown sugars are refined white sugar which has been coloured and flavoured. Sugar syrups, caramel or refined molasses are added to give the characteristic colour and flavour of natural brown sugar.

The varieties of brown sugar are described in Fig. 14.4.

Fig. 14.4 Brown sugars

Natural brown sugars

Name	Description	Uses
Demerara	Clear sparkling crystals of large size. Sticky texture and aroma because of the molasses present. Takes its name from Demerara County in Guyana where it was first produced.	Sweetening coffee. Coating gammon ham. Baked apples, fruit crumbles. Sprinkled on cakes and biscuits before baking.
Barbados or Muscovado sugar	Purified fine crystals of raw cane sugar. Soft, sticky, dark brown because it contains more molasses, has a strong distinctive flavour and should be used with care in baking.	Sauces. Chutneys. Rich fruit cakes, gingerbreads and spice cakes. Christmas puddings.
light Muscovado	Creamy-coloured soft cane sugar crystals with less molasses than the dark sugar. Milder flavour.	Sweetening fruits, flapjacks, ginger biscuits.

Refined brown sugars   These are refined white sugar flavoured and coloured to resemble the natural brown sugars.

Name	Description	Uses
London Demerara	Larger crystals than granulated coloured with cane molasses. Colour is not as clear as the natural demerara and it does not dissolve as easily.	As Demerara
dark soft brown sugar	Small crystals like castor sugar but moister and softer. Tossed in molasses or caramel to replace the flavour and colour taken out in refining.	As Barbados
light soft brown sugar	Crystals like dark soft sugar but milder flavour and paler in colour.	As light Muscovado

1 Which countries in the world supply most of the world's sugar?

2 Examine the brown sugar packets on the shelves of your supermarket and health food shop. Are they natural or refined sugars?

3 Is there any difference between unrefined and refined sugars nutritionally?

4 What are the manufactured foods you buy which contain sugar?

The value of sugar in the diet

As sugar is such a highly refined food it is practically 100% carbohydrate and supplies no other nutrients. Natural brown sugar contains minute traces of minerals but they are too small to be significant.

Sugar is a relatively inexpensive source of energy which is quickly available to the body. It is also valuable because it makes many other foods containing important nutrients more palatable. Young children should not, however, be encouraged to take very sweet foods, as a high intake of sugar may cause problems with obesity (see p. 15). Also too many sweet, sticky foods can cause tooth decay. Bacteria in the mouth convert sucrose into a sticky compound which causes a film of plaque to stick to the surface of the teeth and start decay.

If 1 × 5 ml spoon sugar supplies 20 kcal/83 kJ of energy, how much energy do you obtain from sugar each day if you add it to the hot drinks you have?

What are the other main sources of sugar in your diet?

The uses of sugar in food preparation

Sugar is an important ingredient in many recipes. It has a variety of uses:
- as a sweetener in a wide variety of foods, e.g. beverages;
- it improves the colour of baked products, for example
  (a) in cakes, particularly when brown sugar is used in gingerbread and fruit cakes;
  (b) in breadmaking, where the addition of a small amount of sugar improves the colour of the baked crust;
- it retains moisture and prevents baked products from becoming dry;
- it helps the fat to incorporate more air, giving an increased volume to rich cake mixtures (see p. 219);
- it prevents the development of gluten in cake and pastry mixtures, giving a tender, softer product after baking (see p. 219);
- it provides a readily available food for yeast in yeast mixtures (see p. 219);
- it helps to delay the coagulation of the protein in eggs and gluten. This allows more time for the gases to expand a baked product;
- it strengthens the protein in stiffly beaten egg white and helps the mixture to retain a high proportion of air, e.g. in meringues (see pages 120 and 121);
- it acts as a preservative in jams, marmalades and jellies (see p. 177). These products are examples of boiled sugars (see below);
- it retards enzyme action in frozen products;
- it improves the quality of some frozen products, for example:
  (a) in fruit, it prevents the formation of large ice crystals which cause disintegration of the structure on defrosting;
  (b) in egg yolk, it prevents the coagulation of the protein on freezing;
  (c) in whipped cream, the texture is improved;
- it is used in a variety of cake decorations. These include sprinkled sugar, glacé and royal icings, and more elaborate icings which involve boiling the sugar;
- it is used in preparing a variety of sweets, e.g. toffee, fudge, peppermint creams.

Many of the uses of sugar involve boiling a sugar solution.

Sugar solutions

Sugar is very soluble in water. As the temperature of a sugar and water solution increases, an increasing amount of sugar will dissolve. When no more sugar will dissolve at a particular temperature, the solution is said to be *saturated*. As a saturated solution cools, it becomes *supersaturated*. This means that there is a greater concentration of sugar than can easily be held by the water. This may cause the sugar to crystallise, as in the refining process.

Boiled sugar   When a sugar solution starts to boil, water evaporates away, and the solution becomes more concentrated. The boiling point of the solution rises in proportion to the concentration of the sugar in the solution. For example, pure water has a boiling point of 100°C, an 80% sucrose solution has a boiling point of 112°C. This characteristic is particularly important in making jams, caramel and sweets.

In these mixtures a *sugar thermometer*, which measures the temperature of the solution, should be used. When a specific temperature is reached, the concentration of the sugar solution will be appropriate for its use. See Fig. 14.5.

Fig. 14.5 Fudge and butterscotch

	Weight of sugar	Volume of liquid	Relative proportion	Boiling point
fudge	500 g	250 ml	2 : 1	115°C
butterscotch	500 g	100 ml	5 : 1	150°C

These proportions are recommended, so that cooking-time is not too long to reach the desired sugar concentration. Great care is needed to follow the instructions accurately, in all recipes that require boiling a sugar solution, such as jams, caramel and sweets. If all the water is allowed to evaporate, the mixture produces very small bubbles which turn golden-brown. This is known as caramel. (If heating is continued further, a bitter-tasting charcoal is produced.)

As sugar solutions cool, they become supersaturated. Sugar tends to separate out in the form of crystals. This crystal formation is a nuisance if it occurs in jams, and large crystals make sweets taste gritty.

Crystallisation

A crystal is composed of closely-packed molecules arranged in a pattern. Crystallisation occurs only in supersaturated solutions. The size of the crystal is dependent on the rate of growth of the crystal. The higher the degree of saturation, the more rapid the rate of crystallisation. Crystallisation also occurs rapidly if anything disturbs the stability of the solution. For example, crystals will start to accumulate on the surface of a spoon, if the mixture is stirred.

In *boiled sugar mixtures*, only very small crystals are required. The speed of crystal-formation is critical to obtain the right texture. Crystallisation is most characteristic of sucrose, which is a disaccharide. Glucose, a monosaccharide, does not have the ability to form large crystals.

Crystallisation in sugar mixtures can be prevented by:
- not stirring the mixture whilst the sugar is dissolving or boiling;
- adding glucose, which interferes with the tendency for sucrose to create large crystals;
- adding acid, for example:
  (a) naturally-occurring acid in fruit used in jam-making;
  (b) lemon juice, cream of tartar or vinegar, added to the mixture.

The action of an acid on sucrose when heated is to convert some sucrose to a mixture of glucose and fructose (invert sugar). This is a similar reaction to the action of digestive enzymes which break down the disaccharides to monosaccharides (see p. 42). The presence of invert sugar inhibits crystallisation.

The addition of other ingredients, such as cream, butter and chocolate, also retards crystallisation.

Some sugar mixtures, such as fudge, are beaten as they cool. This encourages the formation of very small crystals, so that a smooth texture is obtained.

Other sweeteners

Treacle is a dark brown strongly-flavoured syrup made from molasses.

Golden syrup is made from the liquid remaining after the sugar has been crystallised.

Maple syrup is obtained from the sap of certain varieties of maple trees. The commerical syrup contains about 65% sucrose and has a characteristic flavour due to the volatile oils it contains.

Honey is made by bees from the nectar of flowers and is stored for their future use in a cell-like structure known as a honeycomb. Before honey can be used all impurities and dirt must be removed. The honey is usually heated to destroy micro-organisms which may cause it to ferment, and the heated syrup is then strained. There is a wide variety of colour and flavour according to the particular flower nectar collected by the bees.

The composition of honey varies; it usually contains about 18% water. The sugar is present mainly as fructose and glucose. This is because an enzyme secreted by the bee converts the nectar, which is mainly sucrose, to invert sugar. Honey containing more fructose than glucose tends to be clear with no crystals. When the glucose content is higher, crystals tend to form.

One important property of honey is its capacity to retain water. Cakes, biscuits and icings which include honey in the recipes remain moist for a long time.

Some people believe honey has some extra nutritive value when compared with sugar because it is eaten in the natural state, but this is not true.

Sugar substitutes

Some other substances also taste sweet and are used in manufactured foods and in the home especially to sweeten drinks. They can be tolerated by diabetics and, as they supply little energy, are also used by weight-watchers.

Saccharin is the most widely used artificial sweetener and is 300 times sweeter than sugar. It was discovered in 1879 and has no food value as it is not metabolised by the body. It may leave a bitter after-taste. Current research suggests that saccharin, if eaten in very large quantities may have a dangerous effect on the body.

Sorbitol is a natural product occurring in some fruits and also produced from glucose. It is metablolised like glucose and has a similar energy value. It is used widely by diabetics and contained in many diabetic foods.

Other substances such as glucose syrup and corn syrup are used commercially.

Storage of sugar and sugar products

As sugars readily absorb moisture from the air it is essential that they are stored in a very dry place. They are very often packed in paper or cardboard packets which are not moisture-proof, and the sugar will form lumps in a damp atmosphere. Sugar should therefore be transferred from the packet to an airtight container. Honey, jams and syrups, unopened, require a cool storage place. Some centrally-heated kitchens may be too warm for long-term storage.

Fig. 14.6 sugar and sugar products: *recommended storage times*

sugar packets	2 months
icing sugar	3 months
jams, jellies, honey and syrup	1 year unopened, a few weeks opened

QUESTIONS

1 Sugar used to be a very expensive commodity. Nutritionists, doctors and dentists may be pleased if it were still bought only as a luxury item.

Explain why this is so and discuss fully the importance of sugar in the diet.
(Welsh, 1976)

2 Write a short paragraph about the use of sugar in the preparation of each of the following:
   (i) cakes
   (ii) preserved foods, including frozen foods
   (iii) home-made sweets
   (iv) drinks.

3 What is the effect of moist heat on sugar?

What happens to a solution of sugar as the water evaporates?

What uses are made of these effects in food preparation?

4 Why is some restriction of the intake of sugar advisable in the diet of
   (i) young children
   (ii) sedentary workers?
What is the value of saccharin as a sugar substitute?
(JMB, 1978)

5 Discuss the value of sugar and sugar products in the diet.
(London, 1981)

Cereals and cereal products 15

Cereals are cultivated grasses. The specific characteristics of each type are described later, but some characteristics are similar for all types. They are grown for their highly nutritious edible seeds, which are known as *cereal grains*. Maize, wheat, rice, barley, rye and oats have been staple foods since the beginning of civilisation. The ability to cultivate cereal crops was important since people changed from a nomadic life to life in a community.

Some form of cereal crops are produced in every area of the world (see Fig. 15.1). Wheat is the largest cereal crop in temperate climates, e.g. in Northern Europe. In soil areas where wheat does not thrive, oats, barley and rye are often grown. In warmer areas, such as America, maize (corn) is an important crop and in moist hot climates such as those of India and China, rice is the staple cereal.

Cereal grains do not deteriorate if kept mature and dry. This means that they can be transported relatively cheaply and easily over long distances.

They are usually milled, refined and processed in factories situated near the ports.

Various kinds of flour, including wheat flour, cornflour and oatmeal are prepared from finely-ground cereal grains. Dried cereal pastes (pastas) have always been important in the Italian diet and increasingly are produced and eaten in other parts of the world. At the beginning of the twentieth century, food technologists developed the processing of cereal grains into ready-to-eat breakfast cereal products. Corn Flakes were the first breakfast 'cereal' to be sold as a convenience food. Now a large variety of breakfast 'cereals' are produced from maize, rice, wheat and oats.

The value of cereal grains in the diet

No other food commodity can compare with cereal grains for their ease of transportation and storage,

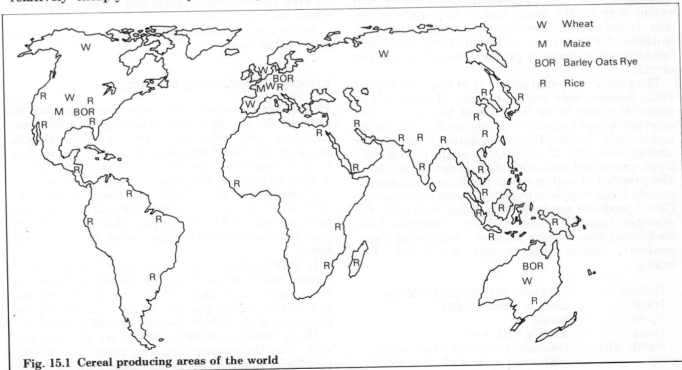

Fig. 15.1 Cereal producing areas of the world

W   Wheat

M   Maize

BOR   Barley Oats Rye

R   Rice

201

their high food value and low cost. Cereal grains have remained relatively inexpensive because they thrive in so many different climates and soils.

In some developing countries cereal grains are a major part of the food intake. In developed countries, they often provide about a quarter of the total energy, protein and iron in the average diet. Cereal grains are also a useful source of calcium, the B-vitamins and dietary fibre.

All cereal grains contain a very high proportion of carbohydrate (70-80%). They also contain 7-14% protein, fat (2-7%) and up to 12% water. The outer layers of the grain, known as the bran, contain complex polysaccharides, and these are not digested by enzymes in the human body (see p. 42). They are, however, a valuable source of dietary fibre (see p. 27).

(a) Carbohydrate in cereal grains

The principal nutrient is carbohydrate in the form of starch. Most of the starch is found in the inner part of the grain known as the endosperm. It is therefore present in both whole grain and refined cereals. Cereal grains and cereal products are therefore a valuable source of energy-giving foods in the diet.

(b) Protein in cereal grains

Although cereal grains are usually regarded as starchy foods, they are also a valuable source of protein. This is because they are eaten in such large quantities. In the developing countries, cereal grains may be the major source of protein in the diet. In countries where rice is the staple cereal, e.g. in India, this may cause some nutritional problems, because rice is lower in protein content than other cereals.

The protein in cereal grains is of lower biological value because only small amounts of some of the essential amino acids are present (see p. 21). For example, wheat and many cereals are deficient in the amino acid lysine. Cereal proteins also contain smaller amounts of the amino acids methionine, tryptophane and isoleucine than do animal proteins. The practice of eating cereal products with animal protein foods supplements the missing amino acids. Cereal products are frequently eaten with milk, for example, breakfast cereals. Many countries have traditional dishes which provide a mixture of cereal products, animal protein and vegetables. For example:

Britain	Cornish pasties, rice pudding
Italy	risotto, pasta dishes
Spain	paella
India	curries with rice
North Africa	couscous (steamed whole wheat with meat stew and vegetables).

(c) Fat in cereal grains

The different types of grains vary in the amount of fat they contain. Oats contain the highest proportion (approximately 8%); rice contains a negligible amount.

In wheat the fat is mainly found in the germ. White flour contains only traces of fat, as the germ has been removed. Wholemeal and wheat germ flours contain 2-3% fat.

(d) Vitamins and minerals in cereal grains

Cereal grains provide some of the B-group vitamins, especially thiamin and niacin. Small amounts of riboflavin are also present. There is vitamin A, C or D in cereals.

Wheat and oats contain a good supply of iron. However, it is not certain how much of the iron is absorbed. Whole cereal grains also contain a substance called phytic acid. This combines with the iron, and the iron is then not absorbed by the body (see p. 37). Appreciable amounts of calcium are also contained in wheat and oats.

(e) Dietary fibre in cereal grains

The outer layers of cereal grains are less digestible, but are a valuable source of dietary fibre. The highly refined cereal products in the western diet are deficient in this fibrous matter. The use of some whole grain cereals or the addition of small amounts of bran to breakfast cereals and bread doughs are therefore recommended.

Some manufacturers also produce white flours with added bran.

Effects of processing on cereal grains

In parts of the world where rice is a major part of the diet, the milling process removes the outer husk, including the fibre, some protein and valuable amounts of the B-vitamins. It is important that special treatments are given to the grains before milling to help the retention of these vitamins.

When cereals are ground into flour, as much as 30% of the grain may be lost if the bran and germ are removed. This part includes valuable amounts of protein, minerals and B-vitamins as well as dietary fibre.

In developed countries, many people prefer highly refined white wheat flour to wholemeal flour. In some countries, flour is fortified to replace nutrients lost in the milling process; it does not replace the protein or dietary fibre lost in the milling process.

Many breakfast cereal products are also enriched with the B-vitamins thiamin, riboflavin niacin, pyridoxin, and folic acid. This makes up for losses incurred in processing. In addition, some breakfast cereal products are enriched with vitamin B_{12}, vitamin D and mineral elements such as iron and zinc.

Types of cereal grain

There are five important staple cereal crops: wheat, rice, maize, oats and rye. In addition, several products are made from barley. Most countries use small quantities of all cereal grains in addition to their staple crop.

WHEAT

Wheat has been cultivated since about 6000 BC. It is thought that cultivation began in Syria and Israel and spread with migrating peoples to both west and east. Today, the important countries growing and exporting wheat are the United States of America, Canada, Russia and Australia.

Many different varieties of wheat are grown to suit different climates and soils. They fall into two main groups, spring wheat and winter wheat:

- *Spring wheat* In countries where the winters are severe (Canada and Russia) the wheat must be sown in the spring and harvested in late summer. Because the ripening period is short, the grains are small and there is less starch and more protein (10-15%) in the endosperm.
- *Winter wheat* In milder climates, wheat can be sown in the autumn because the root system is able to survive the less severe winters and can be harvested the following summer. The longer, slower ripening period means the endosperm is fully developed and has more starch and less protein (7-10%) than that of spring wheat.

Composition of the wheat grain

The wheat grain is a seed and its main purpose is to produce a new wheat plant. The three main parts are:

- *the germ* (2% of the grain) This is the embryo plant and is rich in protein, fat and the B-vitamins.
- *the bran* (13% of the grain) The bran consists of the seed coats which protect the developing embryo and control the intake of water by the seed. It is mainly fibre with some minerals and B-vitamins.
- *the endosperm* (85% of the grain) This is the food reserve on which the young plant lives until it develops a root system. It is composed of starch granules mixed with protein.

whole grain of wheat magnified more than 250 times

grain of wheat cut lengthwise through crease

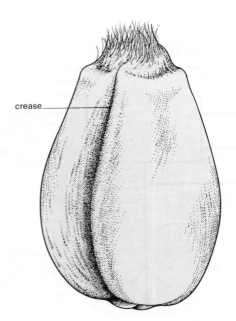

crease

hair (beard)

external part of crease

inner seed coats which control intake of water by the seed

highly magnified

layers of pericarp (tough outer skin)

endosperm cell containing starch granules

bran (pericarp and inner seed coats)

endosperm (food reserve)

the germ (embryo plant)

Fig. 15.2 The wheat grain

The processing of wheat

The whole wheat grain is very hard, therefore for most purposes the wheat grain is finely ground. The grinding process is known as *milling*. Milling is one of the earliest examples of food processing. Several products are made from milled wheat: flour, semolina, pasta and some breakfast cereals.

1 Flour

There are two main types of milling processes which are used to produce flour:
● stone milling:
The grinding or milling was originally done between flat stones by hand. Stone milling was also the first commercial method of milling. The earliest mills were powered by water and later by wind. Steam power followed in the eighteenth century. The method is still used today, but the power is usually electric. The flour produced contains all parts of the grain and is known as stoneground wholemeal flour.
● roller milling:
Developments over the last century have produced

Wheat is crushed between two of these large flat round stones, placed grooved sides together

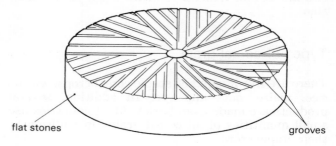

flat stones   grooves

Fig. 15.3 Stone milling

highly automated flour mills which contain special equipment to break open the wheat grains and crush them between steel rollers. Most flour is now produced by this method, which can separate the bran, germ and endosperm from each other very efficiently by elaborate sieving processes. This means that a highly refined flour can be produced. The portions remaining after the extraction of the flour are known as wheatfeed which is used for feeding animals and for making bran products.

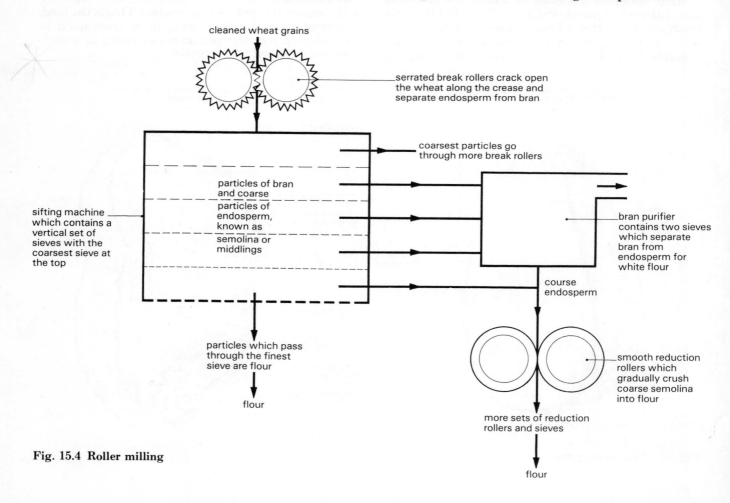

Fig. 15.4 Roller milling

Additives to flour

During the refining process the bran and the germ are extracted. This inevitably means that some dietary fibre, protein and B-vitamins are lost. Consequently, highly refined white flour is different in nutritional value from wholemeal flour.

To overcome some of these problems, some governments require millers to fortify the refined products to replace some of the lost nutrients. In Britain, the following minimum content of iron, calcium, and the B-vitamins, thiamin and niacin, must be present in every 100 g flour.

B-vitamins	thiamin	0.24 mg
	niacin	1.60 mg
mineral elements	iron	1.65 mg
	calcium	$\begin{cases} \text{not less than 235 mg} \\ \text{not more than 390 mg} \end{cases}$

In addition, millers are allowed to add regulated amounts of chemical substances known as 'flour improvers'. These substances improve the whiteness and baking quality of the flour. They include ascorbic acid, ammonium chloride and potassium bromate and potassium persulphate.

Fig. 15.5 Types of flour

Note: The extraction rate is the percentage of the whole grain remaining in the flour after milling.

Wholemeal flour

Extraction rate: 100% (by law it must contain the whole wheat grain)
100 g flour contains 10.8 g bran (dietary fibre).

Description: It is light brown in colour with a characteristic flavour due to the presence of the bran and germ. It may be stoneground or roller-milled. It has a shorter shelf-life than other flours because it contains the untreated fat from the germ. Bread made from this flour is heavy and close-textured because the bran and germ reduce the rise.

Uses: wholemeal bread, pastry and scones

Brown flour (or wheatmeal)

Extraction rate: 80–85%
100g flour contains 8.4g bran (dietary fibre).

Description: Similar in appearance to wholemeal flour but very coarse bran particles are removed in milling. Most brown flours available are of this type because they give a better rise in baking. They may be used mixed with white flour.

Uses: bread, pastry and scones

Wheatgerm flour

Extraction rate: 70% and added treated wheatgerm

Description: These are flours rich in B-vitamins because they must contain at least 10% of processed wheatgerm. The germ is first cooked with salt. This prevents the fat and enzymes present spoiling the keeping quality of the flour.

Uses: breadmaking

Strong, plain white flour

Extraction rate: 72–73%

Description: Has a high protein content (12–15%) and high water absorbency properties. Gives a good volume and light texture.

Uses: yeast cookery, puff and flaky pastries, batters

Plain white flour

Extraction rate: 72–73%

Description: Has a lower protein content (7–10%) and is used where a shorter, finer texture is required. It may be super-sifted in manufacture making the particles fine and separate with less tendency to lump. This is known as *extra fine* flour.

Uses: sauces, batters, short pastry, biscuits, shortbread, very rich cakes: plainer cakes and scones with addition of a raising agent

Self-raising flour

Extraction rate: 70–72%

Description: Soft flour always used (i.e. with a low protein content). Has a fixed quantity of raising agent added by the manufacturer and is suitable for most cakes. Regulations lay down how much carbon dioxide it should produce. Errors in adding raising agent are eliminated and even mixing of the raising agent through the flour is ensured. It should be used only where the raising action is required.

Uses: cakes, scones

Starch-reduced flour

Extraction rate: 70%

Description: A high proportion of the starch is washed out in preparation, leaving behind the flour protein. This flour gives a very light, open-textured product when baked. It is used by people on slimming diets.

Uses: bread and other baked goods

Types of flour (see Fig. 15.5)

The miller selects and blends the wheat grains to produce a large variety of flours, from which consumers may choose the most suitable one for their needs. When choosing a flour, colour and fineness are easy to see. However, there is an even more important characteristic that must be taken into account which is not obvious by appearance. When water is added to the flour, the proteins present (gliadin and glutenin) form another protein called gluten (see p. 216). It is the presence of gluten that makes wheat flour suitable for baking. (Note: other cereal grains do not contain gluten-forming proteins.)

The quality and quantity of gluten formed vary considerably according to the type of wheat grain. The spring wheats tend to produce high protein flours known as *strong flours*. Strong flours contain about 12–15% protein. When allowed to run through the hand, these flours are free-flowing, that is, the particles do not stick together. Winter wheats, which are low in protein, produce flours known as *soft flours* which have a tendency to clump together when handled. Soft flours contain 7–10% protein. The differences in the gluten content of flours can be seen in plate 25.

The use of flour

Raw flours are unpalatable and are always combined with other ingredients and cooked. Chemical reactions take place during the mixing and baking processes. The use of flour is described in detail in chapter 16. Figure 15.5 describes the main types of flour available.

2 Semolina

Semolina is also produced by milling wheat grains. It is produced in the early stages of the milling process when the endosperm is first separated from the bran and germ. The particles of endosperm are slightly gritty and coarse.

The best semolinas are prepared from durum wheat which is grown in Canada, the United States and Russia. It has a large grain with a hard endosperm, containing pigments which give an amber colour to the semolina. It is mainly used for making milk pudding.

3 Pasta

Pasta is the term used for stiff pastes made of semolina or flour and water. Sometimes eggs are added. The pastes are rolled out thinly or extruded into a variety of shapes. The shapes are dried before cooking. Semolina from durum wheat is very suitable for pasta. The pasta made from these wheat grains has a rich amber colour, a smooth surface and a firm brittle texture.

Home-made pasta is very popular in Italy, but most other countries use commercially-prepared pasta. The popularity of pasta is partly due to the fact that it is economical and combines well with many other foods.

Over 100 different shapes of pasta are produced including stars, hoops, butterflies, alphabet letters, etc. Some of the well-known varieties are illustrated and described here. They can be divided into tubular and flat ribbon types.

Convenience forms of pasta

Many canned and frozen varieties of pasta dishes are available and are very popular, such as spaghetti hoops in tomato sauce, and dishes containing pasta, e.g. lasagne.

4 Wheat breakfast cereal

A large number of ready-to-eat breakfast cereal products are prepared from wheat. The whole grains are processed to produce puffed wheat. Wheat flakes and shredded wheats are also prepared. The wheat bran is also processed and sold either as bran or incorporated into a variety of packet breakfast cereal products, e.g. KELLOGG'S ALL-BRAN.

Although commonly called breakfast cereals, these products may be eaten as snacks at other times.

Examine the packets of breakfast 'cereals' in your local supermarket.

How many of them include wheat and/or bran? Why are the breakfast cereals containing bran useful in the diet?

Compare the nutritive value of various breakfast cereals; the composition is usually stated on the packet.

Compare the relative costs of different-sized packages of one breakfast cereal.

RICE

Rice is an aquatic plant and produces most successful crops when grown in water. Therefore high rainfall or fresh water supplies for irrigation are essential for its production. Temperatures must

Tubular types

vermicelli very fine rods, too fine to have a hole through the middle. Used as a garnish for soup.

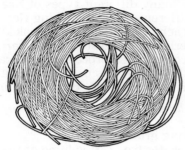

spaghetti (little strings) long rods of varying length and thickness which are cooked whole. Usually served with a tomato sauce (Napolitana) or with a meat sauce (Bolognese).

macaroni long tubes about 5 mm wide which may be obtained whole or cut in lengths or elbow shapes. Usually served in a creamy cheese sauce as macaroni cheese or cooked in milk to make a pudding.

canneloni the widest tubes which after boiling are stuffed with a meat or vegetable mixture, and recooked in a sauce.

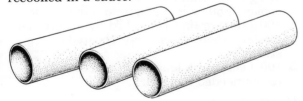

Flat ribbon types

tagliatelli noodles made in various widths may be served with a sauce or as an accompaniment to stews.

lasagne squares or wide strips of pasta which may be coloured green by addition of a spinach purée in the manufacture. After boiling, they are usually layered with a meat sauce and cheese or a white sauce.

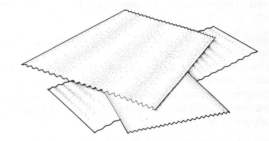

ravioli large sheets of pasta which are not dried but stuffed in little packets when the pasta is in the raw state and then cooked and served in a sauce.

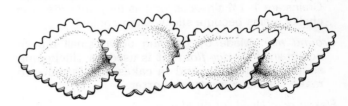

Fig. 15.6 **Pasta shapes**

be very high in the growing season. Ninety per cent of the world's rice is grown and consumed in Asia. Britain imports rice from USA, Italy, China and Australia. It is imported either as raw grain requiring milling, or in various forms as a finished product.

The processing of rice

The milling process removes the outer layers, leaving whole white grains. These are usually used whole and not crushed into flour. The germ and bran are removed by milling. About half the B-vitamins, the dietary fibre and some protein are lost in the process. Where white rice is the staple food in the developing countries nutritional problems are found, e.g. the disease beri-beri, due to a deficiency of the B-vitamin thiamin in the diet (see pp. 32–33).

The types of rice available are listed in Fig. 15.7.

Fig. 15.7 Types of rice

Brown rice: Whole grain with only outer husk removed. A brown coating of bran and some of the B-vitamins remain. Has a nutty flavour and requires longer cooking than white rice.

Long grain rice: (sometimes called Patna rice from days when this type of rice came from a district in NE India) Regular milled rice with all bran removed. Grains are four to five times as long as they are wide. Should be opaque white in colour if they are not to be sticky after cooking. Served with savoury dishes, such as curry. Requires 2 parts water to 1 part rice for cooking.

Easy-cook or parboiled rice: Long-grain rice is treated with steam or boiling water before milling to aid the retention of B-vitamins. It is translucent and yellow-brown. More water is absorbed during cooking (2½ parts water to 1 part rice). A longer cooking time is required but a greater yield is obtained. Grains are more easily kept separate after cooking.

Pre-cooked or instant rice: This is long-grain rice that has been completely cooked and dehydrated. It has a white glassy appearance. It may be called express or instant rice. This type of rice only needs reheating with water to replace the water removed in dehydration. Follow manufacturer's instructions carefully.

Boil-in-the bag rice (long-grain) Pre-cooked rice packed in heat-resistant bags. A 'convenience food', more expensive.

Short or round-grain rice: Used for milk puddings. Grains are 1–1½ times as long as they are wide. The chalky grains become sticky when cooked.

Ground rice: Made by grinding down small broken rice grains into *rice flour*. It is used for thickening soups, in puddings and in cakes and biscuits to make the flour mixture shorter.

Flaked rice: Used for puddings.

Convenience forms of rice

Rice is used to make a number of breakfast cereal products, either alone or combined with wheat. In the puffed form, rice is familiar as KELLOGG'S RICE KRISPIES.

Canned rice pudding is a popular convenience food.

Rice paper is the edible paper-like base used for macaroons and sweets, but nowadays rarely contains rice starch.

Experiment to investigate conditions for cooking rice

There are many different types of rice, and several different ways of cooking rice. The aim is to achieve dry, separate cooked grains. This experiment suggests several variations to the recommended procedure: you can design other variations using different types of rice, or different methods of cooking.

Control sample: *long-grain rice, absorption method*

    100 g long grain rice
    200 ml water (i.e. 2 × volume of rice)
    1 × 1.25 ml spoon salt.

1 What is the cost of 100 g of uncooked rice? Describe its appearance.
2 Weigh the rice. Note the volume.
3 Measure water (i.e. 2 × volume of rice.)
4 Place water, rice and salt in saucepan. Bring to the boil. Put on tight-fitting lid. Reduce heat until mixture is just simmering. Leave to cook (approx. 15–20 mins) until rice has absorbed all the water.
5 Weigh the cooked rice. Measure the volume of the cooked rice.
6 Calculate the cost of 100 g of cooked rice.
7 Comment on the colour, texture and taste of the rice.

Experimental samples:
1 100 g long-grain rice added to a large volume of fast-boiling water. Strain and rinse rice after cooking.
2 100 g long-grain rice cooked by absorption method in the oven. Allow 40 mins cooking time.
3 100 g long-grain rice cooked in a pressure cooker. Follow manufacturer's instructions.
4 100 g long-grain rice cooked by absorption method, then frozen, and reheated by steaming.
5 100 g easy-cook long-grain rice cooked by recommended method.

Observations:
Make a chart to compare colour, texture and taste of rice cooked by different methods.

    Tabulate: cost of 100 g uncooked rice, final volume of 100 g of uncooked rice, cost of 100 g of cooked rice.

Comment on your findings:
● Do all samples of uncooked rice absorb the same amount of water?
● How does the final volume of the rice vary?
● Does the cheapest uncooked rice remain the best value after cooking?

MAIZE

Maize originates from North and South America. Christopher Colombus discovered it in Cuba in 1494, and took the species to Spain. It is now cultivated throughout Europe, wherever climatic conditions are suitable. However, the USA produces 70% of the world's maize. The most important growing areas are the states of Ohio, Indiana, Illinois and Iowa. They are known as the 'Corn Belt'. The cobs of the plant, containing the yellow grains, are also eaten as a vegetable, known as corn-on-the-cob or sweetcorn.

Cornflour The flour produced from maize is practically pure starch and is known as cornflour. It is used for thickening sauces, soups and gravies. It is the main ingredient in custard power and blancmange. As there are no gluten-forming proteins in cornflour, it can be used with wheat to shorten mixtures where extra shortness is required, e.g. shortbread. However, cornflour is unsuitable for mixtures in which the elasticity of the gluten is important, such as cakes and flaky pastry.

Maize breakfast cereals Several types of breakfast cereal products are made from maize, e.g. corn flakes.

Savoury snacks Maize is used to produce a wide variety of savoury snack foods, which are especially popular with children, e.g. corn chips. These are usually sold in small moisture-proof packets to help retain the crispness of the product.

Pop-corn Maize is used to produce pop-corn.

OATS

Oats grow well in cool climates, e.g. Scotland. They are grown largely for animal feed and are not used extensively for human food. The grain contains more fat and protein (12-15%) than other cereals. The protein, however, does not form gluten and

cannot be used for breadmaking. The main products from oats are:

Rolled oats The bran is removed and the grain is steam-treated before being rolled. Rolled oats are used mainly for porridge and in cooking flapjacks and other biscuits.

Oatmeal The grain is ground into a coarse flour after the bran has been removed. Oatmeal is used for porridge and in making oat cakes and parkin. It is also used in haggis.

Oat breakfast cereal products
Rolled oats are frequently used in breakfast cereal products, e.g. they are the main ingredient in muesli, and are often included in other breakfast cereal products.

RYE

Rye is an important cereal in parts of Europe and Russia where it grows better than wheat in poor soil and harsher climates.

Rye has long thin grains which yield a dark coloured flour. This is lower in protein than wheat flour and produces a close, heavy bread. It is also mixed with wheat flour to produce a variety of dark breads. It is often used in the manufacture of crispbreads.

BARLEY

Barley is a very hardy cereal, but is not grown for flour because of its very low protein content. It is grown to produce malt products, e.g. *malt extract* for the brewing industry, and *malt flour* which is added to wheat flour for malt breads.

Pearl barley is the endosperm after the bran and husk are removed. It is used mainly to thicken soups and stews.

Scotch barley has only the outer husk removed: it needs long, slow cooking in stews.

Barley water is a refreshing drink; pearl barley is soaked in water, and often flavoured with lemon or orange.

Storage of cereal products

Cereal products should be stored in a well-ventilated cool, dry place. They absorb moisture in a damp place and may go mouldy. Cereal products are also liable to attack by insects, e.g. from mites and rodents. They should therefore be kept in containers with well-fitting lids.

Flour can be kept in its bag on a cool, dry, airy shelf. New flour should not be added to old flour in a container. The container should be washed and dried before a new bag of flour is added. The storage-time varies according to the amount of fat present in the flour. Wholemeal flour may go rancid if stored for too long.

Breakfast cereals are packed in sealed bags inside their cartons. They should remain crisp for several months in the unopened packet. After a bag is opened it should be carefully folded down inside the carton to help preserve the crispness and freshness of the product.

Fig. 15.8 Cereal products: approximate storage times

flour	● plain	4 months
	● self-raising	2 months
	● wholemeal	up to 2 months
rice		up to 6 months
pasta		up to 3 months
breakfast cereals	● *(unopened)*	up to 12 months
	● *(opened)*	a few weeks

Starches, other than cereal grains, used in food preparation

arrowroot is obtained from the root of a West Indian plant which is cooked, mixed with water, then dried to a fine powder. The arrowroot powder can be used for thickening instead of cornflour when a clear gel is required, e.g. fruit flan glaze (see p. 212).

sago is obtained from the pith of the sago palm. Used in milk puddings.

tapioca is made from the root of the cassava plant. Used in milk puddings.

QUESTIONS

1 What is a cereal?
  What is meant by 'a staple cereal'? Name a staple cereal grown in a temperate climate and one grown in a tropical climate.
  Describe how they are used for food.

2 Explain the meaning and importance of the following:
  cereal fibre
  gluten
  self-raising flour
  strength of flour.

3 Draw a labelled diagram to show the composition of the wheat grain.
  Name three products of the milling of wheat.
  How is the nutritional value of white flour improved before it is sold?
  (JMB, 1979)

4 Why are some cereals unsuitable for making cakes? Give examples.
  (JMB, 1979)

5 Discuss the differences between white and wholemeal flour.
  (AEB, 1977)

6 Give the origins and uses of each of the following:
  (a) pasta (b) cornflour (c) arrowroot (d) cornflakes.
  (AEB, 1977)

7 Discuss the value of ready-to-eat cereals as a breakfast food.
  Which foods should be added to complete the breakfast?

8 The doctor has told his patient to eat more dietary fibre. What advice could you give about this?
  What is the value of eating dietary fibre?

9 Discuss the value of wheat and flour products in the diet.
  (London 1981)

The use of flour 16

1 For thickening liquids

Flour is a particularly useful commodity because:
- wheat, rice and cornflour thicken liquids, e.g. sauces, gravies, custards;
- wheat flour forms the structure of baked products (see p. 216).

These properties are due to the composition and nature of flour.

The main constituent of all flours is the carbohydrate starch. Cornflour, rice flour and arrowroot (see p. 210) are almost pure starch; wheat flour contains a high percentage of starch (see p. 202). When moistened and heated, mixtures containing starch thicken. This process is known as gelatinisation.

Gelatinisation

When examined under a microscope, starch is seen to consist of tiny granules. They do not dissolve when added to a cold liquid. When stirred, the granules are suspended in the liquid. When the mixture is heated, the liquid begins to penetrate the starch granules, causing them to soften. The granules swell to about five times their normal size until they almost touch each other (see Fig. 16.1). This causes the mixture to become thick and viscous. The starch is said to have *gelatinised* and a *gel* has been formed. As a cooked starch mixture cools, there is a marked increase in the stiffness of the gel; for example a cornflour gel may set and form a mould, such as blancmange.

The degree of gelatinisation is affected by
(a) the proportion and type of starch,
(b) the temperature of the liquid,
(c) the effect of other ingredients.

(a) The proportion and type of starch

Each type of starch has granules of particular size and shape. They can be identified under a microscope, as shown in Fig. 16.1. These characteristics affect the properties of the starch in food preparation. For example, arrowroot has a relatively large granule compared with cornflour. Because there are fewer interfaces between cooked arrowroot granules than in a cooked cornflour mixture, light is able to penetrate the arrowroot mixture more easily. Therefore arrowroot gives a clear, transparent gel when thickened. It is most usually used for a fruit sauce or glaze. Cornflour forms a more opaque gel.

The proportion of starch to liquid used affects the thickness of the gel formed, e.g. note the proportions of flour used in the recipes for white sauces of different consistencies (see Fig. 16.5).

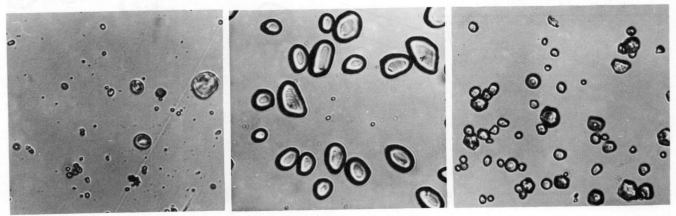

Fig. 16.1 Starch grains in (left to right) cornflour, arrowroot and wheatflour

The process of gelatinisation is important in all starch-thickened mixtures. If this process is not correctly done the mixture may be unpalatable; it may taste raw, be of the wrong consistency, or become lumpy.

Lumps will form in a starch-thickened mixture if:
- dry starch is mixed with warm or hot liquid. On immediate contact with dry starch, the hot liquid will gelatinise the outer starch granules. These starch granules are like a sticky skin which acts as a barrier. The liquid is unable to penetrate to the remaining uncooked starch granules in the lump. If the lump is broken open, uncooked starch will be found inside it (Fig. 16.2(a) and (b)). This is the reason why starch used for thickening is usually blended with a little cold liquid before the hot liquid is added.
- the mixture is not stirred whilst being heated. The starch granules will not remain in suspension, unless the mixture is stirred; instead, they settle in the bottom of the saucepan in groups. The starch granules in contact with the liquid gelatinise and prevent the liquid from penetrating the remaining starch.

(b) The temperature of the liquid

The temperature of gelatinisation varies with the type of starch. Gelatinisation is a gradual process. Look at Fig. 16.3 and note the changing size and shape of arrowroot granules as the temperature rises. Most starch mixtures start to thicken somewhere between 75°C and 87°C, but complete gelatinisation does not occur until the mixture approaches boiling point. It is therefore important to boil mixtures containing starch. Sauces and custards must boil for two minutes to ensure that all starch granules are fully gelatinised. Any ungelatinised starch gives a raw taste to the mixture.

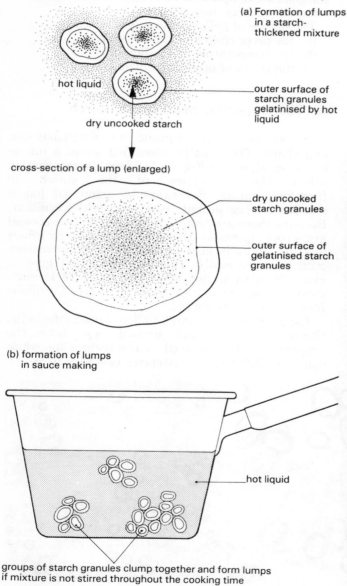

(a) Formation of lumps in a starch-thickened mixture

hot liquid

outer surface of starch granules gelatinised by hot liquid

dry uncooked starch

cross-section of a lump (enlarged)

dry uncooked starch granules

outer surface of gelatinised starch granules

(b) formation of lumps in sauce making

hot liquid

groups of starch granules clump together and form lumps if mixture is not stirred throughout the cooking time

Fig. 16.2 Gelatinisation

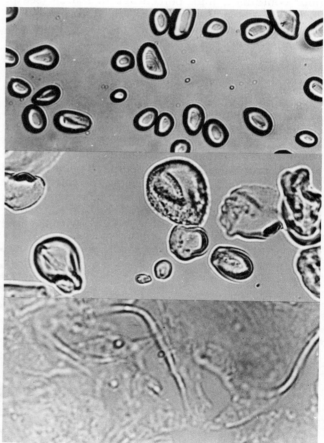

Fig. 16.3 Changes in arrowroot during gelatinisation

(c) The effect of other ingredients

The gelatinisation process may be affected by other ingredients in a recipe. The most usual additions are:

- *acid*, e.g. lemon juice, tomatoes, vinegar. When acids are cooked with a starch mixture they decrease the thickening power of the starch. This is because some of the starch granules are broken down into smaller particles (hydrolysed) by the acid. To avoid this happening, the starch liquid should be cooked and allowed to thicken before the acid ingredient is added, e.g. in a lemon pie filling the lemon juice should be added after the cornflour-and-water mixture has thickened.
- *sugar*, which softens a starch gel, but it does not affect the thickness of the mixture unless it is used in large quantities, e.g. the amount used in custard will have little effect, but the larger quantities used for lemon pie filling may decrease the thickness of the mixture. It is therefore recommended that the sugar is added after the starch has gelatinised.

The effects of these variations on the degree of gelatinisation can be observed in the following experiments.

Experiments to investigate the process of gelatinisation

All starches, when moistened and heated, thicken a mixture. This process, gelatinisation, is used in making gravies, custards and glazes. Follow these experiments and comment on your results.

General method

1 Moisten starch with a small amount of water. Stir until all lumps disappear. Add remaining liquid and stir.
2 Place mixture in small saucepan over direct heat and stir constantly. Note the temperature at which the mixture begins to thicken. Stir continuously until 95°C.
3 Pour mixture into 2 × 250 ml basins. Cool mixture. Freeze one sample and examine at a later date.
4 Measure depth of mould in basin (use a skewer). Turn out on to a plate. Measure depth again. The difference in these measurements indicates the stability of the mould.
5 Cut the mould in half and comment on consistency and clarity of the mould.

6 Record your results on a chart. What difference do you observe in strength, consistency and clarity of moulds made from different starches?
7 Comment on the effect of temperature, sugar and acid on the stability of a cornflour mould.

Experiment 1: to investigate the gelatinisation of different starches

For each sample use 250 ml water with
(a) 25 g cornflour
(b) 25 g wheat flour
(c) 25 g arrowroot

Experiment 2: to investigate the effect of temperature, acid and sugar on the gelatinisation of cornflour

For each sample use 250 ml water with 25 g cornflour.

(a) Temperature: make two samples.
Sample I: heat the mixture only to 85°C
Sample II: heat the mixture to 95°C
(b) Acidity: make two samples.
Sample I: add 30 ml lemon juice before boiling
Sample II: add 30 ml lemon juice after boiling
(c) Sugar: make two samples.
Sample I: add 50 g sugar before boiling
Sample II: add 50 g sugar after boiling

General conclusions

1 When would you recommend the use of cornflour, wheat flour and arrowroot to thicken mixtures in food preparation?
2 What is the effect of adding sugar and acid in starch-thickened mixtures? What advice would you give in making (a) a custard, (b) a lemon meringue pie filling?

The importance of correct gelatinisation of starch granules is clearly illustrated in the making of sauces.

Sauces

Sauces should be smooth, glossy, of the correct consistency and always well-flavoured. These characteristics will be achieved if
(a) suitable ingredients are used in the correct proportions.
(b) an appropriate method of making sauces is followed carefully.

Ingredients

The essential ingredients used are starch and liquid. The choice of these ingredients depends on the type of sauce. Fat is often added to flavour, enrich and give a glossy appearance to the sauce. A variety of flavourings may be added, depending on the type of sauce required, e.g. salt, pepper, cheese, herbs, etc. added to savoury sauces; sugar, fruit, chocolate, added to sweet sauces.

Methods of making sauces

Three methods may be used in the home for the preparation of sauces:
(a) the blending method
(b) the roux method
(c) the all-in-one method.

(a) *The blending method* is used to prepare the simplest form of sauce which does not contain fat. For example:
● custard made from custard powder, blancmange made from flavoured cornflour;
● gravy made from gravy power;
● arrowroot glaze for fruit flans.
Packet sauces are also prepared by the blending method and these may contain fat.
   The starch is blended with a small quantity of the cold liquid to separate the starch granules. The remaining liquid is heated almost to boiling point and mixed into the blended powder. The mixture must be stirred at this stage to distribute the starch granules evenly through the mixture, and to prevent lumps forming. Partial gelatinisation of the starch may take place, but the mixture must be returned to the saucepan, boiled and stirred for two minutes to complete the gelatinisation process.

(b) *The roux method* is used for making:

● white sauces
● brown sauces and gravy

The *roux* consists of equal quantities of fat and flour. The fat is melted, and the flour stirred in. The starch granules in the flour become coated with fat

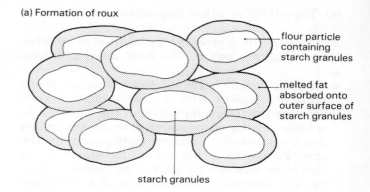

(a) Formation of roux

flour particle containing starch granules

melted fat absorbed onto outer surface of starch granules

starch granules

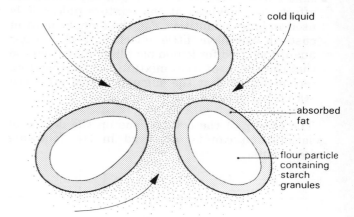

(b) Addition of cold liquid

cold liquid

absorbed fat

flour particle containing starch granules

cold liquid is added gradually to separate the roux

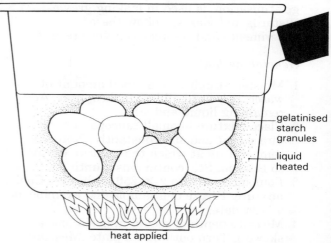

(c) Gelatinisation on heating mixture thickens when heated

gelatinised starch granules

liquid heated

heat applied

mixture is stirred as it is heated, the fat melts and is absorbed by the flour particles as they swell and the starch granules gelatinise to thicken the mixture

Fig. 16.4 Making sauces by the roux method

(see Fig. 16.4). The mixture is cooked over a low heat; great care is needed, as the mixture easily burns. Some gelatinisation of starch takes place at this stage, but most of the starch granules remain uncooked, because there is not enough liquid to complete the gelatinisation process. The fat coating the starch granules helps to keep them separate when the liquid is added. The roux must be taken off the heat and allowed to cool slightly before the liquid is added; this helps to prevent the formation of lumps.

The liquid is added gradually and stirred carefully into the roux; the starch forms a suspension in the cold liquid. The sauce must then be returned to the heat, brought slowly to the boil and stirred continuously whilst boiling to keep the starch granules dispersed. As the temperature rises, the fat melts and is absorbed by the starch: the starch gelatinises, thus thickening the mixture and producing a smooth glossy sauce. The consistency and flavouring of the sauce is dependent on the type of sauce required.

(i) White sauces

The ingredients used are wheat flour or cornflour, milk or fish stock or vegetable liquid, margarine or butter, and seasonings.

Fig. 16.5 White sauces

	flour	liquid	use
pouring sauce	15 g	250 ml	accompaniment, (e.g. served with vegetables, steamed puddings, etc.)
coating sauce	25 g	250 ml	coating for fish, vegetables, and other savoury dishes
binding sauce (panada)	50 g	250 ml	to bind ingredients together, e.g. as in croquettes

---

Look at plate 26(a) to see the differences in consistency between pouring and coating sauces.

The correct consistency is achieved by using the correct proportion of flour and liquid.

It is important that the roux is not allowed to colour. Any slight browning of the flour spoils the colour and taste of a white sauce. The sauce may also be discoloured if a metal spoon is used for stirring in a metal saucepan. A wooden or plastic spoon should be used.

The flavourings, e.g. salt, pepper, cheese, parsley, are added after the sauce has thickened.

A white sauce may also be made by a quick alternative method which does not involve the making of a roux. This method is known as the 'all-in-one' method; see (c) below.

(ii) Brown sauce and gravy

The ingredients used are wheat flour or cornflour, meat stock or vegetable liquor, meat drippings or margarine, and seasonings. The roux is heated until it is golden-brown. (Care must be taken not to allow the flour to scorch or burn, as this gives the sauce an unpleasant bitter taste.) As the flour changes colour, some of the starch is converted to dextrin, which gives a brown sauce its attractive colour and flavour. Dextrin does not thicken as well as starch, consequently, an increased proportion of flour is recommended, e.g. 25 g flour: 250 ml stock for a thickened gravy with a pouring consistency.

After the roux has been made, the liquid is added and the sauce completed as for a white sauce made by the roux method.

In a rich brown sauce, e.g. Espagnol sauce, vegetables are browned in the fat before the flour is added to make the roux. When the liquid has been added, and the sauce thickened, cooking is continued by simmering the sauce. The colour and flavour of the vegetables are extracted into the sauce. The sauce is usually strained before serving to remove the vegetables and produce a smooth glossy sauce.

(c) The all-in-one method

This is a quick simple way to make a white sauce. The ingredients are wheat flour or cornflour; margarine or butter and milk; and fish or vegetable stock. The fat, flour, and liquid are all placed in the saucepan at the same time. The large quantity of cold liquid separates the starch granules in the flour. The sauce should be stirred continuously as it is brought to the boil, so that the starch granules remain separate, and lumps do not form. The fat melts and is absorbed by the starch granules. As the sauce boils the temperature will be high enough to make sure that all the starch is gelatinised. The sauce will taste fully cooked and have the correct consistency.

(a) the ingredients are
placed in the pan

cold liquid

wooden
spoon

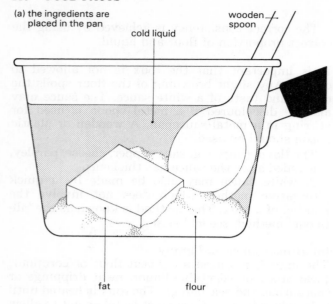

fat

flour

(b) on heating

wooden
spoon

flour particles

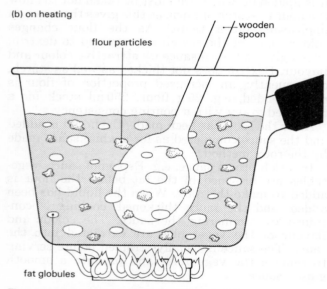

fat globules

The mixture is heated and stirred vigorously; the fat melts and flour
particles are evenly dispersed; fat is absorbed by flour and starch
granules in the flour gelatinise, giving a thickened mixture

Fig. 16.6 Making sauces by the all-in-one method

There are many packet mixes on the market
to make white sauce. How do you account for
this?

Make a white sauce by the roux method.

Make a white sauce by the all-in-one method.

Make a white sauce from a packet mix.

Compare the cost, the time taken, and the
taste and appearance of the finished sauce.

---

2   In baking

Wheat flour is one of the most frequently-used
commodities in food preparation. It is commonly
known as 'flour', and in this section the word 'flour'
refers only to wheat flour. This chapter examines
the scientific principles of the use of plain white
flour. Self-raising flour, that is flour with the raising
agent added in the packet, should only be used
where a recipe suggests it is suitable. Wholemeal
flours may be substituted for white flour in various
recipes. The use of these flours and their interaction
with other ingredients is similar to the processes
described for white flour. Usually an increased
quantity of liquid is required, as the wholemeal flour
absorbs more water than white flour. The main
difference in the finished product will be a coarser,
closer texture, a darker colour, and a 'nutty' flavour.

When flour is used in baked products, the starch
is gelatinised (see p. 211). The starch on the surface
is converted to another carbohydrate, dextrin; this
gives the characteristic brown crust of baked
products. It is, however, the behaviour of the
proteins which makes wheat flour particularly
suitable for use in baked products. When flour is
combined with water, the proteins, gliadin and
glutenin, form another protein, which is known as
gluten (see p. 206).

Gluten formation

When separate from the starch in the flour, the
gluten is seen to be a creamy-beige elastic
substance, rather like bubble gum. When flour
mixtures are heated, the raising agents present
stretch the elastic strands of gluten and so the
mixture rises. On further heating, the gluten
strands coagulate, forming a light brittle sponge
which is the framework supporting the baked
product.

Look at plate 25(c) and describe the texture
of the gluten balls.

The proportions of starch and gluten in a flour
vary with the type of wheat used. Those with a high
proportion of protein are known as strong flours,
and those with a low proportion of protein are
known as soft flours.

The more protein in the flour, the more water it
will absorb and a very elastic gluten will be
developed. When large volumes and light open

Experiment to investigate the gluten content of different types of flour

Flours to be tested

Strong flour, e.g. McDougall's Country Life

All-purpose flour, e.g. Spiller's Homepride

Soft flour, e.g. McDougall's Extrafine plain flour, or special blend cake-flour from a local bakery

Reagent for testing for presence of starch: iodine solution.

Experimental method

1 Weigh 50 g of the three types of flour.
2 Mix each sample with 25 ml of water (distilled, if possible), to give stiff dough. Weigh each sample.
3 Rest each ball of dough under cold water for five minutes.
4 Knead each sample carefully between your fingers under a slow stream of cold running water. At first, the water draining away will be milk-coloured.
5 When the water draining away appears to be clear, collect some of this water in a small bowl and test with a few drops of the iodine solution.
6 If the purple drops of iodine solution turn black, starch is still present. Continue washing the dough until no dark colouration appears when iodine is added to the rinsing water. This indicates that all the starch has been removed.
7 Squeeze excess water out of the remaining gluten ball. Put it to dry.

8 Compare the size and weights of the three gluten balls.
9 Pull each sample between your fingers. Describe the feel of the sample.
10 Place the three samples on a greased baking tray. Bake in a hot over for approximately 15 minutes, until each gluten ball has expanded and is crisp and dry on both the outside and inside.
11 Weigh each sample. Calculate the percentage of gluten in each sample as follows:

e.g. Sample (a): strong flour

original weight = 50 g.

gluten ball weight after baking = x g.

$$\% \text{ gluten in flour} = \frac{x}{50} \times 100.$$

12 Cut each of the three samples in half. Compare the internal texture of the samples.

Observations

1 Explain the differences in gluten content of the three samples.
2 Which type of flour would you recommend for:
(a) making bread
(b) making a cake?
3 In which types of recipe would you recommend the use of an all-purpose flour?
4 Look at plate 25(d); do the results of your experiments resemble these photographs?
5. Compare the results of your experiment with the appearance of an Energen starch-reduced roll.

Fig. 16.7 Baked products (see p. 218)

	Consistency	Characteristics	Examples
Batter	pouring	a thin liquid mixture	Yorkshire pudding, pancakes
	coating	a thicker liquid that will stick to the food	coating for fried foods, drop scones
	dropping	a soft mixture that will fall off a wooden spoon when suspended	choux pastry, cakes
Dough	soft	a soft mixture that can be handled, may be kneaded and shaped by hand	scones, some biscuits and yeast mixtures, e.g. bread
	stiff	a mixture containing more fat and less liquid than a soft dough, and which can be rolled	pastry, biscuits, shortbread

textures are required, as in breadmaking and puff pastry, strong flour is necessary. Too much gluten development is not desirable for cakes, biscuits and some pastries, where shorter, finer textures are preferred. Soft flours should be used for these purposes. The varieties of flour available were described in chapter 15.

Look at plate 25. Compare the quality of gluten from different types of flour.

Fig. 16.8 Proportions of protein and carbohydrate in flour

	Strong flour	Soft flour
protein (gluten)	12-15%	7-10%
carbohydrate (starch)	85-88%	90-93%

Design an experiment to show how the gluten content of different flours would affect the texture of a loaf (see. plate 25(d)).

Baked products

Flour is the basic ingredient in most baked products. It is mixed with some or all of the following ingredients: raising agent, fat, sugar, eggs, liquid and salt. Many other ingredients are used to add interest and flavour, e.g. spices, fruit, cocoa, etc. The difference in taste, texture and appearance of baked products is due to variations in the choice and proportions of ingredients, the method of mixing, and baking temperatures.

Baked products are often classified as batters or doughs, according to the consistency of the uncooked mixture, as shown in Fig. 16.7.

During the preparation and cooking of these mixtures a number of physical and chemical changes take place. It is for this reason that the correct *proportion* of ingredients must be used. Accurate *measurement* is essential in all the baking processes described in the following sections.

Batters

Pouring and coating batters: The role and interaction of ingredients

The essential ingredients in a pouring or coating batter are flour and a liquid, such as water or milk. Eggs are usually added, although in some coating batters they are omitted. The eggs provide additional protein which helps to form the framework of the batter, and they also help to retain air in the mixture, until the batter is set by cooking. A little salt is added to develop the flavour. Sugar and fat (or oil) are added to some recipes to enrich the mixture.

The terms 'pouring' and 'coating' describe the consistency of two types of batter used in food preparation:

Fig. 16.9 Batter: ingredients

	pouring batter	coating batter
flour	100 g	200 g
milk	250 ml	250 ml
egg	1	0 or 1
raising agent	none	baking powder or yeast may be added

A batter contains a high proportion of liquid to flour. The liquid is converted to steam during cooking; this acts as the main raising agent. A little air is included as the batter is mixed. It is essential that plain flour should always be used for pouring batters. Self-raising flour would provide additional raising agent, which would cause the gluten to overstretch and then collapse. Stiffer batters, where smaller volumes of steam are produced, may additionally use chemical raising agents.

In mixing a batter, it is important that the flour and a little of the liquid are blended to a smooth cream before the remaining liquid is added. Mixtures that are initially too liquid are difficult to mix, and liable to form lumps.

Look at plate 26(b) and see the characteristic texture of different batters.

Pouring batters

These are either baked, e.g. Yorkshire pudding, or the same mixture may be fried, e.g. pancakes. Two examples are given to show the importance of accurate cooking methods.

(i) *Yorkshire pudding* should be a well-risen, almost hollow shell. It should be crisp and brown outside, moist but not soggy inside. To achieve these results, bake only a thin layer of batter and preheat the oven, tin and fat to 220°C.

The high temperature is necessary to heat the liquid in the batter rapidly and convert it to steam. This acts as a raising agent, causing the pudding to rise. Simultaneously, gelatinisation of the starch takes place. The high temperature also quickly forms a crust which holds the steam. The crust is formed by coagulation of the proteins in the flour, egg, and milk. Some steam escapes and is replaced by air, but some steam remains inside the pudding. It is important to serve the pudding immediately, or it will collapse because, as it cools, the steam left inside will condense.

(ii) *Pancakes* should be lacy-thin, light, and crisp. To achieve these results, use a very hot, oiled pan and use only a thin layer of batter, so that steam is produced rapidly, creating a lacy, light texture.

Packet batter mixes

Packets of batter mix for Yorkshire pudding and pancakes are available. They contain flour, milk powder, and salt. They are mixed with egg and cold water in the same way as the home-made batter.

Coating batters

These are always deep-fried, e.g. coating batter for fried fish. The batter should be crisp and golden-brown. It provides a seal to prevent juices from escaping from the food. This seal also prevents oil penetrating the food and giving a greasy product. To achieve these results:

- the batter must be thick enough adequately to coat the food.
- the food must be dry to allow the batter to stick to the surface. Pre-coating the food lightly with flour helps the batter to stick to the food.
- the oil or fat for frying must be at the correct temperature for deep-fat frying (see p. 193).

Cakes

The role and interaction of ingredients

The main ingredients in cake recipes are flour and raising agent, fat, sugar, eggs, and possibly liquid. Some spices, dried fruits and other flavourings are added to some recipes.

The choice and proportion of ingredients, the method of making, and accurate baking conditions, are all important to achieve good results in cake-making.

Choice of ingredients

Flour forms the framework of the cake. To obtain a soft, tender crumb, soft flours (low gluten content) are recommended. Self-raising flours are always soft, and frequently used in cake-making as they contain the correct amount of chemical raising agent for most cakes.

Raising agent (see chapter 17)
The type and amount of raising agent used affects the finished texture of a cake. It is important that:
- the correct amount of raising agent is added.
- the raising agent is evenly mixed through the flour.

Fat is important in cake recipes because:
- it has the ability to entangle and hold air in the mixture;
- it adds flavour;
- it improves the keeping quality.
Butter or margarine is usually chosen.

Sugar has several functions in a cake recipe:
- it sweetens the mixture;
- it helps to entangle air in the mixture;
- it increases the volume of the cake;
- it raises the temperature at which the proteins in the egg and flour coagulate. Consequently, the cake can rise evenly at a moderate temperature before the mixture sets.

Eggs are added to:
- enrich the colour and flavour of a cake;
- add protein to help form the framework of the cake;
- entangle air and act as a raising agent.

Liquid is essential for:
- the action of chemical raising agents (see p. 250);
- the gelatinisation of starch (see p. 211);
- the hydration of proteins in the flour to form gluten.

Fig. 16.10 Cake-making: the whisking method (see plate 27(a))

Basic recipe: Swiss roll: 50 g plain flour, 50 g castor sugar, 2 eggs

Action	Reaction	Possible faults
1 Weigh all ingredients carefully.		Inaccurate proportion of ingredients causes faults in appearance, texture and taste of the cake.
2 Place eggs and sugar together in mixing bowl. If a hand whisk is used, place mixing bowl over a saucepan of hot water. This is unnecessary if an electric mixer is used. The mixture should become just faintly warm.	The warmth slightly thickens the egg proteins, allowing the mixture to stretch and incorporate a great volume of air. The electric beater generates more heat than a hand whisk.	Care must be taken not to overheat the bowl. If the mixing bowl touches the hot water, some egg protein may coagulate in the mixing bowl, spoiling the mixture. If the mixture becomes too warm, the sugar dissolves to a syrup, and will not incorporate air. The cake becomes sticky in texture.
3 Whisk the eggs and sugar together until the mixture becomes thick, pale yellow, stable foam. Test: the foam should be thick enough to leave a trail of the mixture across the surface for 30 seconds.	The egg proteins stretch incorporating air into the mixture. At first large bubbles are seen in a frothy foam. As whisking continues, these large bubbles are broken into very small bubbles and trapped inside a very fine honeycomb mesh.	Underwhisking: insufficient air is incorporated, so the finished cake has a poor volume and heavy texture. Overwhisking: most unlikely to happen.
4 Remove bowl from heat if used. Continue beating mixture as it cools.	The mixture become stable and thickens as it cools.	If the flour is added to a warm mixture some starch gelatinises and lumps will form.
5 Sieve the flour.	Sieving makes flour very fine.	If the flour is not finely sieved, lumps may form as it is added to the whisked mixture.
6 Sieve the flour over the surface of the egg/sugar foam.	The flour should remain on surface of the mixture.	If the foam is not sufficiently thick to support the weight of flour, the flour sinks and the mixture loses air.
7 Fold in the flour very lightly using a metal spoon.	The flour is evenly suspended throughout the foam. A metal spoon cuts evenly through the foam and expels less air than a wooden spoon.	Whisking or beating instead of folding at this stage causes the mixture to lose air. It is important not to leave any flour uncoated by the mixture or it will cause lumps of uncooked flour in the finished cake.
8 Pour the mixture into well-greased tins. The tin may also be sprinkled with sugar or flour.	The cake will be easily removed after baking. The outside of the cake becomes crusty during baking.	There is no fat in the mixture and it will stick to the tin if it is not well greased.
9 Bake according to the recipe. Swiss rolls (thin layer, large surface area). Reg. 7 or 220 °C for 7–8 mins.	Oh heating, the water in the egg becomes steam. The air and steam expand, enlarging the bubbles in the mixture. Some small bubbles appear on the top surface of the cake.	If the oven temperature is too low, the air and steam rise through the mixture and escape before the proteins coagulate. This causes a cake with a poor volume and close heavy texture.
Sponge cake (thicker layer and smaller surface area). Reg. 4 or 180 °C for approx. 30 mins.	The starch gelatinises, the proteins coagulate and the cake sets in the risen position.	If the oven temperature is too high the proteins coagulate, setting the cake in position before the air and steam have expanded sufficiently to raise the mixture. Cakes of poor volume and heavy texture are produced.

The proportion of liquid varies with the type of cake. Some liquid is provided by the eggs and fat. No extra liquid is required in the richest cake mixtures.

The method of mixing

This usually depends on the amount of fat used in the recipe:
- no fat: *whisking method*
- less than half fat to flour (plain cakes): *rubbing-in method*
- half to equal quantities fat to flour (rich cakes): *creaming* or *all-in-one methods*

A fourth method known as the *melting method* is traditionally used for gingerbread and some biscuit mixes. The proportion of fat in these recipes is usually one-third to a half quantity fat to flour.

The following step-by-step guide for each method shows what is happening to the mixture and the possible faults that may occur at each stage in the process.

A The whisking method (See Fig. 16.10)

The whisking method is used for making Swiss rolls and spongecakes, which are sometimes known as 'fatless sponges'. Because there is no fat in these types of cake they go stale very quickly. The photograph in plate 27(a) shows the very light, soft, even texture of this type of cake.

The ingredients used are eggs, sugar, and plain flour. It is essential that a great deal of air is incorporated in the mixing. Air and steam from the water in the egg act as raising agents. Plain flour is usually recommended as self raising flour gives a slightly coarser textured cake and the cake may collapse and sink. A little water may be added to Swiss roll mixtures to avoid excessive evaporation from the large surface area of the cake. A Genoese sponge is made by the same method but melted fat is added at the same time as the flour.

B The rubbing-in method: plain cake mixtures (See Fig. 16.13)

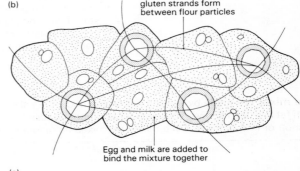

(a)

fat rubbed into thin film around flour particle

flour particle

air is rubbed into the mixture

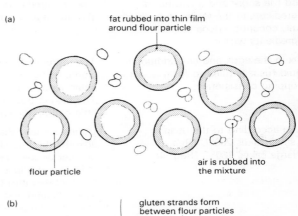

(b)

gluten strands form between flour particles

Egg and milk are added to bind the mixture together

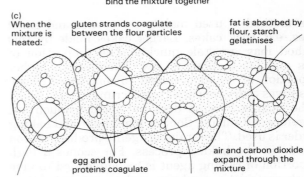

(c)
When the mixture is heated:

gluten strands coagulate between the flour particles

fat is absorbed by flour, starch gelatinises

egg and flour proteins coagulate

air and carbon dioxide expand through the mixture

Fig. 16.12 Cake making: the rubbing-in method

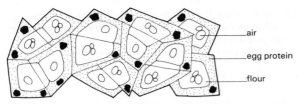

air bubbles

egg proteins

sugar crystals

(a) Egg proteins are stretched, trapping small air bubbles in stable foam

air

egg protein

flour

(b) Flour, finely sieved, is folded into the mixture, adheres to egg protein and also makes a fine, honeycomb structure

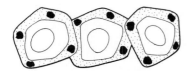

(c) When heated, the air expands and rises, stretching egg and flour proteins; the proteins coagulate, giving the risen, firm structure to the cake

Fig. 16.11 Cake making: the whisking method

Fig. 16.13 Cake-making: the rubbing-in method (see plate 27(b))

Basic recipe: scones: 200 g self-raising flour, 1 × 5 ml spoon baking powder, 25 g margarine, 25 g castor sugar, 8 × 15 ml spoon milk

Action	Reaction	Possible faults
1 Weigh all ingredients carefully.		Inaccurate proportion of ingredients causes faults in appearance, texture and taste of the finished product.
2 Sieve the flour, salt and raising agent.	The ingredients are thoroughly and evenly mixed.	
3 Rub the fat into the flour mixture.	The fat is distributed evenly. A thin film of fat coats the flour particles, forming a waterproof barrier. This inhibits the formation of gluten which would toughen the mixture. Some air is incorporated into the mixture during the process.	Undermixing causes an uneven texture and a tough mixture as the fat is insufficiently mixed. Overmixing is difficult as the proportion of fat is low.
4 Add the sugar and any other dry ingredients in the recipe, e.g. dried fruit, coconut, cocoa. Stir all ingredients well.	These ingredients are evenly distributed through the mixture.	If fruit is too large (e.g. whole cherries) or wet when it is added to the mixture it may sink to the bottom of the cake during the cooking process.
5 Mix in the eggs and any additional liquid (usually milk) to form a soft dropping consistency.	The ingredients are bound together. Some gluten strands are formed when liquid comes into contact with flour. The baking powder starts to release a little carbon dioxide.	If too much liquid is used for small cakes cooked on a baking tray they will spread and join together. More liquid is required for cakes baked in tins or they will be dry and crumbly.
6 Bake according to the recipe: • small cakes 200°C (Reg. 6) • large cakes 180°C (Reg. 4)	During baking, the fat melts. The starch absorbs the fat. The sugar and baking powder dissolve in the liquid. Carbon dioxide is produced. Together with air incorporated into the mixture, these gases expand and rise throughout the mixture. The gluten strands are stretched. The starch gelatinises and the egg proteins coagulate forming the framework of the cake.	Inaccurate oven temperature. If the oven temperature is too high the cakes rise too quickly, the top surface cracks as raising agent gases inside expand. The inside may not be fully cooked, when the cake appears to be cooked outside. If the oven temperature is too low the raising agent gases expand, and escape: there is insufficient heat to set the inside of the cake. When eventually cooked, the cake will have a poor volume and a dense, heavy texture.

Cake mixes are made by the rubbing-in-method. The cake mix contains the dry ingredients: flour, raising agent and sugar to which fat has been added. These mixtures cannot contain high proportions of fat, as this may go rancid during the storage time in the shop or in the home. Cake mixes are mixed as recommended with eggs and liquid.

This method is used mainly for scones and small cakes, e.g. rock cakes. Larger cakes made by this method may go stale quickly. The proportion of eggs and fat to flour is low. Therefore, a higher proportion of liquid is added to mix these cakes. This gives a dry, open-textured crumb.

The mixing process does not include much air. Therefore self-raising flour or plain flour and baking powder is used. These raising agents produce carbon dioxide in the baking process. For scones a high proportion of raising agent is recommended to give the characteristic good rise and open texture, (see plate 27(b)).

C The creaming method and the all-in-one method: rich cakes (see Fig. 16.15, 16.16)

These are the most widely-used methods of cakemaking for rich cakes such as fairy cakes, Victoria sandwich and rich fruit cakes. These cakes contain high proportions of fat to flour (over half fat to flour). A wide variety of flavourings may be added such as chocolate, spices, and fruit.

The cakes should have a light, fine, even texture. They should be well risen with a good volume and a level top.

Traditionally, rich cakes have always been made by the *creaming method*, but the texture of modern fats has meant that cakes can be successfully made by a much simpler method known as the *all-in-one method*. This method has become increasingly popular because it saves time and effort, and can be made very easily by hand or by electric mixer. Taste tests show that almost identical cakes are produced by the two methods.

A Victoria sandwich is used as an example in this section to examine how ingredients combine and react in the preparation and baking in both the creaming and the all-in-one methods. A Victoria sandwich contains equal quantities of fat, sugar, eggs and flour. Air and carbon dioxide (from self-raising flour or added baking powder) act as raising agents. No additional liquid is added. In other rich cake recipes where the proportion of fat and eggs to flour is less, some additional liquid is necessary.

(a) Air in fat foam

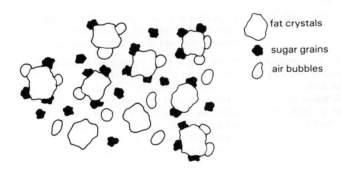

- fat crystals
- sugar grains
- air bubbles

(b) Optimum creaming test

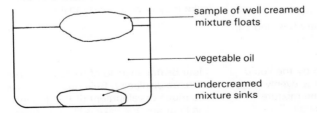

sample of well creamed mixture floats

vegetable oil

undercreamed mixture sinks

Fig. 16.14 Cake making: the creaming method

(c) Addition of egg to creamed mixture

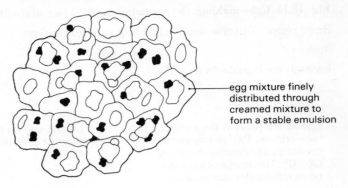

egg mixture finely distributed through creamed mixture to form a stable emulsion

(d) Addition of flour

flour and egg are finely distributed throughout the mixture

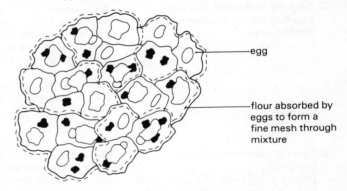

egg

flour absorbed by eggs to form a fine mesh through mixture

(e) Baking the creamed mixture

carbon dioxide   steam   air

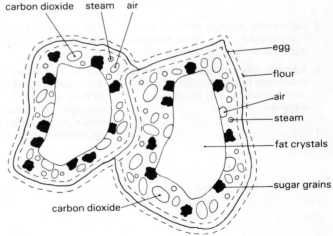

egg
flour
air
steam
fat crystals
sugar grains

carbon dioxide

Fat melts and is absorbed by the flour, the starch in the flour gelatinises
Carbon dioxide is given off from the baking powder in the flour
Air, carbon dioxide and steam from the liquid in the egg expand and rise through the mixture
Egg and flour proteins stretch and coagulate in risen position

Fig. 16.15 Cake-making: the creaming method (see plate 27(e))

Basic recipe: Victoria sandwich: 125 g self-raising flour, 125 g castor sugar, 125 g margarine, 2 eggs

Action	*Reaction*	*Possible faults*
1 Weigh the ingredients carefully.		Inaccurate proportion of ingredients produce faults in the appearance, texture and taste of the finished product.
Ensure the fat is at the correct temperature. Packet margarine should be at room temperature (20 °C). Tub margarine should be at refrigerator temperature.	The creaming can be done efficiently in the shortest possible time.	If the fat is too cold, it is hard and difficult to cream. Insufficient air is beaten in and the cake will have a poor volume. If the fat is too soft or has oiled, the structure of the fat will not allow it to entangle air. The effect is similar to undercreaming.
2 Beat the margarine and sugar together with a wooden spoon or electric mixer.	Air is beaten into the mixture of fat and sugar to form *an air-in-fat foam*. The small, needle-shaped crystals present in the fat (see p. 19) are separated by the abrasive action of the gritty sugar. Individual fat crystals surround the tiny air bubbles and trap the air in the mixture.	If the creaming is not done adequately, i.e. the mixture is undercreamed, the cake does not contain enough air. The result will be a cake with a poor volume and close texture. It is almost impossible to overcream a mixture by hand but this can happen when an electric mixer is used. The effect is the same as when using too much raising agent. The cake will rise too much then collapse when baked.
3 Test for optimum creaming (optional). Float a small piece of the creamed mixture (about the size of a pea) on a bowl of vegetable oil.	The specific gravity of a correctly creamed mixture allows the sample to float on the oil because the mixture has become less dense. The sample should float for at least 30 seconds. An undercreamed sample is heavier and will sink to the bottom of the oil.	
4 Lightly mix the egg with a fork in a separate bowl. Make sure the eggs are at room temperature.	The eggs can be added gradually to the creamed mixture.	Eggs that are too cold solidify the fat and made it difficult to form an emulsion when the egg is beaten in.
5 Add the egg a little at a time. Beat vigorously between each addition, until a smooth, stiff mixture is obtained.	The liquid present in the egg disolves the sugar crystals, allowing the egg to flow in fine channels evenly through the mixture. A water-in-oil emulsion is formed (see p. 000). The air remains trapped in the fat.	If the egg is cold, added all at once or only stirred into the mixture, the emulsion will not form, and the mixture is said to have 'curdled'. (It will look rather like scrambled egg.) An oil-in-water emulsion will form instead of a water-in-oil emulsion and some of the air will escape because beaten egg cannot hold air when fat is present. The cake produced will have a poor volume and a coarse crumbly texture. The crust may flake and the cake may have a greasy taste.
6 Sieve the self-raising flour. (If plain flour is used add raising agent before sieving.)	The flour becomes very fine and can be folded in easily.	
7 Fold the flour into the mixture using a metal spoon.	The flour is absorbed by the liquid in the egg mixture. It is evenly distributed through the mixture without displacing the air. The mixture should have a smooth texture with a soft dropping consistency.	Flour beaten instead of folded in causes air to be displaced. Beating also causes too much development of the gluten in the flour and the cake is likely to peak when it is baked instead of having a flat top. The cake will have a poor volume and a heavy, uneven texture with characteristic large air holes.

Plate 25 Effects of gluten in different types of flour

(a) the dough, the starch is removed, leaving the gluten ball, the gluten is cooked

(b) cross-section of the gluten ball

(c) gluten balls from strong flour, all-purpose flour and cake flour

(d) loaves made with strong flour, all-purpose flour and cake flour

Plate 26 (a) Sauces   (i) pouring   (ii) coating

(b) Types of batter   (i) Yorkshire pudding   (ii) pancake   (iii) fritter or coating batter

Plate 27 Cake making

(a) whisked

(b) rubbed in

(c) all-in-one, white flour

(d) all-in-one, wholemeal flour

(e) creamed

(f) melting method

Plate 28 Breadmaking

(a) stages in raising the dough

(i) initial

(ii) dough begins to rise

(iii) dough risen to twice original volume

(iv) over-risen dough

(b) types of loaf produced using different flours

(i) wholemeal   (ii) granary   (iii) wheatmeal   (iv) strong, plain white

Action	Reaction	Possible faults
8 Bake at 180°C (Reg. 4) for 25–35 mins. NB Rich fruit cakes made by the creaming method are baked at lower temperatures for a much longer time to allow the full flavour of the cake to develop.	The fat melts and is absorbed by the starch in the flour. Air is released into the egg, sugar, flour mixture. The raising agent dissolves in the water from the egg, releasing carbon dioxide. The liquid is converted into steam. Air, steam and carbon dioxide expand. All three gases rise through the mixture. The starch gelatinises and the proteins in the egg and gluten coagulate to form the framework of of the cake.	Inaccurate baking temperature: Oven temperature is too low: some carbon dioxide and air will rise through the cake and escape from the surface before the cake sets. Oven temperature is too high: the proteins coagulate and the cake is set before the carbon dioxide has fully expanded to give a good volume to the cake. A crust forms, which may later crack.

Fig. 16.16 Cake-making: the all-in-one method (see plate 27(c) and (d))

This method is reliable since it avoids the problems asociated with the creaming method.

Basic recipe: Victoria sandwich: 125 g self-raising flour, 1 × 5 ml spoon baking powder, 125 g castor sugar, 125 g margarine, 2 eggs

Action	Reaction	Possible faults
1 Weigh the ingredients carefully. Sieve the flour and baking powder. The temperature of the fat is important: use ● packet margarine at room temperature, ● tub margarine at refrigerator temperature.		Inaccurate proportions cause faults in the appearance, texture and taste. Incorrect temperature of fat causes problems in the mixing process. If the fat is too cold, lumps will remain. If the fat is too warm, the mixture will become oily.
2 Beat all the ingredients together for approximately 2–3 minutes by hand, or 1–2 minutes by electric mixer. 20–30 seconds by food process.	Some air is beaten into the mixture. The sugar breaks down the fat crystals as in the creaming method, and these trap the air in the mixture. Because of the short mixing time, only a little air is included in this way, so additional baking powder is usually included in the recipe.	Undermixing: the ingredients are inadequately mixed, giving an uneven texture. Overmixing: may occur with an electric mixer. If the flour mixture is beaten for too long there is too much gluten development. The texture is spoilt, the cake may peak, and the crust will flake.
3 Bake according to recipe 160°C (Reg. 3) for approximately 30 minutes.	The reactions are similar to the creaming method. More carbon dioxide and a smaller quantity of air raise the cake.	Oven too hot: does not allow enough time for action of raising agent. Overcooked crust, undercooked crumb. Oven too cool: raising gases escape, before crumb is set giving a poor volume, dense-textured cake.

D The melting method is used for gingerbread and some biscuit mixes. (see Fig. 16.18)

These mixtures all have high sugar and liquid content. Bicarbonate of soda can be used as the raising agent in these cakes because the spices and flavourings mask the flavour of any residual sodium carbonate in the mixture (see p. 250).

Fig. 16.17 Cake-making: Melting method (see plate 27(f))

Basic recipe: gingerbread: 225 g plain flour, 1 × 5 ml spoon bicarbonate of soda, 125 g margarine, 4 × 5 ml spoon ground ginger, 125 g soft brown sugar, 200 g golden syrup, 150 ml milk, 1 egg

Action	Reaction	Possible faults
1 Weigh the ingredients carefully.		Inaccurate measurement causes faults in the appearance, texture and taste.
2 Melt the fat slowly with the sugar and syrup.	The fat, sugar and syrup become liquid and are mixed thoroughly.	Overheating of this mixture with high sugar content causes the sugar to burn.
3 Cool the mixture slightly.		If the melted mixture is too hot when it is mixed with dry ingredients, the carbon dioxide in the raising agent is released immediately and a heavy, close-textured cake results. In addition, proteins in the flour are coagulated and starch grains gelatinise, causing a lumpy mixture.
4 Sieve the remaining dry ingredients together.	The ingredients are evenly mixed.	
5 Stir the melted mixture into the dry ingredients.	The ingredients are evenly blended together. The raising agent starts to release carbon dioxide.	Carbon dioxide is released slowly from bicarbonate of soda.
6 Add enough liquid to make a stiff batter.		
7 Bake according to recipe. A low temperature is usually recommended.	The raising agents are given off slowly and raise the cake. The starch gelatinises, the proteins coagulate. The rich brown colour and moist texture are developed.	High temperature would burn the sugar. It also causes too rapid rising, and a cracked surface, which later sinks in the middle.

Fig. 16.18 Cake making: the melting method

(a) The ingredients are melted together

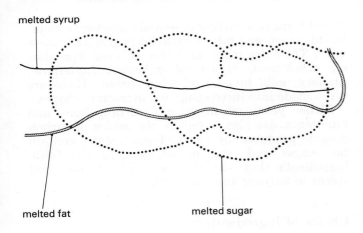

melted syrup

melted fat   melted sugar

(b)   Addition of egg, flour and raising agent and seasonings

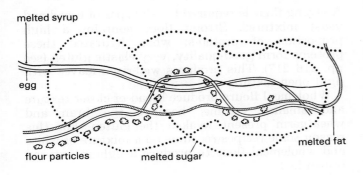

melted syrup

egg

flour particles   melted sugar   melted fat

(c) Baking the melted mixture

carbon dioxide is given off from raising agent

steam is given off from the liquid

flour particles   egg mixture

Fat and sugar syrup are absorbed by the flour
Carbon dioxide and steam expand
Egg and flour proteins stretch and coagulate

Convenience forms of cake

People who do not make cakes from basic ingredients may make them using cake mixes.

Compare a cake mix and a similar home made cake.

What ingredients does the cake mix contain?

Is it necessary to add other ingredients?

What will be the total cost?

Make up the cake mix according to the instructions. Made a similar homemade cake. Compare the two cakes for size, shape, colour, texture, taste and cost. Which cake do you prefer?

List circumstances when it may be useful to prepare a packet-mix cake.

It is also possible to buy many kinds of ready made cakes.

Make a list of all the types of cake available and if possible compare them all with home-made cakes.

What are the important factors to consider in comparing the cakes?

Is there any difference in the nutritional value of the cakes?

General faults in cakemaking

Sometimes the results achieved in cake-making are disappointing. Plate 30(a) shows some of the common faults in cake-making. Figure 16.19 lists the main faults that occur and suggests possible reasons for them. It is hoped that you can avoid these pitfalls and be delighted with the results of the cakes you make.

Fig. 16.19 A summary of general faults in cakes

Fault	Causes
Uneven rising	Mixture spread unevenly in tin.
	Tin placed too near the source of heat in the oven.
	Oven shelves not level.
Peaked, cracked top	Too hot an oven.
	Cake placed too high in the oven.
Sunken top	Too much raising agent.
	Opening oven door during baking.
	Undercooking the cake.
	Moving the cake too soon.
Collar edge on baked cake	Cake has risen too rapidly and sunk.
	Mixture has been spread too carefully on to sides of tin.
Sugary, speckled crust	Too much sugar used.
	Use of granulated instead of castor sugar.
	Too little liquid present and sugar not all dissolved.
	Too cool an oven.
Close, heavy texture	Too cool an oven.
	Insufficient cooking.
	Insufficient creaming or whisking.
	Not enough raising agent.
	Overmixing when flour is added.
	Too much liquid.
Coarse, open texture	Use of granulated instead of castor sugar.
	Too much raising agent.
	Uneven mixing of flour.
Cake very dry	Insufficient eggs or liquid.
	Baked at too low a temperature.

Bread

The role and interaction of ingredients

Bread is made from four essential ingredients: flour, liquid, yeast, and salt. A little fat is also sometimes used. There are many varieties of bread available, e.g. wholemeal, wheatmeal or brown, 'high-fibre', granary, milk bread, and white bread. These are often made into interesting and attractive shapes.

Richer yeast mixtures, e.g. currant buns and croissants, are also raised by the action of carbon dioxide produced by yeast. These recipes contain fat, sugar and egg, in addition to the basic ingredients; they may also contain fruit, nuts, and spices in varying amounts.

Choice of ingredients

Flour (see p. 205)

A strong flour is required for all types of bread and yeast mixtures. Strong flour contains a high proportion of proteins; when hydrated these proteins form good-quality, very elastic gluten (see pp. 216–217). This produces well-risen loaves with light open texture.

Wholemeal flours produce bread of closer texture and smaller volume, because the bran and wheatgerm present weaken the gluten. For this reason some recipes recommend a mixture of white and wholemeal flour to produce a lighter-textured brown loaf.

> Look at plate 28(b), which shows breads made with wholemeal, granary, wheatmeal and strong white flour.

Liquid

The liquid used in basic bread is usually water, but milk or a mixture of milk and water may be used instead. This improves the nutritional value, and also gives a softer, browner crust. The amount and temperature of the liquid used are important factors.

It is important to use the *correct amount of liquid* but it is difficult to state the exact amount required in each case, because this will vary with the type of flour used. Strong flour absorbs more water than soft flour, and wholemeal flour absorbs more water than white flour, thus approximately:

400 g strong plain white flour absorbs 250 ml water,
400 g strong plain wholemeal absorbs 275 ml water.

Too much liquid weakens the gluten, and too little liquid produces a stiff dough which does not stretch, and inhibits rising. The volume of bread produced will be smaller in both cases than when the correct amount of water is used.

The *temperature of the liquid* should be about 25°-27°C, so that it feels warm to touch (i.e. tepid). This is important for the action of yeast. If the temperature of the liquid is too high the yeast will be killed.

Yeast (see pp. 248-250)

The yeast acts as the raising agent by means of a fermentation process to produce carbon dioxide. There are three types of yeast available for bread-making: fresh yeast, dried yeast, and easyblend yeast.

Fresh yeast is the quickest and easiest type of yeast to use. It should be blended with slightly warm liquid before being added to the dough. Some recipes suggest creaming the yeast with sugar. This is not advisable as some yeast cells are ruptured and killed by the high sugar concentration. An unpleasant flavour may be left in the bread after baking, if sugar has been added. The enzymes in yeast are able to provide enough sugar from the flour for the continuing action of the yeast.

Dried yeast is more concentrated than fresh yeast and a smaller amount is therefore required. A general guide to the amount to use is half the weight of fresh yeast stated in the recipe. Recipes for dried yeast recommend mixing it with the liquid at a temperature of 43°C to which 1 × 5 ml spoon of sugar has been added. The mixture is allowed to stand for 10 mins, by which time it should be frothy. This shows that the yeast is activated. If the mixture does not froth it should not be used.

Easyblend yeasts are very simple to use, as they can be added to flour mixtures without any previous soaking. Because of their porous nature these yeasts are extremely light and only about one quarter of the weight of fresh yeast in a recipe is required. Sealed packages ready to use are available and the instructions on the packet should be followed carefully.

Because yeast is a living organism capable of continually multiplying, only small quantities are needed in recipes: only 25g of fresh yeast is used for 1 kilogram white flour in bread-making.

The amount of yeast required for various recipes will be affected by:
(a) the other ingredients present. A richer mixture requires a higher proportion of yeast.
(b) the temperature at which the dough is risen. The yeast is less active at low temperatures.

(c) the time available for rising and proving the dough. If given sufficient time to multiply, a small amount of yeast can be used.

Because the production of carbon dioxide by yeast is controlled by enzyme action (see p. 249), it is important to provide favourable conditions: moisture, food, warmth, and adequate time are essential

The *moisture* is supplied by the liquid in the recipe.

The *food* is provided initially by the small amount of sugar present in the flour. In richer mixtures added sugar may also be used as food. The main food supply is the starch in flour which is converted to sugar by enzyme action.

Warmth is provided by using warm liquid. If possible breadmaking should be done in a warm kitchen. The dough is usually placed in a warm place to rise.

Time is provided for the action of the yeast to take place during the rising and proving periods.

> Look at plate 28(a) which shows the stages in rising bread dough.

Salt

Salt gives flavour to the dough, slows down the action of the yeast and strengthens the gluten. Too much salt kills some of the yeast cells and prevents the dough rising properly. A dough made without salt tends to become sticky.

Fat

Fat enriches the dough and improves the softness and colour of the crumb. It also delays staling of the bread. A very small proportion of fat (25 g of lard or margarine to 1½ kg of flour) is all that is needed to produce these effects. The fat also retards the action of the yeast and weakens the gluten.

Sugar

Sugar is not an essential added ingredient in bread-making. The enzymes in the yeast convert starch in the flour into sugar which then acts as food for the yeast (see p. 249). Sugar may be added in richer mixtures, but it retards the action of the yeast and weakens the gluten. Extra yeast and more mixing may be recommended for these recipes.

Figure 16.20 shows what is happening and the possible faults that may occur at each stage in the process.

Fig. 16.20 Breadmaking (see plate 28(a))

Basic recipe: 500 g plain flour, 2 × 5 ml spoons salt, 25 g fresh yeast, 300 ml water

Action	Reaction	Possible faults
Preparation		
1 Weigh the ingredients carefully.		Inaccurate proportion of ingredients causes faults in the appearance, texture and taste of the product.
2 Rub the fat into the flour.	The fat is evenly mixed into the flour.	
3 Mix the yeast to a paste with a little of the *tepid water* (37 °C). If using dried or easyblend yeast, follow manufacturer's instructions carefully.	The yeast becomes liquid.	Inaccurate temperature affects the yeast. If the water is too hot, some or all of the yeast cells, are killed. This prevents production of carbon dioxide to raise the dough. The bread would be heavy and dense in texture. If the water is too cold, the action of yeast to produce carbon dioxide is slowed down.
Mixing		
4 Mix yeast and remaining tepid liquid into the flour to form a dough.	The flour absorbs the water and gluten is formed. The yeast is distributed throughout the dough.	Uneven distribution of yeast and liquid would cause a lumpy dough that would not rise evenly. Too little liquid causes a stiff dough that will not stretch and gives a loaf with a good volume and texture. Too much liquid causes a sticky, unmanageable dough.
Kneading		
5 Knead the dough until it is smooth and elastic (approx. 10 minutes by hand, 2–3 minutes using a dough hook on the electric mixer).	Kneading: ● traps air into the dough ● develops the gluten in the dough so that it becomes strong and very elastic. This will give the loaf a good volume. ● breaks up chains of yeast cells so that an even texture is obtained in the bread.	If the dough is insufficiently kneaded: ● not enough air is mixed in, which hinders the action of the enzymes in producing carbon dioxide. ● the gluten does not become very elastic. Hence it will not stretch and allow the dough to produce a loaf with a good volume and texture.
6 Place the dough in either an oiled polythene bag or a covered bowl.		If the dough is not covered, the moisture on the surface evaporates and a skin is formed. This prevents the dough rising properly and it forms hard pieces in the dough.
Rising		
7 Leave to rise in a warm place until the dough is doubled in volume. The rising time is dependent on temperature: ● in a refrigerator, up to 12 hours ● in a cool place, up to 4 hours ● at room temperature, 1½–2 hours ● in a warm place, up to 1 hour.	The yeast begins to ferment in the dough and produce carbon dioxide gas. (a) The enzyme diastase in the flour converts starch in the flour into a form of sugar, maltose. (b) Yeast produces an enzyme, maltase, which turns the maltose into a simpler sugar, glucose. (c) Yeast produces another group of enzymes, the zymase complex, which turn glucose into carbon dioxide and a little alcohol. These gases cause the dough to rise. (See pp. 249–250 for a more detailed explanation.)	If the dough is insufficiently risen, the bread will be heavy, and have a dense texture. If the dough is over-risen, the bread will have a very open, coarse texture. The crust may break away from the loaf. If a dough is over-risen, the gluten may collapse and a sour flavour develops. If the temperature of the place chosen to raise the dough is too high, the bread will crumble and go stale easily. A high temperature would kill the yeast and prevent rising.

Note:
A long slow rise gives a better texture and flavour as the yeast works slowly. However, the dough should be allowed to return to room temperature before proceeding with the next stage.

Action	Reaction	Possible faults
Knocking-back 8 The risen dough is kneaded again lightly.	Large bubbles of carbon dioxide produced in the first rising are broken up and distributed as small bubbles throughout the dough giving a fine, even texture. Re-kneading exposes the dough surfaces to fresh supplies of oxygen. This re-activates the yeast for the second rising or 'proving' and improves the volume and texture.	If the dough is not kneaded again at this stage, the finished bread may have a coarse, uneven texture with some large holes.
9 Shape the dough into the type of goods required and place in greased tins.		
Proving 10 Cover the tins and allow the dough to double in volume again in a warm place. This process usually takes about 30–45 minutes for loaves, 20 minutes for rolls. The temperature must not exceed 25°C.	The yeast ferments the dough evenly and a fine texture is produced.	If the dough is not covered, the surface of the dough dries out, forming a skin. This prevents the dough from expanding evenly. If the dough is under-proved the texture of the bread will be heavy. If the dough is over-proved, the texture will be coarse, and the crust may break away from the loaf.
Baking 11 Bake the bread in a very hot oven according to the recipe (230°C, Reg. 7).	At first the dough rises rapidly as more carbon dioxide is produced by the yeast, and the gases inside the dough expand. At 54°C, the yeast is killed. Fermentation ceases, and further rising stops. As the temperature rises, the starch gelatinises and the gluten coagulates to form the framework of the loaf. Some water and most of the alcohol formed in the fermentation process, are driven off through the crust. The action of heat and steam on the starch of the surface form dextrin, which is a sugar. In baking this caramelises and gives an attractive brown colour to the crust.	If the oven temperature is too low: ● the yeast cells will not produce extra carbon dioxide to continue raising the dough in the first stages of baking. A poor-volumed, coarse-textured loaf is produced. The yeast cells are only slowly inactivated; some may still be alive at the end of baking. This produces a sour-tasting loaf. All the moisture is evaporated from the dough during a longer cooking period. This gives a very dry, crumbly loaf. If the oven temperature is too high: ● the yeast cells are suddenly killed, preventing further rising of the dough in the first stage of baking. A poor-volumed, dense-textured loaf is produced. The intense heat evaporates moisture from the surface of the dough rapidly. This forms a skin, which prevents the dough rising evenly. There is too much evaporation of moisture from the surface, which forms a thick, tough crust. The intense heat over-browns the crust before baking is complete.

Short-time doughs

The traditional method of making bread takes quite a long time. However, a process has been developed to reduce the long fermentation period when bread is made commercially. The process is now widely used and is known as the *Chorleywood process*. Chemical improvers, and a few minutes of intensive mechanical mixing, change the elastic properties of the dough. The reactions which develop the gluten into an elastic network are speeded up, and the gases produced by the yeast are retained more easily. The long rising period can be replaced by a short resting period of 5–10 mins.

A short-time method of breadmaking has been developed from the commercial process for reducing the time taken to make bread at home. A small amount of ascorbic acid (vitamin C) is used as a flour improver to reduce and almost cut out the first rising period. The ascorbic acid produces the same effects as the improvers and mechanical kneading used in the commercial process. Ascorbic acid can be obtained as 25 mg tablets from a chemist; one tablet is dissolved in the liquid to add to 600g flour. Only fresh yeast is suitable for this method. The quantity of yeast used should be increased (25g yeast is required for 600 g flour). The quantity of liquid used is slightly reduced.

The basic recipe and method for making a short-time dough is given on p. 243.

> Look at plate 30(b) to see the effects of some common faults in the breadmaking process.

Fig. 16.21 Summary of common faults in breadmaking

Fault	Causes
Heavy close texture poor volume	Flour too soft.
	Innaccurate proportions, method or baking.
	Insufficient kneading or proving.
	Yeast killed by rising in too hot a place.
Coarse, open texture	Too much yeast.
	Too much liquid.
	Over-proving.
	Oven too cool.
Uneven texture with large holes	Dough not knocked-back properly.
	Dough left uncovered during rising.
Sour, yeasty flavour	Over-proving.
	Too much yeast.
	Stale yeast or fresh yeast creamed with sugar.
Bread stales quickly and is crumbly.	Too much yeast.
	Flour too soft.
	Rising too quickly at a high temperature.
	No fat in recipe.
Dough collapses in oven.	Over-proving.
'Flying top' – when top crust breaks away from loaf.	Under-proving.
	Dough surface dried out during proving.
	Oven too hot.
Crust splits at one side of the loaf.	Loaf baked too near one side of the oven.
	Tin too small.
Crust cracks after removing from the oven.	Over-proving.
	Oven too hot.
	Cooling in a draught after baking.

Plate 29   Pastry

(a) shortcrust

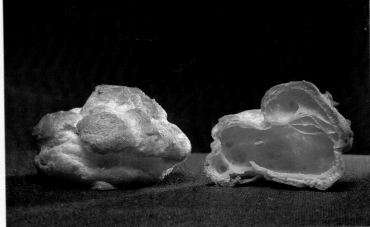

(b) choux

(c) flaky

(d) puff

(e) suet

(f) hot water crust

Plate 30   General faults in baking

(a) in cakes   (i) flour beaten in   (ii) insufficient cooking   (iii) temperature too high

(b) in bread   (i) yeast killed   (ii) insufficient kneading   (iii) 'rising' temperature too high   (iv) oven temperature too high

(c) in pastry   (i) too much water   (ii) insufficient kneading   (iii) rerolling

Pastry

The role and interaction of ingredients

The main ingredients in pastry recipes are flour, fat, water, and a little salt. Rich pastries may contain sugar, eggs, cheese, or other flavouring. There are several types of pastry, each with its characteristic appearance, texture, and flavour (see plate 29).

Shortcrust pastry the most popular pastry for pies, flans, tarts, etc. It should be short, crisp, and light; never hard or tough!

Flaky and rough puff pastry contain a higher proportion of fat. The dough rises in layers or flakes. The two types are very similar, although the fat is added in different ways to the mixtures.

Puff pastry contains an even higher proportion of fat: equal to the weight of flour. It is the richest pastry of all.

Choux pastry is a traditional French pastry. When baked, it should be a light, crisp, hollow puff.

Hot water crust pastry and suet pastry are other varieties used for meat pies and puddings.

The proportions and choice of ingredients, the method of making and baking conditions are different for all the pastries. The step-by-step guide for each method shows what is happening and the possible faults that may occur at each stage.

> Look at the differences in texture of the pastries shown in plate 29.

Shortcrust pastry

Shortcrust pastry is used for making pie crusts, flans and tarts. It can be made either by the rubbing-in method or the fork-mix method.

(a) Rubbing-in method (see Fig. 16.23)

Proportion of ingredients:
- the fat is usually half the weight of the flour.
- 1 × 5 ml spoon water to each 25 g flour.

Choice of ingredients:
- a soft plain flour is used to avoid excess gluten development.
- the recommended fat is a mixture of equal quantities of lard or white fat and margarine or

butter. Lard and white fats shorten the mixture well, because they do not contain any water. However, they do not give a good colour and flavour to the pastry. Margarine or butter are used to give colour and flavour.

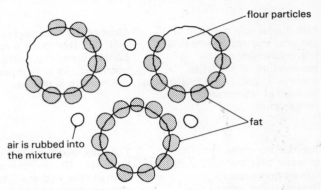

(a) Fat is rubbed into thin films surrounding some of the flour particles

flour particles

air is rubbed into the mixture

fat

(b) Addition of water

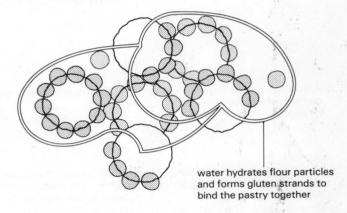

water hydrates flour particles and forms gluten strands to bind the pastry together

(c) Baking

flour particles absorb fat, starch gelatinises

air expands and is given off

gluten strands coagulate

steam is given off from liquid

The fat melts and is absorbed by the flour
Starch swells and gelatinises forming crumbly, short texture
Gluten strands coagulate

Fig. 16.22 Shortcrust pastry: the rubbing-in method

Fig. 16.23 Shortcrust pastry: rubbing-in method (see plate 29(a))

Basic recipe: 200 g plain flour, 1 × 5 ml spoon salt, 50 g margarine, 50 g white fat, 2 × 15 ml spoon water

Action	Reaction	Possible faults
1 Weight the ingredients carefully.		Inaccurate proportion of ingredients can cause faults in the appearance, texture and taste of the pastry.
2 Rub the fat into the flour and salt until the mixure resembles fine breadcrumbs. The temperature of the fat is important. Soft blend fats should be used at refrigerator temperature.	Most of the flour particles are coated with fat. This forms a waterproof barrier. Some flour particles remain uncoated. Air is incorporated during the rubbing-in process.	Fat that is too hard is difficult to rub in. Lumps of fat may remain and too much flour is left uncoated. Too much water will be needed to mix. Fat that is too soft only forms a thin layer round the flour particles. This is not adequate to protect the flour from the water. If the mixture is over-handled, the fat becomes soft and sticky and the pastry will be difficult to handle.
3 Sprinkle the measured amount of water over the surface of the rubbed-in mixture. Bind together using a pliable knife.	The uncoated flour particles absorb the water. Gluten strands are formed. The hydrated flour becomes sticky and elastic and binds the dough together.	If too little water is added, the pastry will not become smooth on kneading. It will crack on rolling. When cooked it will be dry and crumbly. If too much water is added there is too much gluten development and the cooked pastry will be hard and tough. If the water is added unevenly the pastry will be streaky when it is rolled out. The cooked pastry is likely to blister when steam is produced unevenly.
4 Knead the dough together very gently on a lightly floured surface.	The pastry is bound together evenly.	If the dough is heavily kneaded there is too much gluten development and the pastry will be tough. If too much flour is used on the surface, the dough becomes too dry. If the pastry is not kneaded it will crack on rolling.
5 Roll the pastry to the required shape and thickness. Use short light strokes, rolling in one direction only. The pastry should be turned to keep an even shape. Do not handle the pastry more than necessary. Do not re-roll pastry many times. Allow to rest, covered, in a cool place before using, if possible. Resting the pastry relaxes the gluten strands. It is then less likely to shrink on baking.	Rolling causes the gluten strands to stretch. The elastic gluten allows the pastry to be rolled thinly without breaking. If the pastry is turned during the rolling process, short strands of gluten are formed.	Overstretching the dough causes long strands of gluten to form. The pastry will shrink after baking and will be hard and tough. Heavy handling toughens the pastry. The pastry shrinks if it is not allowed to rest before baking. Re-rolling toughens the gluten strands. Re-rolled pastry loses air, and shrinks on baking.
6 Bake the pastry in preheated oven at 200°C–220°C for approximately 20 mins. (If a pie filling has to be cooked for a longer period, the temperature should be lowered to 160°C for the remainder of the cooking time.) It is important that the pastry is just cooked in the hot oven before the temperature is lowered.	On heating, the fat melts. Nearly all the fat is absorbed by the starch granules. The starch granules gelatinise. The air and steam expand and separate the pastry into crumbly layers. These layers become crisp as the gluten coagulates.	If the oven is not hot enough, the melted fat runs out of the pastry. The pastry will be pale in colour and soft and oily to taste. If the oven is too hot the pastry becomes too dark in colour and may have a bitter taste. It will not separate into the light crisp layers.

Fig. 16.24 Shortcrust pastry: fork-mix method

Basic recipe: 200 g plain flour, 125g margarine, 2 × 15 ml spoon water, 1 × 5 ml spoon salt

Action	Reaction	Possible faults
1 Weigh all ingredients carefully.		Inaccurate proportion of ingredients can cause faults in the appearance, texture and taste of the pastry.
2 Place one-third of the flour, all the fat and all the water into the mixing bowl. Blend together well, using a fork. Packet margarine should be at room temperature. Tub margarine should be at refrigerator temperature.	The water is absorbed by the small quantity of flour. The hydrated flour particles are coated by the fat present.	Margarine that is too hard is difficult to blend with other ingredients.
3 Mix the remaining two-thirds of the flour in with the fork.	There is now no water available to come into contact with the flour. It is coated with the fat in the same way that the flour is coated in correctly-made rubbed-in mixture.	
4 Bring the pastry together into a ball with the hands. Knead for 1-2 minutes.	The pastry becomes smooth and silky. This pastry can safely be handled more than the traditional pastry because only the gluten in the hydrated flour can be developed. The pastry will remain short.	If the kneading is not done, the pastry may break up when it is rolled out and be crumbly after baking. If the pastry is not kneaded sufficiently it will crack on rolling.
5 Allow the pastry to relax in a cool place for about 20 minutes if time allows.	The resting makes the gluten relax and the pastry will be easier to handle. The pastry becomes firmer as the fat cools after mixing.	If the pastry is not allowed to rest it will shrink on baking.
6 Roll and bake exactly as for the rubbing-in method.	See comments for rubbing-in-method (p. 234).	

The fork-mix method (see Fig. 16.24)

This method avoids most of the steps which may cause problems in the rubbing-in method. It is a quick, easy and reliable alternative method.

Proportion of ingredients:
● the weight of fat fat is slightly over half the weight of flour
● the proportion of fat to flour is slightly increased in this method, so that the margarine will shorten the mixture without the addition of a white fat
● 1 × 5 ml spoon water to each 25 g flour.

Choice of ingredients:
● a soft flour
● the recommended fat is margarine. Margarines have softer textures than white fats; this enables them to blend easily with other ingredients.

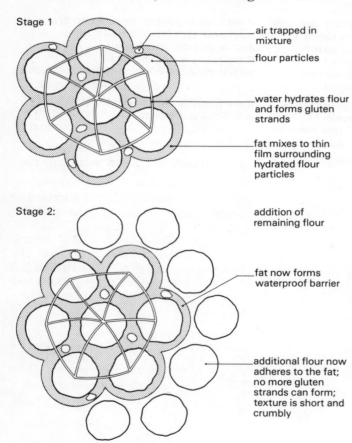

Stage 1

air trapped in mixture

flour particles

water hydrates flour and forms gluten strands

fat mixes to thin film surrounding hydrated flour particles

Stage 2:

addition of remaining flour

fat now forms waterproof barrier

additional flour now adheres to the fat; no more gluten strands can form; texture is short and crumbly

Fig. 16.25 Shortcrust pastry: the fork mix method

Flaky and rough puff pastry (see Fig. 16.28)

Both these pastries are used for making pie crusts, sausage rolls, and cream slices.

These two pastries are very similar. Only the method of adding the fat varies. Both have the characteristic texture of crisp, light layers of pastry. (These are formed by folding layers of dough over layers of fat, and rolling the pastry several times.)

Proportion of ingredients:
● the weight of fat is three-quarters the weight of the flour
● 1 × 15 ml spoon water to each 25 g flour.

A higher proportion of water is used than in shortcrust pastry; this develops gluten that allows the crisp layers to form, and produces steam which acts as a raising agent.

Choice of ingredients:
flour: a strong plain flour is used. The dough must be elastic; more gluten development is necessary than in shortcrust pastry. This gives the elasticity for the pastry to stretch.
fat: a mixture of white fat and margarine may be used. In flaky pastry, margarine with no white fat is sometimes recommended. The fat should be firm but not too hard. It is recommended that the fat should be the same consistency as the dough.
liquid: the water should be chilled; this helps to keep the fat firm, and prevents the dough becoming sticky. *Lemon juice* is added to the liquid. The acidity strengthens the gluten.

Puff pastry (see plate 29(d))

Puff pastry is used for vol-au-vents, cream slices, and where a good rise and flavour are especially important.

Proportion of ingredients:
● the weight of fat is equal to the weight of flour
● 1 × 15 ml spoon water to each 25 g flour.

A hard margarine or butter is used and is added to the dough in one piece. It is folded and rolled nine times in the same way as the flaky and rough puff; this produces a pastry with tender flakes and good flavour.

Since frozen puff pastry became widely available, puff pastry is not freqently made in the home.

Frozen puff pastry

Compare the cost of frozen puff pastry with the cost of making the same amount of puff pastry at home.

Why do you think this convenience product has been so successful?

Discuss its use.

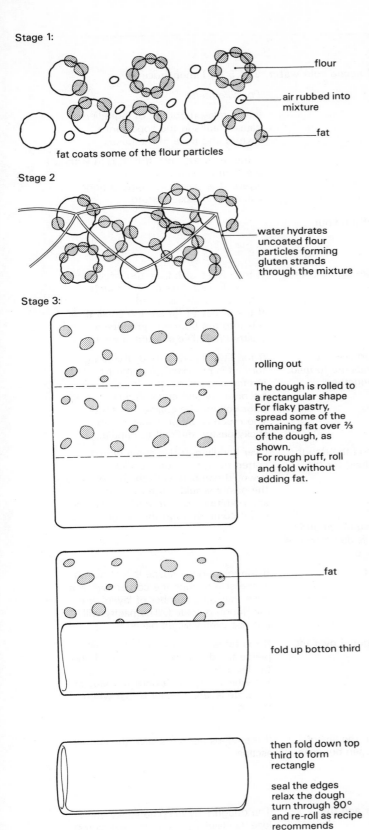

Stage 1:

flour

air rubbed into mixture

fat

fat coats some of the flour particles

Stage 2

water hydrates uncoated flour particles forming gluten strands through the mixture

Stage 3:

rolling out

The dough is rolled to a rectangular shape
For flaky pastry, spread some of the remaining fat over ⅔ of the dough, as shown.
For rough puff, roll and fold without adding fat.

fat

fold up botton third

then fold down top third to form rectangle

seal the edges
relax the dough
turn through 90°
and re-roll as recipe recommends

Fig. 16.26 Flaky and rough puff pastry

Choux pastry (see plate 29(b))

Choux pastry is used for éclairs, profiteroles and savoury choux puffs. Eggs are an important ingredient in this pastry in addition to the flour, fat and water.

Proportion of ingredients:
● the weight of fat is three-quarters the weight of flour
● there is a high proportion of liquid (approximately 50 ml for each 25 g flour). Basic recipe: 65 g flour, 50 g margarine, 2 eggs, 125 ml water.

Method

1 The fat and water are heated in a saucepan, the fat melts and the liquid is brought to the boil. Immediately, the flour is beaten in, off the heat, to form a smooth paste. There is some gelatinisation of starch and a thick *panada* is formed (see p. 215).

2 The eggs are beaten into the mixture. This forms a smooth glossy mixture of piping consistency. Eggs enrich the mixture and provide protein to help form the framework of the pastry, as it does in a batter. Thorough beating is essential to incorporate air and develop gluten in the mixture.

3 This pastry is not rolled, but piped on to tins for éclairs and buns.

4 In the oven this pastry behaves like a batter as the rapid escape of steam forces up the elastic gluten and a crisp hollow shell is formed. Unlike a Yorkshire Pudding, the shells stay puffed after removal from the oven, because the proportion of liquid is lower. It is recommended that the shells are pierced with a knife to allow any remaining steam to escape and prevent the insides of the shells becoming soggy.

(a) Melted fat and hot water form thick panada

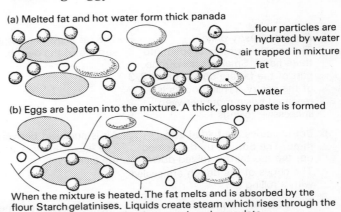

flour particles are hydrated by water
air trapped in mixture
fat
water

(b) Eggs are beaten into the mixture. A thick, glossy paste is formed

When the mixture is heated. The fat melts and is absorbed by the flour Starch gelatinises. Liquids create steam which rises through the mixture. Egg and flour proteins stretch and coagulate

Fig. 16.27 Choux pastry

Fig. 16.28 Flaky and rough puff pastry (see plate 29(c))

Basic recipe: 200 g plain flour, 15 g margarine, 6 × 15 ml spoon cold water, 2 × 5 ml lemon juice

Action	*Reaction*	*Possible faults*
1 Weigh the ingredients carefully.		Inaccurate proportion of ingredients causes faults in the appearance, texture and taste of the pastry.
2 Follow the method you prefer. Make sure the fat is cool and firm.		If the fat is too soft, it blends in with the flour instead of remaining in layers. The pastry will have a poor volume and close texture.
(a) *Flaky pastry* Rub one quarter of the fat into the flour. (The remaining fat is added after the dough is formed.)	The fat coats some of the flour particles.	
(b) *Rough puff pastry* Cut all the fat into small pieces about the size of a sugar lump. Add the flour.	All the pieces of fat are lightly coated with flour.	If the pieces of fat are too large they will be forced through the dough when the pastry is rolled. If the pieces of fat are too small they mix into the flour and produce a pastry rather like shortcrust pastry.
3 Add the liquid. Bind together into a soft dough.	The uncoated flour particles are hydrated. Gluten strands are formed. The dough is bound together.	If too little liquid is used, the dough formed is not elastic enough to stretch and roll several times. It will become dry and crack. It will have a poor volume, be coarse and tough. Too much liquid produces a soft, sticky pastry, difficult to handle.
For *rough puff pastry* mix with a palette knife and handle as little as possible in forming the dough.	All the fat is present and the dough forms a protective coating for the lumps of fat.	Over-handling at this stage would soften the fat, making it sticky. It would combine with the dough, and the pastry would not form layers. If a sharp knife is used to mix, the lumps of fat come through the dough.
For *flaky pastry* knead the dough lightly.	The water is evenly distributed and the gluten in the flour is developed. A smooth dough is formed.	
4 The dough is rolled to rectangular shape.	The gluten is stretched.	If the rectangular shape is lost during successive rollings the corners will not have the same number of layers when the dough is folded. The pastry will not rise evenly when baked.
5 *For flaky pastry only:* The remaining fat is divided into three parts. Small pieces of one part of the fat are dotted on to 2/3 of the pastry. (This process is repeated twice more between successive rollings.)	The fat is evenly distributed over the surface of the dough.	If the fat is too hard the lumps will pierce the dough when it is rolled and the layers will be spoiled. Fat which is too soft does not stay in separate layers, and air is lost when the dough is rolled.
6 Both pastries are folded into three. The bottom third is folded up, the top third is folded down. The edges of the dough are sealed with a rolling pin.	Air is enclosed between the layers. The enclosed air is trapped between the layers.	If the edges are not sealed the air will escape.
7 The pastries are placed in a refrigerator or cool place to relax for at least 15 mins.	The fat becomes firmer and the pastry relaxes.	The dough may become sticky and lose its elasticity if not allowed to rest. It will tend to shrink when cooked.

Action	Reaction	Possible faults
8 The dough is turned through 90° and the rolling and folding repeated twice more before being rolled into the shape required.	More layers of air and dough are formed. The fat is thoroughly incorporated to give a smooth dough.	
9 The edges of the pastry should be trimmed with a sharp knife.		If sealed edges remain they cannot separate into layers in baking. The pastry will rise unevenly.
10 Both pastries are baked at 220°–230°C (Reg. 7) for approximately 20 mins.	The fat melts, and is absorbed by the starch granules. The high oven temperature produces steam from the liquid. The steam and air expand, forcing the layers apart. The starch gelatinises and the gluten coagulates, forming the framework of the risen pastry. The heat and steam on the surface of the pastry change starch to dextrin which caramelises and gives an attractive brown colour.	If the oven temperature is too low, the melted fat seeps out of the pastry, leaving a soggy and greasy underside to the pastry. If the oven temperature is too high, the top surface will burn, before the inside layers are cooked.

Fig. 16.29 Summary of common faults in choux pastry

Fault	Cause
Paste too thin to pipe	Ingredients measured incorrectly. Water not boiling when flour added. Insufficient beating.
Paste too thick	Ingredients measured incorrectly. Liquid boiled too long and allowed to evaporate.
Cooked pastry close and heavy	Self-raising flour used instead of plain flour. Insufficient beating. Oven too cool.
Eclairs badly cracked	Oven too hot.

Suggest ways of using choux pastry in the menu
● for savoury dishes
● for sweet dishes
Compare the food value of shortcrust and choux pastry.

Hot water crust pastry (see plate 29(f))

Like choux pastry, this pastry is also made by bringing the fat and water to the boil before it is added to the flour. The fat used is usually lard or white fat and the liquid is water or a mixture of milk and water. The proportion of flour in this mixture is higher as this is a stiffer paste which can be kneaded and rolled. No eggs are added. It must be used while it is warm as it becomes stiff and unmanageable as it cools. To shape, it is usually moulded by hand over a container. Pies made with this pastry are known as *raised pies* because they are 'raised' or shaped by hand. Some of the starch in the flour is gelatinised by the hot water and this pastry also receives a long cooking time in the oven because the filling is usually raw meat or game. Fat and liquid in the filling help to keep the pastry moist.

Suet pastry (see plate 29(e))

This is the only pastry recipe in which a chemical raising agent is used, either in the form of self-raising flour or baking powder added to plain flour. The suet (¼–½ the weight of flour) should be beef suet which can be grated or bought ready-prepared in shredded form. Enough water must be added to form a soft elastic dough as all the flour becomes hydrated.

This is the only pastry that can be steamed or boiled as the hard fat requires more heat and a longer time to melt it. During steaming, the condensed steam must not come into contact with the pastry or it will be heavy and wet.

If the pastry is baked, the gluten may coagulate before the starch absorbs the fat and the pastry is indigestible.

Fig. 16.30 Summary of common faults in pastry

Pale in colour	Oven temperature too low. Cooking time too short. Too near base of oven.
Dark in colour	Oven temperature too high. Cooking time too long. Too near top of oven.
Burnt edges	Too near sides of oven.
Bitter taste	Overcooked. Oven too hot.
Hard, tough pastry	Too much water added. Pastry handled heavily on mixing. Re-rolling.
Fat runs from pastry on baking.	Too much fat used. Oven temperature too low.
Oily, greasy pastry	Fat too soft. Oven temperature too low.

Look at plate 30(c) to see the effects of some common faults in pastry making.

Storage of baked products

Freshly-baked bread and cakes have moist textures with dry crusts; pastry is crisp. All the products become stale during storage due to loss of, and redistribution of moisture.

- Bread goes stale quickly because it contains very little fat and sugar.
- Cakes which contain fat, eggs and sugar remain fresh for longer.
- Pastry rapidly becomes limp, and is best eaten on the day it is cooked unless it is stored in the freezer.

Bread should be stored at a normal room temperature in a well-ventilated dry breadbin. Air is necessary to keep the crust crisp, and a dry atmosphere discourages mould-growth. If no breadbin is available store the bread in a loosely-closed plastic bag. Do not store bread in a refrigerator as it goes stale most rapidly at refrigerator temperatures.

Cakes should be stored in airtight tins or plastic boxes. The circulation of air is not so important, as they have softer crusts, and the main aim is to prevent than going stale.

The storage-time depends on the richness of the mixture. All plain cakes become stale more quickly than rich fruit cakes. Only cakes containing fresh or synthetic cream should be stored in a refrigerator.

Freezing of baked products

All baked mixtures freeze very well, and may be frozen raw, or cooked. Commercially-produced bread may also be frozen in a partially-baked state. Pastry may also be bought ready-frozen.

Freezer storage is convenient for these products because it is useful sometimes to prepare a large quantity of mixture and freeze some for future use.

Fig. 16.31 Storage chart: bread, cakes and pastry

product	room temperature storage	freezer storage
Bread		
● unrisen dough	not recommended	plain doughs 1 month enriched doughs 3 months
● party-baked dough	not recommended	up to 4 months
Baked bread		
● whole loaves	3 days in a breadbin	up to 6 months
● crisp crusty bread rolls	use same day	1–2 weeks, as crust shales off
● wrapped sliced bread	4 days in a breadbin	up to 6 months
● rich buns	1–2 days	up to 3 months
● teabreads	up to 1 week	up to 3 months
Scones	use same day	up to 6 months
Cakes		
● unbaked mixture	use same day	up to 2 months (not recommended for whisked mixtures)
● baked fresh cream	use same day	1–2 months
● undecorated	3–5 days	up to 6 months
● decorated	3–5 days	up to 3 months
● rich fruit and ginger cakes	1–2 months	up to 3 months (not usually necessary)
Pastry – all types		
● uncooked	cook same day or after 1 day in refrigerator	up to 3 months
● cooked	use same day	up to 6 months
Batter		
● uncooked	not recommended	not recommended
● Yorkshire pudding	use immediately after cooking	not recommended
● pancakes	use same day	plain: up to 6 months stuffed: up to 4 months

Investigation of suitable freezer storage for bread, cakes and pastry

Examine shortcrust pastry, rough puff pastry, choux pastry and suet pastry, and decide which you think would be the most useful way to freeze each of them. Give reasons.

Prepare an all-in-one cake mixture using 250 g flour, 250 g sugar, 250 g margarine, and 4 eggs. Use 15 cm sandwich tins.
1 Freeze 250 g mixture in a plastic box. To examine, defrost, place in tin and bake.
2 Freeze 250 g of mixture in the tin. Bake from frozen.
3 Freeze 250 g mixture in the tin. Defrost before baking.
4 Place 250 g mixture in tin. Bake. Remove from the tin. Freeze the baked cake. Defrost to examine.
Compare the four cakes.
Which do you think is the easiest and best way to freeze cake mixture?

Breadmaking is a lengthy process.
How can you use a freezer to save time and effort in making home-made bread?
How large a mixture of bread could conveniently be made at one time?
Compare a loaf that has been frozen for 3 weeks with a freshly-baked loaf made from the same recipe.
In your opinion, how successful is freezing for bread?

3   Evaluating the quality of baked products

The quality of baked products is judged by the appearance and taste of the product. Appearance is the first sensation that we judge food by: if food does not look attractive, we are not tempted to eat it. The appearance of food is affected by the size, shape, colour and texture of the product. Some things look good but taste poor. Both the appearance and taste are important characteristics in the evaluation of the quality of food.

To achieve successful results in baking, it is important to follow the recipe carefully. Sometimes, results are disappointing. Failures can occur because of one, or a combination of several faults. It is important, therefore, to understand how a recipe is affected by the choice and proportion of ingredients, the method of mixing and baking conditions.

The following experimental plan shows how you can vary one condition at a time in a recipe for making bread. By comparing the experimental sample with the standard recipe, you can see the effect of the variation that causes the particular disappointing result. It is then easy to realise the importance of following a recipe carefully to achieve successful results in baking.

Look at plate 30 to see the faults that can occur if the recipe is not followed exactly.

Design a similar series of experiments based on the standard recipe for other baked products:
- batters, e.g. Yorkshire pudding (see p. 218)
- cakes, e.g. Swiss roll (see p. 221), scones (see p. 222),
  Victoria sandwich (see p. 223), gingerbread (see p. 236).
- pastries, e.g. shortcrust (see p. 233), flaky or rough puff (see p. 236), choux pastry (see p. 237).

Experimental breadmaking: short-time method

NB   In all experiments, you can use white or whole-meal flour.

Control sample	Experiment 1	Standard recipe (as follows)
Variations in ingredients	Experiment 2	Use all purpose flour
	Experiment 3	Use ice cold liquid
	Experiment 4	Use boiling liquid
Variations in method	Experiment 5	No kneading
	Experiment 6	No rising time
	Experiment 7	Leave to rise twice as long as in experiment 1 before baking
Variations in baking conditions	Experiment 8	Low oven temperature (160°C/350°F/ Reg. 4)
	Experiment 9	High oven temperature (230°C/500°F/ Reg. 9)
	Experiment 10	Use microwave oven. Follow manufacturer's instructions.

Bread-making: short-time method

The addition of ascorbic acid to this recipe makes the gluten in the dough more elastic. As a result, the rising time can be greatly reduced. Ascorbic acid can be obtained in 25 mg tablets from a chemist.

Experiment 1: *control sample (standard recipe) – short-time white bread*

To make a small quantity for experimental work, it is essential to weigh and measure ingredients very carefully. It is suggested that the most accurate domestic way to weigh 12.5 g of yeast is to weigh 25 g and cut this into two equal parts.

Ingredients

250 g strong white or wholemeal flour
1 × 2.5 ml spoon salt
1 × 2.5 ml spoon sugar
12.5 g fresh yeast ⎫
150 ml milk ⎬ blended together
12.5 mg ascorbic acid ⎭
(i.e. half a tablet)

Equipment

sieve
large mixing bowl
palette knife
small mixing bowl
measuring jug
measuring spoons and weighing scales
small metal spoon
polythene bag
flour shaker
small loaf tin (750 ml), i.e. base size 13 cm × 8 cm
   oil for greasing tin

Preparation

Oil and flour base and sides of loaf tin. Lightly oil polythene bag.

Method

1 Sieve flour, salt and sugar into large mixing bowl.
2 Boil 50 ml of the milk. Add to the remaining cold milk. The milk should now be very slightly warm (i.e. tepid: 37 °C).
3 Crush half of one ascorbic acid tablet (i.e. 12.5 mg). Blend with the milk.
4 Using small spoon, cream the yeast in small bowl with the milk.
5 Pour blended liquids into dry ingredients. Bind together using palette knife to form a dough.
6 Turn on to lightly-floured table top. What does the dough look and feel like? Describe on your results sheet.
7 Knead the dough well for 10 minutes, until it becomes smooth and elastic. What changes have taken place?
8 Place in greased polythene bag to rest at room temperature for 10 minutes. How does this dough feel and look different?
9 Pull dough into rectangular shape, approximately three times as long as the width of the tin.
10 Fold the dough into three, so that it becomes the same shape as the loaf tin. Rock it on the table top until the top is smooth.
11 Place the dough in loaf tin. Cover with polythene bag.
12 Leave to rise at room temperature until the dough is double in volume, so that it just fills the tin. Describe the changes that have taken place during rising.
13 While your loaf is rising, prepare the oven:
   ● place oven shelf about two-thirds of the way up the oven.
   ● set the oven temperature at 205 °C/425 °F/ Reg. 7.
14 When dough has risen to at least double in volume, brush the top surface with milk or beaten egg and milk.
15 Bake loaf for approximately 25 minutes. Remove loaf from tin. Bake a further 5 minutes on a baking tray. Tap the base of loaf; it should sound hollow when fully cooked.
   Describe the changes in appearance on baking the loaf.
16 Cool on a wire tray, until loaf is cold.

Testing your loaf

The evaluation of the quality of your loaf, and other samples, is a very important part of the experimental session. You must allow sufficient time for observation, evaluation and discussion of all samples. If time is short, freeze the cooked samples, and compare them all on another day.

Test your loaf as shown on the results sheet on p. 244. Compare all experimental samples (see p. 242), with the control sample, experiment 1 (standard recipe).

Do your experimental samples look similar to those shown in plate 31? If not, can you suggest any reasons for the differences?

Experimental breadmaking *Results sheet*

Experiment No. . . . . .   Variation . . . . .

What did the dough look like and feel like before kneading?

Time taken for kneading . . . . . mins.

What changes have taken place during the kneading process?

How does the dough look and feel after the short rising time?

Note the temperature of the rising environment . . . . . °C.

Describe the changes that have taken place during the rising period.

Time taken for rising . . . . . mins.

Describe the changes in appearance on baking the loaf.

Time taken for baking . . . . . mins.

Size: measure side-height and centre-height of cut surface of the loaf.

What is the difference in height?

Has the loaf risen evenly?

Shape: draw the shape of the cross-section of the loaf on a piece of graph paper.

Calculate the surface area of the cut surface of the loaf.

Surface area of cross-section . . . . . sq cm.

Colour: tick as appropriate to describe the colour of your loaf:

crust	pale	golden	brown
crumb	white	grey-white	yellowy-white

Texture: Tick as appropriate to describe the texture of your loaf.

crust	hard	soft	cracked
crumb	coarse	even	sticky
	fine	uneven	dry

Taste: Describe the taste of the loaf:

salty   dry   doughy   yeasty

General comments:

Summary of experimental session

1 Record the results of the experimental session for each sample on a large chart as in Fig. 16.32.

2 Compare all the experimental samples that have been made to investigate the effects of a variation in ingredients.

Comment on each sample. Give reasons for the choice and proportion of ingredients in the standard recipe for bread-making.

3 Make similar observations for all samples that have varied the method of mixing and for all samples that have varied the baking conditions.

4 If possible, take photographs of the experimental samples.

5 If possible, take a photocopy of the cut surface of your samples. This gives a record of the size, shape and texture of your sample.

Cut a slice, about 1 cm thick, across the cut surface of the loaf.

● Place transparent film on the surface of the photocopier to protect the surface.

● Take a photocopy of the cut surface. There will be a grey shadow around the print; this is due to the thickness of the slice. However, you can see the crust line clearly. Trim round the crust line and mount the print on a clean piece of paper.

6 If you wish, you can preserve slices of the samples for future observation. *Note*: **After this treatment they are toxic, and should not be eaten.**

Soak the sample for five minutes in a mixture of glycerine, formaldehyde and water, in the ratio of 1:2:1.

Leave to 'dry' for 3–4 weeks.

Mount the samples on a tray. Label each one. Cover the tray with transparent film.

If you wish to keep samples preserved in this way for a long time, cover the tray with aluminium foil or some other opaque cover, as long exposure to the light bleaches the colour from the samples.

7 Write a report to summarise the results of the experimental session.

Fig. 16.32 Example of experimental record

Control sample	Size	Shape	Colour	Texture	Taste	General comments
EXPT 1						

Variation in ingredients	Size	Shape	Colour	Texture	Taste	General comments
EXPT 2						
EXPT 3						
EXPT 4						

Variation in method	Size	Shape	Colour	Texture	Taste	General comments
EXPT 5						
EXPT 6						
EXPT 7						

Variation in baking conditions	Size	Shape	Colour	Texture	Taste	General comments
EXPT 8						
EXPT 9						
EXPT 10						

QUESTIONS

1 Why are sauces served with foods?
  (a) Explain how you prepare a pouring custard sauce made with custard powder.
      Give a scientific explanation using diagrams to explain the changes that take place during the preparation and cooking of the sauce.
  (b) What do you understand by the term 'roux'?
      Give proportions and ingredients for making a pouring sauce by the roux method.
      Explain the function of each ingredient.
      Name three ingredients that could be added to vary this basic recipe.
      What other ways of making a white sauce could be used instead of the roux method?
(JMB, 1979)

2 What is the effect on the colour and taste of a white sauce, if the roux becomes brown in cooking?
  Give the reasons why a sauce may be lumpy.
  Describe a correctly made white sauce and list the ways in which it may be used in cookery.

3 Explain why the use of a strong flour is preferred in breadmaking, but a soft flour is recommended for cake making.
  What type of flour would you recommend for:
  (a) shortcrust pastry
  (b) choux pastry
  (c) puff pastry?
Give reasons for your answers.

4 (a) Name four basic methods of cake-making, giving two examples of each method.
  (b) Suggest two fats which are suitable for use in the making of cakes; give reasons for your choice.
  (c) What causes a cake mixture to appear to curdle? How does this affect the finished result?
(JMB, 1978)

5 What types of flour are suitable for home bread-making and why?
  Describe the various stages involved when making and baking a loaf of bread, giving scientific explanations where necessary.
(London, 1980)

6 Discuss the use and effectiveness of each of the following:
  (a) the all-in-one method of cake making.
  (b) the all-in-one method of pastry making.
  (c) the all-in-one method of sauce making.

  How do these methods overcome problems associated with the more traditional methods?

7 Give a basic recipe for flaky pastry.
  What are the differences between flaky and rough puff pastry?
  Explain the importance of the correct choice of each ingredient in flaky pastry.
  Describe the preparation and cooking of this pastry, outlining what happens to the ingredients at each stage.

8 State the physical and chemical changes that take place when:
  (i) bread is cooked
  (ii) scones are baked
  (iii) a Yorkshire pudding is cooked.

  To answer this question, refer also to the action of raising agents.

Raising agents 17

For many centuries, flour was made into bread and cakes that were flat and close-textured after baking. The quality of 'lightness' which we normally associate with baked products is a comparatively recent development in baking processes.

To obtain the light, open, palatable texture that is desirable in batters, cakes, bread, pastries, meringues, soufflés, etc., it is necessary to aerate the mixture by adding a *raising agent*.

All raising agents are gases. They may be:
● a gas introduced during the mixing process
● a substance added to the mixture which produces a gas during the preparation and/or baking processes.

The action of raising agents is based on the principle that all gases expand on heating.

Minute bubbles of gas enclosed in the mixture expand in the heat of the oven and cause the mixture to rise. The effect of too little or too much raising agent can be seen in the photographs in plate 30.

The three common raising agents are air, steam, and carbon dioxide. These raising agents are frequently used in combination with each other, for example in a rich creamed cake mixture, the raising agents are air which is beaten in, carbon dioxide released from baking powder, and steam from liquid in the mixture.

Air

Air is introduced into mixtures by mechanical means. It is usually the main raising agent in foods containing beaten egg whites, such as sponge cakes, soufflés (see p. 123). Air is also important in all flour mixtures where it is used in combination with steam and/or carbon dioxide.

The ways in which air is introduced mechanically into mixtures are by:
● *sieving the flour*: this is recommended for all flours, although 'extra fine' flour contains more air between the fine particles.
● *rubbing the fat into the flour*: the mixture should be lifted well out of the bowl to incorporate as much air as possible. Look at the aerated texture of shortcrust pastry on plate 29(a).
● *creaming fat and sugar*: minute air bubbles are introduced into the fat as an air-in-fat foam is formed. Look at Fig. 16.14 which shows how air is incorporated into the creamed mixture.
● *whisking egg and sugar or egg white alone*: this forms a stable foam enclosing a large volume of air. Look at the very light texture achieved in the whisked cake in plate 27.
● *beating a batter*: this introduces a little air, although in a very liquid mixture steam is the main raising agent.
● *folding and rolling of pastry*: in rough puff, flaky, puff and rich yeast pastries, air is trapped between the layers of pastry. Look at Fig. 16.26 which shows how air is layered into these mixture.

Steam

Steam is produced from the liquids added to mixtures. One volume of water produces about 1600 volumes of steam, therefore this is an important raising agent, even in mixtures containing very little water.

Steam also acts in combination with:
● air and carbon dioxide in cakes and bread;
● air in pastry, e.g. shortcrust, flaky, rough puff, and puff pastry.

Mixtures that contain high proportions of liquid, such as batters and choux pastry, depend almost entirely on the steam produced during baking to increase their volume. Look at plates 26 and 29 showing the very light puffy texture of a Yorkshire pudding and choux pastry. These mixtures have characteristic open textures with large pockets of air left after the steam has escaped. They all require a high oven temperature, which rapidly produces steam to raise the mixture. As the steam forces its way through the mixture to escape, it is replaced by air. In Yorkshire puddings, some steam is trapped inside and condenses on cooling; this is why Yorkshire puddings collapse after they have been out of the oven for a while.

Carbon dioxide

Carbon dioxide is produced in two ways.
- biologically from yeast cells as they reproduce (see below),
- chemically from the reaction between bicarbonate of soda and an acid (see p. 251).

Yeast has been universally used to produce carbon dioxide for many centuries. Today, most bread and rich yeast mixtures, e.g. fruit buns, doughnuts, Danish pastries, and croissants are aerated by carbon dioxide produced by yeast.

With the exception of whisked mixtures, most types of cakes and scones are aerated by carbon dioxide released from the chemical reaction between bicarbonate of soda and an acid. This is a quicker, more accurate way of producing carbon dioxide as a raising agent.

Look at the effect of the raising agents on plate 27.

Carbon dioxide produced from yeast

Yeasts are micro-organisms. All yeasts are unicellular and grow and multiply by separating off part of the single cell to form a bud. The bud grows, and in turn forms another bud. Under favourable conditions, chains of yeast cells are produced. The minute cells can only be seen under a microscope. During this process of reproduction, the enzymes in yeast cells obtain energy by converting sugars to alcohol and carbon dioxide. This process is known as *fermentation*.

Wild yeasts are present in the air, on the skins of fruit and in the husks of grain. They have been used for thousands of years to ferment beer. Today, yeasts are specially cultivated for the brewing and bread-making industries. Special strains of yeast are selected for use in bread-making, because of their high yield of carbon dioxide.

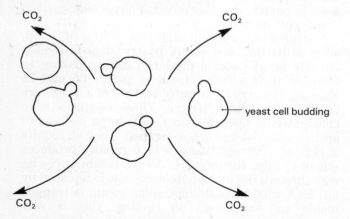

Fig. 17.1 **Yeast budding produces carbon dioxide**

The yeast is placed in a solution of molasses and water. The molasses provide sugar, and the water provides moisture necessary for fermentation. The yeast is allowed to grow under carefully controlled conditions. The cells are extracted from the solution and converted into the various forms of yeast used in baking.

Types of yeast available for baking

Fresh yeast

The yeast cells are mixed with a small amount of starch and compressed into blocks. Fresh yeast is creamy in colour, feels cool and moist to the touch and has a pleasant smell. It is quick and easy to use (see p. 229). Fresh yeast should be stored in a cool place, wrapped in a loosely tied polythene bag, or in a tightly sealed plastic box to prevent it becoming dry. Fresh yeast will keep for ten to fourteen days in the refrigerator. It can be stored in a freezer in measured portions (e.g. 25 g) for up to six weeks. When fresh yeast becomes stale it becomes darker brown in colour, may become dry and cracked or sticky, and has a sour smell. Stale yeast should not be used because many of the cells may have died, and the dough will not rise properly.

Dried yeast

This is widely available, and it will keep in a tightly sealed tin in a cool store cupboard for up to six months.

Dried yeast is produced by passing the cells through a stream of warm air. Small granules or pellets are produced, each with a hard surface. It is necessary to provide moisture, food, and warmth, to reactivate the yeast before it is added to a flour mixture (see p. 229).

Easyblend yeasts

New strains of yeast have recently been developed that can withstand rapid high temperature drying. A fine, very porous yeast is produced which can be added to the flour without soaking. Because of its spongy texture this yeast readily absorbs moisture.

The action of yeast in the production of carbon dioxide

When yeast cells feed on sugar, carbon dioxide is produced. This process of fermentation is a chain reaction in which complex starches, polysaccharides, are split into disaccharides, and then to simple sugars, monosaccharides (see p. 25).

Plate 31 Evaluation of baked products: experimental breadmaking

(a) Control sample, made with strong plain flour

(b) This was made with all-purpose flour

(c) Iced water was used

(d) Boiling water was used

(e) The dough was not kneaded

(f) No time was allowed for rising

(g) Double time was allowed for rising

(h) The oven temperature was high

(i) The oven temperature was low

(j) This was cooked in a microwave oven

Plate 32

(a) A selection of spices

(b) A selection of herbs

borage

dill

basil

thyme

parsley

winter savory

The monosaccharides are finally split to form carbon dioxide and alcohol. The carbon dioxide formed is used as a raising agent. This process is entirely dependent on enzymes in the flour and yeast acting as catalysts in the reactions.

The process can be summarised as follows.

1 Flour contains approximately 80% of the polysaccharide, starch, and 1–2% of the disaccharide, maltose. Flour also contains the enzyme, diastase, which converts some of the starch into more maltose. Maltose is used as food by the yeast. If sugar (i.e. the disaccharide, sucrose) is added to the recipe, it is also used as food for the yeast cells.

2 Yeast contains the enzymes maltase and invertase, which split the disaccharides into monosaccharides:

Disaccharide	Enzyme	Monosaccharide
maltose	(maltase)	glucose
sucrose	(invertase)	glucose and fructose

3 Yeast also contains another group of enzymes, the zymase complex. These enzymes break down the monosaccharides to form alcohol and carbon dioxide in fermentation. Energy is also released and used by the yeast cells.

Monsaccharides

glucose		carbon dioxide +
	zymase complex →	alcohol +
fructose		energy

These reactions can be shown as:

$$C_6H_{12}O_6 \longrightarrow 2\,C_2H_5OH + 2\,CO_2 + energy$$

Oxygen is not required for the fermentation process. This is therefore known as anaerobic respiration. However, if air is introduced into the dough during breadmaking, during the kneading process, some oxygen may be available for the yeast cells. The glucose is then broken down to carbon dioxide and water.

$$C_6H_{12}O_6 + 6O_2 \longrightarrow 6\,CO_2 + 6\,H_2O + energy$$

This process is known as aerobic respiration and is desirable as larger volumes of carbon dioxide are produced. In breadmaking this produces loaves which have good volume and light open texture.

Look at plate 28 to see the effect of carbon dioxide rising through a bread dough.

Factors that affect the action of yeast

Temperature Enzymes are very sensitive to temperature. They are most active between 25°C and 35°C. Above this temperature their activity gradually decreases. At 60°C, the enzymes are destroyed and no further action takes place; below 25°C the enzyme reaction is gradually slowed down, until below 0°C they are inactive. Fresh yeast can be frozen without killing the yeast: on defrosting it becomes active again as the temperature rises. Because of their dependence on enzyme action, yeast cells must have the correct temperature conditions to function. It is important that care is taken in breadmaking to control the temperature of the liquid, the dough and kitchen conditions.

Look at plate 30 which shows the effect of using liquid at incorrect temperatures in the breadmaking process.

Food is provided initially from the very small amount of sugar in the flour, then enzymes break down the starch to provide more sugar as food for the yeast.

Moisture is provided by the added liquid. Care must be taken to ensure that it is at the correct temperature.

Fat/sugar/flour proportions High proportions of fat and sugar slow down the action of yeast. For this reason, rich dough recipes contain higher proportions of yeast to flour.

Salt A high concentration of salt causes water to be drawn out of the yeast cells by osmosis. This causes some of them to be killed. It is therefore important to use the correct proportion of salt which is necessary to give flavour and prevents dough fermenting too quickly.

Yeast under the microscope

Take a very small amount of fresh yeast and make a dilute suspension in water. Transfer a drop of the suspension to a clean microscope slide. Cover gently with a coverslip.

Look at the suspension under low and high power of the microscope. At high power you should be able to see individual yeast cells and you may possibly see budding being carried out.

Experiment to investigate the fermentation action of yeast

Equipment required   *Materials required*

3 water baths   25 g fresh yeast
● one at 0°C   sugar
● one at 37°C   salt
● one at 100°C
5 test tubes
balloons
small heater
standard measuring spoons

Cream the yeast with 30 ml warm water to make a thin paste.
Label the five test tubes A, B, C, D, E and divide the yeast mixture equally among them.
To tube A - add 2.5 ml spoon sugar.
To tube B - made no addition.
To tube C - add 2.5 ml spoon sugar and 5 ml spoon salt.
To tube D - add 2.5 ml spoon sugar.
To tube E - add 2.5 ml spoon sugar.

Place tubes A, B and C in the water bath at 37°C.
Place tube D in the water bath at 0°C.
Place tube E in the water bath at 100°C.

Fit a balloon over the neck of each test tube. Keep the water baths at the correct temperatures for 30 mins. During this time observe if there is any fermentation in the tubes, shown by the production of gas bubbles.

After 30 minutes, what has happened to the balloons on each tube?
From your observations answer these question:
● Which is the best temperature for the action of yeast?
● Does sugar increase the rate of fermentation?
● What effect does salt have on fermentation?

Take the balloon containing the most gas and attach it quickly to a test tube containing lime water.

● What happens to the lime water?
● Which gas has been produced during the fermentation process?

How are the right conditions for production of carbon dioxide by yeast provided in the recipe and method of bread-making?
Why is a hot oven important for all yeast cookery? Look at plate 28.

Carbon dioxide produced from chemical reactions

Chemical raising agents are widely used for many types of cakes and scones. Chemical raising agents are easy to use; they give an accurate and controlled amount of carbon dioxide to aerate the mixture evenly. Small quantities are used in recipes, and they must be measured accurately.
Three types of chemical raising agents are used:
● bicarbonate of soda
● bicarbonate of soda + an acid
● baking powder, which is a commercially-prepared mixture of bicarbonate of soda and several acids.

Bicarbonate of soda

This is the simplest type of chemical raising agent. It is a pure white powder which, on heating, produces sodium carbonate (soda), steam, and carbon dioxide.

$$2\,NaHCO_3 \longrightarrow Na_2CO_3 + H_2O + CO_2$$

The carbon dioxide gas is released, but the soda is left behind in the dough. This may give a sharp alkaline taste and dark yellow colour to mixtures. It is therefore suitable only for use in mixtures where other ingredients in the recipe will disguise these effects, e.g. gingerbread (see plate 27).
This problem of residual soda has led to a search for a substance that would react with it to form a neutral compound. Many dilute acids will do this.

Bicarbonate of soda plus an acid

At first sour milk was used to provide the dilute acid in the form of lactic acid. This is still used today in some scone recipes. The amount of lactic acid in the sour milk varies and cannot be measured, so this method is not very reliable.
Other natural acids such as molasses, vinegar, and lemon juice have also been used. All these substances are unsuitable as they vary in the strength of their acidity, and all leave a residual taste. Several chemical substances that are harmless and would leave a tasteless residue in the mixture were tested.

Cream of tartar, a substance obtained from grapes, was found to be a sutiable substance. It reacted to release all the carbon dioxide slowly from the bicarbonate, leaving a tasteless salt behind.

$$NaHCO_3 + KHC_4H_4O_6 \longrightarrow NaKC_4H_4O_6 + CO_2 + H_2O$$

bicarbonate of soda + cream of tartar → Rochelle salts + carbon dioxide + water

Two parts of cream of tartar are required to react with and neutralise one part of sodium bicarbonate. Therefore recipes using these raising agents should contain twice as much cream of tartar as bicarbonate of soda.

Baking powder

This is now widely used as a raising agent, since it is much more convenient to use a single ingredient. This is also much less chance of error in measurement of the raising agent.

Baking powder was first produced commercially in 1830. The bicarbonate and acid substances are ready-mixed in the correct proportions. The mixture also contains some cornflour or rice starch to absorb any moisture from the atmosphere and stop the reaction taking place in the tin. As the ingredients tend to separate in the tin, it is important to stir or shake baking powder before measuring it.

Several brands of baking powder are available, and each firm produces its own formula for baking powder, but the quality and amount of carbon dioxide produced is controlled by law. Therefore there is hardly any difference between the raising power of different brands.

The acids used in baking powders all have slightly different properties, some release carbon dioxide immediately on moistening, others delay the release of carbon dioxide until the mixture is heated during baking. This double action provided by a mixture of acids is particularly useful as the initial release of carbon dioxide aids the mixing process, and the slowly-released carbon dioxide gives a constant, even rise during the baking process.

The mixture of acids used include:
- tartaric acid, which is released quickly on moistening.
- cream of tartar, which is released at low oven temperatures.
- acid sodium pyrophosphate, which is very stable and releases carbon dioxide only when heated to higher temperatures.

Experiments to examine the constituents of baking powder

Equipment required
6 test tubes
3 watch glasses
beaker or saucepan
4 balloons
standard metric spoons
litmus paper

Materials required
bicarbonate of soda
cream of tartar
baking powder
lime water
iodine solution

Baking powder has three main constituents:
- an alkali: bicarbonate of soda
- an acid substance, e.g. cream of tartar
- starch

(a) **To show which of the three constituents produces the gas**
Take four test tubes and label them, A, B, C and D.
In tube A, place 1×2.5 ml spoon bicarbonate of soda.
In tube B, place 1×2.5 ml spoon cream of tartar.
In tube C, place 1×2.5 ml spoon cornflour.
In tube D, place 1×2.5 ml baking powder.

Add 15 ml cold water to each tube.
Stretch a balloon over the neck of each tube.
Shake the tubes and observe if a reaction takes place.
Place the four tubes in a beaker of cold water.
Heat gently.

Observe what happens to the solutions and to the balloons.
Which substance in baking powder produces the gas?

(b) **To find which gas is produced by baking powder**
Place 2.5 ml baking powder and 15 ml cold water in a test tube.
Place 15 ml lime water in a second test tube.
Heat the tube containing the baking powder and water and allow the gas produced to go into the lime water.

What happens to the lime water?
Which gas has been produced?

(c) **To show why an acid substance is added to baking powder**
Place 2.5 ml bicarbonate of soda and 15 ml cold water in a test tube.
Shake the tube and heat gently.
Observe what happens and, when there is no further reaction, test the solution with litmus paper.

Add 5 ml cream of tartar and shake the tube. Observe.
Heat the tube gently until there is no further reaction.
Test the remaining solution with litmus paper.

Describe what you observed in this experiment and explain why an acid substance is added to baking powder.

(d) To show there is a third ingredient present in baking powder
Take three watch glasses. Label them A, B and C.
On A, place a pinch of bicarbonate of soda.
On B, place a pinch of cream of tartar.
On C, place a pinch of baking powder.
Add a drop of iodine solution to each watch glass and observe what happens.
What is the third main constituent of baking powder?
Why is this substance added to baking powder?

The proportion of baking powder in recipes

The amount of baking powder required in a mixture varies according to the richness of the mixture and the amount of air introduced in mixing. A plain mixture, e.g. scones, requires a higher proportion than a rich cake made by the creaming method, where air plays an important part in raising the mixture.

Self-raising flour contains the raising agent evenly distributed through the flour. The equivalent of 1 × 5 ml spoon of baking powder is added to 100 g flour.

Experiment to compare scones made with different raising agents

It is very important to weigh and measure accurately.
Use standard measuring spoons.
Oven temperature 220 °C, regulo 8-9.
Cooking time 7-10 mins.

Basic recipe
100 g plain flour
1 × 2.5 ml spoon salt
25 g margarine
25 g sugar
60 ml milk

Method
Prepare oven and grease a baking tray.
Sieve flour and other dry ingredients.
Rub in the fat.
Mix to a soft dough with the milk.
Roll the dough out to about 1 cm thick. Cut into six triangles.
Bake the scones near the top of the oven.

Variations
Make up eight batches of scones varying the raising agent as follows:
  (i)   control: no raising agent added.
  (ii) 1 × 2.5 ml spoon bicarbonate of soda.
  (iii) 1 × 7.5 ml spoon bicarbonate of soda.
  (iv) 1 × 2.5 ml spoon bicarbonate of soda + 2.5 ml spoon cream of tartar.
  (v)   1 × 2.5 ml spoon bicarbonate of soda + 1 × 5 ml spoon cream of tartar.
  (vi) 5 ml baking powder.
  (vii) 10ml baking powder.
  (viii) use self-raising flour instead of plain flour.

When the scones are baked place them on labelled cooling racks so that you do not mix them up.
Cut one scone from each batch in half and measure the height. Examine the colour and texture. Taste the scones.

Record your results on a chart like this:

Raising agent	volume and height	colour	texture	taste	order of preference 1 = best 8 = worst
1					
2					
3					
4					
5					
6					
7					
8					

What conclusions can you draw from this experiment?

The action of raising agents in the oven

After mixing, the raising agents should be evenly distributed throughout the mixture. The air introduced will be present as minute bubbles. On heating the raising agents react as follows:

- air expands;
- steam is produced from the water and enlarges the air cells. As the steam escapes through the crust, it is replaced by air.
- carbon dioxide produced by yeast expands, and the yeast produces more carbon dioxide until the temperature becomes too high and the yeast is inactivated;
- carbon dioxide is produced by the action of heat and moisture on baking powder. The carbon dioxide enlarges the air cells and aerates mixtures which do not contain much air. These gases expand on heating.

Flour mixtures are able to stretch as these actions take place, because of the elasticity of the gluten in the flour. All rising must take place before the proteins of the flour and egg are coagulated by the heat of cooking. On coagulation the mixture sets, and baked goods are held in their risen shape.

The choice of raising agent in a recipe is one of the factors that will affect the final texture of baked products. The characteristic textures of several baked products are shown in plates 26-29, and examples are:

- batters and choux pastry raised by steam;
- whisked sponge raised by air;
- scones raised by carbon dioxide, air, and steam;
- rich cake mixture raised by air, carbon dioxide, and steam;
- bread mixture raised by carbon dioxide from yeast cells;
- flaky pastry raised by air and steam;
- shortcrust pastry raised by air.

QUESTIONS

1 What is a raising agent?
  Name the raising agents you would use in each of the dishes listed below. For each state how you would introduce the raising agent into the mixture, and explain what their reaction in the mixture would be.
  (a) a Victoria sandwich cake
  (b) gingerbread
  (c) bread rolls
  (d) sausage rolls made with flaky pastry
  (e) scones
(AEB, 1979)

2 Give explanations for the following:
  (a) the cooking of a Yorkshire pudding in a very hot oven
  (b) the use of baking powder in making scones
  (c) yeast dough can be placed in a refrigerator to rise, but must be placed in a hot oven to cook.

3 (a) Describe three ways by which air may be introduced into a mixture. Give an example in each case.
  (b) Why does a mixture raised by bicarbonate of soda often require the addition of spices?
  (c) Prepare a set of rules for the successful use of chemical raising agents.
(Scottish, 1978)

4 (a) Name four methods which are used in cookery to lighten a mixture, giving the raising agent in each case.
  (b) Select one raising agent and explain its action in detail.
(Northern Ireland, 1978)

5 Give the composition of baking powder.
  State the conditions under which baking powder reacts, and name the products formed.
  What is self-raising flour? When, and for what reasons may self-raising flour be used in cookery?
(JMB, 1978)

6 State three conditions necessary for the growth of yeast.
  How are these conditions provided when yeast is used in breadmaking?
(Oxford 1977)

7 (a) Name the substance which produces carbon dioxide in raising agents.
  (b) Name one substance which reacts with it
      (i) in commercial baking powder
      (ii) in gingerbread.
  (c) What filler is used in commercial baking powder?
  (d) Why is it there?
(London 1980)

Flavour in food

18

People tend to choose food because it looks attractive, but their enjoyment of it is mainly decided by the taste. The flavour or taste of food is as important as the nutritional content. Only foods that taste good will be eaten in sufficient quantity to be a valuable source of nutrients. Foods with an attractive smell and taste stimulate the appetite.

Natural foods have a flavour of their own. Some natural foods, such as strawberries, do not need any additions to be acceptable. Others are made more appetising by the addition of other flavours, as when salt is added in cooking potatoes and green vegetables.

All food loses some flavour in processing. The control of flavour in the manufacture of processed foods is very important. Many flavouring materials may be added to enhance the natural flavour. Alternatively, the flavour of processed foods may be changed completely to create a new flavour, for example by relishes and sauces. All flavourings added to processed foods are tested and must comply with government safety regulations before their use is permitted in foods.

Appreciation of flavour is a very personal matter. Traditionally, people in some countries like bland foods while others prefer foods which are more highly seasoned.

Individuals also appreciate tastes differently. As we saw in chapter 1, the ability to recognise the four basic tastes varies greatly, and for this reason acceptance of food differs. Some substances that alter the taste of food, such as salt, pepper, sugar, vinegar and piquant sauces are therefore served at the table so that everyone is able to add the amount he or she likes to make the food acceptable.

However, in food preparation, a large variety of flavourings is available and should be used by the cook to improve the taste of the dishes he or she prepares.

The added flavourings will:
- strengthen natural flavours, or
- blend natural and added flavours, or
- alter flavours and create a new taste.

The flavouring materials do not add to the nutritional value of the dish as they are used only in small quantities.

The materials used to strengthen, blend or alter natural flavours are seasonings, extracts, herbs, spices, essences, vinegars and sauces. Sugar is also used in larger quantities to improve flavour.

Seasonings

Seasonings are used to bring out and accentuate the natural flavour of the food and sometimes to improve the flavour. Salt and soy are the most widely used seasonings. Traditionally, salt has been used extensively in western countries, and soy in eastern countries, but these patterns are changing as food habits become more cosmopolitan. Pepper is often thought of as a seasoning, and is always served at the table with salt, but it is really a spice (see spice chart, pp. 257-259).

Salt (sodium chloride; see mineral elements, p. 38)

Salt may be obtained from the evaporation of sea water; it is then known as *seasalt*; or it is mined from underground deposits left behind by former seas. When refined, it is available as kitchen salt, in the form of blocks, or cooking salt. Both sorts have no additives. Table salt is refined further and has an anti-caking agent (magnesium carbonate) added to it to keep it dry and make it flow more easily. Salt seasoned with garlic or celery is also available. It is used in cooking when the natural products are not available.

Soy

Finely ground soya beans are fermented with salt, water and barley or wheat flour to produce *soy sauce*. Traditionally, the fermentation process takes about eighteen months, but changes in the manufacturing technique have reduced the fermentation time to six months.

Soy sauce has always has been used extensively in oriental recipes, but it is now also widely used in western countries. Soy sauce is an ingredient in several other sauces, e.g. Worcestershire and barbeque sauces.

Monosodium glutamate (MSG)

This is a white, flavourless substance used as a flavour modifier, as it brings out the flavour of other foods. Traditionally, it is made in eastern countries from soya bean protein, but in western countries it is now made from gluten (i.e. wheat protein) or sugar beet waste. MSG is an ingredient in many manufactured foods, and it is also available for domestic use, e.g. sprinkled on meat or fish before cooking.

Extracts

Flavourings from bones, meat, fish and vegetables can be extracted by prolonged cooking in water. This liquid is known as *stock*. Stock is a well-flavoured base for soups, sauces and casseroles. However, except for chicken stock, it is rarely made in the home today. Commercially, these extracts from meat, yeast and vegetables are concentrated into thick, dark-coloured, highly-seasoned pastes.

They are also available in the dried form:
- together with a thickening agent as *gravy powders*.
- together with herbs and spices as *stock cubes*.
Beef and chicken are the most usual flavours.

Herbs

Herbs are plants, grown mainly in temperate climates, containing aromatic oils which release their flavours during cooking. It is usually the leaves that are used, but sometimes it can be the flower, seed or root of the plant. Herbs have been used in cooking and for medicinal purposes for thousands of years. All herbs can be bought in a dried form and stored. This is a convenient alternative if fresh herbs are not available. It is important to remember that:
- 1 × 5 ml spoon of dried herbs is equivalent to 1 × 20 ml spoon of fresh herbs.

Drying herbs

Fresh herbs may be dried at home. Very fresh herbs are tied in bundles, hung in a warm room or airing cupboard away from strong light. They may also be dried in a cool oven. The dried leaves are rubbed gently and then stored in small airtight containers.

Figure 18.1 shows some of the most common herbs used in cooking.

Fig. 18.1 Common herbs

Name	Description	Uses in food preparation
angelica	A plant rather like cow parsley which grows in northern Europe.	The stalks are candied for use as a green decoration on cakes and desserts.
basil	A strong, pungent herb which is a native of India. It is very popular in Italy because its strong flavour goes well with pasta. It can be grown fresh in summer but is usually sold dried.	Used in salads, especially tomato salad and in sauces for pasta.
bayleaf	The shiny green leaves come from the leaf of the bay tree which is a native of the Mediterranean.	Popular herb for flavouring stews, stocks and sauces and as a garnish for pâtés. Whole bayleaves should be removed before a dish is served.
chives	A plant belonging to the onion family with tubular leaves rather like grass, about 20 cm long; easily grown in the garden. The leaves are used fresh, snipped into small pieces with scissors. The leaves can be frozen. Dried chives are also available.	Give an onion-like flavour in salads, cottage and cream cheese. Also sprinkled on soups as a garnish especially Vichysoisse (leek and potato) soup.
dill	A plant with feathery grey-green leaves which are used fresh. The stalks and seeds are used in pickles. The seeds and dried leaves can be bought.	A very important herb for flavouring fish in Scandinavia. It is also used in soups and with vegetables and goes very well with cucumber.

Name	Description	Uses in food preparation
fennel	A tall plant with feathery leaves which is a native of southern Europe. The swollen bulb base of the stem is used as a vegetable and the leaves and seeds are used as herbs to give a flavour of aniseed.	Like dill, fennel is a fish herb and the leaves are used in sauces for fish and in stuffings. The seeds can be sprinkled on the meat.
garlic	A plant of the lily family with a pungently flavoured, white bulbous stem base which is divided into segments known as cloves of garlic. It is also available in a powdered form and as garlic flavoured salt.	The cloves are crushed and the strongly flavoured juices are added to a variety of dishes: casseroles, sauces, marinades, salads, roast meat, soups. Especially popular in Italian and French recipes.
marjoram oregano	Sweet marjoram is a garden herb with small leaves which grows close to the ground. The wild variety is oregano which has a stronger but similar flavour.	Leaves are used in stuffings for veal and lamb and in casseroles. Oregano is used sprinkled on pizzas and in sauces for pasta.
mint	Many varieties of this herb are found in gardens. They vary in flavour. The common mint is spearmint with oval leaves.	Springs of mint are sometimes added to the water when cooking new potatoes or garden peas. The chopped blanched leaves are used to make mint sauce, and mint jelly. These are traditional accompaniments to roast lamb.
parsley	This common herb is a native of the Mediterranean. There are several other varieties. It can be bought fresh or dried.	A popular garnish for many savoury dishes either as sprigs or chopped. The chopped herb is used in parsley sauce served with fish and is added to stuffings and casseroles. Sprigs can be deep fried for an accompaniment to fish.
rosemary	An evergreen shrub rather like a lavender bush which grows wild in Europe and America. It has hard, narrow spiky leaves and is available fresh, dried or as a powder.	Traditionally the leaves are used to flavour lamb and poultry, either on the roast meat or in casseroles.
sage	A small evergreen shrub. The grey-green leaves have given their name to the colour 'sage green'. The leaves have a strong aromatic smell when they are crushed.	The main use is a stuffing to accompany pork and duck (sage and onion stuffing). It overpowers other flavours if added to casseroles. It is traditionally used to give a green layer to Sage Derby cheese. (see p. 107).
tarragon	The variety most used is French tarragon. It can be fresh, dried or powdered.	A flavouring for vinegar, mustard and sauces. May also be used with poultry, fish and in salads.
thyme	A woody plant with very tiny leaves. There are several varieties including one with a lemony scent. Common thyme is the most widely used.	Thyme is used in stuffings with parsley and also to flavour soups, casseroles and fish dishes.

Name	Description	Uses in food preparation
bouquet garni	A bunch of herbs tied with a string or wrapped and tied in a small square of muslin. The herbs are usually sprigs of parsley, thyme and bayleaf. Peppercorns are added and other herbs may be included. The bouquet garni is always removed before the dish is served.	Very popular ingredient in casseroles, soups and sauces.
mixed herbs	A prepared mixture of dried herbs, usually sage, parsley, thyme and marjoram.	Added to savoury dishes instead of the individual herbs.

Spices

Spices are the dried parts of aromatic plants which come from the roots, bark, leaves, flowers and seeds. Spices grow mainly in the tropics, and have always been associated with eastern countries.

Their use in cookery developed in India, China and South East Asia, where they are still widely used in recipes today. Spices are now available all over the world. In western cooking, some spices, such as pepper, are commonly used; others, such as cardamom, are used occasionally. Some spices, such as chilli powder and mustard, are used only in savoury dishes. Others, such as cloves and nutmeg, can be used in both sweet and savoury dishes.

> Spices have played an important part in trade between countries for centuries. Find out as much as you can about the development of the spice trade.

The most useful spices to have in the store cupboard are shown in Fig. 18.2.

Fig. 18.2 Common spices

Name	Description	Main uses
allspice (also known as *Jamaica pepper*)	The dried or ground berry of an evergreen plant, the pimento tree. It tastes peppery with a blend of flavours of cinnamon, cloves and nutmeg.	Savoury sauces, pickling, marinades, and with some grilled meat dishes
caraway	Sickle-shaped seeds of a plant native to Asia which can be grown in Europe.	Added to bread, cakes and a few cheeses. Very popular in German and Jewish cookery.
cardamom	Black, green or cream pods containing black seeds. Very expensive spice native to India.	In Indian dishes ground cardamom is one of the spices in garam masala and occasionally in curry powder. Whole pods are used to flavour rice puddings.
Cayenne pepper	A hot pungent spice from the dried ground pods of chillies which are red peppers native to Central America. Has a very distinctive red colour.	Very hot. Should be used very sparingly. Added to curries, cheese dishes and shell fish.
chilli powder	Ground chillies mixed with other spices such as paprika, black and white pepper. It has a very pungent flavour.	In curried dishes and chilli con carne. *Note*: Never touch it with hands, as it will cause discomfort, especially on mouth or eyes.

Name	Description	Main uses
cinnamon	A well-known sweet spice from the inner bark of an evergreen tree of the laurel family native to India. Available as sticks or as a powder.	Sticks used to flavour mulled wine and fruits. Ground cinnamon added to fruit cakes, fruit tarts and rice dishes. Also added to savoury dishes of fish, ham and poultry.
cloves (From Latin word *clorus, nail*; whole cloves are nail-shaped)	The dried flower buds of an evergreen plant native to South East Asia. Normally used whole but central head can be ground into powder. Now grown in Indonesia, Tanzania and Sri Lanka. Cloves contain a highly scented oil.	Whole embedded in onion to flavour bread sauce or in the fat of a gammon joint. Also used in apple dishes, pickling and in the fat of a gammon joint. Also used in apple dishes, pickling and in drinks.
coriander	The dried crushed seeds of a plant of the parsley family native to southern Europe but grown in many parts of the world. Indian name is *dhanya*.	Important ingredient of curry powder and curry paste. It is used with lamb and pork and in pickles.
curry powder	A mixture of various hot spices including chillies, coriander, ginger, turmeric and garlic. Various strengths are available.	Used in western countries for preparing meat, fish and vegetable curries. (In India the cook adds the separate spices according to the recipe being prepared and does not use the premixed powders).
garam masala	An Indian spice mixture of black pepper, cinnamon, cumin, cloves, cardamom and mace.	Intended to be sprinkled on Indian food when it is served, to give extra flavour. Sometimes used in cooking like curry powder.
ginger	The rhizome or root stem of a plant which grows in tropical countries and is supplied by Jamaica and India. The fresh root is known as green ginger and it is available dried and ground as a hot spice.	Fresh ginger is used peeled and grated in Chinese and Indian cookery. Ground ginger is used in baking biscuits, gingerbread, etc. and can also be sprinkled on sliced melon.
mustard	Small seeds from three different plants of the cabbage family, which may be black, brown or white. The seeds may be used whole or ground into a powder. *English mustard* powder is prepared from mixed brown and white mustard seeds which are separated from their husks and ground into a yellow powder. When water is added a hot mustard is produced. A little wheat flour is added to soak up the oil in the seeds, and turmeric to turn the wheat flour yellow. *American mustard* is made only from white seeds, so it is much milder. *French mustard* is made from brown seeds, but it is mixed with vinegar or wine instead of water, so it is more aromatic than English mustard e.g. Dijon mustard.	Whole mustard seeds are used in pickling, spice, chutneys and pickles. Mustard powder is added to curries. Prepared mustard powders are used as a condiment with beef or ham and may be added to mayonnaise or cheese sauce. American mustard is served with hot dogs and French mustard is served with hamburgers, beef and in many sauce recipes.

Name	Description	Main uses
nutmeg & mace	Nutmeg is the dried kernel or nut of an evergreen tree native to Indonesia. It can be bought whole or ground. Inside the fruit the kernels are covered with a netlike covering of red tendrils. These blades are known as mace they are dried before use and may be ground.	Nutmeg is used in sweet dishes, e.g. baked egg custard and rice pudding but may also be added to savoury egg, cheese and mince dishes, e.g. moussaka. Mace is used to flavour milk in savoury white sauces and in pickles.
paprika	A red powder made from red sweet peppers which are native to South America. Mildly hot distinctive taste which is very popular in Hungary.	Hungarian goulash and in chicken and veal dishes. A colourful garnish sprinkled on savoury dishes.
pepper	Peppercorns are the fruit of a vine rather like a blackcurrant bush which grows in the tropics. They are exported by Brazil, India, Indonesia, Malaysia and Sri Lanka. *Black peppercorns* are picked from the vine when they are green and unripe. They are dried in the sun until they are black. *White peppercorns* are from the same plant but are allowed to ripen on the vine. When they turn red they are picked and the husk is removed by soaking. The seed inside dries to a creamy white colour. *Unripe green peppercorns* are also available packed in brine.	Whole peppercorns are an ingredient of pickling spice and are added to some casserole recipes. White and black ground pepper are widely used as seasonings with salt. The white pepper is less aromatic than black and is used mainly in white sauces and at the table. Freshly ground pepper has the best flavour.
pickling spice	A ready-made mixture of spices for pickling foods. It normally contains mustard seeds, coriander, cloves, bayleaves, allspice, chilli, ginger and black peppercorns.	Added to foods, e.g. onions that are pickled in vinegar.
poppyseeds	Small, hard, grey-black seeds of the opium poppy which is a native of the Middle East.	Decoration for bread and confectionery especially in Jewish recipes. They are also included in some Indian curry recipes.
saffron	Tiny orange and yellow filaments obtained from the stigma of a crocus. Saffron is a very expensive spice.	Small quantities are used to flavour Cornish saffron cake. Infused in hot water, saffron is used to give a yellow colour to rice in risotto or paella.
sesame seeds	Seeds from the seasame plant, a native of India. Best known as a source of oil. When they are dried the small, pearly-white seeds are used like poppy seeds.	A decoration for cakes, breads and sweets and the seeds are also used in Mexican and Japanese recipes.
turmeric (Indian name haldi)	The rhizomes or root stems of a plant of the lily family, native to South East Asia are dried and ground to produce a bright yellow powder.	An important aromatic spice in Indian cooking and the basic spice of curry powders. It can also be used instead of saffron to give a yellow colour to food.

Essences

Some flavourings are sold as liquid essences. *Real essences* contain alcohol in which the volatile oils from strongly-flavoured plants such as vanilla or peppermint are dissolved. *Vanilla essence* is the most popular flavouring essence used in many sauces, cakes and puddings. It is prepared from the cured pod of a climbing orchid which is a native of Central America. The long, thin, black pods can be bought whole and soaked in milk to give their flavour, but the essence is obtained by soaking the pods in alcohol to extract the flavouring substance vanillin and the colour. Essences are highly concentrated and most recipes require only a few drops of essence to give a flavour. They are sold in small, firmly-sealed bottles.

Synthetic essences, which are less expensive, are also available. These are made from chemicals which have been combined to resemble natural flavours. An example is ethyl acetate which gives a pear-drop flavour. A synthetic vanilla essence can be prepared from the lignin in wood pulp.

Fig. 18.3 Some flavours available as essences

fish	anchovy
fruit	banana, blackcurrant, cherry, lemon, orange, raspberry, strawberry
nut	almond, coconut
alcoholic flavours	chemicals combined to create the flavours of rum, sherry, brandy, kirsch
miscellaneous	coffee, peppermint, vanilla

Vinegars

Vinegar has been used for thousands of years both as a preservative and to give an acid flavour to foods. For flavouring it is used to marinate foods, in dressings for salads and vegetables and it is also used as a condiment at the table.

The word vinegar comes from the French *vinaigre*, sour wine; the first vinegars developed were from wine that had soured naturally. Today the term is also used for other sour liquids produced in the same way, including cider and malt vinegar. Manufactured vinegars more or less follow the native drink of the country where they are made. For example, in England where beer is drunk, mainly *malt vinegar* is produced. France produces most *wine vinegar* and the Americans like *cider vinegar*. Vinegar can also be flavoured with herbs such as tarragon.

The alcohol in the beer, wine or cider is converted into acetic acid, the main component of vinegar, by fermentation with special vinegar yeasts. The strength of the acetic acid varies but it is usually at least 6% for wine vinegars and above 4% for other types.

Sauces

There are several well-known bottled sauces on the market which are also used as flavourings for food, either added at the table or included in recipes.

The most widely used is *tomato ketchup*. There are many varieties available, but the main ingredients in all of them are tomatoes, vinegar and seasonings. Other main flavouring sauces are listed in Fig. 18.4.

Fig. 18.4 Flavouring sauces

Worcestershire sauce	A hot sauce made from an old Indian recipe containing soy sauce, vinegar, tropical fruits, spices and molasses.
tabasco sauce	A very hot sauce made from vinegar and red peppers.
brown sauce	Usually sold under proprietary brand names. This is a blend of fruit and spices in molasses and malt vinegar.
horseradish sauce	The pungent root of the horseradish plant is grated and mixed with cream to serve with cold meats, especially beef.

QUESTIONS

1 Explain the difference between seasoning and flavouring.

How can you ensure a brown stew is well seasoned and well-flavoured?

Write notes on three of the following:
- monosodium glutamate
- bouquet garni
- parsley
- vanilla pod

(Welsh 1976)

2 Write notes on the importance of food colourings and flavourings in food preparation.
(Welsh 1978)

3 Distiguish between herbs and spices.

Give three examples of herbs frequently used in food preparation. Suggest a use for each.

Give one example of a spice used in a savoury dish and one example of a spice used in a sweet dish.

4 Name a substance which is added to table salt
  (i) as a nutrient; why is this considered necessary?
  (ii) to make salt free-running.
(London 1981)

Index